RELIGION IN THE
TWENTIETH CENTURY

BOOKS BY VERGILIUS FERM

The Crisis in American Lutheran Theology
First Adventures in Philosophy
First Chapters in Religious Philosophy
What Is Lutheranism?
Contemporary American Theology (IN TWO VOLUMES)
Religion in Transition
An Encyclopedia of Religion
What Can We Believe?

RELIGION
IN THE
TWENTIETH CENTURY

EDITED BY
VERGILIUS FERM

EDITOR OF "AN ENCYCLOPEDIA OF RELIGION," ETC.

GREENWOOD PRESS, PUBLISHERS
NEW YORK

EDITOR'S PREFACE

AN EDITOR'S preface is supposed to give the reader some conception of the plan and purpose of the new volume for which he is responsible. His own views on the subject at hand are, supposedly, of minor consideration.

I shall follow precedent by stating the general perspective of our purpose; but I shall depart from the customary editorial introductions in expressing an opinion, however minor it may be thought to be in the consideration of the topic as a whole. One cannot plan a volume such as this, with its variety of religious expressions, and read it carefully in typescript, without forming an opinion. And I am sure that those who have freely expressed themselves on matters of their own faith would accord the same privilege to an editor to air his own honest estimate. The fact that so many diverse religious expressions can come together between the covers of one book is but a sure sign of the willingness on the part of all to be in friendly relationships and exchange of opinion, even though religious ideologies seem to create chasms of differences.

First, then, in regard to the purpose and plan of the volume. This book belongs on the shelf alongside a newly issued series of contemporary studies planned by Dr. Dagobert Runes, president of The Philosophical Library press of New York. The series so far has included volumes with such titles as: "Twentieth Century Sociology", "Twentieth Century Psychology", "Twentieth Century English", "Twentieth Century Political Thought", "Twentieth Century Philosophy", "Twentieth Century Education" and the like. Manifestly in such an oceanic subject as religion, not every brand of twentieth-century religious beliefs * could be considered in one volume. Were this possible our book would have taken on the complexion of an en-

---

* While it is true that mass religions expressed by nationalistic loyalties, political faiths and state credos are phenomena characteristic of the twentieth century, they are not peculiar to our day. They cut through and across the old and stable religions and belong to the study of religious psychology. Any adequate treatment of them as such would require a volume by itself, beyond the scope of this book.

cyclopedia which is not its aim. What is in mind is a cross-section of the more important historic living religions which have come down from a long past, together with those younger in age which are thriving healthfully in our day, and an appraisal of these religions in terms of our times. It is not a book on denominations or cults but of the larger divisions of religious ideologies and practices.

For example, Protestantism is covered by its two-fold division of liberal and conservative; Judaism by its three-fold division of conservative, reform, and its recently developed interpretation known as "Reconstructionism"; Catholicism into its three-fold expression, Roman, Greek and Anglo-Catholic; and such Christian religious ideologies as lay claim to special divine revelations, the Latter Day Saints, Christian Science, Swedenborgianism, and the avowedly self-revelatory faith of the Quakers. There is no attempt to follow the old classification of cultism since, in the opinion of the editor, this word has become obsolete by its abuse as a term of scorn by self-appointed orthodox.

Again, no contemporary religious scene would be complete without some representation from the camp of those religious groups which, in this country particularly, have captured the loyalty of thousands both by their vigorous faith and by their enthusiastic activities, such groups as the Salvation Army and the Jehovah's Witnesses; the religious groups which have come upon the contemporary scene in reaction to inherited ideologies, such as the Ethical Culture Movement and Religious Humanism, appealing as they do in increasing measure to the non-conformist type of mind; the religious groups which represent the impact of a non-Christian heritage upon the contemporary scene with a claim to special religious insight, such groups as the Bahaists and the Ramakrishna Order. It had been the hope to have included at least three other groups, the Theosophists, the Rosicrucians and the Spiritualists as certainly worthy of representation but this has met with failure, although invitations were extended these groups. Theosophists and Rosicrucians do not wish to be classified as religions but rather as philosophies. (It is all a matter of definition.) And the Spiritualists do not appear to be concerned enough to join others in a venture such as this.

For the most part it has been the aim to seek out actual representatives of the several faiths. Where this has not seemed possible, it has been the avowed concern to find an interpreter whose scholarship is unquestioned in the field and whose acquaintance with the topic is intimate and sympathetic.

Before each contributor there was placed a prospectus which ran somewhat as follows: *Religion in the Twentieth Century* should offer the reader a clear and concise statement of the main tenets of the religion presented; something as to its history, its scope, its aims and wherever possible a general idea of its present membership (statistics and headquarters); it should raise the query of the peculiar genius of the particular religion, or, what may be regarded as a unique contribution, if any, to the world of religious thought and practice, and give answer; it should state how the religion, as it is interpreted by its representative or spokesman, looks upon other religions, with such questions in mind as "Does it aspire to reach all people or is its mission limited?", "Is it tolerant in principle or competitive?"; it should consider whatever solutions, if any, it may conceive to have to offer to the present pressing questions of our own times, questions like race-relations, the new world of post-war reconstruction, and whatever contributory factors there may be involved in it to man's economic, social, political, literary, educational and cultural interests; it should give the reader a first-hand acquaintance with any recent trends of the religion, pointing toward changes or reform within itself, thus revealing contemporary currents within its own historic framework; and, finally, it should present, without reservation, such interesting and pertinent matters which seem to be of special concern to the religion under discussion and its impact upon modern thought and practice.

The arrangement of the essays follows the pattern of approximate chronology which has, in the judgment of the editor, its patent advantages over other possibilities. Where there is uncertainty either as to exact or appropriate chronological arrangement the decision has been quite arbitrary in view of the slight importance of the matter.

Most readers of such a book as this are students of culture and as such their own interests are not confined to one interpretation, however satisfactory it may be. For this reason, the editor has pressed with insistence upon each writer to present the reader with an appropriate though brief list of the best literature upon the subject for a more comprehensive acquaintance with the religion under discussion. So that one may feel a kind of intimacy with each article, the editor has prepared a brief sketch of the professional life of each contributor in the desire to encourage a more sympathetic understanding of the article itself.

Religion in the Twentieth Century thus presents, it is hoped, a cross-section of the big streams of religious ideas and practices which affect the lives of millions now living, some of whose streams are rivers cut deep by the flow of centuries and some of which are shallow not in substance but only as more recent surgings of the human spirit destined to cut deeper with their contributions, as it is thought, with the passage of time. Though we may not have here a comprehensive picture of contemporary religions, we have, we believe, a representative presentation of the religious landscape of our mid-twentieth-century culture. The book may lay claim to one virtue, not always found in books given to such scope because of the limitations or the prejudices of their single authorships—each religion is authoritatively represented as the biographies of the contributors will bear testimony. To all these men and women who have joined in this publication, the editor expresses his thanks. The contacts with these people, with such divergent backgrounds and, in some cases with such loyal commitments to their religious households, have revealed an underlying sense of comradeship, which, it is hoped, is symbolic of the new day that is dawning upon us at this very late and critical hour in the development of human culture.

Now, as to the editor's own estimate. Were his feeling that his work was only that of a compiler his own interpretation would be altogether superfluous. But it is not in the spirit of compilation that this volume has been born. It has given cause to no end of reflection —an experience which, it is hoped, will be shared by the reader. With so many religions coming up out of the past, so many still vitally affecting the lives of men, women and children, with so many claims to special divine dispensation and with the present world in such awful turmoil and dread of the future—how can one remain neutral to man's search for and his claim to an answer to life's ultimate meaning and destiny? For, after all, this is the characteristic of any religion: it is the expression of man's belief and commitment, fired with emotion, to what he takes to be life's ultimate meaning and the destiny of himself, his fellowmen and of those not yet born. The stronger the conviction, the more is it his feeling that it is of divine sanction. It is the new and terrifyingly uncertain world pressing upon us, with our yesterdays grown ancient almost overnight, that makes the question of religion in the twentieth century a matter not of idle and leisurely speculation but one of agonizing opinion and decision.

It is almost a sickening truism to repeat the fact that our planetary world is fast shrinking. It began almost yesterday and though we know this to be true we are too close to the process to realize the implications. Fate (or shall we say, God?) is moving man closer to man, creating for him, whether he wills it or not, a world neighborhood. This process, let it be sadly noted, has not come by the process of religious brotherliness which has been the dream and the utopia of our greatest religious seers; but it is now a compulsion which has come by way of the much maligned disciplines of modern technological devices and scientific progress. Even the devil of war may be the saint in forcing man to take seriously his long affirmed but little practiced brotherhood. The lines which have long separated men are increasingly growing blurred and we shall, sooner than we realize, find them dimmed out by the erasures of scientific revolutions. Some of these lines were fashioned by nature: mountains, oceans, impassable bulwarks of wilderness and desert—which scientific innovations of communication are fast destroying. Some of them were those long inherited artificial barriers which, by man's own ideological superiority, have been created as islands of isolation and are now, by the same means, becoming anachronistic.

This is only to say that we live in the mightiest era of transition in human history. No other age is comparable. So swift are these changes in economic, political, social and cultural spheres that it is only an honest admission to affirm that we hardly know where in the whirl we are in terms of our earthly destiny and admit our horror of things that may come to pass.

No area of human interest can remain in such a day in quarantine. The age of materialistic sciences (this may be a hard admission for religious people to affirm) has led the way to upheaval. The fierce storms of social unrest, of economic and political revolutions, are upon us; and who would dare to deny that the materialistic sciences in their applied form have been at the bottom to stir men's wants and desires for a fuller share of the earth's offerings. The curse of man's insatiable desires to better himself may well be the blessing in disguise. Even the desire for more material conveniences is a part of the evidence of man's superiority over the things and creatures about him. His religions cannot long remain neutral and unaffected—even though religions move with heavy feet. Any student knows that religions have been conditioned by culture. They have never been born nor have they developed in a cultural vacuum. Changing civilizations have brought about changing religions (granting their reciprocity). What lies in store in the religious field, in our contemporary maelstrom, no one can prophesy. Only one thing can one be certain of: the religions of the world will be mightily affected by the whirlwind that is now surging throughout the ends of the world. What has become of Shintoism over night? How long will the Taoist practices continue with western civilization sweeping in its enlightened practices? How can fundamentalists hold the youth whose public school education has torn them if not adrift at least into the shock of compartmental ideas? How can Christians speak of one mind, of the Christian view-point, with so many affirmed interpretations? How can Hindus and Moslems affirm their spiritual truths in the face of their present brutal conflicts (not to mention the other religious groups)? How can Westerners affirm their spiritual superiority—a doctrine nourished deep in the soil of traditional ignorance? How can the liberal with his new freedom scorn the conservative whose mind troubled by a conscious frailty must lay hold of some stable authority to give balance; and how can the conservative condemn the liberal who has with troubled conscience fought his way up the hill to new freedom, new insights and new vision? How, in the name of a good God, can religions continue to divide, with so many things at stake in the world?

To repeat dead formulae is no answer. To bite the hand of tradition which has nourished so much good is no answer. To be a Hindu or a Moslem or a Christian is in itself no answer. To appeal only to the tradition of one's people is no answer. The answer can only come on the field where the questions are pressed: the field of today, in terms of today's culture, of its own whirlwind. The past may contribute to the answer; but the past is always what it is: the past. To hold that only tradition gives the final answers is to affirm belief in a God who is either a deistic deity or one that is dead. To believe truly in a God is to believe in His being alive in the present, alive with unfolding purposes and no stranger to changes. The prophets have always been believed even by conservatives to have been closer to the Divine (certainly at times of crises) than the priests, although the priests (the better ones) may have had divine functioning in holding on to the gains made from one prophetic interval to the next.

What I am trying to say is this: a look at the various religions shows plainly (if one has a positive belief at all) the work of Deity under two forms: the prophetic and the priestly. Practically all the great religions of the world were launched by good prophets who did not fit their traditions. Practically all of them found their path lonely; many of them died in scorn and disgrace. The second generation becomes the priestly generation, trying to hold the vision; but visions have a way of perishing. They must be re-incarnated in choice spirits, the saints and perhaps the new martyrs. In other words, there are, what I would choose to call, two expressions of religion, as the record plainly shows. The one may be called the *vertical,* the other, the *horizontal.*

The *vertical* is the line in a particular religion that comes up out of the past, through the course of a particular tradition. It may be likened to a river which is traceable, however winding, to its source. To this group belong the priests of religion, the institutionalists, the traditionalists, the vested powers, the succeeding generations of disciples whose main glory is that they belong. The *horizontal* cuts across the past. Tradition means less if not little. The present landscape means more. It is to be likened to the ocean. An ocean has spread and it has depth and it goes nowhere. It just is, regardless of what has flown in or out of it. To this group belong the prophets, the religious innovators of good spirit, the seers and the saviours of mankind. To them there is vested no other power than that of their own conscience and dedication. They are hard to classify as to church or creed or denomination or even by the name of a given religion. They are oceanic and are what they are in themselves. They have stamped upon them the water-mark of their own quality. Always are they the heretics of their times.

These two are discernible in the whole story of religions. (They are also discernible in other fields of human life, in economic, in social and cultural fields.) The two, the *vertical* and the *horizontal,* become conscious of each other when pressing issues are forced. Generally it is the priest who wins the skirmish; but the prophet is content with anonymity in the conviction that right has a way of working itself out eventually because it belongs to reality (deity).

The *horizontal* approach to world religions has not even begun to be appreciated for what it is worth by those whose vision is circumscribed to the *vertical*. But in a world that is fast shrinking—*the horizontal view is destined more and more to come to its majority*. This, I take it, is the answer that the religions of the twentieth century must begin to find, however hard it may be to see and to realize and to practice. The *horizontal* view means that no one religion can claim monopoly of truth, either the truth of man or of God. The Divine communication has not been confined to one religious group, nor even to the particular field called religion. No universal truth or value can be circumscribed to one people unless God be a tribal deity. The values that are eternal in character are found in diverse places and on many tongues and in many traditions. It is this "look around" (the *horizontal*) rather than the "look to the past", that will bring to man his crowning religious achievement, in his spiritual struggle to understand himself and all men and even his God. *Our present age is thrusting this truth home,* whether we welcome it or not. Isolationism or special prerogative in religion is a passing though long chapter in human cultural history. It is nourished on provincialism and ignorance, both of which are sprinkled with deep sincerity, and it breeds misunderstanding, suspicion and bigotry. That kind of religion belongs to the pre-atomic age. It is the horse and buggy type. The new world must have less of this, else it is done.

I find startling confirmation of all this in the record of the greater religions. The vision of their founders and best expositors saw across their traditional borders, the sunlight of God's truth and value among other sons of men "not of the fold". Even the outcast Samaritan, sparse in theology and wearer of no blue-ribbon sanctioned by his social group, had what the elect lacked, said Jesus of Nazareth.

The question whether one religion is as good as another strikes me as curious. It is curious because when one reads the history of religions one sees, unless one is too prejudiced by a theory, that each and every religion is plural in itself. What is called Christianity, for example, has been historically a great variety of thought and practice. The religion of its founder was certainly much simpler than many subsequent interpretations and expressions. The same is true for

Zoroastrianism which (as is shown in the essay in this volume) was for Zoroaster a far different thing than for the Zoroastrians who followed with their manifold and stringent interpretations. The same for Mohammed and Buddha and Laotze; and the same (shall we say?) for many of the prophets who followed them. It is this prophetic, *horizontal,* expression of the several religions that needs comparison, if comparison is wanted. But prophets and the greater founders tend to proclaim, amidst the provincialisms of their times, fundamentals which cut across the traditional and *vertical* lines and, by the same token, belong much more together than those who solidify their own and their fathers' views into dogmas, into inflexible doctrines and practices and crown them with the sanctity of the founder's name. The question of comparison certainly is not one of one religion over against another, but rather whether the vision of the founders and their prophets through the centuries matches those universal ideals which the spirit of God, we must believe, has been proclaiming in the hearts of men of good will everywhere. Qualities bear their own water-mark and do not depend upon any extraneous authority and they cut *horizontally* across all traditions. With some there may be more quantity of quality which makes for pre-eminence. The ideas may be expressed in ways which hide those fundamental qualities; and it is a lack of spiritual vision not to see them. For example, the Nirvana of Buddha spiritually is not far removed from that ultimate union interpreted in the Christian Fourth Gospel which speaks of the utter one-ness of disciples with their Lord, though the phrases tend to hide such similarity. The Golden Rule spoken negatively need not be less significant than when it is spoken positively. The spiritual unity of mankind need not be less significant when spoken of in terms of the Absolute as when it is symbolized by the happy figure of Jewish family life. Men will always speak in terms of their culture and surroundings but that does not mean that they are utter strangers to the same divine impulses. The prism of man's life darkens and dulls or sharpens and brightens the indwelling Spirit of the Universe. Some religious prophets and the better priests have prisms which shine with crystal clearness; others have prisms which are dulled by ignorance and superstition and by religious myopia. The *horizontal* view finds the prisms of truth and value everywhere wherever eternal values pierce the limited horizons. Eastern and Western people can unite only in this manner in the one kind of union that is worthy of the name, the union not of identity but the union that comes by the recognition of these fundamental values, the common spirit which reveals the common God. The doctrine of plural spiritual incarnations of God, with one supreme perhaps in the quantity of quality, is the sounder basis for the kind of unity in religious tradition in the one world that by necessity is now to be fashioned, the prophetic voice in religion for our generation.

All of us have come up out of a certain religious tradition. No man ever lives apart from his inherited social pattern. We are all drenched with the customs and the ideology of our caste, our point in time and in space, and by the same token we all are potential prisoners of the overwhelming power of group pressure. Conforming to society will always make the way of the conservative the easier and the smoother path. Even nature reflects the principle of conservatism: a tree cannot grow too high, an animal must not develop too large a body, a stream cannot be too powerful. It is not conservatism or traditionalism in itself that can be held to be nature's curse. It is the traditionalism that blocks the ever flowing *elan vital* of life itself which is the curse, the stubborn resistance to the very principle of change and creative power that is in life.

Our era reflects this creative power in a mighty surge. Any attempt to halt it now is an invitation to death. The religions of the world need not be ashamed of their several heritages but only of any disposition to self-conceit which blocks progress and suppresses its prophets. A man's heritage may be respected but it need not be an idol to be worshipped as above the immanently working God. The world that is opening up is insisting that all values be recognized, whatever the heritage. The chief sin that will beset religiously committed men is the worship of their heritage to the degree that they are blind to the creative values thrusting themselves upon us and giving us our sacred opportunity. To be specific, a Christian who believes in the supreme spiritual worth of Jesus of Nazareth even to the point of a Trinitarian theology need not make his loyalty to the Jesus of history and theology a cause greater than loyalty to what he must believe, if he is honest with himself, to be the universal spirit of Christ wherever found in any traditional faith. A Scripture becomes genuinely sacred in so far as its appeal touches the soul of man of whatever faith; the sacredness which tradition gives to it is far less significant. This is only to say, again, that the world of value is fundamentally an oceanic world, one that is *horizontal* fundamentally and self-authenticating.

Our times are making many issues live options. The religious live option is the *horizontal* approach. The option has not come, we repeat, by the front door of religions themselves; it has come by the back door of technological advances. It is no time for bickering over small issues. It is an age for prophets who see bravely and optimistically beyond the turmoils of transition the vision of things eternally fundamental by whatever the name or the heritage. The twentieth century era which began only yesterday (shall we date it when hell broke out on Hiroshimo?) will not last out its expected life span unless the lesson of warning is heeded: there is to be one world or none. Such an era desperately needs a religion that can bring men together. To this end the various religious households must transcend their provincialisms and each, after its own kind, give voice to that in its heritage which reflects the Universal Spirit brooding upon all sons of men of genuinely good will everywhere.

VERGILIUS FERM

Mercer Lake
Mercer, Wisconsin

TABLE OF CONTENTS

LIST OF CONTRIBUTORS

VERGILIUS FERM

SWAMI NIKHILANANDA

IRACH J. S. TARAPOREWALA

SHRI KRISHNA SAKSENA

ANANDA KENTISH COOMARASWAMY

WILLIAM JAMES HAIL

CHAN WING-TSIT

CHARLES A. HART

DANIEL CLARENCE HOLTOM

SALMA BISHLAWY

GEORGE PETROVICH FEDOTOV

HILDA WIERUM BOULTER

ANDREW KERR RULE

HOWARD HAINES BRINTON

WILLIAM FREDERIC WUNSCH

CONRAD HENRY MOEHLMAN

W. NORMAN PITTENGER

LₑROY EUGENE COWLES

MIRZA AHMAD SOHRAB

LOUIS ISRAEL NEWMAN

SIMON GREENBERG

HENRY NEUMANN

DONALD McMILLAN

ARTHUR JAMES TODD

NATHAN HOMER KNORR

SWAMI SATPRAKASHANANDA

ROY WOOD SELLARS

MORDECAI MENAHEM KAPLAN

HINDUISM

Swami Nikhilananda was born in 1897 in a small village called Noakhali, in Bengal, India. He attended high school and college and worked as a journalist prior to his joining the Ramakrishna Order of monks. This Order is a branch of the Hindu religion, founded by Swami Vivekananda in 1897. (An article on the Ramakrishna Movement appears in this volume.)

The word "swami" is a title given to the world-renouncing monks, meaning literally "master" or "lord." It is used in the same way as the title "father" in the Roman Catholic faith. A "swami" monk takes the vows of celibacy, poverty and renunciation of all worldly ties.

Swami Nikhilananda was ordained as a monk of the Order in 1924 and given his present name. He spent several years in the Himalayan monastery of his Order, the Mayavati Advaita Ashrama, during which time he made a study of Hinduism and other systems of philosophy and religion. After making an extensive tour of India delivering lectures he was sent, in 1931, to America to preach "the universal ideas of Hinduism." His first assignment was at Providence, R. I.

In 1933 the Swami founded the Ramakrishna-Vivekananda Center of New York and remains its spiritual leader. The congregation consists almost entirely of Americans. Among his literary productions are "The Gospel of Sri Ramakrishna," a translation (1942); "The Bhagavad Gita," a translation (1944); "Self Knowledge" (1946); and "The Essence of Hinduism" (1946).

Editor

HINDUISM

SWAMI NIKHILANANDA

THE RELIGION practiced by over two hundred millions of men and women living in the vast subcontinent of India from a prehistoric past is known as Hinduism or Brahmanism. Both words are of foreign origin. The word *Sindhu*, the Sanskrit name for the river Indus, flowing into the Arabian Sea, was distorted into *Hindu* by the Persians and later on changed into *Indos* by the Greeks. The country east of the Indos was called India; its inhabitants became known as Hindus, and their religion, Hinduism. The word *Brahmanism* was coined by early European travelers and Christian missionaries, who found the brahmin caste dominating Hindu society and religion. But the Hindus prefer to call their religion the *Sanatana Dharma*, the Eternal Religion, because it is based upon eternal principles; or the *Vaidika Dharma*, because it is founded on the teachings of the Vedas. The country of the Hindus is known to them as *Bhārata* or *Bhāratavarsha,* derived from Bharata, an ancient Indian king, the son of Dushyanta and Sakuntala, immortalized by Kalidasa in his great drama *Sakuntala.*

The origin of Hinduism is lost in the haze of antiquity. This much, however, may be stated with a certain amount of truth, that it is the oldest religion in the world which has produced in an unbroken succession a large number of prophets and philosophers who have demonstrated by their lives and experiences its cardinal doctrines and principles.

Hinduism cannot strictly be called a historical religion. It was not founded by any historical person or persons. It is based upon the teachings of the Vedas, which, according to Hindu tradition, consist among other things of certain spiritual laws describing the nature of Ultimate Reality, the individual soul and its hereafter, the universe, and the relationship between man and his Creator and his fellow beings. These laws, eternal in nature, were revealed to those

3

spiritually developed persons known as *rishis,* who lived, at a very early period of history, on the banks of the Indus and the Ganges. Great prophets of olden times like Rama and Krishna, or of medieval times, like Sankara and Chaitanya, or a modern prophet like Ramakrishna, were upholders and demonstrators of these spiritual laws during critical periods of India's history. They were not their originators. According to the Vedas, seers of Truth are found among both sexes and in all religions.

The Vedas are the scriptures of the Hindus and the ultimate authority concerning spiritual experiences. They are roughly divided into two parts: the *karmakanda,* dealing with rituals, sacrifices, and other methods of worship, by which the gods are propitiated for the purpose of gaining happiness and prosperity; and the *jnanakanda,* which discusses philosophical truths bearing upon transcendental experience. The latter part is also known as the Upanishads, whose instructions were given both in forest retreats and in the crowded courts of kings.

The goal of the Vedic teachings is twofold: first, the enjoyment of prosperity in the world, both here and hereafter, through the pursuit of ethical and religious disciplines; second, the attainment of the highest good, known by such terms as immortality, liberation, and the supreme bliss. Further, every individual is asked to realize four ideals in life. They are the ethical virtues (*dharma*), economic pursuit (*artha*), the enjoyment of esthetic and sensuous pleasures (*kama*), and freedom (*moksha*). The second and third ideals must be based on *dharma,* or righteousness. Otherwise they degenerate into greed and voluptuousness. Abiding peace and blessedness are possible through the attainment of the fourth ideal, namely, liberation.

In order to realize the above-mentioned four ideals in life, the Hindu philosophers have divided it into four stages (*ashramas*). They are known as *brahmacharya, garhasthya, vanaprastha,* and *sannyasa.* During the first stage a man leads the austere life of a celibate student, conserving his physical and mental energy. During the second stage he becomes a householder. He marries, begets children, and fulfills his duties to the family, the community, and the country in accordance with his power and capacity. After fifty, he hands over the charge of the family to his children and retires with his wife to a holy place in order to lead a life of reflection and

meditation. And during the last stage, he renounces all ties and
becomes a free soul. The great Hindu poet Kalidasa says that boyhood should be devoted to the acquisition of knowledge, youth to
the enjoyment of material happiness, old age to reflection, and the
last moments of earthly life to communion with God.

The division of Hindu society into four castes shows that the
ancient Hindus valued the spiritual qualities more than military and
economic power. The *brahmins* were the custodians of learning and
spiritual lore; the *kshatriyas* were the kings and military protectors;
the *vaisyas* controlled the trade and economic life; and the *sudras*
supplied the manual labor. The four castes, working in harmony,
preserved Hindu society for a long period in history. All of them
were indispensable for the preservation of the social structure. Their
welfare and security were interdependent. The *Bhagavad Gita*
defined as follows the duties of the four castes: "Control of the
mind, control of the senses, austerity, cleanliness, forbearance, and
uprightness, as also knowledge, realization, and faith—these are the
duties of a *brahmin,* born of his own nature. Heroism, high spirit,
firmness, resourcefulness, dauntlessness in battle, generosity, and
sovereignty—these are the duties of a *kshatriya,* born of his own
nature. Agriculture, cattle-rearing, and trade are the duties of a
vaisya, born of his own nature. And the duty of a *sudra,* born of his
own nature, is action consisting of service." (*Bhagavad Gita* XVIII,
42–44.)

The Vedic culture is spiritual, because it believes that the universe is revealed, when Truth is known, as a spiritual entity, and
also because human life has a spiritual end. Some of the main
doctrines of the Vedas are briefly described below.

The tangible universe did not come into existence at any particular point of time. It is without beginning and without end. What
is called creation is only a manifestation of names and forms from
an unmanifested seed state; and dissolution is a return to that state.
Manifestation presupposes a previous non-manifestation. Creation
and dissolution represent an unending process, often described as
the "breathing of the cosmic soul." Time, space, and causality are
concepts of the phenomenal universe; they do not belong to eternity.
A world period, when the names and forms are manifested, is called
a cycle (*yuga*). According to a Vedic statement, the names and
forms repeat themselves in every cycle. The soul's liberation does

not lie in identification with the world process, but in going beyond it.

As the universe is without beginning, souls are also without beginning. What is the soul? What is its nature? The soul is the unchanging and immortal substance in every living being. It is of the nature of Spirit and consciousness. It is the detached witness of the changes that take place in the body and the mind. A man's unrighteous or righteous actions may obscure or reveal the nature of the soul, but they can never destroy it. The same soul shines equally in the highest man and the lowest creature, the difference being in the degree of manifestation. Everyone will eventually realize the divinity of his soul. The body, the sense-organs, and the mind are the instruments through which the soul manifests its light in the outer world. They themselves consist of insentient matter. Behind the physical body there are, according to the Hindu mystics, the subtle and the causal bodies. The soul is described in the Vedas as the "eye of the eye," the "ear of the ear." "That which cannot be seen by the eyes but by which the eyes see—know that to be the soul." The experiences of the mind are detached from one another like the pictures in a movie-film. The unchanging soul, like the screen, gives the idea of continuity to those experiences. Without the presence of an immutable substance in man, the activities of the senses and the mind could not be coordinated.

The soul cannot be affected by the laws of matter—temporal, spatial, or causal. Hence it is immortal and deathless. Birth and death are related to the body and not to the soul. The *Katha Upanishad* says: "The soul is not born, nor does it die. It has not come from anywhere, nor has it produced anything. It is unborn, eternal, everlasting, ancient; it is not slain though the body is slain. If the slayer thinks of slaying the soul, and if the slain person thinks that the soul is dead, both have missed the truth. The soul slays not nor is slain. The soul, smaller than the small and greater than the great, is hidden in the hearts of all living creatures. A man who is free from desires and free from grief sees its majesty through tranquil senses and mind. Though sitting still it travels far; though lying down it goes everywhere. Wise men, having realized the incorporeal, great, and all-pervading soul dwelling in perishable bodies, do not grieve."

The soul, which is not limited by time and space, is necessarily one and without a second. Duality is seen only in the realm of matter. The soul is Spirit. The different souls seen in the relative universe are reflections of one soul in various material objects, like the reflections of the sun in many waves. In spite of this apparent multiplicity the soul always remains non-dual.

In the Vedas the soul is described as existence-knowledge-bliss absolute (*sachchidanandam*). Its oneness with the Godhead is the essence of the Vedas. This oneness is revealed by such statements as "Thou art That," "I am He," "Consciousness is Brahman," "This very soul is Brahman." This unitive knowledge is the true knowledge. There are three main interpretations of the Vedic philosophy, known as Dualism, Qualified Non-dualism, and Absolute Non-dualism. They all agree about the spiritual nature of the soul, though they differ about its relationship with the Godhead.

Why does the infinite, perfect, and immortal Spirit appear as a finite, imperfect, and mortal creature? Why does the One appear as the many? This is the result, says Hinduism, of its identification with finite, material forms. What is the cause of this identification? The Upanishad describes it as *maya*, or ignorance. Maya is the inscrutable and indescribable power inhering in Ultimate Reality itself, which at first conceals its true nature and then projects the material universe and all the material forms contained therein. The Spirit identifies itself with these forms and appears as finite beings subject to birth, death, and similar physical changes, hunger and thirst, pain and pleasure, and the other pairs of opposites. Such illusion is experienced in a man's everyday life. Under its spell he sees the mirage in the desert, takes a rope for a snake, and while asleep regards his dreams as real. But the appearance of water in the desert or the snake in the rope is illusory; that is why it cannot alter the real nature of the desert or the rope. Likewise the false identification of the soul with material forms cannot change its real nature. It is always and under all conditions pure, perfect, and non-dual. The discovery of the spiritual nature of the soul and its non-duality is the goal of religion.

Thus Hinduism speaks of two souls, as it were: the real soul and the apparent soul. The real soul is pure Spirit. The apparent soul is identified with a material form. It is the latter that is aware of good and evil, that acts righteously and unrighteously, that experiences rewards and punishments here and hereafter. The Vedas speak of different courses that the apparent soul may follow after death. The meritorious soul enjoys happiness and the wicked soul is punished, through divine or subhuman bodies. After these experiences are over, it again assumes a human body on earth and resumes its journey to its spiritual goal. The Vedic doctrine of *karma* and reincarnation does not apply to the real soul, which neither is born nor dies. In the relative world the law of *karma,* or cause and effect, determines a man's thought and action. Good produces good, and evil produces evil; and this law operates after death as well. That men are born with dissimilar physical and mental traits is the result of their past actions. Neither God nor fate is responsible for this. We should accept our present misfortune with calmness, but, at the same time, we should now act in a righteous way so that our future may bring us only good.

The goal of life is absolute perfection through the unitive knowledge. As this exalted condition cannot be attained in one life, the Hindu philosophers speak of reincarnation. In each birth a man adds a little more to his merit. In the end he realizes his true nature, goes beyond the illusory law of cause and effect, and thus attains immortality and freedom.

The Godhead, or Ultimate Reality, is described in the Vedas as Brahman, or the Absolute. Devoid of name, form, or sex, Brahman is sometimes referred to as He and sometimes as It. Brahman is Spirit and consciousness, the unchanging Reality behind the changing universe. It is both transcendent and immanent. It alone exists: when Truth is known, names, forms, and material objects are realized as nothing but the Godhead. The world is rooted in Reality. It is not unreal in the sense that a barren woman's son or a castle in the air is unreal. Everything in it should be regarded as filled with Divine Spirit. Material objects appear real because the Godhead, which is the only Reality, forms the inmost essence of all. Without It nothing whatsoever can exist. It is the purest freedom. By realizing It man is released from the bondage created by ignorance. It is the essence of love. Because It is the indwelling Spirit of all, human beings feel attracted to one another. It is the essence of beauty. Physical beauty is only a reflection in matter of the beauty of the Spirit. The abode of blessed qualities alone, It is totally free from anger or passion. The Godhead does not punish or reward. Man alone is responsible for his suffering and his happiness. Though the

wind of divine mercy blows for all—the sinful and the virtuous—
only the pure in heart are benefited by it.

Hinduism declares that Brahman is unknown and unknowable.
Man thinks of It according to his inner understanding. To some, who
are beginners, It appears as the extra-cosmic Creator of the world,
the efficient cause and the giver of rewards and punishments. To
some, who are more advanced, It is the Power manifest in the universe, immanent in the creation, the material cause of the world
and the Soul of all souls. Brahman is the whole and living beings are
parts of It. And to a few, who have attained the final stage of spiritual evolution, Brahman, soul, and universe are one. They are con-
vertible terms. "I am He."

As the supreme Godhead is unknown and unknowable to the
finite mind, the Hindu religion prescribes various symbols through
which one can contemplate It. Thus the Vedas speak of such symbols as *Agni, Vayu,* and *Indra.* These, however, were replaced later
by the popular deities of the *Puranas,* such as *Brahma, Vishnu, Siva,
Kali,* and *Durga.* The Vedas are never tired of reiterating that all
these are manifestations of the impersonal Absolute in time and
space. By contemplating the Godhead through these symbols the
aspirant ultimately realizes the Absolute. Hinduism believes in
Divine Incarnations. The *Bhagavad Gita* says that whenever virtue
declines and vice prevails in the world, the Godhead is born in a
human form for the establishment of righteousness and the punishment of the unrighteous. Though unborn and immutable, yet Brahman, through the help of Its own inscrutable maya, appears to be
born as a man so that men may realize their divine nature. Rama,
Krishna, Buddha, and others, all born during critical periods of
India's spiritual history, are regarded as Divine Incarnations. A
Hindu accepts Christ, too, as an Incarnation. God can be worshipped
through them as well. When the nameless and formless Brahman
manifests Itself in time and space and appears to be endowed with
human attributes, It is called the Personal God. The Gods of the
different religions, from the tribal deity of the primitive people to the
one God of the monotheists, are only different aspects of the Absolute revealed to men's limited minds.

According to Hinduism every soul is potentially divine. This
divinity is hidden on account of ignorance; it can be manifested
through knowledge. The manifestation of the soul's divinity is the

whole of religion. God can be seen and must be seen; which means that a man can be perfect and must be perfect. Religion is not mere believing or reasoning; it is being and becoming. It is a unique experience between the eternal Godhead and the eternal soul. Then alone "the knots of the heart are destroyed and all doubts set at naught."

The method of spiritual unfoldment is called *yoga* by Hindu philosophers. The word means union of the individual soul with the universal soul, or Godhead. It also means the method by which this union may be achieved. Though inflexible regarding the nature of Ultimate Reality, Hinduism is very catholic regarding the choice of spiritual paths, which are determined by the aspirant's inborn tendencies. For the active type Hinduism prescribes *karmayoga,* or the method of right activity. The aspirant must perform every action regarding himself as God's instrument. He must surrender to God the fruits of all his actions, whether philanthropic or ritualistic or those he performs every day for the maintenance of his body. A true *karmayogi* serves others, seeing in them a manifestation of God. He regards with holy indifference success and failure and the good and bad results of action. He cultivates a spirit of detachment from all worldly objects. To him every work is a form of worship and therefore sacred. Though busy with his body and mind, he maintains an inner calmness, being aware of his indissoluble relationship with God. Through the performance of action in the spirit of *yoga* the aspirant purifies his mind and ultimately attains the knowledge of God.

For the emotional type Hinduism prescribes *bhaktiyoga,* the path of divine love. The aspirant on this path is called a devotee or lover of God. His ideal is the Personal God in the form of a Prophet or a Divine Incarnation; or he may worship a Deity without form but endowed with human attributes. The devotee establishes with God a human relationship, regarding Him as his Father, Master, Friend, or Beloved, according to his prevailing mood. Rituals such as the offering of flowers and food, and the burning of lights and incense, characterize the path of divine love, especially during its earlier stages. Love of God is the secret of this path. But divine love, unlike human affection, is free from fear, desire for reward, or any other ulterior motive. A true devotee does not worship God because he is afraid of punishment after death or because he expects happiness on earth or in heaven. It is the natural inclination of his mind to love God, since the essence of God is beauty and blessedness. To him the form of God that he loves is the perfect ideal, however differently it may be regarded by another person. Formal and ritualistic devotion practiced for a long time with sincerity and earnestness is gradually transformed into spontaneous and ecstatic love, which destroys all the impurities of the devotee's heart and reveals to him the ultimate oneness of love, lover, and Beloved.

The third type of *yoga, rajayoga,* is based upon *Samkhya* philosophy, propounded by Kapila. According to him the *purusha,* or soul, is pure consciousness, by nature perfect and immortal. There are innumerable *purushas* corresponding to the individual souls. *Prakriti,* or matter, is one and inert. Through non-discrimination the soul identifies itself with matter and experiences birth, death, and the other miseries of relative life. Through right knowledge it realizes its isolation from matter and attains freedom and perfection. Rajayoga describes the practical disciplines by which this freedom is attained. It consists of eight steps. The first two deal mainly with ethical disciplines, such as non-injury, truthfulness, continence, contentment, study of scripture, and devotion to God. The third and fourth describe postures and breathing, which help in the practice of concentration and meditation, discussed in the remaining steps. Through the practice of ethical disciplines the aspirant gradually weakens his violent desires, which, like waves, disturb the surface of the mind. It is this mental agitation that prevents a man from seeing his inmost self. Through concentration the aspirant strengthens the mind and cultivates inwardness of spirit. Through the one-pointed mind he practices contemplation, analyses the different layers of consciousness, and at last realizes the true nature of the soul and its freedom from matter.

Jnanayoga, or the method of discrimination, is suited to the philosophical temperament. It is discussed in *Vedanta* philosophy. Its purpose is to enable one to attain undying bliss and a cessation of misery through the perception of the illusoriness of names and forms and the realization of the sole reality of Brahman, which is identical with *Atman,* or the soul. The follower of this path must possess keen power of reasoning, by which he can distinguish the unreal from the real, the unchanging from the changeless. He also must develop indomitable will-power to detach himself from the unreal and the changing. He cultivates such disciplines as control over the mind and the senses, inner calmness, forbearance, faith, and concentration. Above all he must have an intense longing for freedom through the knowledge of Truth. Such an aspirant repairs to a qualified teacher and is instructed about the identity of the soul and Brahman. He reasons about this instruction and then contemplates its meaning. Through uninterrupted contemplation for a long time he at last attains an exalted state of superconsciousness in which he realizes oneness with Brahman. As his ignorance is destroyed he sees the entire universe and all beings to be the same as Brahman. The realization of non-duality is the goal of *jnanayoga.*

It is said in the Vedas that the ultimate Truth is supramental. The Godhead cannot be perceived through the senses nor comprehended by the mind. Yet the teachers of *yoga* never ask their students to surrender reason. They declare that through the practice of *yogic* disciplines, such as self-control and contemplation, the mind acquires a higher power, sometimes called intuition or inspiration, which is beyond reason and through which the supersensuous Truth is directly realized "like a fruit lying on the palm of one's hand." Then a man lives in the world as a free soul. He is no longer deluded by the mere appearance of things. He is not a victim of false fear or false expectation. Realizing all beings in himself and himself in all beings, he loves all and never becomes a cause of fear or pain to anyone. After death his soul, which has already been freed from ignorance, desire, and attachment, merges in the Supreme Spirit and thus attains complete liberation.

Hinduism is noted for its catholic and universal outlook. Its toleration and respect for other faiths mainly result from the fact that it regards the Godhead, or Ultimate Reality, as unconditioned by time and space. Religion itself is not the Godhead but the means to Its realization. According to the Vedas Truth is one, though the sages call it by various names. The *Bhagavad Gita* declares that all religions are strung on the Lord like pearls on a necklace. In whatever way people offer their worship to the Lord, He accepts it. All religions lead to the same Truth. Ramakrishna repeatedly said that the different religions are only different paths leading to the same spiritual experience of peace and blessedness. Every religion is thus a vista which ultimately opens on the infinite horizon of universal religion. This universality is not, however, to be found either in the myths or in the rituals of religion, which are necessary in so far as, like the shell of a seed, they protect the kernel of religion and gradually drop off as the Truth breaks out in the devotee's heart. The Godhead alone, which is the goal of all faiths, is the universal religion. It can be realized by the deepening of the spiritual consciousness through the practice of the disciplines laid down in all faiths. The Hindu attitude toward other religions is that of respect and not of mere tolerance, much less of rivalry.

The cardinal principles of Hinduism may be stated as follows: the divinity of the soul, the unity of existence, the oneness of the Godhead, and the harmony of religions. As the soul is divine, everyone is entitled to respect, no matter how his body may look or his mind may function. This is the true basis of democracy and all decent human relationships. The unity of existence is the real foundation of ethics. Violence, hatred, and malice toward others ultimately injure oneself. One cannot be truly happy by hurting other beings, whoever or wherever they may be. The surest way to one's own happiness is to work for others' happiness. Ethical laws dictated by expediency, political or otherwise, do not serve a useful purpose in the long-range view of things. The different Gods are different facets of the one Truth. Therefore those who desire religious harmony must never destroy or pull down. Malicious words must not be used against any faith, though constructive criticism is allowed. A man should be taken where he stands and then given a lift. This is the application of the democratic principle in religion.

Hinduism cannot be described in terms of fixed dogmas or stereotyped creeds. Remaining loyal to fundamental principles, it has shown amazing flexibility of forms to meet the demands of changing conditions both from within and from without. Patterns of worship have indeed changed, but the spirit of adoration always remains the same. In every century, from time out of mind, Hinduism has produced great spiritual geniuses who have preserved untarnished the basic truths of their religion when Hinduism was shaken by internal upheavals or by such external causes as contact with the Greeks, the Sakas, the Huns, the Scythians, the Moslems, and the Christians.

The *Upanishads* registered a protest against the excessive monopoly of the priests officiating in the rituals described in the Vedas. They preach that liberation is to be attained through the cultivation of knowledge and not through the performance of sacrifices. The *Puranas* developed the idea of a Personal God, the Divine Incarnation, and the path of *bhakti,* or divine love. The *Bhagavad Gita* shows the harmony of different spiritual disciplines, emphasizing however, selfless work as an easy way to the realization of Truth. Buddha, who was born in a Hindu family and was recognized later by the Hindus as an Incarnation of the Godhead, protested against many of their time-honored religious and social beliefs, such as the infallibility of the Vedas, the caste-system, and the Vedic sacrifices. He stressed the cultivation of the moral virtues, the suppression of longing for material things, the renunciation of the world, friendship for human beings, and compassion for animals. Sankaracharys (A.D. 788–820) rescued Hinduism from the confusion that attended the downfall of Buddhism in India. He preached the austere philosophy of the *Upanishads,* the supremacy of the unitive knowledge acquired through discrimination, detachment, and self-control. He reinterpreted the *Upanishads,* the *Bhagavad Gita,* and the *Brahmasutras,* the three authoritative books of the Hindus, in the light of Non-dualism. Ramanuja (1017–1137), the founder of Qualified Non-dualism, preached a combination of knowledge and love. According to him the universe and its living beings are the different modes through which Brahman manifests Itself, the three together forming the complete Reality. The cultivation of ecstatic love for the Lord and the surrender of one's actions and desires to His will have an important place in Ramanuja's scheme of salvation. Maddhva (1199–1276), in southern India, and Chaitanya (1486–1533), in Bengal, were preachers of Dualism and taught love of God as the only means to salvation. Contact with Islam produced such religious reformers in northern India as Kabir and Nanak (1469–1583).

Hinduism came in real contact with Christianity in the eighteenth century, after the British conquest of India. The impact with this new, dynamic religion shook it almost to its foundation. In the nineteenth century two movements of reform were started which succeeded to a great extent in stemming the tide of the alien faith. The *Brahmo Samaj,* founded in Bengal by Raja Rammohan Roy (1774–1833), was dedicated to the worship of "the Eternal, the Unsearchable, the Immutable Being, who is the Author and the Preserver of the universe." The Raja, though born in an orthodox brahmin family and well versed in the Hindu scriptures, studied Islam and Christianity with respect. He went to Tibet in search of Buddhist mysteries. Two other great leaders of the Brahmo Samaj were Maharshi Devendranath Tagore (1817–1905) and Keshab Chandra Sen (1838–1884). The members of the *Samaj* were generally recruited from the English-educated Hindus. The movement itself, under its powerful leader Keshab, compromised in several respects with Christianity. It was an intellectual and eclectic faith. It preached against image-worship and the caste-system and confined itself mainly to social reform work. The *Brahmo Samaj* undoubtedly prevented many Hindus with an English education from embracing Christianity.

The *Arya Samaj* was founded by Swami Dayananda (1824–1883) as a bulwark against both Islam and Christianity. The movement was launched in Bombay in 1875 and soon its influence was felt throughout western India. Dayananda was a pugnacious preacher. He attacked the worship of images in Hindu temples and reintroduced the ancient Vedic rites among his followers. Like its sister movement in Bengal, the *Arya Samaj* also employed its strength to introduce such social reforms as the remarriage of Hindu widows and the abolition of the caste-system and the early marriage of Hindu women. It took the lead in liberating Hindu women from ignorance and seclusion. The cause of education in general received a special impetus from the *Arya Samaj*.

The nineteenth century also saw the birth of the great Ramakrishna * Paramahamsa (1836–1886), who was described by Romain Rolland as the fulfillment of the spiritual aspirations of the two hundred millions of Hindus for the past three thousand years. Through his spiritual experiences he beame a living witness of the truths of Hinduism embodied in the *Upanishads,* the *Puranas,* and the *Tantras.* He impressed everyone with his complete mastery of the body and the senses. In him one sees the triumph of Spirit over matter. He practiced the different faiths, including Christianity and Islam, and found that the same Truth is the goal of them all. He is respected everywhere today as the prophet of harmony.

Ramakrishna's disciple Swami Vivekananda (1863–1902), after the fashion of the Buddhist missionaries of olden times, carried the message of the Eternal Religion of the Hindus outside the land of

* See article "The Ramakrishna Movement."

its birth. He was the first religious preacher of India to present Hinduism before the Western world. In the year 1893 he represented his ancient faith at the Parliament of Religions held in Chicago in connection with the Columbian Exposition. It was he who founded the monastic Order of Ramakrishna, whose members take the vows of dedicating themselves to the realization of Truth and the service of humanity. During his short but dynamic career he reiterated the time-honored wisdom of the *Upanishads*. He taught that the culmination of spirituality is reached when one realizes the Godhead within oneself and then sees It in others. This ideal, expressing itself through various forms of social service, appears to be the present trend of Hinduism.

BIBLIOGRAPHY

NALINI KANTA BRAHMA, *Philosophy of Hindu Sadhana* (London, 1932).

SURENDRANATH DASGUPTA, *History of Indian Philosophy,* 3 vols. (London, 1932).

M. HIRIYANNA, *Outlines of Indian Philosophy* (New York, 1932).

S. RADHAKRISHNAN, *The Hindu View of Life* (London, 1931).

————, *Indian Philosophy,* 2 vols. (New York, 1927).

SRI RAMAKRISHNA, *The Gospel of Sri Ramakrishna,* translated by Swami Nikhilananda (New York, 1942).

ROMAIN ROLLAND, *Prophets of the New India* (New York, 1930).

F. MAX MULLER, translated by, *The Upanishads. Sacred Books of the East* (London, 1926).

SWAMI VIVEKANANDA, *Complete Works of Swami Vivekananda* (Mayavati, Himalayas, 1932).

SWAMI NIKHILANANDA, translated by, *The Bhagavad Gita* (New York, 1944).

ZOROASTRIANISM

Replying to our invitation to have a part in this volume, Dr. Taraporewala wrote: "I shall be very happy to contribute on Zoro-astrianism because of two reasons: (1) I am born a Zoroastrian and profess that faith and (2) I have studied our Scriptures in the original during well over thirty years. I have just completed my life's work with a revised translation of the Gathas (Songs) of Zoroaster. Therein I have found answers to all life's questions."

Irach Taraporewala has pursued the academic life as student, professor and research scholar continuously since the turn of the century. In 1903 he won his B.A. at the University of Bombay; from 1904 to 1909 he studied in London and then was called to the bar at Gray's Inn. He was awarded the Government of India Sanskrit scholarship in 1911 which brought him to the University of Cambridge and then to Germany where he later won his Ph.D. degree at the University of Würzburg; during this period he conferred with many of the leading European scholars on matters of philology and ancient literatures. After a period of teaching in India, he became, in 1917, professor of comparative philology at the University of Calcutta. In 1930 and for ten years he was principal of the M. F. Cama Athornan Institute, Andheri and the next two years director of Deccan College Post-Graduate and Research Institute, Poona, until his retirement in 1942.

Dr. Taraporewala was born in 1884 at Haiderabad, Deccan. Besides his mother tongue (Gujarati) he is at home in more than a dozen languages: Marathi, Hindi, Urdu, Bengali, English, French, German, Italian, Dutch, Sanskrit, Pali-Prakrit, Avesta, Greek, Persian, Pahlavi, Latin, with an acquaintance with Arabic and Chinese. His more than sixty published papers and books have dealt with subjects ranging from Indian Ideals of Education, the Parsis, San-skrit Dipthongs, ancient philology to his well known work "The Religion of Zarathushtra."

Editor

ZOROASTRIANISM

IRACH J. S. TARAPOREWALA

ZOROASTRIANISM is unique among the living religions of the world in two respects. First, it is perhaps the oldest faith which is "living." Secondly, it has the smallest number of adherents.* Zoroastrianism was contemporary with the ancient faiths of Egypt and Babylon. The date of the Founder cannot be fixed with any certainty, nor can any reliable account of his life be given.** Judging by the *language* of the most ancient documents of the faith, as found in the *Gāthās* (reputed to be the actual words of the Founder himself), Zoroastrianism seems to have been contemporary with the Vedas of India. Very probably the language of the *Gāthās* represents a slightly earlier stage, because we find in it words and grammatical forms which had already become obsolete in the Vedic period.

In any case the *Gāthās* are the foundations of all Zoroastrian beliefs and practice. The Zoroastrians look up to them as the very words of the Prophet. All the remaining Scriptures *** may be taken as deriving their inspiration from them and carrying forward their message.

* The total is less than 130,000 in the whole world. Of these more than 100,000 live in India (over 50,000 in the city of Bombay). Some 20,000 (or less) live in Persia. The remaining (a few hundreds) are scattered over the other lands of the world.

** The traditional life of the Prophet was composed about 2,000 years after his time.

*** These are in three languages, Avesta, Pahlavi and Persian. The Avesta Texts consist of (1) the *Yasna* (in 72 chapters, of which 17 are the *Gāthās*); (2) the *Visparad* (a sort of liturgical supplement to the *Yasna*); (3) the *Vendīdād* ("the Laws against the Demons," a work of much later composition, containing details of ceremonial and "purification"); and (4) the *Khordeh-Avestā* (a miscellaneous collection of hymns and litanies and prayers). The Pahlavi Texts were all composed much later, between the 3rd and the 10th centuries of Christ. They consist of translations of the Avesta Texts with a running commentary, and also of a number of theological treatises embodying the beliefs and dogmas of the Sāsānian age. The Persian Texts are mainly the *Revāyats,* which are answers to theological questions sent from India to Zoroastrian priests in Persia regarding details of ritual and daily life.

As has happened in the case of every religion, the purest and highest form of the faith is to be found in the days of the Founder and in his own inspired words; in other words, in the earliest Texts. In later days influences from other races and other beliefs begin to creep in and the faith undergoes an enormous change. Naturally the later priests would make attempts to find sanctions for their own later beliefs in the authentic teachings of the Founder. Thus in the later Zoroastrian Scriptures we find two sentences fairly regularly repeated: (1) "Zarathushtra asked Ahurā-Mazdā, 'O Ahurā-Mazdā, Spirit most holy, Creator of this material world, what is . . . ?'"; and (2) "Thereupon Ahurā-Mazdā replied, 'O holy Zarathushtra, it is . . .'" In this way every superstition and every practice of later ages was justified and doubly sanctified by invoking the sacred names of the Founder, Zarathushtra, and of the Supreme Being Ahurā-Mazdā.

During the third and the fourth centuries of the Christian era all the ancient Avesta Scriptures of Zoroastrianism were collected and translated into Pahlavi, which was the language of the people in those days. The original language of the Scriptures was Avesta, which was the language of ancient Bactria (in East Iran). This language was very near in structure and vocabulary to the Ancient (Vedic) Sanskrit of India. From internal evidence it is proved that the whole of these Avesta writings cover a period of several centuries —probably well over a thousand years. The *Gāthās* represent the oldest stage of the Avesta language. Hence it is obvious that at least a thousand years have intervened between their composition and the Pahlavi renderings and commentaries. There are very clear indications that the Pahlavi writers have not understood the grammatical construction of the ancient Texts and a number of Gāthā words have been given the meanings they had acquired in the later Pahlavi days. The result is that these Pahlavi renderings cannot by any means be taken as entirely reliable. The Pahlavi translators and commentators were certainly Zoroastrians by faith, but they looked at the teachings of the Prophet in the light of the beliefs and practices of their own days. Naturally, therefore, we get a somewhat distorted picture of the fundamentals of Zoroastrianism from these Pahlavi works. All the work on the *Gāthās* done so far by Western scholars has depended ultimately on these Pahlavi treatises. Even thus we get a picture of the Prophet and of his Teaching which is very noble and sublime. But to get an accurate picture the *Gāthās* must be studied in their own light and in the light of the ancient traditions they embody. The closest to them, both in language and in thought are the contemporary Vedic Texts of India, the Hymns for the language and the earlier *Upanishads* for the thought and for the ancient Aryan tradition.

For the Iranians, among whom Zoroaster was born, and to whom his Message was addressed, were a branch of the ancient Aryan people. They were proud of being Aryans and of their Aryan heritage. This heritage forms a sort of background for the *Gāthās*. It consisted of a set of beliefs concerning life and its meaning, and a system of customs and social usage. The Aryans had a system of Nature-worship and adored a set of Nature-gods. These are seen fully developed in the Hymns of the Vedas. And above and beyond these Nature-gods the Aryans did recognize a Supreme Being, "the One Reality," whom "the Wise call by many names" (*Rig-Veda,* i.164.46). Zarathushtra took firm hold of this "One Reality" and held Him up as the Supreme Being, *Ahurā-Mazdā.* He eliminated all other Deities of the Aryan pantheon. Even when in later days some of the older Nature-gods came back into Zoroastrian theology, the supremacy of *Ahurā-Mazdā* remained unchallenged.

The Aryans seem to have had some sort of social organization. Both in Iran as well as in India this developed into the four hereditary "classes" of (1) Priests, (2) Warriors, (3) Agriculturists (and commercial people) and (4) Craftsmen (and servants).

The distinguishing dress of the Zoroastrians today is made up of three items: (1) the "sacred shirt" (the *sudreh*); (2) the "sacred girdle" (the *kustī*) and (3) the cap covering the head. This was the ancient Aryan dress, and goes back to pre-Zoroastrian days. The investiture of every Aryan child (whether boy or girl) took place sometime after the age of seven. After this investiture the religious education of the child began. This investiture constituted the "second" or the "new birth" of the child, and hence in India all true Aryans (belonging to the first three classes) were called the "twice-born."

To these Aryans of Iran Zarathushtra brought his Message. This can best be understood by considering it point by point. The first essential Teaching of the Prophet is that Ahurā-Mazdā alone is the Supreme Being and as such deserves our obedience and worship. The first thing to note is that the name itself is *double*. In the *Gāthās* we find that the Supreme is addressed in four ways: (1) *Ahurā* or (2) *Mazdā* (both single) or (3) *Mazdā-Ahurā* or (4) *Ahurā-Mazdā* (the last two being double). The last name has become stereotyped in later Avesta literature and in all Pahlavi and later theological works. As a matter of fact the use of the first three variants definitely marks out *Gāthā* passages. Indeed, out of the four variants the combination *Ahurā-Mazdā* is the least used in the *Gāthās* themselves. Since in the earliest Achaemenian Inscriptions of Darius the Great we find the form *Aurā-mazdā* alone, we may confidently assert that these Inscriptions were contemporary with the later Avesta Texts and that therefore the *Gāthās* are certainly pre-Achaemenian.

This double name is full of significance. *Ahurā* (Sanskrit *asura*) means "Lord of Life." He is the Creator and Upholder of all Life, and thus represents the Spirit-side of the universe. *Mazdā* may be explained as made up from *maz* (Sanskrit *mah*) and the root *dā* (Sanskrit *dhā*), and the word may be translated as "Creator of Matter." * So the double name *Ahurā-Mazdā* signifies "Lord of Life and Creator of Matter." Thus this name brings out the fundamental duality of our visible universe—Spirit and Matter. And this name implies that the Supreme Being is the Creator and Upholder of both these great principles. This fundamental dualism runs through all Zoroastrian writings, and is in fact at the root of the teaching about the Twin Spirits which is often pointed out to show that Zoroastrianism is "dualistic." For this wrong notion the really responsible people were the Pahlavi writers who identified the "Good" Spirit with the Supreme Creator and made the "Evil" Spirit His eternal adversary. But this is certainly not the original teaching of the Prophet.

This Supreme *Ahurā-Mazdā* is necessarily invisible and intangible to our physical senses. He can only be "seen" through "the eye of the/Spirit" (*Yasna* 45.8). For the average human being He must necessarily remain a mere name. To understand Him, therefore, Zarathushtra has pointed out a method through the *Ameshā-Spentā* (usually translated as the "Holy Immortals"). In later ages these

---

* The Pahlavi writers seem to have confused this with another root *dā*, to know, and so have explained the name *Mazdā* as meaning "Lord of great Wisdom."

have been understood as almost equivalent to Arch-angels, Deities standing next to the Godhead in rank, each with a special "department" of the universe assigned to look after.

Western scholars have tried to explain them as "personified qualities of the Godhead," but that seems somewhat inadequate. To begin with they are six in number, divided into two groups of three each. In one group all three bear names in the *feminine* gender and represent the Mother-side of the Supreme. In the other group the names are actually in the neuter gender, but they stand for *masculine* concepts and represent the Father-side of the Supreme. Thus we have amongst the highest Divinities two clear groups, one representing the active side, the Fatherhood, and the other representing the passive side or the Motherhood of the Supreme. These two also correspond respectively to the *Ahurā* and to the *Mazdā* aspects of God.

It must never be forgotten that all these six are not *different* Beings, nor even the "creations" of the Supreme. They are in very truth *aspects* of *Ahurā-Mazdā*. A better comparison would be with the "rays" of various colors which make up the white light of the Sun. These six "Holy Immortals" together with *Ahurā-Mazdā* Himself make a *Heptad,* who are known in later literature as the "Seven Ameshā-Spentā." But the phrase used for these seven in the *Gāthās* is very significant—they are called there "the *Ahurā-Mazdās*" (in the plural number). (*Yasna* 30.9 and 31.4.)

The three "aspects" of the Supreme on the Father-side are named *Asha, Vohu-Manō* and *Kshathra*. These names have been usually translated as "Righteousness," "Good Mind" and "Power" (or "Dominion"). But these renderings convey but a very faint idea of all that these signify in the *Gāthās*.

Asha stands for the Knowledge of the Law of God, and for the Law itself. In many places *Asha* stands for the *Eternal Law of God,* which is identical with Righteousness, the Righteousness about which Jesus had preached. The deeper significance of the word has been lost in later writings and today the word is used to describe a man who is "good" in the ordinary sense of the term and in the eyes of the world. But the original concept of *Asha* is far above mere worldly goodness and physical purity. It also implies mental and spiritual purity. In the earlier texts we read of the Divine Beings occupying their exalted positions "through *Asha*"; and in one passage (*Yasna* 57.4) *Ahurā Mazdā* Himself is described as having "advanced the furthest through Asha." The finest definition of *Asha* is contained in the last stanza of Tennyson's *In Memoriam*:

> That God, which always lives and loves,
> One God, one law, one element,
> And one far-off divine event,
> To which the whole creation moves.

In *Asha* lies the consummation of our human life and effort. By understanding *Asha* and by realizing what He stands for we may understand the Supreme. *Asha*, therefore, is the Eternal Law of God, the Law of Truth and Righteousness, which none may thwart, which none may defy. This *Asha* is the very foundation of Zoroastrian Religion.

In later theology *Asha-Vahishta* (the Highest *Asha*) becomes identified with the Sacred Fire, the physical symbol of Zoroaster's religion. There is an oft-quoted sentence which says, "There is but one Path, the Path of *Asha*; all the others are False Paths." This sentence fittingly closes the Book of *Yasna*. And in another place (*Yasna*, 60.12) the worshipper expresses this wish: "Through the highest *Asha*, through the best *Asha*, may we catch a glimpse of Thee, may we draw near unto Thee, may we be in perfect union with Thee."

Asha, in short, is the Righteousness of the Father in Heaven, which we should seek first so that all other things "shall be added" unto us.

The next step after understanding *Asha* or the Law of Righteousness is the cultivation of *Vohu-Manō*. The usual rendering "Good Mind" is very weak and entirely colorless. The adjective *vohu* is derived from an obsolete root *vah* (*vas* in Sanskrit) which means "to love." We find derivatives of the same root in the Vedas also. So the correct rendering of the name of the second "ray" of *Ahurā* should be "Loving Mind" or *"Love."*

In the *Gāthās* no doubt *Asha* ranks first, but all through later theology *Vohu-Manō* stands next after *Ahurā-Mazdā*. As a matter of fact even in the *Gāthās*, *Vohu-Manō* has been mentioned nearly twice as often as *Asha*. Love is the supreme fact of Life, the Power that sways our human destiny. In the *Gāthās* the aspirant expresses his desire that he may reach up to *Mazdā-Ahurā* "through *Vohu-Manō*" (*Yasna* 28.2). In another passage (*Yasna* 46.2) the Wor-

shipper and the Worshipped are called "the Lover and the Beloved." Herein lies the first germ of the exquisite mystic poetry of
the Sufis.

When *Vohu-Manō* rises in the heart of a human being it is expressed either as Devotion to the Father of All or as Love for our
Brother-Man. The supreme manifestation of Love in human life is
seen in the union of man and maid in wedlock. This earthly Love
can be sublimated into spiritual Love. There is a beautiful verse in
the *Gāthās* (*Yasna* 53.5):

> These words I speak to maidens truly wed
> And to their comrades young; bear these in mind,
> And understand them deep within your Souls;—
> Bring down Vohu Man' in your lives on earth,
> Let each one strive the other to surpass
> In Asha's Truth, in Vohu Manō's Love;
> Thus each one surely shall reap rich rewards.

Wedded life and wedded love is the first step on the Path towards *Ahurā,* for in that condition alone the man or the woman
begins to think for the first time of some one else. Hence the wedded
state is regarded as distinctly *holy*; and it has been stated that a
married person is dearer to *Ahurā-Mazdā* than an unmarried one
(*Vendīdād* 4.47).

In Zoroastrian Texts five great Lords and Masters have been
enumerated. These are: (1) the Lord of the House; (2) the Lord
of the Town; (3) the Lord of the Province; (4) the Lord of the
Country, and (5) the Lord of Religion. These five imply ever-
increasing circles of love and responsibility, and the last holds the
whole of Humanity within the circle of his Love.*

The Love of *Vohu-Manō* extends even beyond Humanity, and
takes into its fold "our younger brothers," the Animals. In later
theology *Vohu-Manō* is depicted as the Guardian Angel of the Animal Kingdom. Zoroastrians as a rule are meat-eaters, but even today
orthodox Zoroastrians abstain from flesh on the days consecrated to
Vohu-Manō.

Achieving the Understanding of the Eternal Law of Righteousness and realizing the All-embracing Love of *Ahurā-Mazdā,* the

---

* This foreshadows in a way Wendell Willkie's "One World."

aspirant should now translate both these—this Knowledge and this Love—into Action. He must seek the help of the third "Aspect" of the Lord, *Kshathra,* who represents the Strength of the Lord bestowed upon those who truly *serve* their brothers. Loving Service—*Vohu-Kshathra*—follows directly from Love. He also represents the Creative Activity of the Supreme. In human life the only activity worthy to be called "creative" is.Service done to Humanity, inspired by Love. As an eminent worker once put it, "the best reward for Service is the opportunity to do greater Service." And this is exactly what has been promised to the Zoroastrian, when he is told (*Yasna* 27.13) that:

> Ahurā's Kshathra surely cometh down
> On him who serves with zeal his brother meek.

Every act of service rendered to the meek (who according to Zarathushtra also "shall inherit the earth") brings a greater outpouring from above.

The three "Aspects" of the Supreme on the Mother-side are not so prominent nor so clear. They represent the firm, unshakable Faith in the Eternal Law and the resulting rewards.

Ārmaiti (usually translated "Piety") is the counterpart of *Asha* on the Mother-side. She represents the firmness of Faith in *Mazdā* and His Law. She resides in the heart of every human being and "stands by to solve our doubts" (*Yasna* 31.12). She is our "Rock of Ages," and we must keep our ears ever open to listen to Her whisper within our hearts. She is the "Daughter of Ahurā-Mazdā" (*Yasna* 45.4), and our ultimate Refuge. In our hours of tribulation and sorrow She brings us strength and comfort. In later theology *Ārmaiti* is the Guardian Angel of the firm and stable Mother-Earth.

The remaining two are mostly mentioned together. They are named *Haurvatāt* (Wholeness or Perfection) and *Ameretāt* (Immortality). They are clearly and definitely "allegorical" concepts. They bestow upon man the blessings of "Life renewed" and "Strength of Soul," and these gifts come only to those who have realized *Vohu-Manō.*

This wonderful and poetic Teaching of the Holy Immortals may be summed up thus: Every human being must understand the Eternal Law of God of Truth and Righteousness. He must realize the Power of Love. And he must translate both these into Acts of

Loving Service. All through his striving he must hold fast to Faith and thus attain the Goal of Perfection and Immortality.

The entire Message of Zarathushtra, as contained in the *Gāthās* revolves around the Holy Immortals, and he has taught us the way to realize them in our life on earth and thus realize *Ahurā-Mazdā*.

Besides these Seven of the *Heptad* Zarathushtra also mentions two other Deities as worthy of worship. These are Fire (*Ātar*) and *Sraosha*. Both are clearly "allegorical" personifications.

All through the history of Zoroastrianism the Fire has been understood to be not so much the physical Fire as the Spiritual Fire within each human being. It is the Divine Spark in man. Zoroastrians have been wrongly named "Fire-worshippers." The real object of their worship is the Inner Spiritual Fire, who

> lights the Faithful clearly through Life;
> But, Mazdā, in the hearts of Infidels
> He sees the hidden evil at a glance. (*Yasna* 31.4)

In Zoroastrian Temples to this day the Sacred Fire (the outer symbol of the Inner Reality) is kept constantly burning. At Udvādā (about 100 miles north of Bombay) there is the Holiest Shrine of the Fire of Iran (the *Īrānshāh*), which has been blazing for well over ten centuries. But ever above and behind this physical Fire there is present the idea of the "Divine Spark," for the Fire is always called "*Ātar, the Son of Ahurā-Mazdā*" (*Yasna* 62). He is literally a "Spark" from the Divine Fire. Nowhere in all the numerous references to Him in the *Avesta* Texts is He ever conceived as purely physical.

In later theology, *Sraosha* is the greatest Divinity after the "Holy Immortals." The name means literally "Obedience" and implies the willing and understanding obedience of man to *Mazdā's* Will and to His Law. *Sraosha* has been called in the *Gāthās* (*Yasna* 33.5) "the Greatest Servant" of *Mazdā*. It should be clearly understood that the Obedience which the Prophet expects from every man is not the blind obedience of the fanatic, but the *willing* obedience of an *understanding* mind.

The most notable contribution of Zoroaster to the religious thought of the world is his solution of the Problem of Evil. The Prophet does, indeed, see clearly that Evil and Suffering are stark realities of human life, and he never tries to minimize this patent fact. But he has given a very rational explanation of the Existence of Evil in a world created by the benevolent *Ahurā-Mazdā*. This he has developed in his Teaching about the Two Spirits. He says in very clear words that both Good and Evil have been *"created by Mazdā"* (*Yasna* 30.1), just as elsewhere he speaks of "the Great Architect," who fashioned Realms of Light and also Realms of Dark" (*Yasna* 44.5). The verses of the *Gāthās* where the Two Spirits "created by *Mazdā*" are first described are worth quoting in full (*Yasna* 30.3–5):

> The First-created were the Spirits Twain,
> As Twin Co-workers they reveal themselves;
> Yet, in each thought and word and deed these Two
> Are ne'er agreed;—one's Good, the other Bad;
> And of these Two the Wise do choose aright,
> The Unwise choose not thus,—and go astray.

> And when together did the Spirits Twain
> Foregather at creation's early dawn,
> *Life* did One make, the Other made *Not-Life*;

> And thus Creation's purpose is achieved;
> Dark is the mind of those that cling to False,
> But brightly shines the mind that holds to Truth

> Of these Twin Spirits he that was the False
> Did ever choose performing evil deeds,
> But Righteousness did choose the Holy One:
> He who would clothe himself in Light of Heav'n,
> He who would satisfy Lord Ahurā,
> Let him through deeds of Truth choose Mazdā's Way.

The essential difference between the Two Spirits is seen in their respective Creations, *Life* and *Not-Life*. The *negative* form of the latter is to be particularly noted. For this brings out clearly the essential characteristic of the "Evil Spirit." Like Mephistopheles in Goethe's *Faust* the Evil One is the Spirit of Eternal Negation, the Spirit which evermore denies, and which claims as his own peculiar preserve

> all the elements which ye
> Destruction, Sin, or briefly, Evil, name.

Again Mephistopheles tells Faust that he is

> part of that power which still
> Produceth good, while ever scheming ill.

This is exactly what Zarathushtra had taught many centuries before Goethe. The purpose of all Creation is the attainment of the Good by all Souls, and this can be achieved only if Evil exists. But this Evil is essentially negative and hence cannot be everlasting: in the end Good shall assuredly triumph. The victories of Evil are always shortlived.

Then again it is the sign of Wisdom to choose the Path of Good. People choose the Path of Untruth because they are ignorant, because they "find it pleasanter to go astray" (*Yasna* 53.6). So all "sin" is rooted in ignorance, and that has to be overcome by the Divine Wisdom of *Asha*. In the early *Avesta* Texts the greatest opponent of *Asha* is *Druj* (Falsehood).

Another point in this exposition is that when a man chooses to follow Evil his *mind* becomes dark, while "brightly shines the *mind* that holds to Truth."

Yet another point emphasized here is that the Path of Good, "Mazdā's Way," is to be sought "through *deeds* of Truth." Zoroaster has always stressed *deeds*. His three Commandments are, Good Thoughts, Good Words, Good Deeds. Thoughts necessarily come first, and last but not the least are *Deeds*.

The most valued Teaching of the Prophet of Iran is where he asserts that each human being is *perfectly free* to choose one of the Two Paths. He says in very clear words:

> Hear with your ears the Highest Truths I preach,
> And with illumined minds weigh them with care,
> Before you choose which of Two Paths to tread,—
> *Deciding man by man, each one for each;*—
> Before the great New Age is ushered in
> Wake up, alert to spread Ahurā's Word. (*Yasna* 30.2) . . . .

This is Mankind's Charter of Spiritual Freedom. The Prophet has nowhere said that his teaching *must* be followed; he flourishes no Divine sanctions in our faces. He only enunciates *Mazdā's* inexorable Law. He says that *Mazdā* has given to human beings

Bodies with Souls within that can perceive (*Yasna* 31.11),

and out of his Thought *Mazdā* gives us "power to think." These three, Body, Soul and Mind, are the greatest gifts of the Supreme to Man, and the most glorious of the three is Mind. Zoroaster wants all of us to use our "illumined minds." Each human being must utilize to the fullest this greatest of Divine gifts. And just because Man has Mind—the faculty of distinguishing Right from Wrong—therefore, he has the fullest freedom to choose his Path in Life. He is absolutely free to go to Hell if he so chooses. True Strength of the Soul can come only through such perfect freedom; only thus can Man rise to the height of his Divine Stature and be "as perfect as his Father in Heaven is perfect." This is the noblest Teaching of Zarathushtra.

As the immediate corollary of the perfect Freedom of Choice follows the inexorable Law of Action and Reaction, the Law which lays down, "as ye sow, so shall ye surely reap," what the Philosophers and Sages of India have called "the Law of *Karma*." The results which follow the choice, good or evil, are clearly described in the *Gāthās*. This is the unchangeable Law of *Ahurā*—"Evil to Evil, Good to Good" (*Yasna* 43.5). He states in very clear words that

> Falsehood brings on age-long punishment,
> And Truth leads on to fuller, higher Life (*Yasna* 30.11).

These Laws of *Karma*, "of Happiness and Sorrow," are inexorable. No one can intercede. Again and again the Prophet asserts that one's "own evil thoughts and deeds" prove a bar to further progress.

The Twin Spirits indicate the fundamental difference between Spirit and Matter, between things mundane and things heavenly. Human beings in their ignorance are led astray by earthly joys, which are in their very nature fleeting. They do not "choose aright," the Prophet says,

> Because the Arch-Deluder close to them
> Approached as they disputing stood in doubt;
> Thus did they choose the Spirit of Worst Thought,
> Misled by him they rushed away to Wrath,
> And thus did they pollute our mortal Life (*Yasna* 30.6).

The Arch-Deluder is always near by to delude and mislead us when our ears are filled with the "songs of the Earth" and are deaf to the voice of *Ārmaiti* within. We stand "disputing in doubt" endlessly.

We are then attracted by things of this earth and when we fail to get these the sense of frustration converts our "desires" into Wrath and Hatred. That is exactly what has been happening to the Nations of the Earth all these years; and thus we have all polluted Mother-Earth and our mortal Life. The Demon of Wrath, *Aēshma* (the Asmodeus of the *Book of Tobit*) is stalking abroad today. He is described in Zoroastrian books as being next to the Evil One himself. The *Gāthās* very strongly admonish us,

> Keep Hatred far from you; let nothing tempt
> Your minds to violence (*Yasna* 48.7).

These words are full of meaning for the World today. One of the verses of the *Gāthās* might be the cry of Humanity today (*Yasna* 44.20):

> Mazdā, why are the Wicked powerful?
> I further ask, Many for selfish ends
> Have flung our Earth to Hatred, Strife and Woe;
> Bound her to men both deaf and blind to Thee:—
> Could these not make her safe in Asha's hands,
> And full of Peace and Love lead her to Thee?

The upward Path of *Asha* is difficult and long, but it leads to the "Abode of Vohu-Manō," the Heaven of Love, for "the Path of Truth is but the Path of Love" (*Yasna* 49.3). And with the aid of Ahurā's *Vohu-Manō* and with Faith (*Ārmaiti*) in the heart every man shall tread this Path and reach the final Goal "where Ahurā rules supreme." Every human being is destined ultimately to reach this Blessed Abode, even the most wicked of mankind. For just at the height of his triumph "the follower of Falsehood" sees his victories crumbling to dust, "and all his triumphs brought to naught by Truth." Then, "from that time shall his mind retrace its steps" (*Yasna* 30.10). Then he shall begin to replace the Hate in his heart by Love;

> Then, Mazdā, Lord of All, Thy Law Supreme
> Shall be revealed to them by Vohu Man',
> Then, O Ahurā, shall they learn, indeed,
> To give all Falsehood into Asha's hands (*Yasna* 30.8).

This ultimate redemption of even the wicked ones is the most heartening feature of the Message of Zarathushtra.

After long years of tribulation, of frustration and of mental agony in this "Abode of Untruth" (our earthly home) the Soul learns his lesson and retraces his steps, surrrendering himself utterly to the guidance of *Vohu-Manō*. Hatred is thus literally conquered by Love.

This life upon earth, with all its strifes and all its temptations is the great school for the aspiring Soul. The *Gāthās* describe this as the "Ordeal of molten metal"; this is the "Fiery Test of Truth" which burns up all Evil within us.

The Sages of India have emphatically asserted that repeated births in human shape are needed before Perfection can be attained. As a matter of fact the various Religions of India have made the doctrine of Reincarnation a fundamental one in their teaching. In the *Gāthās* there is but one single verse (*Yasna* 49.11)—only one verse out of 239—which speaks clearly of a "return to this Abode of Untruth":

> But Souls whose Inner Light continues dim,
> Who have not yet beheld the Light of Truth,
> Unto this House cf Falsehood shall return,
> Surrounded by false Leaders, Egos false,
> By those who think and speak and act untrue.

Zarathushtra all through has emphasized *deeds,* and so, quite consistently, he has hinted at the possibility of a man's attaining Perfection and achieving Immortality *in one single life,* by deeds of Truth and Love. He has promised that:

> Within the span of this *one* life on Earth
> Perfection can be reached by fervent souls,
> Ardent in zeal, sincere in their toil (*Yasna* 51.12).

Toil and *Action* are the keynotes of Zoroastrian life. This activity must be motivated by true Knowledge of God's Plan and by Love for all. He has taught that each one should choose "all deeds of goodness as His worship true" (*Yasna* 53.2); and we are further told deeds should be done "out of Love for Lord of Life" (*Yasna* 27.13). All actions must be performed in the Name of *Mazdā* and not for selfish ends. The life of a Zoroastrian has to be guided by four principles: (1) removal of all quarrels and differences; (2) lowering of weapons; (3) self-reliance and (4) righteousness. The main objects of human life should be, in short, "Peace on Earth and Goodwill to man."

To attain these objects it is necessary to cultivate certain activities which are typified by the first three Holy Immortals. These three most necessary activities for any human being are *to know, to love, to serve*. All these three have to proceed simultaneously and have to be developed harmoniously in order to attain Perfection and Immortality. This would be the truest worship of the Holy Immortals and through them of *Ahurā-Mazdā*. There is hardly any idea of *individual* freedom from sorrow and tribulation. The governing idea is the forwarding of *Mazdā's* plan for the universe by doing one's best wherever one happens to be. The worshipper prays (*Yasna* 43.11):

> And through this Teaching I grow true and wise.
> When difficulties come my faith in man
> Leads me to be and do what Thou hast taught—
> To be my own true self and do my best.

Zarathushtra speaks of the dangers from "Evil Teachers," who for their own gain deliberately "distort Mazdā's Word" and lead men astray. He calls such teachers "devourers," and warns all to be on their guard against them and their teaching. But however hard these Teachers may try, they are ultimately doomed to failure. The Prophet says:

> Such persons in these ways defile our lives;
> Dazzled by worldly grandeur they regard
> The wicked as the great ones of the Earth;
> They hinder all fulfilment here below;
> O Mazdā, from the highest Goal of Life
> They turn aside the minds of righteous men.

> They through their teaching try their very best
> That men may leave the honest Path of Work;
> But Mazdā gives them retribution just;
> With chants alluring they mislead all life,
> Until not Truth we meet but hungry Wolves,*
> Deaf to all else, and maddened by Untruth.

* Cf. what Milton wrote more than two thousand years later in his Sonnet to the Lord General Cromwell about "hireling wolves whose gospel is their maw."

Whatever hopes these Wolves have to attain
Power in realms of Lies and Evil Minds,
This pow'r itself destroys their Inner Life (*Yasna* 32.11–13).

All this strong condemnation seems to have been directed
against the ritual-ridden priesthood of the earlier faith. He calls
this ritual a "rotting mass of Lies" (*Yasna* 48.19) and wishes that
it may "dissolve." To the Prophet Right Thought and Right Action
means far more than any ceremony or ritual.

Such was the glorious "Faith of Mazdā-worship, taught by
Zarathushtra." Such was his Message which was in truth a Message
for all mankind. It was a Message of Universal Brotherhood and
moral uplift, based on Knowledge, Love and Service. Zarathushtra
was certainly among the earliest of the Saviours of mankind.

As has happened in the history of every great religion, the
Faith of Zarathushtra declined slowly but steadily in the course of
ages from its pristine purity. He had gathered round himself a band
of ardent Disciples, who formed the famous Maga-Brotherhood,
the Magi described by Greek and Roman historians. After all,
Iranians were human beings, having their full share of the failings
of lust and greed and wrath, owing to which the religion declined.
The history of Zoroastrianism shows two very sudden declines
and falls.

However strongly the Prophet may have spoken against mere
ceremonial and ritual, the average human mind always desires some
tangible show, some appeal to his senses and emotions. This in fact
is the *raison d'être* of all ceremonial. So we find that soon after the
passing of the Prophet all the ancient ceremonies and the worship of
the ancient Aryan Nature-gods returned to Iran. The supremacy of
Ahurā-Mazdā, however, remained unchallenged and the lofty ethics
of Zarathushtra have never been entirely forgotten. As time went
on the "Holy Immortals" became more and more anthropomorphic,
many of the older Aryan Deities came back, and moral and ethical
concepts like *Daēnā* (Inner-Ego), *Ashi-Vanguhi* (Good-Blessing)
and *Manthra-Spenta* (Holy-Word) became installed as Deities.

Soon after the Prophet's days the texts of Zoroastrianism were
collected together in 21 separate treatises called *Nasks*, arranged
subjectwise. Later on, it has been recorded that Darius, the Great

(B.C. 521–485), the Achaemenian, had three copies of these *Nasks* inscribed on parchment and had them deposited in safe places. One of these was kept in the palace of the King of Kings at Persepolis.

The later Achaemenians were certainly Zoroastrians, and of the earlier rulers both Cyrus the Great (B.C. 549–529) and Darius I (B.C. 521–485) were probably Zoroastrians. But in any case the Achaemenian rulers were neither bigoted nor narrow-minded. They ruled over a vast empire made of many nations, followers of various Faiths. Both Cyrus and Darius have been mentioned with gratitude in Babylonian and Egyptian chronicles as restorers of the hoary religions of these lands. And the very valuable and timely aid given by Cyrus and by Artaxerxes (B.C. 465–425) to the Jews is well authenticated.

It is absolutely certain that the other religions and beliefs of the vast Empire of the Achaemenians have left a very deep impress on Zoroastrianism, the national religion of Iran in those days. In particular the Spring festival of both Babylon and Egypt was introduced into Persia and it was soon transformed into the Iranian cult of *Mitra-Anāhitā*. No doubt the closely similar Dionysius festival of the Greeks had also a share in moulding this Iranian cult. We find *Mithra* and *Anāhitā* (both early Aryan Deities) mentioned in the later Achaemenian Inscriptions side by side with the Supreme *"Auramazdā."* The orgies connected with the *Mithra-Anāhitā* cult did indeed sap the vitality of the nation and loosened their moral fiber. Thus the spread of this cult was one of the major causes of the collapse of the Achaemenian Empire.

The influences of Greek thought and culture had penetrated Persia long before Alexander's conquest. One very noteworthy characteristic of the Iranians was their faculty of assimilating foreign customs and cultures. The Hellenic influences had already begun their work long before the conquest of Alexander and so the subsequent process of hellenizing Persia was comparatively swift and easy.

Alexander burnt down the palaces at Persepolis (B.C. 330) and with them perished the priceless copy of the Zoroastrian Scriptures. Zoroastrians have never forgiven Alexander for this act, and in all subsequent Zoroastrian writings he has always been called "the Vile" or "the Damned."

But it seems that at least one of the three copies made by the command of Darius was carried off to Alexandria in Egypt. It was lodged there for several centuries until the great Library there was burnt down (B.C. 48).

In any case the ancient Zoroastrian Scriptures were now entirely lost to Persia. Their contents, however were preserved in the memories of priests, in fragments of ritual and in a few scattered manuscripts. The ancient Religion and its ritual were kept alive during the five centuries after Alexander by a line of devoted Priest-Princes who ruled at Persepolis under the suzerainty of the Parthian Emperors.

For five centuries after Alexander the political history of Persia is chaotic. Zoroastrianism had disappeared as the official State-religion of Persia, but there were many in high places who followed that ancient Faith, if only in name. Notable among them were the Rulers of Pontus and of Armenia. Practically all the Rulers of the Arsacid (Parthian) Dynasty were Zoroastrians, at least in name. But all these highly placed people were clearly hellenistic in their outlook and many of them took pride in calling themselves "phil-hellene."

Naturally the practice of Zoroastrianism suffered many and strange transformations among the masses. Foreign influences were working practically unchecked among them all through these centuries. The greatest undoubtedly were from Greece. Then also there were influences from Buddhism, which was a considerable cultural factor in East Iran. From the north came the strange superstitions brought in by the Parthian peoples, relics of a primitive Shamanism, with a vivid belief in hosts of demons who must be placated. Then there were the superstitions, magic and astrology of Babylonian beliefs. There were the Jews with their insistence on ceremonial purity. And last of all came Christianity, which had already begun its onward march by the end of the Parthian period.

Zoroastrians had spread extensively all over Asia Minor and Syria during the Achaemenian days. A great many had emigrated eastwards into Central Asia, China and India. Some had scattered over North Africa and there were some Zoroastrians in Italy during the Parthian days. The Zoroastrianism these emigrants practised was strongly tinged with Mithraism. But this Mithra-worship was now purged of its orgies and its excesses and was confined to the worship of *Mithra,* the Lord of Light, the *Sol invictus,* the invincible Lord of Truth and Justice. This style of worship appealed strongly to the well-disciplined Romans and through them Mithraism spread extensively over the Roman Empire. As a matter of fact *Mithra* was the greatest and most formidable rival of Christ in the early days of Christianity.

The Parthian Emperors were always too much occupied with their wars to pay any attention to religion. They had always on hand some war with Rome or with the wilder tribes on the eastern and northern frontiers. Or else they were busy with dynastic and fratricidal wars. But Valkhash (Velegeses) I (A.D. 51–77) was an exception inasmuch as he was a man of peace. He was a Zoroastrian not merely in name but he actually strove to put into practice the teaching by loving his brothers and not fighting with them. He conceived the grand idea of restoring the ancient Zoroastrian Faith as the State-religion of Persia. For that purpose he sent for Zoroastrian priests and learned men from all over his empire and ordered them to help in restoring the Texts of the original 21 *Nasks.* This move sent a thrill through the faithful Zoroastrian community ruled by the Priest-Princes of Persepolis. But long before these learned men could come together and start work Valkhash died. Parthia was once again plunged into a terrible struggle with Rome, in the course of which the capital city, Ctesiphon, was sacked and destroyed three times within one hundred years by the Romans. These events were most severe blows to the national and racial pride of Iran. To make matters worse the Parthian Emperor Ardavān (Artabanus) V (A.D. 209–226) had betrothed his daughter to the "heathen" Roman Emperor, Caracalla. This, in the eyes of the Zoroastrians, was an unpardonable offense. The Priest-Princes at Persepolis were already dreaming of a truly Zoroastrian Empire. So they raised the standard of revolt against the Parthian Ruler and they found a capable leader in Ardashir, son of Pāpak, of the House of Sāsān. He himself was an ordained priest of Zoroastrian Faith. He met Ardavān in battle, gained a complete victory, and proclaimed himself King of Kings. Thus the Sāsānian Empire was founded.

Ardashir I (A.D. 226–240) and his son Shāpūr I (the conqueror of Valerian) (A.D. 240–271) were both very staunch Zoroastrians and were both priests; for by now priesthood had become definitely hereditary in Zoroastrianism. Both these rulers carried forward and successfully completed the work begun by the Parthian Valkhash. The original Texts of the 21 *Nasks* were restored, largely from memory. And both these rulers went much further than Valkhash ever intended. They ordered that the ancient Scriptures, written in the now forgotten Avesta language, should be translated into Pahlavi, the language of the common people of those days. All the ancient Texts were accordingly translated and extensive commentaries on these were compiled by learned priests.

Of course this restored Zoroastrianism of the Sāsānian Empire was based on the fundamental teachings of the Gāthās of Zoroaster. But the many centuries that had passed since the days of the Prophet had transformed the Faith enormously. The priests of Sāsānian days naturally read into the Texts of the Gāthās the beliefs and customs of their own days. Judging by these translations and the accompanying commentaries the Zoroastrianism of these days was largely mixed with a very complex ritual and tinged with beliefs in a Demon-host who were a constant source of danger to the faithful. Countless ceremonies were prescribed to placate these Demons, and to counteract their activities. Every little act of human life, like the cutting of hair or paring of nails, had to be performed to the accompaniment of an elaborate ritual. This sort of Sāsānian Zoroastrianism is rather depressing when compared with the vigorous and robust teaching of the *Gāthās*. The *Gāthās* picture man as a warrior, strong in Love and Truth, girt for the fight against Hatred and Untruth, whereas the Sāsānian theologians picture man as going about in constant fear of the Demons that surround him and threaten him continuously. In fact these Demons are an obsession all through the Sāsānian period.

In the days of the early Sāsānian Emperors there was the characteristic zeal of a renaissance in the nation and its momentum carried the people to great heights of happiness and material prosperity. Both Ardeshir I and Shāpūr I were supermen and born rulers. The system of government established by the Founder of the Sāsānian Empire was frankly a Theocracy, with the main power concentrated into the hands of the priesthood. Besides this there was a graded Feudal System which set up a powerful landed aristocracy. Ardeshir I had set up this constitution after long and earnest consideration; but the inherent weak point in this system was that its successful working depended entirely upon a very strong Ruler at the head. Under weak Kings the clergy and the aristocracy were certain to consolidate their own power at the expense of the masses. The excessive power concentrated in the hands of the clergy necessarily led in course of time to a narrowing view of religion and to a growing fanaticism. To add to these difficulties inherent in a Theocracy came the very ill-considered action of Constantine of Byzantium. He declared himself to be the Head of all Christians of the world, including those of Persia. This made matters worse, for the Ruler of Persia at that time was Shāpūr II (the Great) (A.D. 309–379), the proudest of the Sāsānians, and he could not tolerate such interference with his own sovereign rights over his own subjects. The net result of this move of Constantine was that the Christians of Persia were put in a very false position, torn between two loyalties, and they were looked upon with grave suspicion in their own land. A merciless persecution of these unfortunate people was the result and many thousands were massacred. There were reprisals and Iran was torn by civil strife lasting for nearly two centuries. Both sides reviled at each other in books and papers written in the most blistering language. Some of this controversial literature from both sides survives and this gives us a fair idea of the great bitterness prevalent at that period. Both sides forget utterly the fundamental Teachings of their Prophets about *Vohu-Manō* and about Charity, and both sides became utterly intolerant and dogmatic. This feeling always provided a *causus belli* for fighting Rome. All this had a very serious effect when in years to come Persia and Rome stood face to face with the new and more vigorous Gospel of the Prophet of Arabia.

The first two Sāsānian Emperors were succeeded by a set of weak Rulers during whose rule the vested interests consolidated their own power. There were, however, a few very strong rulers, like Shāpūr II (the Great) (A.D. 309–379), Behrām V (Behrāmgor) (A.D. 420–440) and Khusrav I (the Just, also surnamed Noshīravān) (A.D. 531–579). All these were strong enough to restore order and bring back justice and some measure of happiness to the masses. Still on the whole the condition of the masses was definitely deteriorating, and in place of true Knowledge and Strength from religion they were given a mass of ceremonial and dogma.

Two movements during the Sāsānian period indicate very clearly how matters were shaping in Persia. The first was the eclectic movement of Māni at the beginning of the period and the other was the

Communism of Mazdak which came very near the end of this age.

Māni's move was more or less intellectual, and it was a deliberate move to reconcile the doctrines of the three great religions of Iran in his day: Zoroastrianism, Buddhism and Christianity. Māni chose the best from each and presented a sort of composite Faith. Fortunately for him the Ruler at that time was Shāpūr I, who was also his friend, and so Māni managed to get out of Iran safely. But when he returned after the death of Shāpūr I, he was promptly executed and his followers were scattered.

The Communism of Mazdak was not intellectual but purely a social and political revolt. The causes that produced it were exactly the same that produced the great French Revolution and the Bolshevik movement in Russia. "By their fruits shall ye know them" may very well be said of the priests and aristocrats of Iran against whom Mazdak raised his standard. The movement spread like a forest fire all over the Sāsānian Empire. The Ruler at that time was Kobād I (A.D. 487–531), and he sympathized with it. But he was helpless against the vested interests; he was forced to renounce his throne for some years (A.D. 498–501) and when he was restored he had perforce to persecute the communists. He was succeeded by his son Khusrav I, the greatest of the Sāsānians, if not the greatest Ruler in all Iranian history. He was wise enough to see the real roots of the Communism of Mazdak and he was also strong enough and bold enough to take immediate steps to remove the root causes of this discontent. He was merciless to the Communists, but he was equally adamant toward the vested interests and he insisted that strict justice be meted out. So he got the surname of *Adl* (the Just). He succeeded in restoring law and order throughout his realm and under him the masses were happy. It was his grateful nation that gave him the produest title any Monarch ever received, the title of *Noshīravān* (he of the Immortal Soul).

After the death of Khusrav I there was a sliding back into the good old ways where the vested interests had all their own way. There was a last flicker of greatness under his grandson Khusrav II (surnamed *Parvez*, the Victor) (A.D. 590–628). But the successors of Khusrav II plunged Iran into bloody civil wars while the Arabs were literally knocking at their very gates.

Only three pitched battles were fought and the Sāsānian Empire, which had lasted for over four centuries crumbled to dust (A.D. 642). Zoroastrianism ceased to be the national Religion of Persia and Islam stepped into its place.

The Arabs were on the whole a tolerant people, though they were drunk with their conquests. Though Zoroastrians went over to Islam in large numbers, still many thousands were permitted by the Arabs to follow the Religion of their fathers on payment of the *jeziya* (the poll-tax).

Under the Arabs also the Iranians showed their characteristic adaptability. They made the Arabic language their own and some of the greatest masters of Arabic literature were converted Zoroastrian Persians.

When the purely Semitic Arab domination of Persia was replaced by the Abbasid Caliphs of Baghdad (A.D. 749), there was another rejuvenation of Iranian Culture, which reached its zenith in the "Golden Age" of Haroun al-Rashid (A.D. 786–809) and his illustrious son al-M'amūn (A.D. 811–833). It was under the wide-hearted encouragement of the latter that the most important Pahlavi work on Zoroastrian theology, the *Dēn-kart* was composed.

Unfortunately very soon after al-M'amūn the Rulers of the Islamic world in Persia changed to dogmatic ways. One of his successors al-Mutawakkil (A.D. 847–861) launched relentless persecution against those who were not orthodox Moslems. This led to the emigration of the persecuted Zoroastrians to the West coast of India.

The cultural connections of Iran and India go back to prehistoric ages. Many thousands of Iranians had for one reason or another settled down in India, which possessed a kindred culture. In the course of ages these emigrants got absorbed among the teeming millions of India.

But this band of persecuted Zoroastrians who emigrated to India as a result of the persecution of al-Mutawakkil and his successors persisted in holding themselves aloof from the Indian population of Western India, amongst whom they had come to settle almost a thousand years ago. Their descendants are the modern Parsis of India. The first "Pilgrim Fathers" who had left their native land for the sake of religion were very staunch and this characterizes most of their descendants to this day. For nearly nine hundred years they lived in comparative obscurity as farmers and petty traders. When the Britishers came to India the Parsis began to come forward. They were not bound by the rigid rules of caste and of food which stood in the way of the Hindus. Besides this advantage the Parsis had inherited the adaptability of their Persian ancestors. They took very kindly to British manners and customs. Added to this the Parsis possess a keen sense of humor to which the Britishers at once responded and a facility for learning foreign languages. The Parsis also possess a certain modicum of honesty and more than an average share of organizing ability. Hence it is that though they are but 100,000 among the 400 millions of India they have been pioneers in almost all the modern movements in India. In the field of Social reform and of Political advancement the Parsis have led the way. In commerce and in industry the Parsis have been literally the founders of the greatness of the city of Bombay. Even today the largest industry of the country is the Tata Iron and Steel works at Jamshedpur. That is a concern founded by Parsis and it ranks among the biggest Iron and Steel works of the world.

Naturally the Religion of Zarathushtra has undergone various transformations during this long sojourn in India. A number of Hindu Social customs and superstitions have crept in. With the impact of the West began a movement of "reform" which aimed at discarding all un-Zoroastrian accretions. The result was a reaction against Religion itself, for in those days the tide of materialism was running full. The intellectual leaders at that time were rather proud of their materialistic and "rational" outlook. About thirty-five years ago a natural reaction set in and the bulk of the Parsis today are decidedly going back to the ancient Zoroastrian beliefs of the Sāsānian age. This, however, does not quite suit the intellectuals, who are steeped in Western ways of thought. So among them recently a movement has started of going "back to the *Gāthās*." They want the *Gāthās* in their pristine purity to be the inspiration of their lives. In short they want a Religion of sturdy Faith and manly Action based on Truth, Love and Service. This is the most hopeful sign today. And the younger generation, too, seem whole-heartedly for the movement of "back to the *Gāthās*" because they all sincerely believe that Zoroastrianism still has a Message for the World today.

BIBLIOGRAPHY

I. J. S. TARAPOREWALA, *Selections from Avesta and Old Persian.* Part I. (No date.)

————, *Selections from Classical Gujarati Literature.* Vols. I–III. (n.d.)

————, "History of the Parsis in India." In Vol. II of *Cambridge History of India.* (n.d.)

————, *The Religion of Zarathushtra.* (n.d.)

————, *Some Aspects of the History of Zoroastrianism* (Cama Oriental Institute, 1927).

————, *Some Principles of Gathic Interpretation* (Fifth Oriental Conference).

————, *Some Aspects of Iranian Studies in India* (Presidential address in the Iranian section, Seventh Oriental Conference, n.d.).

————, *The Arrival of the Parsis in India and their subsequent History* (Ahmedabad, 1936).

M. N. DHALLA, *History of Zoroastrianism* (1938).

L. H. GRAY, *The Foundations of the Iranian Religion* (1929).

J. H. MOULTON, *Early Zoroastrianism* (1913).

J. C. PAVRY, *The Zoroastrian Doctrine of a Future Life* (1926).

(Above List prepared by Editor)

JAINISM

Dr. Saksena knows the religion of the Jains intimately. A life-long student of this native religion of India and of India's rich philosophic thought he has eminently qualified himself as one of India's notable scholars and educators. It has been his ardent desire to bring the West and the East into closer cultural relationships and to this cause he has devoted himself. He is head of the department of philosophy in Hindu College, Delhi, and reader in philosophy in Delhi University. Besides authorship of scholarly studies which have appeared in numerous philosophical journals and periodicals he has published in India a work entitled "Nature of Consciousness in Hindu Philosophy".

Born in 1903 Dr. Saksena received his education at Allahabad and in London, England. He took his master's degree in philosophy at the University of Allahabad with honors. In 1939 the University of London conferred upon him the Ph.D. degree for his expert knowledge of and researches into the field of Indian philosophy.

Just recently he has taken over the editorship of the Quarterly called the "Perspective," a journal published by the Department of Information and Broadcasting, Government of India and intended to inform the Western world about the cultural, social and literary aspects of Indian life.

Editor

JAINISM

SHRI KRISHNA SAKSENA

THE TERM Jain is derived from *Jina* meaning the victor—or the conqueror, implying conquest or final victory over the bondage of the ailments and ills of life. The Ideal or the Supreme purpose of Jainism is, therefore, the realization of the highest or the Absolute perfection of the nature of man, which in its original purity is free from all kinds of pain or bondage. Jainism does not consider it necessary to recognize any other perfect being besides man or any being more perfect than the perfect man. It is thus a religion of the perfect man. A being higher than the most perfect man is not considered necessary for either the creation of the world or the moral regulation of the universe. It is for this reason that Jainism is usually characterized as atheistic. But the term with its fixed connotation in Western thought, is likely to be misleading here; for while it is true that Jainism has no place for a God as a creator or a governor of the universe, it would be truer to call it a heretical sect of the Vedic faith, which had its origin in revolt from the tradition and the authority of the Vedas. It is well known that amongst the early adherents of the Vedic faith, differences in course of time arose on the question of "animal sacrifice"—or the killing of animals for the sake of *Yajna*. The *Ahimsā Dharma* and its opposite had a theological tussle from the earliest time. And though the Jain tradition claims its faith to be eternal, it is more than likely that its earliest founders must have belonged to the sect that rebelled from the idea and practice of taking life. It is interesting to note that in the traditional line of the Vedas, those on the side of animal killing are all *Brāhmaṇas,* while the dissenters belong to the *Kshatriya*—or the warrior class; and that the perfect souls—or *Tirthānkaras* of Jainism are all *Kshatriyas.* Jainism should, therefore, be characterized as a heretical sect of the Vedas, with predominantly monastic leanings, though its teachings are enjoined on all alike. Its peculiar genius lies in its emphasis on equal kindness towards all life, even towards the meanest. It is *par excellence* a religion of love and kindness.

HISTORY OF JAINISM

It has already been said that, according to the Jains, their faith is eternal, for *Ahimsā Dharma* is eternal; but as time, which is infinite, is measured in cycles of evolution and dissolution called the *utasarpaṇī* and *avasarpaṇī* and as each again is divided into six eras, it was in the fourth of the second cycle that the twenty-four *Tirthānkaras* or perfect souls arose. These *Tirthānkaras* are supposed to have attained their perfection and absolute freedom from all bondage, and preached Jainism to the world. The first *Tirthānkara* was Riṣabha who was the real founder of Jainism. The name occurs in the Vedas and the Purānas also, but very little else is known of him, and the last was Vardhamāna, otherwise Mahāvīra who was also an elder contemporary of Lord Buddha. The following are the names of the *Tirthānkaras*—

Riṣabha, Ajita, Sambhava, Abhinandan, Sumati Padmaprābhā, Supārsva, Chandraprabhā, Pushpadanta, Sitala, Sreyāṅśa, Vasupujya, Vimala, Ananta, Dharma, Śānti, Kunthu, Ara, Maltī, Munīsuvṛta, Nami, Nemi, Pārśva, and Vardhamāna.

This is the fifth era—with Mahāvīra ended the fourth era. Mahāvīra was indeed not only not the founder of Jainism, but actually comes last in the galaxy of his other well-known predecessors. His predecessor Pārśvanātha or the 23rd *Tirthānkara,* is known to have died in 776 B.C. Neminātha, or the 22nd *Tirthānkara,* is supposed to have preceded Pārśvanātha by some 5,000 years. Contemporary researches have made it unnecessary to refute any doubt regarding the existence of Jainism as an independent sect much earlier than either Hinduism or Buddhism. (*Vide* Dr. Jacobi's introduction to *S.B.E.* Vols. 22 & 24 and works of other scholars).

Lord Mahāvīra was born in 599 B.C. (The two sects of Digāmbara and Śvetāmbara, however, slightly differ about this time) in the family of a ruling *Kshatriya* chief of the *Naya* Clan. (The Buddhists call him *Nātaputra* which means the same.) He was born in the republic of Vaiśālī (Behar) at the site of the modern village of Basārh about 27 miles north of Patna (the modern capital of Behar). After being a house-holder for about 28 years during which he had a daughter born to him, he bade farewell to his family and retired to solitude. There he meditated upon the miseries of life and the means for final emancipation. After fourteen years he attained his objective when he decided to preach Jainism. (It would be observed that the life history is almost parallel to that of the founder of Buddhism). During the course of a wide travel and wandering, he preached for about 30 years, and attained his final *Nirvāṇa* in 527 B.C., at Pāvā-purī (also in modern Behar). Pāvāpurī is, since then, one of the chief places of Jain Pilgrimage. It is a small place in the midst of beautiful surroundings where a number of Jain temples have sprung up. Diwali—the annual day of the Hindu illumination—is the day of this pilgrimage; for Lord Mahāvīra is supposed to have attained *Nirvāṇa* on this day. The main temple contains the sacred foot-marks of Lord Mahāvīra.

THE SECTS OF JAINISM

Jainism is one and undivided so far as its philosophy is concerned; but a little earlier than the Christian era, the Jains began to split, on the points of certain rules and regulations for the monks, in the two well-known sects of the *Śvetāmbara* or the white-clad and the *Digāmbara* or the sky-clad.

The points of difference between the two are just minor ones. They are:

(a) That the *Digāmbaras* hold that a perfect saint goes without food.

(b) That he should own nothing, not even clothes, hence the practice of going naked.

(c) That salvation is not possible for women. They have no nuns.

Later on, other minor sects called the *Sthānakavādī* and the *Lūnikās* were also formed, on idol worship and similar matters. Not believing in a God or Avatars, the Jains are not an idol-worshipping sect, but that has not prevented them from erecting and carving statues in honor of their *Siddhas* or perfect souls.

CANONICAL LITERATURE OF JAINISM

The preaching of Jainism, till and much after Lord Mahāvīra, must have been by word of mouth transmitted from generation to generation. The Jains relied entirely on memory for the propagation and preservation of their faith. They were also called *Nirgranthas*— or those having no books. It is generally believed that after the death of Mahāvīra, knowledge of Jainism as it was first preached gradually began to disappear and it was only much later that it was again restored.

According to Śvetāmbaras, the canon was reduced to systematization by the council of Pātli-Putra about the end of the 4th Century B.C. But it is generally agreed that it was given final shape only after 800 years, i.e., in 454 A.D. (There is, however, some minor difference among scholars about the exact date.)

The systematized teaching of Mahāvīra consists of:—

    (a) 12 *Aṅgās,* the last *aṅga* being sub-divided into
    (b) 14 *Pūrvas*
    (c) 5 *Prakaraṇās,* along with other *sūtra* literature.

Among later works, mention should be made of *Lokaprakāsa,* an encyclopaedia of Jainism, compiled by Vinaya-Vijai in 1652 A.D. Most of the canonical texts have now been published in India and English translations of at least seven of them are now available. The language of their canonical literature is *Ardha-Māgadhi,* a blend dialect of the province of Magadha (Modern Behar), but it would be better to call it *Apabhramśa* or *Jain-Prākṛt,* a corrupt form of Sanskrit. Jain literature has also contributed much towards the expansion and evolution of new forms of language. The above, however, is according to the *Śvetāmbara* belief. The *Digāmbaras* hold that the entire literature was destroyed about 789 A.D., and this carnage is ascribed to Śankarāchārya—the illustrious Vedantist (though no evidence exists for it). Some of the books, however, were saved in Nepal and in Śravanabelagol (in Mysore), the Jain headquarters of south India, and the second most important place of Jain pilgrimage where a colossal statue of Lord Gomteśvara exists.

JAIN METAPHYSICS

It would thus appear that the simple spirit of Jainism is not to be identified with the long vicissitude of Jain literature, for the Jain philosophy in its ultimate analysis is simplicity itself. It can be summed up in a few sentences. First, there are living beings, second, there is non-living matter, third, there is contact, fourth, as a result of these, there is an inflow in the soul of a *Karmic* energy, causing in the *Jiva*, the bondage of life and its experiences. And lastly, this inflow can be stopped resulting in the final *Mokṣa* or liberation which is the ultimate goal or the aim of life. Jain metaphysics, is thus, a dualistic system dividing the universe into the two ultimate, eternal and independent categories of the living and the non-living, i.e., the *Jiva* and the *Ajiva*. Besides the *Jiva*, the other substances are the five kinds of *Ajivas*, i.e., *Pudgala* or Matter, *Dharma* and *Adharma* and *Akāśa* and *Kāla* or space and time. We have thus the six *Dravyas* or the substances of Jainism. The soul which is always mixed up with matter except at the highest stage, is further sub-divided into mobile and immobile, for even trees and stones are supposed to have souls. The soul possesses nine qualities in all, out of which consciousness or *Cetanā* is the chief quality. Souls are also classified according to the number of sense-organs they possess. Man possesses five senses along with the mind, the lower animals successively scale down from five to one sense-organ alone. About both soul and matter, Jainism adopts the common-sense view of their being innumerable. Their metaphysical system is thus pluralistic also. The soul is regarded as an active principle as distinguished from the mere knower of the *Sānkhya*—Yoga system. The powers of the soul are limitless and its striving for perfection is continuous. There being no power higher than that of the soul, the entire scientific and material progress of the world, is but an infinitesimally small expression of the latent powers of the soul only. Souls are again divided into those that have attained perfection, i.e., *Mukta* and those that are still in bondage, and are struggling for freedom or the *Baddha*. Of the former, there are five classes in order of merit, the foremost being the *Siddha*, then *Arhat*, and three others. These five are called the *Pañcaparameśthina* or the five Lords of Jainism.

As Jainism is a system designed primarily for the achievement of the perfection of the soul, it would be interesting to know what, by virtue of this achievement, a perfect soul is supposed to acquire. Every *Tirthānkara* is a perfect soul and acquires the following ten qualities:—He

(1) averts famine in an area of 800 miles radius;
(2) remains raised above the ground whether walking, standing or sitting;
(3) seems to be facing everyone in all the four directions;
(4) destroys all destructive impulses in persons around him;
(5) is entirely immune from all possibility of pain and disturbances of any kind;
(6) is able to live without food;
(7) possesses mastery of all arts and sciences;
(8) nails and hair do not grow;
(9) eyes are always open, lids do not wink;
(10) his body does not cast shadow.

In addition to these, he enjoys the four attributes of infinite perception, infinite knowledge, infinite power, and infinite bliss. These perfect souls are of two kinds—those with bodies and those without bodies.

Of the five *Ajīvas,* those of space, time and matter are concepts common to other systems of thought. But *Dharma* and *Adharma* are the two most peculiar concepts of Jain philosophy. No other system of thought has anything like it. Unfortunately, the term *Dharma* has a variety of meaning in Hindu and Buddhist thought and the Jain *Dharma* and *Adharma* are quite unlike the accepted meaning in either. An exposition of the Jain concept of *Dharma* and *Adharma* has, therefore, naturally suffered from this confusion. But in itself the idea is quite plain. By *Dharma* and *Adharma* are meant the principles of movement and rest. A principle of movement has to be conceived as an uncreated and eternal substance for, otherwise, with other eternal substances alone, it would be impossible to explain the universe. But they do not mean "that which moves" but, rather a condition providing for movement and rest, i.e., if a substance had the principle of movement in itself, they provide the necessary condition for it. Besides the above two categories of *Jīva* and *Ajīva* and the six substances, from a different standpoint, these substances are further classified as being either *Astikāya* or *Nāstikāya. Asti* means existence and *kāya* means volume or magnitude, technically called the *Pradeśa*. Except *Kāla* or time, all other substances including the *Jīva* are *Astikāyas*. Time alone has no *Pradeśa*. There are thus five *Astikāyas*. Thus, while on the one hand, the classification of categories is on the basis of the life and no-life principle, on the other hand, it is on the basis of their possessing *Kāyā* or magnitude. The next most important concept of the Jains is that of *Karma* and the *Karmic* matter. As regards *Karma*, in common with other Indian systems, Jainism holds that every effect has a cause. *Karma* is that general energy of the soul which is the cause of its attachment with matter and its subsequent defilement. It is the link of union between the soul and the body. Since a God has no place in Jainism, *Karma* comes to occupy a very important position, indeed, in this system, for most of the functions of God are appropriated by the soul and its potential power. Connected with the doctrine of *Karma*, are the doctrines of re-incarnation and transmigration which are also held. There is no short-cut to life's perfection, the law of *Karma* being inexorable. Any meditation of Divine Grace or Forgiveness is, according to Jainism, only an oversimplification of the problems of sin, suffering and redemption, for a *Karma* can be destroyed only by another *Karma*. Jainism, therefore, specializes in an elaborate classification of the kinds and qualities of *Karma*. There are eight kinds of *Karma*, and as many as 148 of its sub-divisions. Karma takes its start from the contact of the living and non-living, which is responsible for an inflow of the *Karmic* matter in the soul. This inflow attains fruition in course of time; and, by a reverse process, this inflow and fruition are to be stopped, and the *Karmas* finally extinguished. Technically, this function of the *Karma* from beginning to end is marked by five stages, called *Aśrava* or inflow of *Karma*, *Bandha* or bondage, *Samvara* or fruition, *Nirjarā* or stoppage and *Mokṣa* or liberation. Jainism works out a very imposing psychological superstructure of the spiritual destiny of man from start to finish. The Jains believe in five bodies or sheaths of the soul instead of the three or four bodies of the other systems. As the *Karmas* are destroyed bit by bit, the body acquires new qualities shedding off its grosser manifestations; and as the bodies perish one after the other in the soul's ultimate march towards perfection, it passes through fourteen well-marked spiritual stages, called the *Gunasthānas*.

To sum up, there are the two ultimate categories of *Jīva* and

Ajīva, the six substances (one *Jīva* and five *Ajīvas*), the five stages of *Karma* with the two ultimate categories (called *Tattvas* or principles); and finally, if merit and demerit, i.e. *Pāpa* and *Puṇya*, are added to these seven principles, we have the nine *Padārthas* of Jainism. These are the fundamental principles of Jain metaphysics. Some critics of Jain metaphysics have found fault with this kind of cross division implying that the Jains had no clear concept of how many substances they really believed in. But such a criticism is founded on a lack of understanding, although Jain metaphysics is not very clear about the process of the creation of this actual world from these eternal categories and substances. This may be regarded as a weak thread in its metaphysics.

Jain ethics is a direct consequence of the Jain philosophy of Soul and *Karma*. Since the primary duty of man is the evolution and perfection of his soul as well as of his fellow creatures, the principle of *Ahimsā* or 'non-hurting' of life irrespective of its distinction into higher and lower, is the cardinal principle of Jain ethics. Even the principle of truth may be sacrificed for the principle of *Ahimsā*. "Hurt no one" is a positive injunction enjoining love and compassion towards all fellow creatures. Jains alone build asylums and resthouses for old and diseased animals where they are kept and fed until they die a natural death. With a view to attainment by humanity as a whole, of its cherished goal of *Mokṣa* from all bondage, Jainism prescribes perhaps the most elaborate rules for practical everyday conduct. *Samyag Chāritra* or right conduct must follow *Samyag Darshan* and *Samyag Jyāna* or right faith and right knowledge, and these three form the "three jewels" or the *triratna* of Jainism.

Jain ethics is the most glorious part of Jainism. In one respect, it is quite simple, as the primary duty of man is the strict observance of the principle of *Ahimsā*. But, in another respect, it is anything but simple. For the rules of conduct prescribed are perhaps the most elaborate and complicated. Even for the guidance of the practice of *Ahimsā*, cruelty is analyzed into as many as nine kinds, each subtler than the other. The number of rules to be observed in everyday life are too many and their discipline and rigor are about the hardest. Life is divided into a number of stages according to the evolution of the soul and a great many vows, such as, non-killing, non-stealing, chastity, non-possession and daily worship, etc., have to be taken even at its earliest stages. These rules of conduct are for all classes of persons, for the ascetic as well as for the house-holder and are, of course, much stricter for the former, though they are, by no means, lax for the latter. But as there is no conflict recognized between the true interest of the individual and humanity, it cannot be denied that even these rules are not without great social value. And since no ideal short of the absolute and perfect happiness of all living beings is conceived, Jainism, in a way, may be regarded as a bold and daring fore-runner of modern theories of utilitarianism, which, in comparison strike as but pale and feeble attempts at evolution of only a limited variety of humanitarianism. Criticism is often made of the impracticability of the exalted ideal of Jainism, but no one has set limits to practicability excepting man himself.

JAIN LOGIC

The most distinctive contribution of Jainism is, however, in the realm of logic, and lies in its doctrine of *Naya*, which means "point of view". According to Jainism, the Buddhistic doctrine of change and of nothingness was contrary to facts, and so was the Advaitic theory of absolute identity. Their foremost logical position, therefore, is what is called *Anekāntavāda* or the theory of many-sidedness. It can be one thing and different also from different stand-points. This is what is called *Anekāntavāda* or the theory of many-sidedness. It is obvious that about anything, from one point of view, it can be said that it exists, while from another point of view, with equal truth, it can be said that it does not exist. Again, from another point of view, the predication of both existence and non-existence can be made, while, from yet another standpoint, it can be said that the thing is indescribable. If we combine the last standpoint with the first three we have in all seven *Nayas* or points of views about a thing. That is why the Jains like to prefix every proposition with *Syād* or "maybe." The following would thus be the seven *Nayas*:—

(1) *Syād Asti* . . . . May be, it is.
(2) *Syād Nāsti* . . . . May be, it is not.
(3) *Syād Asti Nāsti* . . . . May be, it is and it is not.
(4) *Syād Avaktavya* . . . . May be, it is inexpressible.

(5) *Syād   Asti   Ca   Avak·* May be, it is and it is inex-
tavya .... pressible.
(6) *Syād   Nāsti   Ca   Avak·* May be, it is not and is inex-
tavya .... pressible.
(7) *Syād   Asti   Nāsti   Ca   Av·* May be, it is and it is not and
aktavya .... it is inexpressible.

From these seven modes of expression, the theory derives the much-reputed name of *Saptabhaṅgīnaya*. While the modes of expression are seven, knowledge itself, according to Jainism, is of five kinds: *Mati* or the ordinary perceptual knowledge; *Śruti* or the scriptual knowledge; *Avadhi* or a kind of clairvoyant knowledge; *Manaḥ-parayāya* or telepathic knowledge; and, finally *Kevala jyāna* or the absolute knowledge. The Jain doctrine of *Anekānta-vāda* is a unique contribution; and, as in the realm of conduct, it preaches love and respect of all living beings, in the realm of thought, it affirms only relative or conditional validity to all propositions. No judgment, according to Jainism, is absolutely false, as none is absolutely true.

PRESENT POSITION

Jainism, like Hinduism, after stagnating for centuries petrified itself into sheer ritualistic and formalistic practices. The spirit, having left, the body continued to be artificially fed by blind adherence to dead formulae, until towards the end of the nineteenth century, India turned to a general awakening of the cultural and religious glory of its past. A wave of renewed enthusiasm for acquaintance with and study of its forgotten sources of inspiration swept the educated and the sensitive; and Jainism also shared in this revival, though not to the same extent. Jain Sacred Text Societies were formed, which discovered, edited, and published authentic texts. Young Men's Jain Associations sprang up in the north and south of India, and a number of Jain Gazettes and Periodicals began to be issued. With a view to reform and propagation, a large number of popular books have also been written by able scholars in various languages of the country. It is true that Jainism has no economic or political plan for the world, since it does not think in terms of multiplication or complication of the physical needs of man. Although it is indifferent to the forms of Government, so long as it is in spirit a Jain Government, i.e., inspired by the un-conditional love and respect for life, Jainism has not been neglectful of the educational and cultural betterment of mankind. While Jain literature and scholarship, both religious and secular, are themselves of no ordinary status, they have also taken due share in the development of arts in the country. They erected monumental *Stupas,* Gate-ways, Umbrellas and Pillars in honor of their Saints. In the richness and quality of their architecture or carving in stone, Jainism would have few parallels in the world. Excellent examples of these exist in Junagadh, Osmanabad and in Girnar. While Mount Abu in Rajputana "carries to its highest perfection the Indian genius for the invention of graceful patterns and their application to the decoration of masonry," Satrunjaya is one of the "loveliest temple-cities in the world." In the realm of religion and philosophical outlook, it preaches universal tolerance. Jainism sees no reason for wrangling amongst religions and faiths. Like Hinduism, it is a non-proselytizing faith and enjoins on its followers the same respect for a different faith which it has for its own. This aspect of Jainism is worthy of greater attention than it has, hitherto, received at the hands of its admirers and critics. Its attitude towards other forms of religion is that of perfect non-criticism. Jainism is not competitive, and has not, at all, cared for the spread of its faith. Its followers hardly totalled 1,500,000 in 1941. It has already been said that the message of Jainism is for all humanity. Its love extends not only to humanity but to all living creatures; and, shorn of its handicap of an utterly unsuitable rigidity of its ritualistic observances, the growth of *Ahimsā*—or the "spirit of Jainism"—should have a great future and a great message indeed for a world today torn with growing hostility and uncontrollable violence.

BIBLIOGRAPHY

Dr. J. Burgess's Edition of Buhler's *On the Indian Sect of the Jainas* (London, 1903).

A. B. LATHE, *An Introduction to Jainism* (Bombay, 1905).

U. D. BARODIA, *History and Literature of Jainism* (Bombay, 1909).

H. L. JHAVERI, *First Principles of Jain Philosophy* (London, 1910).

H. WARREN, *Jainism* (Madras, 1912).

SINCLAIR STEVENSON, *The Heart of Jainism* (Oxford & London, 1915).

JAGMANDAR LAL JAINI, *Outlines of Jainism* (Cambridge University Press, 1940).

BUDDHISM

There is probably no one in America better qualified to interpret the first principles of the Buddhist faith to the Occidental mind than is Dr. Coomaraswamy. Our knowledge of Buddhism is far from complete and there are controversial interpretations even among scholars. He has had the decided advantage over many students of the subject in that, during his life-long studies, he has worked with the original sources and is a theologian at heart. He is widely recognized as an expert in the field of early Buddhism, particularly canonical Buddhism.

His many books deal with oriental art, theology, philosophy and culture. His recent work "Hinduism and Buddhism" (1943) is well known, as are his earlier volumes "Buddha and the Gospel of Buddhism" (1916) and "Elements of Buddhist Iconography" (1935).

Dr. Coomaraswamy was born in Colombo, Ceylon, in 1877. In 1906 he became director of the mineral survey of Ceylon; later, he initiated a movement in India for national education and was in charge of the section on art at Allahabad, 1910–11. Since 1917 he has been a fellow for research in Indian, Persian and Mohammedan art at The Museum of Fine Arts in Boston. In 1904 the University of London conferred upon him the degree of Doctor of Science.

Besides fulfilling numerous lecture engagements, Dr. Coomaraswamy continues the work of scholarship. His most recent task is the writing of a comprehensive introduction to a book on the Buddha's "logoi" which is being edited by the secretary of the Pali Text Society in London.

Editor

BUDDHISM

ANANDA KENTISH COOMARASWAMY

1. *HISTORY:* The Buddhist scriptures speak of the Buddha—Gotama, thus distinguised by his family name from former Buddhas and Buddhas yet to come—as having been a man who, in his last birth, attained the goal of Full Awakening (*sambodhi*) and Despiration (*nirvāna*) for which he had prepared himself in the course of the long series of his residences in "former habitations." The recorded events of his life as a *Bodhisatta* before the Great Awakening are largely, however, the echoes of much older myths; and the recorded teachings of the later life are to a very large extent transpositions and reaffirmations of the older Brahmanical doctrines pertaining to the Ancient Way that he claims to have followed; and these facts, taken together with those of the Buddhology of the canonical texts make it entirely possible that what he represents is really another revelation to men and gods (he is always the teacher of both) of the Eternal *Avatar* and Light of lights, who is spoken of as Fire and Sun.

As a historical person, the exact date of Siddhattha's birth is uncertain; it may be 483 B.C., but it is hardly possible to say more than that the Buddha's life-span of eighty years, of which thirty-five precede the Awakening, or *Nirvana,* * covers the greater part of the fifth century B.C. The Bodhisatta was born at Kapilavatthu as the son of king Suddhodana and his queen Mahā Māyā, thus not as a Brāhman but as a *Khattiya*; this incarnation taking place by a deliberately willed descent from the Tusita heavens in which the future Buddha Maitreya now resides. In referring to him as a "prince" it must be understood that while he must have been brought up in luxury, the "kingdom" was really a sort of republic with a royal president, and that the "parliament-procedure" of

* "Nirvana" has long been a naturalized English word, and is therefore employed in this Sanskrit form, rather than as Pali *nibbāna*. All other terms are cited in their Pali forms.

Buddhist monastic assemblies was really modelled on that of the secular councils.

The Bodhisatta's birth was miraculous; as such it was already compared by Hieronymus to that of the Christ, and it may also be mentioned here that the Christian legend of St Josaphat ("Bodhisatta") is really the story of the Buddha's life. The child already bore the marks of a "Great Person," and it was foretold of him that he would become either an Emperor or a World Teacher; in effect, he was "both king and priest," and could speak of himself as a "Brahman," not by birth, but in the full sense of the word, by knowledge, and of himself as a king in leadership. He was married to his cousin Yasodā, and had a son, Rāhula, who later on received ordination and so became his spiritual son in the sense in which the Buddhist monks are "Sons of the Wake."

On the day of the child's birth the Bodhisatta for the first time came into contact with the fact of the universal liability of all men to sorrow, old age, sickness and death; and thereupon determined to devote himself to the search for a "medicine" for this sickness unto death, all the more dangerous in that men are ever striving to forget their misery; to devote himself, in other words, to the quest for a kind of knowledge and a way of life that might ensure to those who would practise it a state of inviolable happiness and an assurance of immortality. So the Bodhisatta, not yet a Buddha, or "Wake," abandoned his home and all family ties, as many had done before him, as many have done since and still do. He became the disciple of Brahmanical teachers, finding much, but not all that he sought for. He practised the most extreme austerities, and had his own followers. But he found no help, and decided to follow the Middle Way between the extremes of luxury and self-mortification; his disciples then abandoning him. At last the time was at hand: taking his seat at the foot of the Bodhi-tree, at the navel of the earth, with his back to the tree facing the east, he firmly resolved never to rise again, though the flesh should wither on his bones, until the goal should be reached. Then follows the conflict with *Māra*, the principle of Love and Death, who claimed the sovereignty, and would not "let go"; the Bodhisatta's victory is a recension of the ancient Vedic myth of the conquest of the Dragon, *Namuci*, "Holdfast," Death. Then, passing through ever deeper and deeper states of consciousness, and recalling his "former habitations," the Bodhisatta at last obtained that complete understanding of Causal Origination, and that Awakening after which he is called the Buddha, "Wake."

At first the Buddha hesitated, fearing that none would be found able or willing to grasp the hard-won truths; but persuaded by Brahmā and moved by pity, he became an itinerant teacher, preaching the First Sermon ("The World is on Fire"), or more literally "Setting in Motion the Wheel of the Eternal-Law" (*dhamma*), before his former disciples, in Benares, and thereafter gradually winning from all classes of society an ever-increasing following of disciples, known as *bhikkhus* (mendicants or almsmen) or *samaṇas* (ascetics, workers), composing the Buddhist order or community (*sangha*) of monks; many of these became *Arahants* ("Worthies," *digni*) and having accomplished their Nirvana can be referred to as "Awake" (*buddha*), like their Great Teacher, who nevertheless remains uniquely *the* Buddha of the age. An order of nuns, parallel to that of the monks, was later established; it is expressly admitted that women are no less capable of spiritual attainment than are men.

After the Buddha's death, which is thought of as the shattering of the bodily investment, his teachings, at first transmitted orally (and by no means therefore inaccurately), were brought together in the books of the Pali canon. These embrace the *Tipitaka* (i.e. *Vinaya*, five *Nikāyas*, and *Abhidhamma*), *Dhammapada, Itivuttaka, Udāna, Sutta Nipāta, Thera-therīgatha* and a few others. Of the extra-canonical Pali texts the most important are the *Milinda Pañha, Jātaka,* and still later Buddhaghosa's commentaries, in particular the *Visuddhi Magga*. English versions of all these have been published by the Pali Text Society. The earliest of these books may date from the second century B.C., the latest from the fifth A.D. In the present writer's opinion their fundamental consistency justifies the view that the Canon at least is a reliable report of what had actually been taught; he puts no trust in the kind of "higher criticism" that tries to distinguish what the Buddha "must" or "ought" to have said from what he is reported to have said. In any case they are a reliable source for the content of "Early Buddhism." Differing schools of interpretation had arisen already within a few centuries of the Founder's death; of these, the *Sautrāntikas*, as their name suggests, seem to have been the most orthodox.

The first great impetus to the spread of Buddhism in and beyond India proper was given by the renowned Emperor Asoka (272–232 B.C.), who was not only himself a practising Buddhist and famous for the rock-cut and monolithic pillar Edicts in which he both expressed his own repentance for previous wars of conquest and enjoined on his subjects the earnest practise of Buddhist ethics, but also for having dispatched Buddhist missions to more distant lands, and in particular by his son Mahinda to Ceylon, where Buddhism more or less in its earliest form has survived to the present day. Later rulers amongst the Kuṣāhas, Guptas and others likewise supported Buddhist doctrines and institutions; but it must not be supposed therefore that there was ever a "Buddhist India" in any exclusive sense of the words or that Buddhism effected any changes in the outward forms of Indian society. The Buddhist layman is a Buddhist in faith and conduct, not by virtue of any kind of institutional revolution; just as, also, in the case of Buddhist art, which flourished from the second century B.C. onwards, there is iconographic adaptation, but no Buddhist style or technique different from that of contemporary Brahmanical or Jaina art.

Before the beginning of the Christian era the Buddhist Order was no longer one of merely itinerant monks, but one of monastic communities living in monasteries, the larger of which were at the same time universities. One of the greatest of these was that of Nālandā, well known by its remains and by the accounts of it given by the Chinese pilgrim Hsuan Tsang. In India proper, Buddhism during the Middle Ages gradually declined; surviving, after the destruction of Nālandā by the Moslems about 1200, only in Nepal, Sikhim and Bhutān. Meanwhile, as the result of colonizations and of missions, Buddhism side by side with Hinduism, or sometimes therewith combined, already long established in Ceylon, spread eastwards from India to Burma, Siam, Cambodia, Malaya, Sumatra, Java and even to parts of Borneo and the Philippines, and survives to the present day in Burma, Siam, Cambodia and (with Hinduism) in Bali. As the result of royal alliances and missions Buddhism became the religion of Tibet; and mainly as the result of the visits of Chinese pilgrims to India, and partly also by the settlement of Indian teachers in China, Buddhism and Buddhist art spread throughout the Far East, China, Korea and Japan. Practically all the Buddhist texts were accurately translated by bodies of qualified scholars, and these Tibetan and Chinese sources still retain their independent value. The total number of Buddhists in the world has been estimated at something like a fifth of the world's population.

The main divisions of Buddhism are those of the *Hīnayāna* and *Mahāyāna,* respectively the "lesser" and the "Great" Way or Vehicle; sometimes also, but rather inaccurately called "Southern" and "Northern," the *Hīnayāna* having best survived in Ceylon. The scriptures of the Hīnayāna are in Pali, those of the *Mahāyāna* in Sanskrit. As known from existing texts, the *Mahāyāna* develops from the beginning of the Christian era onwards; and as a whole is a scholastic, metaphysical, epistemological and also theistic and devotional aspect of Buddhism. It would take more than the whole of the present article to summarize its history. The most important texts are those of the *Mahāvastu,* ostensibly the *Vinaya* of one of the older *Hīnayāna* sects; the *Lalita Vistara,* in which the Buddha's divinity is strongly emphasized; the various *Prajñāpāramitās,* of which the famous *Vajracchedikā* ("Diamond-cutter"), which became the leading text of the *Shingon* school in Japan, is the briefest; the *Samādhirāja;* the *Suvarnaprabhāsa;* the *Laṅkāvatāra;* the *Saddharmapuṇḍarīka* ("Lotus of the True Law"); the *Karaṇḍavyūha,* in which the doctrine of the *Ādi* Buddha is developed, and the subject of a long series of sculptures at Borobudur; and the *Amitāyurdhyāna* and many other *Sūtras;* all of these range from the 2nd to fifth centuries, and the majority exist in Tibetan and Chinese as well as Sanskrit versions. The names of the great *Mahāyāna* doctors are Nāgārjuna, Aśvaghoṣa, Aryadeva, Śāntideva, and the brothers Asaṅga and Vasubandhu.

2. *Doctrine and Way:* The basic and essential doctrines, ostensibly and probably stated really in the Buddha's own words, are enunciated in the *Hīnayāna* Pali Canon. The doctrine in its briefest form is one of causality (*hetuvāda*); all phenomea are parts of a beginningless causal series,—"this being so, that becomes; this not being so, that does not become." Other brief statements are: "Of all things causally come to be, the Buddha has told the cause"; "Whatever has had a beginning must also cease (i.e. "death is certain for all born beings")"; "Just this is what I set forth, Ill, and the ceasing of Ill"; "All things composite are transitory"; "All beings are nourished by food, all are composite."

The great importance of the principle of causality for what is really a medical diagnosis, is this, that if no cause of "Ill" (*dukkha,* the misery of existence subject to origination, change and decay) could be pointed out, no way of putting an end to this intrinsic infirmity of "life" or "becoming" (*bhava*) could be found. The cause of Ill is "Ignorance" (*avijjā*); that is, our congenital blindness to the true nature of the phenomenal world of which we are a part and to which, for so long as we do not realize its "vanity" (*suññatā*), we are bound by our "desires" (*kāma*) and "thirst" (*taṇhā*) as if to a mirage. The very notion of "possession" (*mamatā,* "mineness") is a delusion, for "it is of the very nature of all things dear and attractive to be various, that we must be bereaved of them, and to change. How, then, is it possible to 'have' them?" Birth and death are not merely first and last events of life, but of its very substance. The characteristics of life are misery (*dukkha*), transience (*anicca*), and the absence-of-any-persistent individuality (*anattā*). Ignorance is the "original sin" because of which beings are born. This does not mean that a Buddhist could wish he had never been born, or might commit suicide; birth as a human being is the supreme opportunity for making an escape from all necessity of ever being born again.

Life as a psycho-physical process is one of combustion, requiring the continued supply of physical and mental food or fuel if its feverish heat is to be maintained; the fires are those of passion, malice, and delusion (*rāga, dosa, moha*). But if their fuel is withheld by detachment from all pursuits, the fires no longer "draw" (breath); and the result of that "despiration" (*Nirvana*) is precisely that reduction of temperature and state of nonchalance on which all true and stable happiness depends; we find, accordingly, the words *nibbuto* (despirated) and *sītibhūto* (cooled) in constant apposition. The word Nirvana (Pali *nibbāna*) itself has led, perhaps, to more misunderstandings than any other Buddhist term. Certainly, it implies a "death" of some sort: the fire is "quenched" and "goes out." But if we are to avoid the great error involved in any rendering of *Nirvana* by such words as "annihilation" (which would be to beg the whole question of the meaning of Buddhist "immortality," and contrary to the Buddha's express repudiation of all "annihilationist" heresies) it must be observed that the reference of *Nirvana* (or *Parinirvana*) to physiological death is only a special case of its general meaning; the common references are to the *completion* of stages in a continued life,—each of the transformations of which involves the arrest of or death to a previous condition and a going on in some other and superior condition. For example, when first Yasodā sees Prince Siddhattha she aspires to be his wife, and refers to that *end* of her girlhood as a *Nirvana,*—not an extinction (though she will be a girl no more) but a consummation and a fulfilment; and similarly, the successive stages in the training of a royal stallion (analogous to the training of the human individual) are referred to as so many *Parinirvanas,* which is as much as to say that the colt is dead, the steed perfected. Thus we "rise on stepping stones of our *dead* selves"; and when the word *Nirvana* is used absolutely with reference to the Great Awakening of any *Arahant,* this is merely the last step, and implies that the whole work of self-naughting has been accomplished. This is the end of all becoming and beyond all states of being; when "all has been done that there was to be done" (*katam-karaniyam*), and the heavy burden of existence has been dropped, there is no more a return to any conditioned existence in which to be at all one must be *so,* or *such.* This end and *summum bonum,* equally so for men and for the highest of the personal gods (whom we should now call angels), is attainable either (and preferably) here and now, or at the point of death, or hereafter from whatever position in heaven one may have earned by the practice of moral or habit of intellectual virtues. For so long as the goal has not been reached there remains the possibility of an ultimate fall from even "the summit of contingent being" (*bhav'agga*).

It is often asked: What is the condition of the Buddha, or Arahant, after death? And although annihilation is expressly denied ("to say of a monk thus set free [*vimutta*] that he neither knows nor sees would be improper," D.II.68; after death, the Buddha "is," though neither here nor there, Mil.72), it is always answered that words (inasmuch as their application is only to things that have beginnings and ends) are inadequate, and that none of the phrases "is" or "is not" or "Is and is not" or "neither is nor is not" is applicable,—even in this life, indeed, a Buddha is beyond our grasp, and how much more so when the body is no more. Further discussion of what is therefore "untold" is refused. It is just because of the limitations of "logic" that there must be (as also in Christian theology) a resort to the *via negativa* even when referring to the most positive reality; for example, it can be told what liberation is *from,* but not what an absolute independence *is.* The arrest of becoming (*bhava-nirodha*) is *Nirvana*; and what this implies can only be illustrated by analogies (*upamā*) such as that of "the way of a bird in the air, leaving no track." The ultimate reality is "void" (*suñña*) of any psychic (*attanīya*) essence, and of all the defects that pertain to it; hence the "Void" is synonymous with *Nirvana.*

The great work to be done is, then, one of self-naughting; one of the eradication, root and branch, of the notion (*māna*) "I and mine,"—*denegat seipsum.* For all suffering is bound up with the concept, I am this, or that; and to have laid down this burden is a beatitude than which there can be no greater.* Of all the delusions that men are attached to the greatest is that of their conviction of the constancy and reality of their "name and shape" (*nāmarūpa*), Ego (*aham*), or "self" (*attā*)—Behmen's "that which thou callest 'I, or myself' "—with which the "untaught many-folk," animists (then, as now) identify themselves; and the most dangerous aspect of this belief is that of the identification of Self not with the visible body (an evident inconstant) but with the invisible "soul" of which the persistence throughout our life, and even thereafter, is assumed. A great part of the Buddhist teaching is therefore devoted to the destructive analysis of the postulated (*sammuta*) "self" or "soul" (*attā*) or "being" (*sattā*); and it must be clearly understood that this is no mere matter of being "unselfish" but one of a quite literal self-denial—of which "unselfishness" in the ethical sense will be only a natural consequence and symptom.

The psycho-physical "self" is a bundle of five "stems" or composite of five "elements": visible body (*rūpa, kāya*) and invisible sensibility (*vedana*), recognition (*saññā*), constructions (*saṅk*

---

* It may make this more intelligible if we point out that modern psychologists have asserted in almost the same words that the concept or postulate of individuality is "the very mother of illusions" and that any person would be "infinitely happier if he would accept the loss of his individual self"; "individuality and falsity are one and the same." Cf. also St. Paul's "I live, yet not I"; the O. Fr. "morir vivant"; and Islamic "Die before ye die" and "dead man walking"; Angelus Silesius' "Stirb ehe du stirbst." "How can that which is never in the same state be said to 'be' anything?" (Plato, *Cratylus* 439 E). Almost always and everywhere it has been realized that our life is a dream from which we may sooner or later *wake.*

hārā),* and consciousness, discrimination or valuation (*viññāna*); or more briefly, of body with consciousness, the latter term then including the other four components which correspond to the "soul" with its contents. Whoever would not be deceived must know this composite "as become" (*yathā bhūtam*), viz. as a causally determined process of which the peculiarities exhibited at any given moment are the consequences of past events, this man So-and-so being the "inheritor" of past acts (*karma*); the composite is not "ours" because "we," who are "swallowed up in it," cannot say "let it be thus, or thus" but must take it as it is. It is demonstrated that the contents and the whole of this "self" are inconstant, never the same from one moment to another; "the life of a mortal lasts for so long as it takes one thought to succeed another"; and the analysis invariably ends with the words, "That's not mine, I'm not that, that's not my Self."

These words are a negative definition of the Self that I *am*.

Once at least the analysis is followed by the injunction, "Make the Self thy refuge, or resort" (*kareyya saraṇ'attano*, S.III.143), familiar also in the Buddha's well known saying, "Make the Self your lamp, the Self your refuge" and paralleled in the concept of a Self to be sought for as opposed to that of a self to be rid of. It is evident that the Self thus referred to cannot be equated with the unreal, composite, mortal self that was analyzed and by which we are overburdened already. It must be realized, if the Buddhist formulae are to be understood, that just as in every other traditional metaphysics, "there are two (selves) in us," and that the one word *attā* (Sanskrit, *ātman*) may refer to either of these "selves" according to the intention of the context; just as the one word "soul" may refer either to the fleshly "life" or to the "Spirit," i.e. "Soul of the soul"; or as "self" may refer to the outer and "selfish" man or to the inner and "selfless" Man, the "Man in this man"; we have already made this distinction by printing, in accordance with a well established convention, on the one hand "self" and on the other "Self" with the capital.

Buddhist references to the Self are explicit; for example, "Self is the Lord of self, Self self's goal." The Great Self (*mah'attā*) or

---

* Here, the notions, postulates, beliefs, opinions and *idées fixes*—e.g. "progress"—that are the convictions of individuals or parties; but in other contexts, more generally any or all of the composite things that "become."

Fair Self is distinguished from the petty or foul self, and is the latter's judge or conscience; the two selves are at war with one another, until self has been tamed or conquered. So it is asked, "With which self (*ken'attanā*) does one reach the Brahma-world?" and to this there are variously formulated answers, e.g., "with the purified Self," "with Self made-become," "with Self Brahma-become" (or "Brahmā-become," as the sense may require). The Buddha knows the Brahma-world, and all the roads that lead to it, as one who was born and bred there. But it cannot be said of the Self that it "is" or "is not," or "is and is not," or "neither is nor is not"; and here "self" is synonymous with the *Tathāgata* (Truth-finder), i.e. the Buddha.

The Way (*magga*, an old word implying the following of foot-prints), not indeed of the Buddha's invention, but an "Ancient Way" reopened, has been taught, but it is for everyman individually to "swelter at the task" until it has been accomplished; it is followed for the sake of what has not been, because it cannot be, taught. Until the "end of the road" has been reached, the pilgrim remains a learner (*sekho*), but having reached it, becomes an "untaught" (*asekho*), i.e. adept or expert; short of "World's End," not to be reached "by paces" but within you, there will be no escape from Ill. At this point the meaning of "Faith" emerges. Those who have not yet "heard" hold all sorts of mostly false "beliefs" (*ditthi*, views), and it is only because of his *faith* in the authority of one who *has* reached the goal that a man will be led to adopt the homeless life of the *peregrin* for the sake of an end as yet unseen; only if we believe in the credibility of a witness do we act accordingly, especially if the action demands a great renunciation. On the other hand, the adept, who has actually reached the goal, is no longer "faithful," no longer a disciple "walking by faith"; "gnosis (*ñāṇam*) is better than faith." *

The practice of virtues, notably of generosity, by the householder leads to rebirth in the happy heaven worlds, not of itself to liberation; the household life at best is a "dusty path," involved in worldly cares. The Way taught by the Buddha and that, by a variety of images, leads overland to World's End, or overseas to the Farther Shore, or upstream to its Source, or downstream to the Sea in

---

* "Habent illa duo certam veritatem: sed fides clausam et involutam, intelligentia nudam at manifestam": St. Bernard on *Consideration*, V.3.6.

which the rivers "lose their names and definition," or in any case to
the attainment of higher and higher conditions of existence and at
last (whether now or hereafter) to an end beyond all conditions,
is the life of "Walking with God" (*brahma-cariya* or *dhamma-
cariya*) to which the Buddhist monk commits himself under a
Master. The monastic discipline regarded as a training in self-
control by Self is a life of purification (*sujjhana,*—katharsis, *via
purgativa*) from all that is not-Self, and especially from all those
foul issues or fluxes (*āsava*) by which the Self is outwardly con-
taminated. The following of the Way, in addition to the avoidance
of all worldly attachment and of all incontinence, sexual or other,
requires a practice of all the virtues ordinarily demanded by any
monastic rule of moderate severity. But the procedure is by no
means only negative; it is one at the same time of ethical and intellectual development; i.e. in Buddhist terms, one of the "fostering"
or "making become" (*bhāvanā*) of desirable qualities, the work of
self-naughting coinciding with that of the "making-become" of the
Self, one whose self has been "cast off" (*atta-jaho*) being equally
one whose Self has been "made become" (*bhāvit'atto*). This
"making become" is a deliberate and controlled procedure, to be
sharply distinguished from the unregulated "becoming" that is characteristic of any mere existence and from which a deliverance is
sought. "Making become" is essentially a way of contemplative
practice (*jhāna*, Sanskrit *dhyāna*, becoming in Chinese *ch'an*, and
in Japanese *zen*),—ethical and intellectual, because in fact liberation has these two logically distinct aspects, and should be realized
in both ways, that is to say as regards the will (*ceto-vimutti*) and
as regards the understanding (*paññā-vimutti*).

The ethical contemplation consists in the practice of the four
brahma-vihāras or "godly states,"—a willed pervasion of the entire
universe and an extension to all living beings whatever and wherever
of feelings of love, sympathy, tenderness and impartiality,—desiring,
"May every living thing become a beatified Self" (*sukhit'attā*).
Needless to say that this devotion includes the love of one's enemies;
against whom, whatever the provocation, no monk may feel anger.
The practice of the "godly states" is a purification of the heart and
establishes the habit of a perfect charity.

On the other hand, the contemplations (*jhāna*), four in which
an objective image persists and four "without image," are attain-

ments of degrees or stations of consciousness (*viññāna*) in the hierarchy of states of being beyond that in which the practitioner normally functions; synthesis (*samādhi*) being a state of unified consummation reached on any one of these levels. The states of contemplation are analogous to the stations of "mystic experience," but differ in this respect, that the contemplative (*jhāyī, dhīra, yogī*) is only considered proficient (*kusala*) when he is able to reach, remain in or abandon any one of them and to pass from one to another in either direction *at will*. Each degree of this ladder is a liberation of its kind, but all, with their respective advantages and disadvantages, come short of the final goal by the very fact of their relativity; no Comprehensor would wish to remain in any one of these states for ever. Miraculous powers (*iddhi*) such as that of walking on the water or passing through solid obstacles are accidental results of contemplative practice, but are not to be sought for their own sake, nor may they be publicly exhibited.

There are also what may be called meditations, or rather "recollections" (*satī*) than contemplations. In the "recollection of death" (*maranasatī*—"memento mori"), practised sometimes in the presence of a decaying body, one pays attention to the liability of all things and all men to change and decay and on the inexpressible brevity of life under any conditions. In the "recollection of former births" (*jāti-sara*), which at the same time is a recollection of past aeons (*kappa*), one recovers to the degree of one's ability (possessed absolutely only by a Buddha) the memory of the stages of the long road that has been travelled in past aeons and in the course of which more tears have been shed than would fill the sea. This recollection introduces us to the difficult subject of "reincarnation," and here it must be made very clear, what has been recognized by many scholars but has rarely been understood, that Buddhism knows nothing of a "reincarnation" in the presently accepted sense of the rebirth of an identical "soul" in another body on earth; explicitly, "there is no being (*sattā*) that passes over from one body to another as a man might leave one village and enter another." What takes place is the reintegration of a consciousness (*viññāna*) under conditions predetermined by past actions (*karma*), which are only to be regarded as those *of* the new consciousness in the sense of possession by inheritance. What is transmitted and regenerated is aptly symbolized by the lighting of one fire from another; what is renewed is not an entity but a process. The ignoramus thinks, "*I was in the past, am now, and shall be in the future*"; but in reality the "former habitations" that one remembers were no more than one's present enceinté anything but the five-fold aggregate "that I am not, nor is it mine"; and no enlightened monk would be so foolish as to say that "in time past I was So-and-so, or am now, or shall be So-and-so." The expressions "I" and "my," and "a being" (*satta*) are merely *conventions* and *façons de parler*, permissibly used by a Buddha or any enlightened monk in everyday life for practical purposes, but are not to be taken for assertions of a corresponding reality. There is, thus, a clearly realized distinction of pragmatic (*sammuti, vohāra*) from absolute (*paramattha*) truth, of which the latter alone is really valid, "one, without a second." A man of knowledge "does not worry about what is unreal" (*asati na socati*);—i.e. "himself," or anything else that "is not my Self."

One further point respecting the realization of the saint's intrinsic "purity," of which the familiar *exemplum* is the old likeness of the smooth lotus-leaf that is not wetted by the water it grows in and rests upon: in the same way the Freedman (*vimutto*) is uncontaminated by human qualities, i.e. by any of the contraries on which experience rests and between which our ethical choices are made; he knows neither likes nor dislikes, and is as little stained by virtue as by vice. The making of choices as between good and evil is an absolutely indispensable means of procedure, but of no more use to one who has arrived than is a boat to one who has "crossed over" and is now safe ashore; all attachment, whether to vice or virtue, is a barrier to the taking of the last step.

As the Buddha often points out, he teaches his Law (*dhamma*) always in terms of the mean (*majjhe*), avoiding both extremes (*antā*); refusing to say, for example, of things, that they "are" or "are not" or of apparent identity that it remains in the sequence of cause and effect "the same" or "not the same"; so much depends on what we mean by "is" and what by "same." The most interesting application of the principle of the "Middle Way" is to time: the moment without duration that separates past from future embracing the whole of any existence, which is no longer the same but another as the flux of moments continues without a break. The moment (*khaṇa*, "glance") remains the same; it is we who change. Eternity is not in time, but now; it follows that this indivisible now is man's ever-present opportunity, that gateway of immortality that the Buddha "threw open" by his "Turning of the Wheel of the Law" (*dhamma-,* or sometimes *brahma-cakka*), and at which the disciple "stands knocking."

The *Mahāyāna* is often sharply contrasted with the *Hinayāna*; but in the present writer's view the *Mahāyāna* represents a perfectly orthodox and by no means "degenerate" expansion of doctrines already enunciated in the Canon; those, for example, of the Middle Way, the Void, the Moment, and that of the distinction of pragmatic from ultimate truth; there is little difference between Buddhaghosa's canonical position in the fifth century and that of the *Śūnyavadins* or *Mādhyamikas.* The difficulties inherent in the *Mahāyāna* dialectic arise from the universally recognized truth, that *Trasumanar significar* per verba *non si poria;* all the discussions of actions without an agent, knowledge without a knower, and impossibility of the knower knowing himself (as the finger cannot touch itself) revert to this. In the end, one becomes aware of the impossibility of *knowing* anything,—objects, because they never stop to be, our own reality, because this is not an object. Relative knowledge of the "facts of experience" in terms of subject and object— implied by the "consciousness" that in the parable of the raft is indispensable as means but of no further use when the end has been reached—is bound up with and appropriate to the existential nature that presupposes it; but is a veritable ignorance when envisaged in the light of the absolute understanding (*paññā*) that is not derived from objects perceived. *This* knowledge is not *of* the Suchness or Truth (*tathatā*) but *is* the Truth. As such the Truth, already synonymous with "Buddha," "Dharma," "Brahma," is all-inclusive, the infinite not other than the *finite,* and this is the sense of the famous aphorism, *"Samsara* and *Nirvana* are one and the same." That the relative is thus never really out of touch with the absolute at the same time leaves room for the cult of images and relics as supports of contemplation and for the concept of the Buddha's compassion or grace (*karuna*). It would be an error to realize *only* the transitoriness of the existent, or *only* the timelessness of *Nirvana;* negation and affirmation are both no more than partial truths, between which the Middle Way is one of silence. One who has reached the end holds no views, "in him there is no assumption, and no rejection"; this had already been enunciated in the Canon. One learns to think

of "oneself" and other "things" in terms of process; and having
outgrown a belief in their positive entity, understands also that it
cannot be said that they have no existence whatever; and when at
last the problem "is" *or* "is not" no longer presents itself, and can no
longer be asked, there remains no distinction of the resultant gnosis
from the residual gnostic; this is the Buddhist "peace that passeth
understanding."

3. *Buddhology:* Who was the Buddha? In a statistical sense,
the question is meaningless: "useless," as he himself says, "to ask my
name or parentage,—I wander in the world a nameless nobody."
This represents a "return,"—if we bear in mind that according to the
old doctrine of which the Buddhist teachings are only a new version,
"this one who is neither born nor dies, the eternal, hath not come
anywhere nor become anyone." Asked from another point of view
(as in the *Upanishads,* "Which is the Self?"), the question, Who?
can only be answered in terms of the impersonal epithets that must
be many if only because there are so many points of view from which
That can be regarded. Amongst all these, very many are the old
names that were those of *Agni* or the Sun in the Vedic tradition; and
it must not be overlooked that the name of the future Buddha,
Metteya, itself implies a "scion of Mitra", i.e. of the Sun or Fire,
that "Eye in the World" that is one of the Buddha's well known
designations. Amongst the names that he shares with the great
Brahmanical divinities are those of Supreme Person, Great Hero,
Dispenser, Physician, Charioteer, and God of gods; in his own words,
he is freed from all those conditions that might make him a god
(angel), spirit, daimon, or human being, one amongst others; he is
a Buddha, and as such out of all categories; just as all others "gone
home" can no longer be accounted for.

However, the most significant of the terms in which the Buddha
is referred to are those of *dhamma-bhūto* and *brahma-bhūto,* "become the Eternal Law" and "become Brahma," which occur repeatedly in apposition. The Buddha says of himself that "He who
sees me sees the Eternal Law, and he who sees the Eternal Law sees
me"; and he refers to himself and is referred to as "He whose name
is Truth" (*saccam*). Now, for the essentially Brahmanical audiences
to whom the Buddha preached (and we must put ourselves into
their position if we want to understand him who always preached

ad hominem) these principal names had all along been those of one and the same eternal essence, an essence, moreover, identical with that of the immanent Self in all beings. That the Buddha himself is this Self, that his is that very nature that should be served (*bhatti,* Sanskrit *bhakti*) and made-become within you is suggested by the appellations *Vissantara* and *Vessantara;* and it is more than once asserted that "the wakened Self is the Wake" (*buddh'attā yeva buddho ti).* Buddhahood, then, represents a potential goal finally attainable by anyone who takes upon himself the vows of a *Bodhisatta* and fulfills them. In some cases a *Bodhisatta's* final release may be delayed by the very nature of his resolve to function as a Savior "until the last blade of grass shall have been set free."

The universality of the Buddha-nature is explicit in the *Mahā-yāna,* where also in the elaborated pantheon we find the conception of an *Ādi* (primal) Buddha, of whom all other Buddhas ("human" or "contemplative") and *Bodhisattvas* are the diversified manifestations, while the *Tārās* (feminine Saviors) who are their consorts represent their "Wisdom" and correspond in all their forms, notably in that of the supreme *Prajñāpāramitā,* to the Christian *Sophia.*

In the epithet "Brahma-become," *brahma-* is grammatically ambiguous, but in apposition to *buddha,* and in many expressions synonymous with *dhamma-,* cannot be understood to mean Brahmā, the supreme *personal* deity of the age. For not only has the Buddha already in former births, before he was a Buddha, been a Brahmā or Mahabrahmā, but, great as the glory and long as the life of a Brahmā may be, it is repeatedly emphasized that the knowledge and understanding of even a Brahmā are very limited if compared to those of a Buddha; the Buddha is a teacher of Brahmās, not they his; and he is explicitly "far more than a Mahābrahmā." It is emphasized that merely to have reached the empyrean Brahma-worlds, however great a reward, is not the "final escape"; in former lives, as a *Bodhisatta,* the Buddha had taught only the Way to these worlds, but as a Buddha, "Brahma-become" himself, he knew and taught the way of the final escape from all circumstantial existence in any mode, whether human or divine.

4. *Cosmogony:* The scheme of the succession of cycles is not only of great intrinsic interest, but is to be envisaged as the tremendous

background against which the whole drama of liberation is enacted. "There are these four incalculable aeons (*kappa*): those of involution, state of involution, evolution, and state of evolution." These all together make a Great Aeon *(mahākappa)*; our world, having long ago evolved, is now in a cycle of involution, i.e. dissolution, and will finally be destroyed either by fire, water or wind; such destructions extend as far as to the Brahma-worlds, in which all living beings remain latent until the evolution of worlds begins again from the highest level affected by the dissolution; then beings descend from the *Ābhassara* to the lower Brahma-worlds, and in due course to lower and lower realms as these appear in descending order of progressive materialization. This whole beginningless process constitutes the "conflux" (*saṁsāra*) or cycle of becoming (*bhava-cakka*) of which the Buddha is omniscient and from which he teaches the way of escape; the Freedman (*vipamutto*), *Arahant,* "transcends the aeons"; the Eternal Law with which the Buddha identifies himself is "intemporal."

5. *In conclusion:* Some of the greatest of European "mystics" have asserted that "God is properly called 'Nothing' " (*nihil*): Meister Eckhart speaks of the freedom of the Godhead "in its non-existence." It would be difficult to distinguish this "nihilism" (which is only another aspect of the Scholastic "realism") from the Buddhist "nihilism" that equates *Nirvana* with the "Void" and at the same asserts that this "unborn, unmade, unbecome, incomposite *is,* and were it not, there would be no way of escape from the born, the made, the become and composite." In other words, the "Vacancy" into which the Freedman escapes is "empty" not by privation inasmuch as it does not contain any of those "things" that are in themselves privations and of which the veritable non-entity has been realized by the Freedman who now "transcends the aeons"; the "rest" and "peace" that are synonymous with *Nirvana* and beyond our understanding are, literally, man's holy day and *vacation,* open here and now to anyone whose work of self-naughting has been perfected, or if not now, then hereafter, when the task has been completed, and all potentiality has been reduced to act (*kata-karaṇīyam*).

Buddhaghosa can say that *Nirvana* is a passing away or destruction (*khaya*):

> For there is Ill, but none to feel it;
> For there is action, but no agent;
> And there is peace, but none enjoys it;
> A way there is, but wayman none

but he is equally careful to say, and equally orthodox in saying, that there is no passing away or destruction of anything but of passions, defects, and all possible delusions. As Meister Eckhart says, "Behold the soul divorced from every aught," or, again, "The soul must put itself to death." These are "hard sayings"; but it must be realized that such a "mystical theology" as this, like that of Dionysius, cannot be grasped apart from the "ascetic theology" that it involves. The Way is "for those whose wants are few," and only for them. The Forerunner asks us to abandon all our "great possessions," material and mental goods, vices and virtues together, to follow him to an end of the road beyond all values whatever, to the realization of an Eternal Worth that is not a value, but on which all values depend. The Buddha might have said with Meister Eckhart that "What the tyro fears is the expert's delight."

BIBLIOGRAPHY

Most valuable are the texts and translations published by the Pali Text Society, together with *The Sacred Books of the Buddhists* published by the Oxford University Press. Mrs. Rhys Davids' many books on Buddhism are of high value but must be read with reservations. Amongst other works available in English may be cited: Vols. X, XI, XIII, XVII, XIX, XX, XXI, XXXV, XXXVI, XLIX of the *Sacred Books of the East* (Oxford); Vols. 3, 28–30, and 37 in the *Harvard Oriental Series;* E. B. Cowell, ed., *The Jātaka* (Cambridge, England, 1895–1907); E. H. Johnston, *The Buddhacarita* (Calcutta, 1935–6); and *The Saundarānanda* (Oxford, 1928, 1932); E. W. Burlingame, *Buddhist Parables* (New Haven and Oxford, 1922); E. Foucaux, *Le Lalita Vistatara* (Fr. tr.), (Paris, 1884, 1892).

I. B. HORNER, *The Early Buddhist Theory of Man Perfected* (London, 1936).

A. K. COOMARASWAMY, *Hinduism and Buddhism* (New York, n.d.).

A. B. KEITH, *Buddhist Philosophy* (Oxford, 1923),—best for the Mahayana.

I. BABBITT, *The Dhammapada . . . with an Essay on Buddha and the Occident* (Oxford and New York, 1936).

Sir C. N. E. Eliot, *Hinduism and Buddhism* (London, 1921)

J. Legge, *A Record of Buddhistic Kingdoms . . . by Fâ-Hien* (Oxford, 1886).

J. Beal, *Life of Hiuen-Tsang by Hwui Li* (London, n.d.), and *Buddhist Records of the Western World . . . Si-Yu-Ki of Hiuen Tsang* (London, n.d.).

D. T. Suzuki, *Açvaghosa's Discourse on the Awakening of Faith in the Mahāyāna* (Chicago, 1900); *Outlines of Mahāyāna Buddhism* (London, 1907).

————, *The Lankāvatara Sūtra* (London, 1932).

————, *Studies in the Lankāvatara Sūtra* (London, 1930)'.

————, *Essays in Zen Buddhism* (London and Kyoto, 1928–1934)'.

W. Gemmell, *The Diamond Sutra* (London and New York, 1913).

L. D. Barnett, *The Path of Light . . . Bodhicharyāvatāra of Sānti-Deva* (London, 1909).

Bendall, *Cikṣāsamuccaya of Cāntideva* (Petrograd, 1902).

————, *Buddhist Texts from Japan* (Oxford, 1881).

E. H. McGovern, *A Manual of Buddhist Philosophy, I. Cosmology* (New York and London, 1923).

L. de la Vallée Poussin, *The Way to Nirvāna* (Cambridge, Eng., 1917), and (in French) *L'Abhidharmakosa of Vasubandhu*

Th. Stcherbatsky, *Buddhist Logic* (Leningrad, 1932). (Paris and Louvain, 1923–1931).

G. Tucci, *Indo-Tibetica* (Rome, 1932–1941).

Marco Pallis, *Peaks and Lamas* (London and New York, 19— etc).

W. Y. Evans Wentz, *Tibetan Yoga and Secret Doctrines* (Oxford, 1935).

J. Bacot and H. I. Woolf, *Three Tibetan Mysteries* (London and New York, n.d.).

Lama Yongden, *Mipam* (London, 1938).

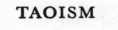

TAOISM

The name of Dr. Hail is familiar to students of Oriental history. His research on "Tseng Kuo-fan and The Taiping Rebellion", published in 1927, and for which Yale awarded him his Ph.D. degree in 1921, has remained a standard work of reference for students of Chinese history.

He was born in Osaka, Japan, in 1877. At the age of fifteen his family returned to this country, where he received his higher education. He earned his B.A. degree at Missouri Valley College, Marshall, Missouri, in 1899, which institution conferred upon him, in 1921, the honorary Doctor of Divinity degree. After a year's teaching at his alma mater he returned to Japan to teach for one year at the Japanese Imperial Naval College. Three years followed at the Yale Divinity School where he was given his B.D. degree in 1904. Two years later Yale conferred upon him the master's degree and the same year he began his long teaching career in China with the College of Yale-in-China (1906–1927). He served as dean of Yale's Middle School in China for ten years and dean of its College for five years. During a furlough (1920–1921) he became visiting professor of history at Yale.

Since 1928 he has taught at The College of Wooster, holding the Michael O. Fisher professorship in history and the headship of its department of history. In 1946 he retired as professor emeritus to the quiet life of a scholar in anticipation of further literary work.

Editor

TAOISM

WILLIAM JAMES HAIL

TAOISM HAS had the most chequered career of any of the three religions of China. Once it commanded respect among the mighty, but Confucianism ultimately replaced it as the guardian of the State Religions. Then for a time it appealed to the religious needs or hopes of the more religious folk who would cultivate their spiritual life, or even prolong this life, but Buddhism eventually replaced it there, and it had to take its stand among the ignorant and superstitious who invoked its magic working powers to avoid disease, death, or trouble from vengeful spirits in the other world.

It began, so far as the official accounts go, in the same conditions and with the same backgrounds that produced Confucianism—the war torn feudal age of the waning Chou Dynasty, during the last three centuries of its weakening career, which ended when the Ch'in Dynasty (221 B.C.) with the powerful Shih Hwangti or "First Emperor" set up a centralised government which formed the pattern of later Chinese government, followed soon, and for four centuries by the Han, and thereafter until the fall of the Manchus in 1912.

Of the numerous Chou thinkers whose systems contained possibilities, only Confucianism and Taoism remained to contend for preeminence; the ideas of other masters were integrated into one or the other of these two philosophies or were laid aside. The day of free discussion was gone, though there was enough to permit accommodation between the two predominant philosophies.

We know that Confucianism, pondered by many teachers and brought to its height by Mencius in his writings, attempted to secure integrated personality, right social relations, and good government. Virtuous rulers fulfilling the Mandate of Heaven and of people alike were to be like fathers who cared for a peaceful, prosperous people. The religions of the classics were, of course, a part of the Chinese heritage and must be observed with great care, but Confucius disclaimed any knowledge of that Spirit world and its mysteries.

The reputed founder of Taoism is one surnamed Li, who presumably was a senior contemporary of Confucius. He is known in later ages by the title conferred on him in admiration by Confucius himself: Lao Tzŭ or Old Master, (or, better, Old Philosopher). There is some dispute about his historicity, or the date at which the chief writing of Taoism,—the *Tao Teh Ching*—was composed. But whoever the author, he had interests quite distinct from those of Confucius. Government, ethics, virtue or its opposite, he seemed to ignore, save as they moved along the current of existence. He wanted to penetrate the mysteries of the universe. He contemplated the matrix out of whose quiet depths came the universe itself, God, and the numerous good and evil influences which the ancient Chinese attributed to the antagonisms and eternal struggles between the benevolent spirits which were known as *shen,* and the demons known as *kwei,* from whom came good or bad fortune. Much of the Chinese civilization of the earlier days had been concerned with soothsaying and formulas to appease the one group and beat back the other. The world was filled with witches, necromancers, and fortune tellers, and there was a literature dealing with these matters which none of the masters could ignore.

Lao Tzŭ is credited with being the founder of Taoism and the author of the classic of Taoism, the *Tao Teh Ching* (Classic of the Way and Virtue). Eventually scholarship will have to clear up the question of date and authorship; it will also have to resolve some of the even more difficult questions of the origin of some of the concepts in the philosophy of Lao Tsŭ. Some of these are unquestionably from the older Chinese classics which Confucius claimed he transmitted but did not write, especially the *I Ching* so precious to diviners because it embodied the *yin* and *yang* philosophy of dualism which in one form or other prevailed for centuries all the way from China to Greece. How much prehistorical interchange of ideas was there, and where were the ultimate sources of Lao Tzŭ's concepts?

In brief, his view was comprehended in the thought that back of all the process of change in the universe was what he can only call "The Great Tao," and that this *Tao* is powerful but with a latent power not yet brought into activity. Somewhere and somehow it begins to unfold and move along in its course producing somehow the universe of gods and spirits and human beings. Apparently God himself would simply have evolved in the flow of this power which itself had none of the attributes of personality, yet moved irresistibly forward as a stream towards the mighty ocean. The term *Tao* itself means way or road or course, but like the Greek word *Logos,* it comes to mean both the course of evolution, and the power that was once apparently chaos, but now pervades the entire universe.

Since men and spirits alike are borne like drops of water down this mighty stream, all human striving is useless. Virtue, which to Confucius is achieved by a lifetime of self discipline is, in the *Tao Teh Ching,* just a quiet submission to the power of the *Tao.* Riches, fame, honor and power for which men strive are, in the view of this philosophy, only matters that produce strife and war. His conclusion is that the *Tao* and human conformity to it resemble water in being content to flow into the low places; and just as water which is one of the softest of substances can wear down rocks, so is the man who is borne down the current of *Tao.* Through the feminine virtues of humility—the gentleness that makes one bold,—and a shrinking from taking precedence over others, whereby one becomes a vessel of honor, this quiet yielding to the Absolute, the *Tao,* carries one to his destined place.

The figure of water that overpowers the rocks as it flows quietly in its descent to the low places, and eventually to the ocean, is carried forward by later thinkers to the figure of the mighty force of stormy ocean waves as they dash against the rocky coast.

As the Absolute, *Tao* cannot be defined. "The *Tao* that can be trodden is not the enduring and unchanging *Tao.* The name that can be named is not the enduring and unchanging name. (Conceived of as) having no name it is the Originator of Heaven and earth; (conceived of as) having a name, it is the Mother of all things. . . . Under these two aspects, it is really the same; but as development takes place, it receives the different names. Together we call them the Mystery. Where the Mystery is the deepest is the gate of all that is subtle and wonderful." I : 1 : 1, 2, 4.

In the usual Chinese view of the universe, Heaven seemed to be at once the overruling power, sometimes impersonal, sometimes, perhaps usually, the presiding deity over the array of gods and spirits, at any rate supreme. But the *Tao Teh Ching* rarely refers to Heaven, and only once to God, where speaking of the *Tao* it exclaims: "How pure and still the *Tao* is. I do not know whose son it is. It might appear to have been before God." I:4: 2b, 3.

As the debates between rival schools of thought continued through the years and a partisanship produced more positive views on each side, Chuang Tzŭ late in the fourth century B.C. emphasized Taoism against the crystallizing views of the Confucian school which reached their clearest expression in a contemporary of Chuang Tzŭ, namely Mencius. In many different ways the superiority of conformity to the *Tao,* even to the point of avoiding all strife, over the views of the Confucianists (who still accentuated statecraft and ethics, and were moving towards their destined position as guardians of China's chief system of thought and expounders of the rites and ceremonies so essential to the rulers in the state religion) is urged with a considerable display of literary strife.

But even the champion of Taoism has to admit that there is a cleavage between the pure Taoism of Lao Tzŭ and a "human Taoism." The *Tao Teh Ching* had hinted that through the quiet yielding to the *Tao,* the softness and humility of water in human life would end in firmness and power. Probably under the pressure of the popular and more practical difficulties of life, some of the less speculative and philosophical Taoists dealt with the human side of the matter, trying by breath control and other devices to prolong life. Perhaps already, and certainly after the First Emperor of the Ch'in Dynasty and his later successors in the Han, the thought prevailed that certain substances contained much of the *yang* and others more of the *yin.* (All through the spirit world and the animal and vegetable kingdoms, as well as in the heavens and in the world below, everything contained one or the other or a mixture of the *yang,* which stood for light, summer, benevolent spirits and gods—known as *shen* —the male sex, and the *yin* under which darkness, winter, evil spirits, or *kuei,* and the female sex were grouped. The five elements fell into one or the other of the two groups, and the various possible combinations were represented in the venerated *I Ching* by diagrams made up of some 64 possible combinations of long lines for the *yang* and broken ones for the *yin.* From these diagrams soothsayers had been able to determine lucky days, favorable or unfavorable prospects for a proposed marriage, and many other matters of concern to individuals and families. And the belief had for generations been implicit that God spoke through some form of divination: through oracle bones during the earlier ages, through other means later, but with the *I Ching* serving as the standard treatise on divination.)

During these times the more practical Taoists addressed themselves to the task of seeking out all the elements that were largely *yang* and using them as food, or amulets, or adornments or furniture, and of avoiding whatever was substantially *yin*. But far more significant was the thought that there was some elixir of immortality, and some way to transmute baser metals into gold. After the days of Chuang Tzŭ the quest for these things received imperial support, and Shih Huangti founder of the Ch'in Dynasty, was reported to have sent a number of young men and girls for the elixir of immortality into the Eastern seas, whose destiny, it was believed, was to settle in Japan.

From now on the philosophy of the *Tao Teh Ching* meant little, and the constantly growing trend of Taoism was in the direction of specializing on the determination of such questions as diviners usually answer, and to use what powers they had to win the favor of the *shen* and drive out the *kuei*. To be sure there were those who still read what books the philosophers had left behind, and they deprecated the descent from quiet and submission to the *Tao* to the support of magical powers to secure even such desirable aims as long life and good fortune. They were at heart more like the Buddhists whose earliest teacher had sought to escape the evils of existence through the enlightenment which follows the overcoming of desire. As the Buddhists would retire from the world to quiet retreats so would these more spiritual Taoists retire to lives of simplicity and contemplation in some isolated nook. But the rank and file lived on an animistic level, and Taoism more and more catered to that side of religion.

Eventually Buddhism did arrive in China, first as a trickle, but before the end of the Han Dynasty in a great deal of strength. The more enlightened Taoists found in it a far more attractive form of what they believed, for it came with a finished ritual, with numerous *sutras,* and an underlying philosophy like theirs; it came chiefly in the *Mahayana* form with numerous divinities, a promise of bliss in the Western Paradise after death and many hells for evil doers.

In spite of its being a foreign religion there were aspects of universal appeal in it. The Taoists who had already lost prestige by the adoption of their rival cult as the official system, now saw that they had met a new competitor in Buddhism: one that satisfied religious needs which neither of the other cults met. During the Later Han Dynasty a minor Taoist sect followed one Chang Tao-ling in a rebellion in the Szechuan-Shensi area, held it for a time, but, far more important, began from that stronghold to organize Taoism into an ecclesiastical realm. His family continued to hold power in that religion, and to this day produce the "Taoist Popes."

Under their regime, which thus began at the end of the second Century A.D., Taoist writings copying Buddhist techniques, setting up a Taoist Trinity which has not always contained the same three, but in general consisting of the Jade Emperor 'Yü Huang Shangti', P'an Ku who assisted in the creation of Heaven and Earth, and Lao Tzŭ. Numerous gods of the upper and lower world were appropriated and rituals and other items from Buddhism or akin to it introduced. In spite of all such efforts, however, Taoism found itself losing ground in competition with Buddhism as that religion became naturalized. The missionaries of the foreign faith studied Taoism and made the most of the similarity of the two philosophies. From among the converts to Buddhism must have been numerous intelligent and educated Taoists who felt that geomancy, necromancy and other magic working "sciences" were a degradation of Taoism, and that it would be better openly to renounce it and espouse some of the numerous more or less attractive Buddhist tenets. We know definitely that in the formation of Chinese sects which still exist today former Taoists played their part—for instance in the development of the Ch'an or Meditation sect. Here two Fourth and Fifth Century Taoists, Tao Sheng and Hui Yüan led in the revolt against ritualistic Buddhism and eventually there emerged the sect which emphasized what in Christianity might be called the Inner Light, secured by sustained contemplation.

The Pure Land or *Amida* sect in which merit is gained by simply repeating over and over the simple confession of faith in *Amida* is another Chinese development ascribed to the former Taoist Hui Yuan mentioned above. This simple passport to Paradise opened a future life of happiness to the coolie on the street and the peasant who must stay at home and assume the responsibilities of every day life. Many centuries later this simple faith penetrated Japan and along with the Zen (*Ch'an*) faith swept away many of the older and more formal sects. The point here is that Buddhism won away from

Taoism much of its remaining prestige and intelligent personnel, and left it to become what some have regarded as a much degraded form of religion, in spite of all the efforts of the Taoist Pope and his followers. The manufactured Taoism they tried to develop did not have the ring of the genuine.

We are very apt to think that indeed Taoism had degenerated from the lofty ideas of Lao Tzŭ and Chuang Tzŭ, or even the alchemy and ranks of would be immortals among whom searchers for an elixir were included. Yet I suspect that the case is not that simple and that there is a possibility that what happened was that the older animistic faiths of China which centered in Ancestor Worship and in the intricate possible patterns of the *Yang* and *Yin* which called for expert or divine guidance were really back of the whole religious life of China, making it necessary for Confucianism to sponsor every form of public worship, and for some other religion to care for a diagnosis and cure for the crises of daily life, accident, sickness, death and the life beyond. From remotest antiquity, as recorded, for example, in the *I Ching,* divination was resorted to by great and small folk, and the organization of the Chinese family life with right relationships essential between the living and between those who had passed into the spirit world and their descendants opened a wide range of professions for those who dealt in the occult, from witches and necromancers, locators of lucky sites for graves, and fortune tellers who could advise common people on their prospects for luck, to more gifted wonder workers who could reach the unseen powers and secure blessings or avert curses.

To this earlier and still potent superstitious faith of the common people all three of the ruling religions bowed, but especially Taoism, since they were left only that field. Some writers are reluctant to burden Taoism with all the superstitious practices whereby witchcraft, fortune telling, communication with the dead and the like are allied, but at least they fall more under that religion than under any other. Yet there is a special form of service which the Taoist monks and priests are called on to perform that ordinary wonder workers shrink from. They are often called in to help drive out demons of sickness, and when death befalls, their services are in demand to secure the repose of the departed spirit through prayers and other devices to prevent their becoming vengeful *kuei.* They also assist in the purification of homes where demons lurk, and in writing potent charms and making powerful amulets to protect people from evil spirits, and secure aid from kindly ones.

However, it must be remembered that, in spite of the array of *sutras* and the profound philosophy of some of the Buddhist sects, they too cater to many of these needs of ignorant followers, and often both Buddhist and Taoist monks assist at desperate crises and preside at funerals, each bringing his own form of power from the invisible world. And even the almost agnostic Confucian magistrates in the old regime came forth to invoke strange spirits when the welfare of a province or county was threatened by the spirits through drought or flood or pestilence.

In these respects they all confess that the real religion of the masses moves about on a plane far lower than the philosophies and dreams of religious speculators. It is not merely the men like Confucius, Mencius, Lao Tzŭ or Chuangtzu or Buddha that must be reckoned in considering Chinese religion, but the notions, fears, and needs of the Changs and Lis and Lius who form the masses of China. If even the more dignified religions have had to cater to these practical needs, Taoism, driven in retreat from its place beside Confucianism and its priority to Buddhism, has been more or less forced, like water, to flow along with the tide and take the lower and humbler duties of serving the common people.

.But it is today threatened again by a rival. For modern science is working havoc with the trade of the Taoist priest or the near Taoist diviner. It substitutes techniques of meeting sickness, not by incantations, but by skilled treatment of ascertained causes of disease in the physical realm while psychology rolls back the mental roots of many forms of sickness. The area of accident and chance happenings still furnish room for religion, but profounder religions than Taoism are in the field.

Yet, China is still mainly rural and, in the cities, a poverty stricken proletariat. Among them Taoism remains in the forms of groping for any form of deliverance they can find, from disease, from "hants" and "hexes." They call hopefully on the Taoist priest for amulets and charms for themselves or their children, and so long as these things are needed or desired, the Taoists will have a field of service. But they are in retreat everywhere and it is doubtful if they will ever regain respectability since their true seekers after the mysteries of the universe left them for Buddhism and made them flow down to the lower levels of daily life among the ignorant and superstitious.

Though no future seems to open to them—unless perchance civilization itself perishes—yet they have not been without great influence. Chinese folklore bristles with tales of immortals (ranged by the Taoists into three groups), and of the power radiating from the five sacred peaks, especially the Eastern, T'ai Shan, stones from which are as potent among China's evil spirits as Solomon's seal was among the Moslems in its romantic tales. There are hundreds of materials that bring good luck, such as jade the peach tree and many another *yang*-filled substance; likewise there are many dangers of destruction, say from the fox which can change into the form of a beautiful maiden who lures some bewildered victim out to a remote mountain or moor and there abandons. There are a thousand practices of daily life which have their origin in animistic or Taoistic beliefs. It will be generations before the genius of the Chinese civilization can be understood without understanding the evolution of her religions.

Probably no one will ever know how to estimate the numbers of professing Taoists there are; in the confusion of present day China probably there is no way even to tell how many priests and monks serve the Taoist Pope. There are relatively few temples; little or no attempt to follow modern techniques in attracting people in masses to preach to them as Christians and some sects of Buddhists do. There appears to be very little effort to engage in what we call social service. If Confucianism revives, if Buddhism rises again and adapts its teachings and practices to modern methods, and if science and learning take the field and dispel fear of the *kuei*, what remains for Taoism?

Perhaps we may hope for a re-study of Lao Tzŭ's penetrating philosophy as fitting into the evolutionary hypothesis. Perhaps we may some day appreciate his aversion to strife and warfare as cogently and tersely stated in the *Tao Teh Ching:* "There is no calamity greater than lightly engaging in war." II:69: 2a.

Since in a sense on their popular side, or in the concessions they must all make to the strong survivals of primitive faiths among the Chinese—Confucianism and its state worship, Buddhism and its assurances of mercy and happiness in Paradise, and Taoism with its manipulations of the spirit forces—it is not surprising that they exist peacefully side by side. Perhaps since for the time being they are all more or less discredited they feel like comrades. At any rate the various sects of Buddhism and Taoism seem more like schools of philosophy than persecutors under the skin. I have been in small country temples where all three religions were housed though in three separate rooms, each with its appropriate symbols, and all served by the self-same caretaker. In that same way they all seem to exist together and serve different religious and social needs as specialists do among our physicians.

But whenever you gaze on a Sung picture or a Ming vase the chances are that you see the influence of Taoism, or of Buddhism as Taoists have modified it—a serene mountain or seaside scene, rocks, mountain peaks, a stream and a philosopher crossing that stream. The trees in the foreground and background are undoubtedly those having plenty of the *yang* element. Or it may be that a bowl or vase is adorned with the lines representing combinations of the *yang* and *yin,* and perpetuate the days when Taoism was a proud religion, embodying from the side of humbler folk, the universal desire for a quiet and orderly world where good should overcome evil and the power of the Great *Tao* prevail. If its spirit marches on under the banner of Buddhism perhaps Lao Tzŭ would accept its eclipse as one of the stages along the Way.

BIBLIOGRAPHY

I. Sources:

The Texts of Taoism, comprising translations of the *Tao Teh Ching* and Chuang Tzu's writings: volumes XXXIX and XL of *The Sacred Books of the East* (Second impression. New York, 1927).

L. Wieger, *Taoisme* (Two volumes Hsien hsien, 1911–1913) including translations of the above two works and Lieh Tzu, and a list of the sacred Taoist books.

H. A. Giles, *Chuang Tzu, Mystic, Moralist and Social Reformer* (2d edition, Shanghai, 1926).

II. General discussions and accounts, in which Taoism and popular religions are considered:

J. J. M. de Groot, *The Religious System of China, its Ancient Forms, Evolution, History and Present Aspect.* 6 vols. (Leyden, 1892–1910). (Also briefer books by the same author: *The Religion of the Chinese* and *Religion in China* (1910 and 1912).

W. E. Soothill, *The Three Religions of China* (London, 1913).

M. Kennelly, *Researches into Chinese Superstitions* (being a translation of a more extensive work in French by Henri Dore), 8 vols. (Shanghai, Tusewei Press, 1914–1926).

Witter Bynner, *The Way of Life According to Laotzu* (1944).

J. K. Shryock, *The Temples of Anking and Their Cults. A Study of Modern Chinese Religion* (Paris, 1931).

The most up to date discussion of Chinese religions, ancient and modern, where comprehensive bibliographies are to be found is:

Kenneth Scott Latourette, *The Chinese, Their History and Culture* (third edition revised, 1946).

CONFUCIANISM

Dr. Chan is Professor of Chinese Culture in Dartmouth College. Born in South China in 1901, during his early years he received a Confucian education and thus writes with personal knowledge upon the subject of this essay. He was later trained in modern schools, earning his B.A. degree at Lingnan University, Canton. He did graduate work at Harvard University, where he received his M.A. in 1927 and his Ph.D. in 1929.

Returning to Lingnan University, he served as dean of its faculty from 1929 to 1936. The next six years he taught at the University of Hawaii, holding the professorship of Chinese Philosophy and Institutions in its Oriental Institute. Since 1942 he has been on the faculty staff at Dartmouth.

Professor Chan has lectured extensively before college and university groups, always most favorably received as a platform speaker. Although no longer a Confucianist, he has helped many of the younger generation of Westerners better to appreciate the greatness of Confucius' teachings and to understand the mind and the culture of ancient and modern China. The clarity of his writings matches the brilliance of his public speaking. He has contributed many essays in the field of his specialty to published volumes, among which are: "Twentieth Century Philosophy" (1943), edited by D.D. Runes; "Philosophy: East and West" (1944), edited by C. A. Moore; and "China" (1946), edited by F. H. MacNair. For the recently issued "Encyclopedia of Religion" (1945) he wrote the major articles dealing with Chinese Religions, Confucianism, Buddhism and Taoism and their terminologies.

Editor

CONFUCIANISM

CHAN WING-TSIT

CONFUCIUS (551–479 B.C.) has been called founder of a religion and an agnostic. He was neither. In ancient China, Lao Tzu, the naturalist, represented the left wing in the matter of religion, and Mo Tzu, the vigorous promoter of the ancient faith, represented the right wing. Confucius followed the middle course, with tendency towards the right. He found the worship of Heaven and ancestors conducive to morality and social order and therefore encouraged it. But he would not discuss life after death. He discouraged praying to spirits. He opposed human sacrifice. In the worship of ancestors he preferred simple to elaborate ceremonies. The fact was Confucius was primarily interested in human affairs. Consequently he "did not talk about spirits" but said that "if we cannot serve man, how can we serve spirits?" He advocated true manhood (*jen*) as the highest good, the superior man as the ideal being, and cultivation of life (*hsiu shen*) as the supreme duty of man. He emphasized moral perfection (*chih shan*) for the individual and moral and social order (*li*) for society. These are to be attained by the practice of *chung*, or being true to the principle of one's nature, and *shu*, the application of those principles in one's relationship with others. *Chung* and *Shu* form the "one thread that runs through" the entire Confucian teaching. The total objective is *chung yung*, the Golden Mean or Central Harmony, that is, "the central basis of our moral being and harmony with the universe." To this end, knowledge must be directed, names rectified, and social relationships harmonized. The whole program involves the investigation of things, the achievement of knowledge, sincerity of the will, rectification of the heart, cultivation of the personal life, harmony of family life, national order, and finally, world peace.

Mencius (c. 371–c. 289 B.C.) carried this moralism and humanism further. He held that we not only should be good but must be good, since human nature is originally good. A man must "develop his nature to the fullest" and "exercise his mind to the limit." Hsun Tzu (c. 335–c. 288 B.C.), on the other hand, believed that human nature is originally evil and stressed moral discipline and education, especially through rules of social conduct (*li*).

In the Han dynasty (202 B.C.–220 A.D.) Confucianism was first strongly influenced by the *Yin Yang* philosophy. As advocated by Tung Chung-shu (177–104 B.C.), man and nature have direct correspondence. As the cosmic order results from the harmony of *yin* and *yang* or the negative and positive universal principles in nature, so the moral order results from the harmony of *yang* and *yin* in man, such as husband and wife, human nature and human passion, love and hate, etc. Human affairs and natural events were both explained in terms of a neat macrocosm-microcosm relationship. In the end Confucianism was thoroughly infested with the "science of catastrophies and anomalies." Not until Liu Hsin (d. 23 B.C.) was Confucianism purged of this superstition.

Confucianists in the T'ang period (618–907) were largely concerned with the problems of human nature and how to cultivate it, especially as Confucius and Mencius saw them. Under the stimulus of Buddhist metaphysics, Confucianism developed into a new phase in the Sung dynasty (960–1279), inaugurating an extensive movement, Rational Philosophy, usually called Neo-Confucianism in the West, which was to dominate Chinese thought to the present day.

The Confucian Rational Philosophy developed in three stages, namely, the Reason School in the Sung period, the Mind School in the Ming period (1388–1644), and the Empirical School in the Ch'ing period (1644–1911). The central idea of the movement is focused on the Great Ultimate and Reason. The Great Ultimate moves and generates the active principle, *yang,* when its activity reaches its limit, and engenders the passive principle, *yin,* when it becomes tranquil. The eternal oscillation of *yin* and *yang* gives rise to the material universe. Thus reality is a progressively evolved and well-coordinated system.

This dynamic and orderly character of the universe is due to Reason and the Vital Force (*ch'i*). As the Ch'eng brothers (Ming-tao, 1032–1086, and I-ch'uan, 1033–1077) said, "All things have the same Reason in them." Thus, Reason combines the Many into One, while the Vital Force differentiates the One into the Many, each with its own "determinate nature." Reason operates through, and is embodied in, the Vital Force. It is this coöperative functioning of theirs that makes the universe a cosmos, a harmonious system of order and sequence. As such the cosmos is a moral order. As the greatest of the Neo-Confucianists, Chu Hsi (1130–1200), put it, "the Great Ultimate is nothing but the Reason of ultimate goodness."

In order to appreciate fully the meaning of the universe, man must comprehend Reason by "investigating things to the utmost," that is, by "investigating the Reason of things to the utmost." When sufficient effort is made, and understanding naturally comes, one's nature will be realized and his destiny will be fulfilled, since "the exhaustive investigation of Reason, the full realization of one's nature, and the fulfillment of destiny are simultaneous." When one understands Reason, he will find that "All people are brothers and sisters, and all things are my companions," because all men have the same Reason in them.

When it came to the Ming period, especially in Wang Yang-ming (1473–1529), Reason became identified with Mind. Mencius' doctrine of native knowledge was revived and made the basis of his theory of the identity of knowledge and conduct and the sacred duty of man to "fully exercise his mind" and to "manifest his illustrious virtues."

Wang Yang-ming considered desire as an obstacle to the mind. The Neo-Confucianists of the Ch'ing period, especially Tai Tung-yuan (1723–1777), however, argued that since desire is part of our nature, it has its rightful place, just as the Vital Force has its rightful place beside Reason. As a matter of fact, Reason can only be discovered in daily events and experience, or in short, in the Vital Force itself.

In a rationalistic and humanistic system such as Confucianism, its religious position is difficult to define. There is nothing in the system to justify the Western habit of calling Confucianism a religion in the conventional, occidental sense. The Chinese do not call it a religion, but *ju chia* or *ju chiao,* meaning the School of the Learned or the Doctrine of the Learned, respectively. It is a system of training which involves education, government, rules of social conduct (*li*), and religion. The system itself has no priesthood, no church, no Bible, no creed, no conversion, and no fixed system of gods. This being the case, no Chinese should be labeled a Confucianist as a Chinese monk is called a Buddhist or a Chinest priest a Taoist. A Confucianist is one who upholds the Confucian way of life or who specializes on the Confucian Classics, but not a member of any religion. In a sense all Chinese are Confucianists, including those who oppose the Confucian way of life, just as all Westerners may be called Aristotelians, inasmuch as Confucianism has dominated Chinese government, education, home and society for the last two thousand years, even more than Aristotelianism has dominated the West. With respect to religion, a typical Chinese is one who synthesizes all religions as "different roads to the same destination."

This does not mean that Confucianism is not religious. While the Confucian outlook of the universe is obviously naturalistic, the universe is conceived as a moral order to which man's destiny is closely tied. It is true that Confucian scholars, being strongly rationalistic and humanistic, have remained aloof from superstitions and idol worship, leaving these to ignorant people. It is also true that they have not shown any high degree of piety. It is likewise true that they have no use for fanaticism and irrational beliefs and take external religious observance and formal religious organization very lightly. Nevertheless, they believe human nature to be fundamentally good, although there have been many divergent views. To them this goodness of human nature comes from Heaven, whose outstanding quality is *jen* or love, as evidenced by the unceasing production and reproduction of things. As a matter of fact, all Confucianists agree that the "ancient sages founded teaching (*chiao*) on the way of gods." More than this, they have accepted and promoted the worship of Heaven, the worship of ancestors, and the worship of Confucius so strongly that the three religious traditions have become identified with Confucianism. We shall briefly survey these three institutions.

(1) The Worship of Heaven. Confucius said that a superior man stands "in awe of Heaven" and that "at fifty he knew the will of Heaven." He declared that "It is only Heaven that is grand," and that "If you have committed sin against Heaven, you have not got a god to pray to." These utterances certainly reveal him as a believer in a purposive, supreme, personal Heaven. At the same time he asked, "Does Heaven speak? The four seasons pursue their courses and all things are continually being produced, but does Heaven say anything?" This saying suggests that Confucius was inclined to a naturalistic interpretation of Heaven. Evidently the Confucian conception of Heaven was both deistic and naturalistic. Mencius, leader of right-wing Confucianism, developed the deistic tendency. He repeatedly spoke of "paying sacrifice to Shang-ti," the Lord of Heaven, and "serving Heaven." In this he followed the *Chung Yung,* or *Golden Mean,* attributed to the grandson of Confucius, which is the most religious of all Confucian Classics. The leader of left-wing Confucianism, Hsun Tzu, on the other hand, firmly asserted that "The course of Heaven is constant." As Confucianism developed, its conception of Heaven became increasingly naturalistic. Even in the *Chung Yung,* the will of Heaven is interpreted in terms of human nature. "Being true with (or sincere to) one's self is the way of Heaven, and trying to be true to oneself is the way of man." Likewise, Mencius said the way to serve Heaven is to "develop one's mind to the utmost and nourish one's nature." In *The Book of Changes* (c.300 B.C.) Heaven is equated with the creative process operating through the two universal forces of *yin* and *yang.* Even in the T'ang period (618–907) when religious atmosphere was strongest in Chinese history, Han Yu (767–834) declared that reward and punishment did not come from Heaven, and Liu Tsung-yuan (773–819) identified Heaven with what was metaphysical.

This naturalistic tendency was carried to great heights throughout the Neo-Confucian movement. To Chang Heng-ch'u (1021–1077), "The concentration and the dissipation of the vital force of Heaven and Earth are many and varied, but its principle or Reason is never wrong," and "Heaven is that according to which the Great Ultimate and *yin* and *yang* attain their nature and unity." Shao K'ang-chieh (1011–1077) declared that "There is no Heaven outside of Nature," and that "Heaven and Earth are merely the greatest of existence; since they exist, they have a limit." To the Ch'eng brothers, "Heaven is the universal Reason," "unconsciously producing and transforming things." Chu Hsi considered Heaven as "nothing but the vital force," that is, "the pure aspect of the material principle." As such it is moral, for it is characterized by *jen* or love because "it is constantly producing things."

Curiously enough, this naturalistic tendency has strengthened rather than weakened the deistic tendency. Since the foundation of things is Heaven, it merits our respect. Hence the worship of Heaven has been supported by Confucianists. The worship of Heaven goes back to time immemorial. In the earliest authentic historical period, the Shang (c. 1523–c. 1027 B.C.), Heaven (*T'ien, Ti,* or *Shang-ti*) was worshiped by the emperor as a personal, purposive, perfect deity who rewarded the good and punished evil and was responsible for the rise and fall of dynasties. This practice was continued in the Western Chou (c.1027–770 B.C.). In the Eastern Chou (770–256 B.C.), *T'ien* (Heaven) and *Ti* (Lord) were distinguished, the former referring to the Lord in the sense of omnipresence and all-inclusiveness and the latter referring to the Lord as the directing and governing power. The custom of Imperial worship of Heaven, however, continued to modern times. It was the duty of the emperor to worship Heaven on the winter solstice as the representative of the people. Fasting, special music, and elaborate ceremonies were required. Since 1531, the annual worship took place in the Altar of Heaven, outside of Peiping, architecturally a supreme artistic achievement. While few educated Chinese actually took part in the worship of Heaven, whether in the Altar of Heaven or in any open space, they supported this Confucian tradition as a meritorious expression of respect for the Origin of the universe. In 1912 the annual imperial worship was given up as a part of the imperial system which was then terminated. The Chinese masses, however, continue to worship Heaven either as the supreme being or as one of many gods.

(2) The Worship of Ancestors. "As the foundation of things is Heaven, so the foundation of man is the ancestors." This is the basic reason for the institution of ancestor worship strongly supported by Confucianism. As we learn from inscriptions on oracle bones of the Shang period, ancestor worship was highly developed at that time. Historical beings of great virtue and achievement, not necessarily one's own ancestors, were worshiped as predecessors. In the Chou dynasty, only one's own ancestors were worshiped, and in the case of the Imperial family, were worshiped in the Hall of Light where Heaven was worshiped, thus making ancestor worship fully as important as the worship of Heaven. Confucius encouraged this practice but denounced the worship of other people's ancestors as flattery. Up to the Christian era, the worship was performed before a person, usually the grandson, who impersonated (*shih*) the deceased. Later wooden tablets were used instead of personification. From ancient times up to the eleventh century, worship took place before dawn

when candles were burned. From the seventh century on, paper money has been offered and the custom of burning incense, a borrowing from Buddhism, was established. Throughout history to this day, these customs of burning candles and incense and offering paper money have been observed as have been the building of ancestral temples, the elaborate systems of burials and mourning, the extensive practice of visiting graves, the observance of birth and death anniversaries, the offering of food, and the libation of wine on anniversaries and festivals.

As has been said, Confucius did not talk about spirits. He even detested the worship of spirits. The belief in spirits as controlling powers over human fortune and misfortune was extremely strong in the Shang but was declining in the Chou. Whatever survived was continued and promoted by Mo Tzu and his followers. Confucianists, on the other hand, gave spirits a strictly rationalistic interpretation. Both the *Chun Yung* and Mencius did say that "The virtue of spirits is perfect." However, they understood spirits as the mystery of the universe instead of ghosts controlling human lives and natural events.

Spirits are called *shen* and *kuei* in Chinese, which are usually mentioned together. Etymologically *shen* consists of the radical *shih*, which means indication from above (sun, moon, and star), and the stem which gives it the pronunciation *shen*, and which means extension, that is, bringing about the myriad things. *Kuei*, on the other hand, means to return. In *The Book of Changes, shen* is understood as "spiritual power which is unfathomable," or "what is unfathomable in the movement of *yin* and *yang*." In other words, "*Shen* refers to the mystery of the myriad things," that is, "the unity of things." Throughout ancient and medieval Chinese philosophy, *kuei* and *shen* were interpreted in terms of *yin* and *yang*. "The concentration of the vital force of *yang* to produce things is an extension of *shen*, whereas the dissipation of the positive and negative aspects of the soul, resulting in a change, is the *kuei* that is returning (to the elements)." According to the Neo-Confucianist, Chang Heng-ch'u, "*Kuei* and *shen* are the native and good ability of the two vital principles of *yin* and *yang*," in the sense that "coolness is an example of *kuei* while hotness is an example of *shen*." "To come into being from non-being is the nature of *shen*; to change from being to non-being is the nature of *kuei*," he said. To Ch'eng I-ch'uan *"Kuei* and *shen* are the traces of creation," or "the operation of the universe." For Chu Hsi, "*Kuei* and *shen* are the increase and decrease of the two universal forces of *yin* and *yang*." "From the standpoint of the two forces or principles, then *shen* is the efficacy *of yang* and *kuei* is the efficacy of *yin*. From the standpoint of the one universal force (*ch'i*), then what has departed and returned (to its origin) is *kuei*." He said also, "The vital force of Heaven is unceasingly producing things; that is *shen*. . . . The vital force of human beings returns to the elements (at death); that is *kuei*."

The foregoing Neo-Confucian interpretations are summed up by Chang Shih: "Generally speaking, what has become but is unfathomable is *shen*, and what has gone is *kuei*. Specifically, the vital force of Heaven, Earth, mountain, river, wind, snow., etc., is *shen*, whereas what is worshiped in an ancestral hall or temple is *kuei*. With reference to man and things, what has concentrated and come into being is *shen*, whereas what has dissipated and passed away is *kuei*. With reference to a person, the vital force of the positive aspect of the soul is *shen*, whereas the vital force of the negative aspect of the soul is *kuei*."

This philosophical interpretation of the conception of spirits is beyond the understanding of the Chinese masses who worship thousands of spirits of all descriptions to give their thanks, to express their devotion, to ask for favors, and to array their fear. Both Taoist and Buddhist religions have fostered this superstitious worship but it has found no encouragement from Confucianism. Educated Chinese of the Confucian tradition consider the worship of spirits a superstition, a darkness to be removed through education and an expediency to be tolerated very much like children's belief in Santa Claus is to be tolerated.

However, Confucianists have made one important exception, ancestors. They are not only to be worshiped, but are to be worshiped with all seriousness. Confucius said, "When parents are alive, they should be served according to the rules of propriety (*li*). When they are dead, they should be buried according to rules of propriety. After they are dead, they should be sacrificed to according to rules of propriety." He offered sacrifice to his ancestors "as if they were present bodily."

Confucius and his followers emphasized sacrifice to ancestors because of its psychological importance. Hsun Tzu explained the meaning of sacrifice quite clearly. "Sacrificial rites," he said, "are the expression of man's will, emotion, remembrance, and love. They represent the height of loyalty, faithfulness, love, and respect. . . . With sorrow and reverence, one serves the dead as he serves the living, and serves the departed as he serves those present. What is served has neither appearance nor shadow, and yet the social order is completed in this way." As the *Li Chi (The Book of Rites)* puts it, "Sacrifice is not something coming from outside, but issues from one's heart." "The heart of sacrifice means that externally all things attain their utmost, and internally the will attains its utmost. This is the true spirit in sacrificing."

Why is sacrifice so important? It is important because, first of all, it is a fulfillment of human relationship. Confucius said, "To serve those now dead as if they were living, and those departed as if they were still with us: this is the highest achievement of true filial piety." In other words, ancestral worship is the extension of filial piety. When the educated Chinese goes before the altar of his ancestors, he does not go there to seek blessing or longevity as does the ignorant person, or to supply his ancestors with daily needs as Westerners believe him to do, but purely to demonstrate his filial piety. Both material offerings and ceremonies are to him purely symbolic. Even whether the objects of worship are really there or not makes no difference, so long as he feels "as if they were present."

Sacrifice is important also because it helps one to "remember his origin." According to the *Li Chi,* "All things originated from Heaven and all men originate from their ancestors. . . . The sacrifice . . . . is to express gratitude towards the originators and recall our beginnings." Hsun Tzu said, "Rites are rooted in three things. Heaven and Earth are the origin of life; ancestors are the origin of human beings; and rulers and teachers are the origin of ordered government. . . . Hence the rites are to serve Heaven above and Earth below, honor our ancestors, and make eminent our rulers and teachers. These are the three foundations of the rites." Even the extremely naturalistic Wang Ch'ung (27–c. 100 A.D.) echoed, "We trace our origin and serve the dead, because we dare not forget our origin. . . . There are not necessarily spirits to enjoy the sacrifice." Sacrifice, then, is an expression of gratitude, a reminder of our origin.

But the most important reason for sacrifice is that it is the "foundation of moral teaching." As already pointed out, sacrificing to ancestors has a moral effect on filial piety. According to Confucius' pupil, Tseng Tzu, "If people are careful about funeral rites and remember their ancestors in sacrifice, then morals of the people will resume its proper excellence." To put it differently, sacrifice helps people to have a right attitude and to behave. This is the meaning of the ancient saying that "The ancient kings established teaching on the basis of gods."

The practice of ancestor worship is now declining. Whereas formerly practically every home had an ancestral altar dominating its central hall, many modern dwellings are without it. Whereas practically every Chinese, regardless whether his favorite deity was Buddha or Lao Tzu, bowed before ancestral tablets and visited ancestral graves, many Chinese no longer do so. A number of ancestral halls are neglected or even used as barracks. It is wrong, however, to assume that ancestor worship in China is a thing of the past. The majority of the masses continue to practice it as they did in the past. What will likely happen is that the external aspects of the worship, such as altars and tablets and offerings, will be replaced by more informal expressions of honor and reverence.

(3) The Worship of Confucius. Just as the Chinese honor their parents, so they honor their teacher, Confucius. In his lifetime, Confucius was but one of many scholars who traveled from state to state trying to influence rulers. He was politely consulted but no ruler would put his moral doctrines into practice. He was even sent away from Ch'i, threatened in Sung, driven out of Sung and Wei, and surrounded between Ch'en and Ts'ai. Retired wise men ridiculed him. The *Tso Chuan* describes him as "knowing good manners but having no courage." Elsewhere he was described as desperate "like a dog of a mourning family." Thus contemporary opinion of him was not entirely complimentary. His pupils did compare him with the sun and the moon, and they claimed that "Our Master cannot be attained to, just in the same way as the heavens cannot be gone up to by the steps of a stair." But even among his pupils there was no effort to regard him as a superman. For at least centuries, his doctrines were criticized and attacked by opposing schools, first by the Taoists and Mohists and later by the Legalists. It was not until the Chinese people revolted against the totalitarian and dictatorial state of Ch'in (221–207 B.C.), organized and directed by Legalists,

did Confucian moralism begin to gain favor. Ultimately Confucianism became the supreme system in Chinese history.

For centuries after his death, Confucius was worshiped by his own descendants as was any ancestor. In 195 B.C., the founder of the Han dynasty personally offered sacrifice before Confucius' tomb. He was the first ruler to pay Confucius such honor, but his visit was hardly more than political gesture. In 136 B.C., however, largely through the influence of Tung Chung-shu, Wu-ti established the Confucian College of Doctors, consisting of the five faculties corresponding to the five Confucian Classics, thus establishing the supremacy of Confucianism that was to last until 1905. In 125 B.C. these Classics were made the basis of civil service selection, and later, examination, thus assuring Confucian supremacy in Chinese government and education. Since then special Imperial honors have been conferred on Confucius. In 8 B.C., title and land were granted to direct descendants of the sage. In 1 A.D., Confucius himself was given the posthumous title of "Duke." In 59 A.D., sacrifice in his honor in all schools in larger cities was decreed. In 175, the Five Classics were engraved on stone slabs by Imperial order and placed in the Temple of Confucius at the capital, Ch'angan. In 442, a Temple of Confucius was erected in his birthplace. In 609, the title "Foremost Teacher" was conferred on him. In 628, he was promoted to be "Foremost Sage." In 630, all prefectures in China were ordered to build a Confucian temple. Seven years later, it was decreed that images or portraits of Confucius were to be set in place in schools throughout the empire. In 739, the title "Wang" or Prince was conferred. In 1012, the titles Foremost Sage and Prince were combined. In 1308, he became "Prince Wen-hsuan, Grand Perfection and Ultimate Sage." In 1370 the emperor took away all official titles given by the State to all gods except Confucius. In 1530, all Confucian titles of nobility and all his images were eliminated. In 1747, music and ceremony appropriate to the emperor were used in the worship of Confucius. And finally, in 1906, the same sacrifice was made to him as to Heaven.

In a sense the worship of Confucius was a state cult, as state worship was accorded him ever since the Han dynasty, except in the T'ang and Yuan (1280–1368) periods, when Taoism and Lamaism, respectively, were popular with the rulers. The term state cult, in the case of China, however, meant nothing more than official sanction of and participation in the worship of Heaven, ancestors, Confucius, etc. It was different from the state cult of Imperial Rome or Japan. Theoretically the emperor was the son of Heaven and the head priest of the people. But this did not imply the theory of divine right or governmental control of religions or exclusion of other cults. The emperor's part in the worship of Heaven and Confucius was purely ceremonial. Government regulations of religions were political rather than religious. It is true that each dynasty fixed its own order of worship. The Ch'ing dynasty, for example, paid grand sacrifices to Heaven and Earth, the Gods of the Ground and the Grain, the past emperors, and Confucius; paid secondary sacrifices to the spirits of Heaven, famous rulers of antiquity, great Confucianists, and outstanding historical persons; and paid ordinary sacrifices to other deities. This classification, however, had little meaning to the people at large. It is also true that in all state capitals, the emperor himself was worshiped in the Temple of Long Life. But there was no idea of the divinity of the emperor as in Japan, the worship being merely an expression of hope for the sovereign's longevity. So far as the state was concerned, the worship of Confucius was limited to offering of titles and Imperial participation in worship. The term "supremacy of Confucianism" implies no religious exclusiveness, but rather the idea that from the Han dynasty up to the Republic, the Chinese government was at least theoretically based on Confucian concepts, namely, that the empire should be a harmonious unity with an emperor on top; that the emperor should be regarded as and act like a parent to his people; that he should rule by moral example instead of by force; that he rules by the "mandate of Heaven," but if he fails to bring about order and peace, it is an evidence that he has failed to live up to this mandate and should be overthrown; that the government should be in the hands of virtuous and able men; that ranks, titles, and functions should be clearly defined and strictly adhered to; that governmental affairs should be simple and punishment should be light; and that conquests and wars should be denounced except punitive expeditions.

The supremacy of Confucianism, therefore, was based on Confucius' ideas, not on his superhuman qualities. It is important to remember that while the Chinese have honored Confucius as they have honored no other man, they never made him a god, except by the very ignorant. One could argue that since Confucius has been worshiped in some temples with Lao Tzu and the Buddha, both of whom were definitely deified, Confucius was regarded a god. But it is doubtful whether even in such cases the worship is anything more than hero worship. Unlike Lao Tzu and the Buddha, Confucius has not been believed to have worked miracles, to have ruled in any heaven, or to have led a hierarchy of gods, or to have exercised control over human or natural events. It is significant that in 1074 the petition to call Confucius *Ti* (or Lord of Heaven) was rejected by the government. To Confucianists, the sage was the "foremost teacher," an example of man.

Not only was there no idea of Confucius as a god, there was even no idea of him as a savior. When Confucius said he knew the will of Heaven and when he sighed that if his way was not to prevail it was the will of Heaven, he said so as any sincere social reformer would say. Mencius did try to spread the theory that every five hundred years a "kingly man" would appear in history to save civilization and that Confucius was such a man, but his appeal went unheeded. There have been surprisingly few legends about Confucius, and those few have not been taken seriously by the educated. Biographies of Confucius have been absolutely honest about Confucius' limitations and failures. He has been looked upon as thoroughly human but a great teacher of mankind.

Today the respect for Confucius as a great teacher and an example of man is weakening. The old educational system, under which the Confucian Classics were required texts for two thousand years and all government officials were to be selected through examination on these Classics, was abolished in 1905, and with it went the Confucian domination on Chinese government and education. The Empress Dowager's futile attempt in 1906 to call Confucius "the match of Heaven and Earth" did not strengthen Confucianism, for everyone knew that it was a desperate political move to salvage the hated and foredoomed regime. Some forty years ago, the last of the great Confucianists, K'ang Yu-wei (1858-1927), believing that Western powers became strong partly because they had a state religion, or what he thought was state religion, sought to establish Confucianism as a state religion. Columbia educated, Ch'en Huan-chang acted as his chief lieutenant. Societies of the Confucian Religion were organized both inside and outside China. Some of these societies still thrive in the United States. The movement became quite powerful by 1915 and almost succeeded but it finally failed because the Chinese were not in the mood to make Confucianism a religion, much less a state religion. In 1914, Yuan Shih-k'ai restored the worship of Confucius on par with Heaven. He also failed partly because the Chinese people knew his sinister motive of preparing himself to become an emperor, partly because any state worship was contrary to the spirit of freedom of worship guaranteed by the constitution, and partly because Confucianism itself was fast losing its hold on the Chinese people. With the advent of the Intellectual Renaissance beginning in 1917, Confucianism has been condemned as the chief cause for China's downfall. The cry "Destroy the old curiosity shop of Confucius" was universal. Not only the worship of Heaven, ancestors, and Confucius, but Confucian doctrines as well, seem to be on the way out.

It is wrong, however, to suppose that a system so closely woven into the fabric of Chinese culture such as Confucianism will pass out of the picture. Sun Yatsen, in no way a Confucianist, was influenced by Wang Yang-ming in his theory that it is "easy to act but difficult to know." He loved to quote the Confucian saying that "The world is a great commonwealth." It is safe to say that this saying has become a conviction in contemporary Chinese political thought. The most important development in Chinese philosophy in the last decade has been the emergence of the New Rational Philosophy by Fung Yu-lan. His works, notably the *New Rationalism,* the *New Inquiry on Man,* the *New Investigation into the Way,* etc., represent an attempt to synthesize Confucian philosophy and Western objectivism. As the world feels more keenly the need of peace and democracy, the Confucian sayings that "All men are brothers" and "There is no class distinction in education" are becoming more and more familiar quotations. Just what will happen to the religious institutions promoted by Confucianism, time will tell. It is safe to say, however, that the basic Confucian concept, that Heaven is rational, moral, purposive, and good, and other religious concepts arising out of this basic conviction, will continue to enlighten the Chinese.

BIBLIOGRAPHY

The most scholarly and reliable account of Confucianism as a state cult is John K. Shryock's *The Origin and Development of the*

State Cult of Confucius (New York, 1932). The most interesting and illuminative story of Confucianism from the religious point of view is Y. C. Yang's *China's Religious Heritage* (New York, 1943). W. E. Soothill's *The Three Religions of China* (Oxford University Press, 1923) is outdated. One would do well to avoid books by Doré and de Groot. For brief accounts on Chinese religion, Confucius, Confucianism, Neo-Confucianism, heaven, etc., see my articles on those subjects under the general topic "Chinese Terminology" in *Encyclopedia of Religion,* edited by Vergilius Ferm (Philosophical Library, New York, 1945). In this essay I have freely drawn material from these articles.

ROMAN CATHOLICISM

The author of this strong exposition and defense of Roman Catholic faith and polity is nationally prominent in the activities of his church and well known in academic circles. An ordained priest, he is associate professor of philosophy at The Catholic University of America, Washington D. C., and at the College of Notre Dame, Baltimore, Maryland. He is also the national secretary of the American Catholic Philosophical Association. Radio listeners have heard his voice over the national networks in "The Church of the Air" and "The Catholic Hour." Among his many activities mention may be made of his association with the Speakers' Bureau of the National Conference of Christians and Jews and his founding, in 1931, and continued directorship of the Washington Catholic Evidence Guild.

Dr. Hart was born at Ottawa, Illinois, in 1893. His education first began in the public schools of that city and continued at St. Viator College, St. Paul Seminary, Catholic University of America and at Columbia. He holds, besides his bachelor's and master's degrees, divinity degrees (S.T.B. and J.C.B., 1920) and his Ph.D. from Catholic University of America (1930). The honorary Doctor of Laws degree was conferred upon him by St. Viator College in 1936.

His authorship includes: "Thomistic Concept of Mental Faculties" (1930); editor and contributor to "Aspects of New Scholastic Philosophy" (1931); Philosophy and Society" (1936); "Philosophy of the State" (1940); and the editorship of "Proceedings of the American Catholic Philosophical Association." He has also contributed many articles to professional journals and to such well-known symposia as "Builders of American Culture" (1947) and "The Role of Religion in World Peace" (1947).

Editor

ROMAN CATHOLICISM

CHARLES A. HART

"ANIMA EST naturaliter Christiana!", the soul is naturally Christian, exclaimed Tertullian, one of the most distinguished converts to Catholicism in the primitive Church. He was noting how easily its teachings upon man's supernatural life could build upon the natural. The soul of today is just as easily Christian when it is faithful to the first and most ultimate principles of intellect. Christian principles are perfectly in harmony with sound reasoning. Nevertheless, Catholic faith is definitely a supernatural gift from God. Pertaining to the very nature of man in his relation to God, the principles transcend all time and are always timely and contemporary. Catholic theology is the most current of all twentieth century theologies. It produces the same holiness, the same heroic virtues among the multitude of those who truly practice it in this century as it did in the first, or second, or third century. It meets the changing conditions of today with the same unique assurance as in the age of its birth. No other religious faith affects the lives of its followers to the degree Catholicism changes its real members. No other religious system has even remotely approached Catholicism in its impact upon human affairs. Its position in contemporary religious life is as unique as its position in religious history. That is because it is God's way for man's fulfillment of man's greatest obligation, his duty to his Creator. It is God's way for man's salvation.

This brief article cannot possibly give anything more than the most sketchy outline of a system so all-embracing. We shall speak only briefly of its main tenets, its history, its peculiar genius, its attitude towards other religions, the solution it offers for some of the chief present day problems, and likewise some of its present trends as indicative of its timeless vitality.

Roman Catholicism is the name of a theology and a religious way of life established by Jesus Christ, who was truly God and truly man through a union of the divine nature with a perfect human nature brought about by the Second Person of the Trinity of Persons in the Divine Nature. Hence, such a union is known as the Hypostatic (i.e. Personal) Union. Jesus Christ, which means Savior Anointed, is the name of the human nature and Second Person or Son designates the Divine Nature, who was thus incarnated or united with human life. Thus all the human acts of the Founder of Catholicism, though truly human, were infinitely meritorious since they were performed by the Second Person of the Divine Nature who acts in both natures. Originally the human race as represented by its first human beings, Adam and Eve, were endowed with the gift of supernatural life, that is, with a power given freely to them and in no way due to them naturally, by which they were able to know God as God knows Himself, i.e. as Father, Son and Holy Ghost, as well as knowing Him through the limited natural way of grasping Him through His effects; and of loving Him according to such supernatural knowledge. In a word, man participated in the Divine Life. This supernatural life had also the privileges or preternatural gifts of integrity of all faculties and personal immortality. All these gifts made by God to the whole human race through its progenitors were lost by the latter's disobedience. But man thus losing his supernatural means of grace to attain his continuing supernatural destiny, was promised a restoration of such means in due course of time. His Savior or Redeemer was Jesus Christ who through His life and death upon a cross, acts of infinite merit, brought about the Atonement (at one-ment) of the sinful human race with their Creator, whereby man could have his supernatural gifts restored. This central event in all human history began in a little village of Bethlehem in Judea, in Asia Minor, when the Second Person or Son of the Divine Nature took human flesh in the womb of a Jewish virgin, Mary, espoused to Joseph, both of whom were of the line of family of an earlier king, David, and his son, King Solomon, of that country. Thus Jesus was born of a virgin under the power of the Third Person, the Holy Spirit of the Trinity of Persons in the Divine Nature. By being the Virgin Mother of Jesus Christ, Mary was also truly the Mother of God. By reason of her high office, and as a special divine favor, Mary was preserved free from the effects of the original sin of the first parents of the human race and so was not conceived in a state of loss of the supernatural life as were all other descendants of Adam and Eve. From the moment of her conception through the marital union of her parents, Joakim and Anna, she was thus free from this loss of the supernatural life and the effects of the loss. In a word she was immaculately conceived. These historical events took place nearly two thousand years ago and because of their transcendant importance they divide human history into the period before the birth of Christ (B.C.) and the period after that birth (A.D.).

Shortly after the birth of Jesus Christ his Mother and fosterfather went to dwell in the town of Nazareth in Judea. Hence Jesus is often called a Nazarene. There he dwelt in complete obscurity, subject to His creatures, for thirty years with only one public appearance at the age of twelve when, in a visit to Jerusalem with His parents, He became separated from them and was found later discoursing on the Law of the Old Testament with the Jewish doctors in the Temple of that city. At the age of thirty, approximately, Jesus began a public ministry or teaching period in Judea which had a Jewish ascetic, John the Baptist, as its fore-runner or announcer. The ministry is generally estimated to have lasted around three years, beginning with the miracle of Jesus changing wine into water at Cana and ending with His death by crucifixion. This latter occurred on a hill outside Jerusalem called Calvary, at the command of the Roman ruler of Judea, Pontius Pilate, who was urged to do so upon the false accusations made by certain Jewish priests that Jesus was in insurrection against Roman authority. In their own court He was falsely accused of the blasphemy of making Himself equal to God but as members of a subject people the Jewish priests could not themselves condemn Jesus to death. The accusation of blasphemy was false for the reason that Jesus was truly united with God and could not be blasphemous in declaring the truth about Himself. Pilate himself attested he could find no truth in the charge of treason against Jesus.

During His public ministry Jesus performed many well authenticated miracles demonstrating His complete power over the forces of nature, over life, and death, including finally His own physical resurrection after His Crucifixion, to demonstrate that He was truly the promised Messias or Redeemer, true God and true Man. In his life also was found fulfillment of the many prophecies concerning His coming in the Testament the Jewish people received from God.

He selected twelve disciples called Apostles (messengers) of whom
Simon (renamed Peter) was designated as chief and made supreme
head of the Church which Jesus outlined as the means whereby
mankind might have its gift of supernatural life restored to it. "Thou
art Peter (a rock) and upon this rock I shall build My Church."
The first requirement was an act of faith in Jesus Christ as Son of
God and Savior. Thereafter, the followers of Christ accepted His
Church, founded on Peter, as their teacher and spiritual director.
Such a follower must be baptized i.e. receive the Sacrament of Baptism or Rebirth instituted by Jesus Christ, whereby to his natural
state of birth in the sinful race of Adam the supernatural life is
restored. "Unless a man be born *again* of water and the Holy Ghost,
he cannot enter the Kingdom of God." The baptized becomes a
Christian, a member of the Church of Jesus Christ, which is Christ's
own Mystical Body functioning in the world to carry out what Jesus
Christ did during His earthly life, and acting in His name. It is this
Church which is designated as Roman Catholic, or more properly
the Holy Roman Church, because its first head, Peter, selected by
Jesus Christ, came to Rome from Jerusalem and established himself
there as the first Vicar of Christ in accordance with Christ's command. Since his time 261 selected successors of St. Peter, the Roman
Pontiffs or Popes, have continued unbroken that apostolic succession
of authority. No other Christian groups, since separated from the
Church Christ founded on Peter, even claim such succession, having
had their origin by merely human action of a founder in no way
authorized by Jesus Christ. To His own Church alone, the Roman
Church, founded upon Peter, the Founder gave promise of everlasting life and inerrancy in teaching. "Thou art Peter (rock) and
upon this rock I shall build My Church and the gates of hell shall
not prevail against it. And to thee I give the keys of the Kingdom
of Heaven." "And whatsoever thou shalt bind on earth shall be
bound also in heaven. . . . And behold I am with you all days even
to the consummation of the world." . . . (Matthew XVI, 18–20
and XXVIII, 20.)

To this infallible Church Jesus Christ gave the ordinary means
whereby man might be restored to his lost supernatural life. This
restoration must have beginning for each man in this life in order
that it may have fulfillment in the Beatific Vision, or life with God,
after death. In addition to the Sacrament of Baptism for rebirth in

His Church, i.e. His Mystical Body, He instituted six other Sacraments for the strengthening of the baptized Christian's supernatural life at every stage of his earthly existence or for a restoration of it if lost by his own personal sin. These Sacraments over which His Church has exclusive jurisdiction as to the condition of their administration are, in addition to Baptism: Confirmation, or fixing of the Christian in his status in the Mystical Body; Holy Eucharist, or the Body and Blood of Christ which have been effected by the power Christ delegated to His ordained priests to change the substance of bread and wine into His Body and Blood; Penance for restoration of supernatural life lost by man's own personal sin against God's law; Holy Orders, by which priests are ordained and bishops consecrated; Matrimony, for sanctification of married life and the family; Extreme Unction, whereby a special grace is given in the face of death. Baptism, Confirmation and Holy Orders leave indelible marks on the soul and cannot be repeated. Thus the Sacraments use various material things as outward signs to convey grace to the supernaturally reborn soul: bread, wine, water, and oil. In addition there are sacramentals which bear some relations to Sacraments, such as holy water; prayer e.g. Our Father and liturgical prayers; anointings; acts of confession; alms in the name of the Church; blessings of Churches, houses, bells, rulers, candles, ashes, medals, images, crucifixes, et cetera. If used rightly in accordance with the mind of the Church, they are means of actual grace to do good and avoid evil, of protection to soul and body, and for remission of venial or lesser sin. Thus like Sacraments they use material objects as signs of spiritual processes, and emphasize the truth of the union in man of matter and spirit. But they differ from the seven Sacraments in that the latter are fulfilled not merely by the fact that one believes in them but by the fact that they are performed with the necessary disposition of soul and with the intention of doing what the Church does. The effects of the sacramentals, however, are dependent entirely on the mercy of God regarding the prayers of the Church and the good dispositions of those who use them.

In organization the Catholic Church is an hierarchical monarchy with the Pope, the Bishop of Rome, and successor of Peter, as supreme in authority and infallible when, exercising his office as pastor of the Universal Church, he means to define matters pertaining to faith and morals. The other bishops, named by the Pope from the ordained priests as successors of the other Apostles to govern a designated territory or diocese, derive their authority at least immediately from the Roman Pontiff. A union of a number of dioceses in the Western Church form a province and the bishop in the province who has authority, limited and defined by Church law over the others therein, is designated as archbishop and metropolitan. The others are so-called suffragan bishops. In the Eastern Church, both Catholic and dissident, most archbishops have no suffragan dioceses under them. Below the episcopal rank is that of ordained priest who receives the Sacrament of Holy Orders from a bishop and from whom he receives authority and jurisdiction. Among his chief offices are those of offering the Eucharistic Sacrifice called the Mass which repeats the Sacrifice of Jesus Christ on Calvary in an unbloody manner by command of Christ Himself. In this Sacrifice the bread and wine are offered and changed by the power delegated by Jesus Christ, into the Body and Blood of the Savior. They are thereafter consumed, usually under the form of bread only by the faithful, as a compietion of the Sacrifice to God for the sins of man and to secure God's mercy. This is the central and supreme act of worship in the Catholic Church. The priest with the bishop and by the bishop's authority, also administers Sacraments, preaches, teaches the Church's doctrine, and carries on other labors for the advancement of the Church's work of salvation of its members. In the Western Church the priest binds himself to celibacy, and in both Western and Eastern Churches, he is obliged to recite daily the official prayer of the Church, known as the Divine Office, as contained in the compendium called the Breviary. Preliminary steps preparing the candidate for priesthood known as Minor Orders and subdiaconate include door-keeper, lector, exorcist and acolyte have been instituted by the Church though with their offices much restricted in modern times. In many of the Catholic and dissident Eastern Churches several of them have disappeared. They are not a part of the Sacrament of Holy Orders. Tonsure, or clipping of the hair, is not even a Minor Order. Major or Holy Orders include those of deacon, priest and bishop. They are also called hierarchical or sacred orders and are conferred by the imposition of hands of a previously consecrated bishop. The candidate must advance to the rank of priest before he can offer the Eucharistic Sacrifice, or Liturgy, as it is called in the Eastern Churches. The Sacraments of Bap-

tism and Confirmation confer also on all Christians a real participation in the priesthood of Jesus Christ through which alone they
can fulfill their obligation to offer sacrifice. But the Holy Orders of
the priesthood differ from these, among other things, in imparting its
own particular indelible character and power to minister divine grace
to the laity both by the Sacraments and by word. Priests subject to
a bishop of a diocese and engaged primarily in parish work are
known as secular priests. Those subject to a superior of a religious
community or Order of men, though ordained by a bishop, are
known as religious priests. They carry on the special works of their
group, such as teaching and special preaching. Groups of women
known as nuns or sisters carry on similar Church work. The women,
of course, do not receive Holy Orders.

Also connected with the administration of the Roman Church
are the oecumenical or general Councils convened by the Pope after
inviting all the bishops of the world. When confirmed by the Pope's
authority its solemn decrees are invested with the same infallibility
in matters of faith and morals as are such decrees of the Pope himself apart from a council. Beginning with that of Nicea in 325 and
down to the Vatican Council in Rome in 1869–70, not yet technically adjourned, there have been recognized twenty such world
councils. In addition, and chiefly for disciplinary purposes, there
are provincial and diocesan councils or synods. Their acts must be
approved by the Holy See, that is, the Pope, before the acts may
be promulgated in their respective territories. To assist him in the
government and administration of the Church, the Pope names a
Sacred College of Cardinals, generally from the list of bishops, or
at least, since 1876, from the clergy in priesthood, to serve as his
privy council. The College also administers Church affairs between
pontificates and elects a new Pope. There are representatives from
all nations by order of the Council of Trent, with a preponderance
of Italians from the requirements of the government of the Church
being seated at Rome. Even the non-Italians must reside at Rome
unless they are bishops of a foreign see. The College is in no sense
a parliament. The Cardinals constitute, with assisting officials, the
fourteen Roman Congregations for the transaction of the head-
quarter business of the Church. The three Roman Tribunals or
Courts; i.e., the Penitentiary, the Rota, and the Signatura; and the
Curial Offices of the Chancery, Dataria, and Apostolic Camera are

also under direction of various Cardinals as are also the six permanent Commissions, e.g. the Biblical Commission, and likewise the three secretariates. The totality of these organized bodies makes up the Roman Curia, or Courts of Church administration. In all cases the Curia exercises delegated authority, the Pope being responsible for all that is done properly by it. A similar but simpler Curia is also set up in each of the dioceses of the Church to assist the bishop in the administration of his diocese.

The historical growth of the Catholic Church through the two thousand years of its existence from the time of the chosen twelve and a few disciples to its present membership of between 350 and 400 million members, approximately one-fifth of the world's population, is truly phenomenal. With the exception of the traitor Judas, whose place was taken by Matthias, chosen by lot, the Apostles under their head, St. Peter, began their apostolic labors after the visitation of the Holy Spirit upon them on Pentecost, the fiftieth day after the Resurrection of Jesus from the dead, as He had foretold during His public life. Perhaps the most powerful aid in their work of evangelizing the world of the Roman Empire was a convert Jewish persecutor of the early Church, Saul of Tarsus, who was miraculously chosen by God as an additional Apostle: "one chosen out of due time." Renamed Paul he was the great theologian and the Apostle to the Gentiles who insisted that the primitive Church break the confining bonds of the Old Law and begin fulfillment of the command of Christ: "Going therefore teach ye all nations, all things whatsoever I have commanded you." His three amazing journeys through Asia Minor, Greece, and Rome led to the establishment of numerous Churches. To these Churches and to his associates he wrote his eleven notable inspired epistles expounding Christian doctrine, counselling the converts against the evils around them, and urging their perseverance. Similar inspired epistles were written by Apostles Peter, who moved from Jerusalem to Rome to make that capital of the world of that day also his headquarters; by John, by Jude, and by James. Two of the Apostles, Matthew and John, with Mark, the disciple of Apostle Peter, and Luke, disciple of Paul, also wrote inspired biographies of their Master for teaching purposes. They are known as the four Gospels. Luke wrote in addition a history of the first years of the Church, known as the Acts of the Apostles. John also wrote a book of revelations of the future and especially the end of the world, under the form of symbolic visions called the Apocalypse. These twenty-seven writings, known as the New Testament, were written before the close of the first century and circulated separately at first. They were finally collected as the Books of the New Testament. The First oecumenical council of the Church at Nicea in 325 A.D. made an official list of what were the genuinely inspired books for both the Old and the New Testaments. This is known as the Canon of the Old and the New Testament. Both together constitute our present Holy Bible. The Old Testament list contains the forty-six inspired books written before the coming of Jesus Christ for the Jewish Church. They contain only the beginning of God's revelation but prophesy its fulfillment in the coming of the promised Redeemer of Mankind, Jesus Christ. Their moral teaching is far below that of the fulness of divine revelation in the New Testament described above. The Catholic Old Testament contains the seven so-called deutero-canonical books of Tobias, Judith, Wisdom, Ecclesiasticus, Baruch, First and Second Maccabees, and parts of Esther and Daniel which Protestant Bibles reject because they are not contained in the Hebrew Bible of later Jews.

In Catholic doctrine, reaffirmed at the Council of Trent, there is no difference in inspiration in these so-called deutero-canonical or second canon books. They are so-called because the Jews before Christ held them as inspired but later Jews rejected them. The Protestant Reformers denying the infallibility of the Church joined with the later Jews in a rejection which is unwarranted. The whole Bible of seventy-three books constitutes the inspired historical documents of the Catholic Church. By inspiration is meant a direct influence of God on the mind, will, and executive faculties of the human writer by which he mentally conceives, freely wills to write, and actually writes, correctly, all that God intends him to write and nothing else, so that God is always truly the author of the book and man the instrument in God's hand though still retaining his own character or personality. The writer need not know, nor do others necessarily know, of the inspiration of his writings, but the Church by divine revelation is the sole guarantor of its inspired character with its absolute absence of error as being incompatible with God's veracity. The contents of the writing need not include any new truths and hence facts of natural science and history can be expressed within the limitations of human knowledge, provided such statements do not include any error. There are no degrees of inspiration, as inspiration is an absolute grace. It is equal in all books and all parts thereof. Yet it so affects the will of the human writer as to leave it free as to style, diction, and general mental outlook. Thus does the Catholic Church regard the Bible which it collected and alone preserved for all mankind through the centuries by vast effort. It is literally God's word. Yet it is not the sole rule of faith. It could not have been that in the critical first century of the Church when the New Testament was being written, nor for a considerable time thereafter before the Catholic Church collected the dispersed writings into a single book. Nor could it ever be the sole rule of faith for the vast multitudes through all ages who could not read it, or even if they could read, could not possess it until the invention of printing in the fifteenth century made multiple inexpensive copies possible. The rule of faith is not a book but the Catholic Church as a living teacher, preserving every precious written word of the Bible as God's word and preserving also the words of the first followers of Christ which oral tradition has brought down to us. The Bible has exactly the same place now as it had when it was being written and gathered together. In its tradition also there has been no essential change. Hence the making of the Bible the sole rule of faith in the sixteenth century was a complete break with the Bible's own history. With St. John at the close of his Gospel the Church says: "Many other things Jesus Christ said and did which are not written in' these books . . . but these are written that you may believe that Jesus is the Son of God and believing you may have life in His name." No less an authority than St. Peter himself warned against private interpretation of the Scripture without an inerrant living teacher when even in his early day he spoke of' those who "wrestle with the Scriptures to their own destruction."

The first epoch of the Catholic Church known as Christian Antiquity is generally given as extending from the death of Christ in 30 A.D. to the crowning of the Emperor Charlemagne by Pope Leo III on Christmas Day 800 A.D. as "Emperor of the Romans and Most Faithful Protector of the Apostolic See in all things." At the time St. John, the last of the Apostles (died about 96 A.D.), the only one of the twelve not put to death by the torments of martyrdom, there were Christian communities in Palestine, Syria, Mesopotamia, Asia Minor, Macedonia, Greece, Italy, Spain, Ethiopia, and Egypt, with converts from every class from the highest to the lowest. About the time of the destruction of Jerusalem in 70 A.D., as predicted more than forty years before by Jesus Christ, the ten general persecutions enumerated by St. Augustine began. The first was under the Roman Emperor Nero, mainly in and around Rome, from 64 to 68 A.D. With periods of relative quiet lasting as long as from two to forty-three years, emperor after emperor vented his fury against this new force within his empire, sometimes for only a few years and then at times for as many as twenty years, as in the cases of Trajan and Marcus Aurelius. The last persecution was under Diocletian from 303 to 305 A.D. Finally in 313 A.D. the joint emperors Licinius and Constantine issued the famous Edict of Milan "allowing each individual to practice whatever religion he professed." This action resulted largely from the fact that a year previously Constantine gained the notable victory of the Milvian Bridge after he had prayed to the God of the Christians. After praying he and his army beheld a cross in the heaven with the words: ʼεν τούτω νίχα—"in this conquer." Added to the imperial persecutions were the attacks of the various pagan philosophers which were met by the early Christian apologists notably Justin Martyr (166 A.D.), Irenaeus (180 A.D.), Tertullian, Cyprian, Clement of Alexandria and Origen.

From the earliest times, even while the Apostles still lived, heresies, i.e. rejections of truths revealed by God, appeared. Among the earliest, Gnosticism and Manicheism were really a return to paganism. Simultaneously with the battle against these heresies the primitive Church was establishing its hierarchy through the direction of the Apostles, as they were instructed by Jesus Christ. They provided the triple gradation of power, the apostolate (or episcopate), the presbyterate (priesthood) and the diaconate, with definite powers assigned to each order. Very early celibacy of the priesthood appeared as a laudable voluntary following of St. Paul's injunction to his disciple Timothy (I Tim. 3/2). In the West it was universally required but not in the East. The unity of doctrine in all the early churches was most of all established by the recognition of the primacy of the Bishop of Rome where Peter, Chief of the Apostles, had established his headquarters.

With the Church established by the Edict of Milan in 313 A.D. as a legal institution in the Roman Empire external and official opposition ceased, but internal strife in the form of almost every conceivable heresy sought to destroy the deposit of faith received from the Son of God as the Church's Founder. These heresies are generally grouped as: (a) *theological* or *Trinitarian heresies* concerning the Blessed Trinity of Persons in the Divine Nature of God; with the denial by Arius, a priest of Alexandria, and his followers that Jesus Christ is truly Son of God and Second Person of the Trinity. He is said to be called Son only by grace. This heresy was condemned in the presence of the Papal Legate Hosius by the Council of Nicea (325 A.D.) convoked by the Emperor Constantine, with the so-called Nicene Creed expressing the true position. (b) The *anthropological heresies* concerning man's human nature and the gift of divine grace; with the denial by the British monk Pelagius and his followers, that man lost his original supernatural life by the sin of our first parents, and the assertion, therefore, that he could lead a sinless life and attain eternal salvation without Christ or His grace, these latter being superfluous. St. Augustine, who had personally experienced this heresy, was its great opponent. It was officially condemned by the third Oecumenical Council at Ephesus in 431 A.D. (c) The *Christological heresies* concerning the natures and person of Jesus Christ; with the denial by Patriarch Nestorius of Constantinople, of one divine person for both the divine and human natures and the insistence on two persons, one human and one divine, and hence the denial that Mary was Mother of God. An opposite extreme of this, held by Abbot Eutyches, held that there was no true humanity in Christ. The Catholic position, mediate between the two, insisted as we have previously noted, that the Second Person, uniting both the human and the divine natures, acted in both of them, supplying a divine person for the human nature which was without human person. The Nestorian heresies were condemned also at the Council of Ephesus and the Eutychian heresy, known as Monophysitism, at the fourth Ecumenical Council at Chalcedon in 451 A.D. and the sixth Ecumenical Council at Constantinople in 680 A.D. In the overcoming of all these heresies the Church greatly developed her theology as a true science and raised up most distinguished defenders in both the East and West, notably St. Athanasius, St. Basil the Great, St. Gregory Naziansen and St. John Chrysostom, known as the Greek Fathers in the former, and St. Ambrose, St. Augustine, St. Jerome, and St. Gregory the

Great, known as the Latin Fathers, in the latter. This was the period also of the rise of the monastic orders, those religious communities of men which exerted such a profound influence upon the subsequent ages of the Church. St. Basil the Great was the great founder of monasticism in the East and St. Benedict of Nursia in the West. The monasteries were the great sanctuaries of civilization in the chaos of the barbarian invasions of the coming centuries as well as the great teachers of the arts and sciences to the invaders.

In the period from the fifth to the ninth century, the Church's great activity was transferred from peoples already highly organized and civilized to the barbarian Germanic tribes of western and northern Europe who swept down over the whole of the ancient Roman civilization. The work of converting, educating, and civilizing the Goths, the Vandals, the Franks and the Saxons in all the countries of Western Europe was perhaps the greatest feat of mass education in human history. Alone the Church in her monasteries and cathedral schools preserved the art and culture of Greek and Roman antiquity along with Christian revelation, to pass them on to mediaeval and modern civilization. The culmination of the task came with the revival of the Roman Empire in the West under the great Charlemagne as Emperor in 800 A.D. It was the beginning also of the temporary power of the Church. These centuries saw also the rise in the East of the great rival religion of Mohammedanism of the Arabs, in which region it destroyed most of the work of the Church and sought to subdue Europe as well. It was checked in one of the great battles of the world, the Battle of Tours, in 732 A.D. with Charles Martel as leader of the Christian forces.

With the death of Charlemagne the period of great decline of the ninth and tenth centuries set in for both Church and Empire. This was the time of the Greek Schism, or breaking away of the Eastern Church, under the unscrupulous Patriarch Photius who was excommunicated by Pope Nicholas I. The schism was healed by the eighth Ecumenical Council of Constantinople (869 A.D.) but the break was renewed by the Patriarch Michael Cerularius in 1054, chiefly for political reasons. This breach, the first great break in Christian unity, continues to the present. The eleventh century, however, witnessed a great revival of the power of the Papacy'in the West and its extension throughout the whole of Europe. The monk Hildebrand, elected to the Papacy as Gregory VII in 1073, was the initiator of this revival and reform which was destined to last to the beginning of the fourteenth century. During these centuries the Church carried on the Seven Crusades, those remarkable military attempts of the Western Church to bring about deliverance of the Holy Land and repel the Saracens who threatened Christian Europe. They did not attain their first objective but they did secure Europe against the power of Mohammedanism. They also stimulated great intellectual development, fostered the religious spirit of knighthood, and promoted the spirit of unity among the nations of Europe. They weakened the feudal system of serfdom of the masses to baronial rulers, and gave great impetus to commerce between the East and the West. The period had its culmination in the thirteenth century, often called the Church's greatest century, which witnessed the founding of the Mendicant Orders of Franciscans and Dominicans, and other religious organizations, the high point of the great universities, and the highest development of theology and philosophy under such profound teachers and writers as St. Albertus Magnus, St. Thomas Aquinas, St. Bonaventure, and John Duns Scotus. The following fourteenth and fifteenth centuries, bringing the mediaeval period to a close, saw another great period of decline with the removal of the papal court to Avignon in France under Pope Clement V in 1309 and its continuance there for seventy years, a period known as the Babylonian Captivity. This low ebb of the Papacy was the signal for the so-called Western Schism (1378–1417) with its rival claimants to the papal throne holding forth at Avignon, Rome, and Pisa. This was the period also of the revolt against the Church's authority and doctrine by John Wyclif (1324) in England and John Hus in Bohemia (1415), forerunners of the Great Revolt of the sixteenth century which was destined to effect a destruction of Christian unity in the West which has lasted to the present. The heresies of these centuries, such as the Albigenses, were particularly violent, anti-social, and a menace to the order of the State as well as in opposition to the truth of Catholic doctrine. To avoid arbitrary action against followers of such heresies the third Lateran Council in 1179 and the fourth Lateran Council in 1215, organized a systematic method of legal investigation or inquiry, in charge of Dominican theologians, and hence known as the Inquisition. The Church never claimed power to inflict physical punishment, this being the exclusive prerogative of the State. It should be noted that the death penalty was added by the impious Emperor Frederick II certainly for no zeal for religion, which he condemned, but strictly for political reasons. From our twentieth century vantage point the Inquisition's sanction for the state's severe penalties seems very cruel, especially since it so easily led to hypocrisy. However, we must remember that in the Middle Ages, and indeed long after that period, Church and State were intimately united. In the public mind heresy was equally dangerous to both and indeed was often disruptive of civil order. The severe punishments for disrupting of that order were typical of a violent age. It was just as typical in Protestant countries in modern times after the break-up of Christian unity. Even today many of the immoralities like those advocated by the heretics are punished by imprisonment and sometimes death. Finally the number punished by the Inquisition had been greatly exaggerated. In Rome the death penalty was seldom invoked and State excesses elsewhere were repeatedly condemned by the Church. It is also to be remembered that the Inquisitions in Spain, Venice, and other countries were chiefly civil tribunals, not identified with the ecclesiastical tribunals. Their excesses cannot be attributed to the Church. In 1519 Pope Leo X excommunicated all the Inquisitors of Toledo where the political Inquisition was used chiefly to extend royal power and suppress the influence of the Church. Even in these civil set-ups nearly 99% of those classed as being sent to the *Auto da Fé* had merely to perform a work of penance. Persecution of Jews, often on charge of usury and other crimes, was not approved by the Church but was repeatedly condemned by Popes Innocent II, Clement VI, Paul II and many local bishops. Such eminent Protestant historians as Ranke and Guizot recognize that the Spanish Inquisition became a purely political institution.

The modern era beginning in the sixteenth century, which witnessed the opening of the vast western hemisphere to Christian influence, was also the century of the break up of Christian unity with the revolt against the Church's authority and the progressive rejection of its doctrine. Misnamed the Protestant Reformation it was led by a rebellious Augustinian monk, Martin Luther, in Germany, by the Catholic priest Ulrich Zwingli and John Calvin in Switzerland, by Francis I and the Huguenot Party in France, William of Orange in the Netherlands, by Henry VIII and Queen Elizabeth in England, and by John Knox in Scotland. In England the break was originally political. In the North Countries the reigning rulers were also in the main the sources of the disruption through primarily political actions. Everywhere the break was accompanied with fierce violence, spoliation of Church property, cruel persecution of those who remained faithful to the Church, alliance of the so-called reformers with civil authorities, the latter of whom saw in the movement an opportunity to enhance their own political power by breaking the influence of the Church. Originally Luther's heresy in doctrine concerned the nature of justification. Rejecting sixteen centuries of traditional teaching of the Catholic Church, he taught that justification was attained simply by an act of faith, or trust, in Jesus Christ as Divine Redeemer. It was something external, like the act of a judge declaring a man to be innocent, and did not require any cooperation of the recipient, such as a change in his way of life. It was simply a garment put on over the sinful man. Faith alone sufficed. Acts of religion such as good works were not necessary. Since St. James insisted in his inspired epistle that "faith without works is dead" Luther rejected it as an "epistle of straw." This false view of the nature of the supernatural life logically led to the progressive rejection, one after another, of the seven Sacraments as causes of sanctifying man's soul by additional graces at various stages of the individual's life for his cooperation with the gift of grace. Luther also offered the Bible as the sole rule of faith, rejecting the living authority of the Church.

Undoubtedly the revolt could not have made such rapid progress had there not been many abuses within the Church, such as the ignorance and wickedness of many bishops, priests and religious; the State's insistence on appointment of political favorites to high ecclesiastical posts with the benefices attached to them. This was particularly true in the center of the movement in Germany. Everywhere these evils caused resentment. The new movement further offered avaricious civil rulers an excellent opportunity to enhance their own power by destruction of the Church; to have excuse for seizing Church lands for their own enrichment and that of their leading supporters. The ignorant were deluded by the clever practice of the reformers of keeping old Catholic names for their heretical doctrines. For the lower classes it often seemed a chance to cast off all authority. For the strongest princes it was an opportunity to band against the authority of the Emperor and make themselves supreme in their own territories. Hence, arose the excessive absolute national sovereignties that plague the world's desire for peace today. Political unity was destroyed with religious unity. The violent civil wars and the subsequent Thirty Years War were a set-back to art, virtue, and civil and religious liberty. In the long run, whatever abuses within the Church may have been corrected were negated by the manner of the so-called Reformation, the character of the reformers, and the evil effects upon the religious, social, or political life of the people. Hence, the movement could not be said to be that which the reformers claimed for it, a work of God. If the reformers were sincere they would have undertaken the reform of the Church of the Son of God from within rather than by substituting distinct man-made churches. Such an inner reform was initiated by the nineteenth Ecumenical Council of Trent (1545-1563) quite soon after the beginning of the revolt. Indeed everyone of the twenty Church councils is specifically for the purpose of necessary reform of the human agencies and elements in a divine Church. The Council of Trent undertook a complete restatement of the whole of Catholic doctrine, practically every part of which had been progressively rejected by the succeeding reformers.

If the Protestant Revolt was a dark page in the Church's history in that very century and those following, with its multitudes falling away from the old faith, a compensation was had in other multitudes who were being converted in the New World just then being opened by the remarkable European explorations. Of the countries remaining faithful to Catholicism, Spain and Portugal provided religious missionaries to accompany explorers to bring the Catholic faith to Central and South America and what is now southwestern and southeastern United States. The French missionaries worked mainly in what is now eastern Canada and through the center of the present United States as far as the mouth of the Mississippi. Protestant missionaries from England and Holland worked along the Eastern seaboard of the Atlantic. One Catholic group however was early (in 1634) established in what is now Maryland under the English Catholic Lord Baltimore and the English Jesuits. It early passed the first law of religious toleration in the New World. Portuguese and Spanish missionaries, especially the great Jesuit, St. Francis Xavier, also carried on notable evangelization in India, the coast of China, the Philippines, and Japan, and many of the South Sea islands. Later pagan persecutions often destroyed their vast labors. What the Church lost in Europe it more than gained in the Americas and in Asia.

Space permits saying only a few words of the history of the last century and a half. The close of the eighteenth century saw the violent French Revolution which almost destroyed the Church in France. Almost equal oppression came from Joseph II in Austria. Similar action was taken in Spain, in Germany, and in the Italian kingdoms. Napoleon proclaimed Rome a republic and took Pius VI prisoner to France. The three pontificates in the first half of the nineteenth century were equally turbulent. In the reign of Pius IX (1846–1878) the Italian King, Victor Emanuel of Piedmont, succeeded in uniting the various Italian states in a war against Austria which the Pope would not sanction. Emanuel then seized the Papal States and made Rome his capital. The Pope withdrew to the Vatican Palace where he remained a voluntary prisoner until the Lateran Pact in 1929 ended the dispute with the Pope's temporal sovereignty being recognized in a small territory around the Vatican and St. Peter's Cathedral. During this pontificate of Pius IX the last of the twenty ecumenical councils, the Vatican Council, was called. It proclaimed the doctrine of the infallibility of the Pope in defining doctrines of faith or morals. It declared the rational foundations of faith against the so-called Modernists who, following Kant, denied that reason could prove God's existence and also denied that Christianity had any real historical basis. The Council is still not closed. Prior to the Council, in 1854, the formal dogma of the Immaculate Conception was proclaimed, namely, that the Blessed Virgin was conceived free of the stain of the original sin of our first parents.

The long reign of Leo XIII (1878–1905) brought a brilliant revival of the prestige of the Papacy. In a series of profound encyclicals Leo outlined the social and political philosophy of the Church in such advanced liberal positions, for example, as the encyclical on the rights of labor in "The Conditions of the Working Class." He also restored the philosophy of St. Thomas Aquinas to the Catholic universities and seminaries of the world. Piux X succeeded him in 1905. Pius instituted many reforms in the inner life of the Church, set up the commission for the codification of Canon Law and proclaimed a ringing denunciation of so-called Modernism in his encyclical *Pascendi Gregis.* Succeeding pontiffs, Benedict XV, Pius XI, and Pius XII made every effort to avert the two World Wars which have rocked civilization since the turn of the century. In this first half of this present century the Church has suffered many vicissitudes in all the countries in Europe that have remained Catholic and has had a like history in South America. The absolute sovereignty of these modern states has sought continuously to destroy the spiritual autonomy of the Church but without success. In the United States and Canada, the Church has had a phenomenal growth. Today the Catholic Church has nearly 25 million communicants in the United States, approximately one-sixth of the population, and more than one-half of the whole number professing any church membership in this country. The missionary activity of the past one hundred and fifty years, and particularly since the turn of this century in Asia and Africa, has been one of the most consoling movements amidst many disappointments. In China, for example, there are today nearly four million Catholics. At the present there is comparative peace between Catholicism and Protestantism. The Catholic Church considers secularism, with its denial of any place for religion in human affairs and with its positive efforts to destroy religious influence in modern life, as its greatest enemy. It views atheistic Communism as the most complete embodiment of that secularism. Never in the history of mankind has any nation equalled the Union of Socialist Soviet Republics in its vast effort to destroy every vestige of religion in the mind of its citizens and those of its satellite states. As it exists today communism is the irreconcilable foe of the Catholic faith in its official ideology.

Such are the main tenets, history, scope, and aims of Roman Catholicism. It is a remarkable history which demonstrates its vitality. Despite the most powerful efforts of states and its religious enemies in every century to destroy it, this Church stands today as the most powerful spiritual and moral force in the world. Its world wide organization is the one source of unity among warring nations and conflicting ideologies. It alone has kept alive the true sense of the supernatural in the lives of men. It alone has refused to compromise with the age in giving up any portion of the fundamental dictates of the moral law. It is unique in standing for the supremacy of human reason in the establishment of the rational foundations of religion. It is the one truly world religion, making equal appeal to every class of mankind and in every condition, from the black natives of Africa and the islands of the Pacific, lately perchance converted from cannibalism, to the intellectuals of European and American universities. Its hundreds of thousands of converts each year number many of the most distinguished of citizens. It meets each class on its own level and seeks to raise them to the high supernatural level of sons of God, joint heirs with Jesus Christ, Son of God. Its deposit of faith, received from God, remains unchanged through the two thousand years of its history, the development of its doctrine being simply by way of deeper understanding of the doctrine's significance and its appropriateness for the solution of the problems of each succeeding age. Like its Divine Founder, it is the most hated and persecuted, and yet most beloved, of institutions in human history. In view of its established claim that it alone is the Church the Son of God, founded for man's salvation, it can never consent to place itself upon the same level as the multitude of other religions which are man-made. Catholicism however considers all men as its potential members and feels bound by the solemn mandate of its Divine Founder to bring them all into its fold, which is the Mystical Body of Jesus Christ, living today to do His work of sanctifying and saving mankind. All men of good will, seeking to do what God has ordained for their salvation, insofar as God has enlightened them, though not of the formal Body of Christ's Church, are considered members of the Soul of the Church. The Body embraces all the baptized both in the Church on earth called the Church Militant, the Church Suffering in Purgatory, and the Church Triumphant, those already in the presence of the Beatific Vision. The Catholic Church recognizes without question the sincerity of millions of persons everywhere who do not accept its divine character and the truth of its doctrine but follow their conscience, always man's supreme guide, as conscience enlightens them. Today in the face of world-wide decay of morality and the rejection of God and His moral law the Popes of the Catholic Church have been seeking for the cooperation of all men of good will, of whatever faith, for the joint task of preserving the primacy of the spiritual in human lives and the universal acceptance of the dictates of the moral law as given by right reason to the souls of men by God, their Creator.

The Catholic Church considers the chief source of disorder in present day society to be the result of secularism with its complete rejection of God and hence the rejection of His moral law for man's direction. Thence follows the rejection of the supernatural grace of God. As the Creator of the Universe God is the only true ordering principle in human affairs. Without an understanding of their relation of dependence for existence upon God, men cannot understand their own nature. They lose their essential dignity as children of God and seek to construct a universe with man as its center. The law of God for the direction of man to his ultimate end has thus disappeared as the universal measure of the morality of actions of man and of the state. Man, denying God, seeks to deify himself in the state which is his collective self. Thus has arisen the absolute state which recognizes no law above its own arbitrary dictates. Thus has the moral unity of the human race been broken and physical force, with its familiar concentration camps, torture chambers, secret police, and the many other forms of violence and terror, that disgrace contemporary civilization, have logically followed. Even many of those who call themselves ministers of God are so confused and debauched by their secularistic environment as openly to espouse the race destroying unnatural artificial birth control. The intrinsic malice of this practice lies in its denial of God as Creator of the human soul by which man is a person and its satanic placing of man, who is God's instrument for the continuance of the human race, in the place of God, at least to the negative extent of saying life shall not come. Actually the gift of life as well as its denial is the exclusive prerogative of the Creator. Thus the Catholic Church opposes this violation of the natural law just as it would oppose murder or stealing or adultery, even in the face of an overwhelming erroneous public opinion to the contrary. Morality is not made by counting noses. The Catholic Church's position is an insistence on the full rational implications of the Creator-creature relation between God and man which is the basis of even natural religion.

In view of its complete opposition to secularism and an insistence on the spiritual unity of the human race, a principle the present reigning pontiff Pius XII proclaimed as the very keynote of his pontificate in his first encyclical *Summi Pontificatus* (On the Unity of the Human Race), the Catholic Church, in its fundamental doctrine and in its practice, to the extent it can do so, considering its human instruments, opposes all forms of race discrimination which would put certain races in a sub-human position.

Where such discrimination against Negroes or Jews, for instance, is practiced by members of the Catholic Church, it is done so in clear violation of the constant teaching of the Church. It insists upon inalienable rights of every human person simply because of his personality bestowed on him by God in His creation of the human being.

The Catholic Church looks with highest favor upon every effort of mankind to form a world society in view of its teaching upon the unity of the human race. Its history shows it has been the chief influence for the formulating of a truly international law upon which alone an international society may be based. It has always been opposed to the absolute sovereignty of any state as involving the state making itself independent of the moral law of God. Whenever it has had the influence the Church has rebuked such arbitrary civil power. In requiring its children in conscience to render to Caesar the things that are Caesar's through respect for legitimate civil authority, it has equally insisted that all men as members of the human race, which transcends any state, shall render to God the things that are God's. The clear pronouncement of its Divine Founder is the source of its doctrine of Church and State as two perfect societies, each having its authority from God and each independent in its own respective eternal and temporal spheres. The Church's doctrine of a truly international society led to the greatest degree of political unity the then civilized world ever witnessed when the Church's influence was at its height in the Middle Ages. Christian unity was its basis. The break up of that unity has issued in the extreme nationalism that thwarts our present efforts for peace. Further, the Church sees the human race, not simply as a natural society by reason of the unity of the human species, but what is far more important, in the Providence of God, as a supernatural society. All men, as we have explained, are actual or potential members of the Mystical Body of Christ, which is His Church. This binds them together on a far higher spiritual level than that of their physical unity arising from the unbroken continuity of human generations from the first human beings to the present moment. The 400 million actual members of the Body of the Catholic Church are today the greatest international society in the world with "one Lord, one faith, one baptism," one spiritual head on earth and appealing to similar moral standards despite a multitude of cultures, languages, nationalities, and economic conditions. Yet this international society is built upon the priceless value of every individual soul in the sight of God and hence it surrounds that individual with every possible protection of the inalienable rights with which his Creator endowed him, consonant with the preservation of the rights of every other individual.

In the economic and social field the Church's philosophy is based on the primacy of the rights of person over rights of property. Long before so-called liberal modern states acknowledged human labor as that of a person was not a mere commodity, the Church sought to integrate that truth into the relations between the modern employer and employee. At the same time, the Church has been the principal and most consistent proponent of the natural right of private property as an adjunct of the human person, and the natural means whereby man, as a spiritual being projecting himself into the future, could have that security without which he could not proceed peacefully in his labor. Hence as a natural right, the private property right is rooted in the spiritual nature of man. Modern industrial civilization with its vast disparity of wealth and the concentration of the expensive means of production in the hands of relatively few owners of capital goods has meant the dispossession of the multitudes who have now only a wage for labor as their sole means of sustenance. Early in the Industrial Revolution, and long before any state, the Catholic Church insisted upon the personal character of human labor and the impossibility of free contract in modern capitalistic societies without collective bargaining of laborers through labor unions. More than fifty years ago, in 1891, Leo XIII proclaimed the Magna Charta of the wage earner of the industrial era, in his great encyclical, *Rerum Novarum* (On the Condition of the Working Classes). Pius XI brought that great document of human rights up to the present in a similar encyclical, *Quadregesimo Anno* (Forty Years: Reconstructing the Social Order). After recounting the benefits to labor of his predecessor's efforts in their behalf he notes the changes in economic conditions which forty years have brought about; reaffirms the right of property and the obligations of ownership due to the social as well as individual character of such property, and again condemns economic systems which would destroy it. But now the greatest concentration of wealth in the hands of a few which has followed from the extreme individualistic spirit in economics has meant the death of free competition and the substitution of economic dictatorship. "Unbridled ambition for domination has succeeded the desire for gain; the whole economic life has become hard, cruel and relentless in a ghastly measure." There is no more trenchant criticism anywhere of the abuses of capitalism. Yet the pontiff does not consider Communism as the alternative. Property must recognize its social obligations. A private property system must correct its own abuses. It should be noted that the Socialism which both Leo XIII and Pius XI condemned as conceptions of society and social character foreign to Christian truth is today more properly included under the term Communism. The latter espouses the philosophical position of dialectical materialism of Karl Marx, with its atheism and its denial of man's spiritual nature in addition to its economic doctrine. Today in Europe the Socialism of the British Labor Party and Socialistic parties in a number of countries on the continent have rejected all this philosophical materialism and proclaimed a purely economic policy of socialization of the great industries, such as transportation, mining, banking, et cetera, without denying private property rights. In view of the collapsed economy of most of the countries of Europe following the Second World War, no other course seems open. Not a few Catholic economists feel that such a position is in no sense condemned by Pius XI. They distinguish between Communism, with a doctrinal position on human nature attached to extreme socialization of all property on the one hand and the moderate so-called Socialism with its limited socialization of great industries and in no way connected with the Marxian economic determinism of history on the other.

Politically, the Catholic Church in the encyclicals of Pius XI, has offered the most penetrating criticisms and rejections of Nazism (*Mit Brennender Sorge*), of fascism (*non Abbiamo Bisogno*), and of communism (*Illi Redemptoris*), as equally denying the rights of the human person and being similar in their totalitarian claim of complete possession of the citizen and in their rejection of the right of the Church in spiritual affairs. The making of concordats or agreements with such governments, be it noted, in no way implies acquiescence to their political philosophies any more than the sending of an ambassador to Russia implied the acceptance of communism by the United States. The concordats such as those made with Italy and Germany, are simply agreements whereby the Church may be permitted to minister to Catholic citizens in such countries. In the Catholic viewpoint separation of Church and State does not mean the State may ignore a church's independent right to exist and function in any state. The state has an obligation to see that religion may carry on its work without interference in view of the state's obligation to secure the general welfare which includes the eternal welfare of all citizens. In countries practically or entirely Catholic, a union of Church and State has frequently been effected in view of the common membership of the citizens in both institutions. Where mixed religions prevail, separation of Church and State in the sense here indicated is acceptable as for the best interests of all the citizens. The Catholic Church does not insist on any particular kind of relation between itself and the state in which it exists. One of the greatest Catholic churchmen in the history of the Catholic Church, in America, Cardinal Gibbons, was very enthusiastic for what he considered the ideal relations between the Catholic Church and the American Republic. Incidentally the Catholic Church has not sought diplomatic relation with the United States. The personal representative of the President is at the Vatican City State at the President's initiative because he believes such representation of this country is to its advantage. It was not sought by the Pope. Hence, the unfairness of many Protestant leaders in accusing Catholics of desiring union of Church and State in the United States when these accusers demand that the President withdraw his personal representative from the Vatican City State. Finally, the Church teaches the moral obligation of citizens to support the authorities of a legitimate government, that is, a government in office by due process of the law of the land. Obedience is a matter of conscience so long as the government has not clearly come into power by unlawful means and is not clearly opposed to the common good. It is this obligation of the state to secure the common good in temporal affairs that requires it to interfere in the conduct of an economic system which perpetrates notable economic injustice to any class in the state.

Even the foregoing exceedingly brief history of Roman Catholicism has shown that the Church considers education one of its greatest duties, placed upon it by its Divine Founder Himself. Indeed the Church is fundamentally a teaching magisterium. It can never cede this divinely imposed duty to the State. It exercises the duty by its own right and not simply by sufferance of the State. During long European periods it was the only teaching institution. The monastery and cathedral schools, and the mediaeval universities came into being under its aegis. In the United States it has built up a vast educational system from the grades to the university. More than two and one half million attend its parochial schools; three hundred thousand its high schools. Nearly two hundred thousand are enrolled in its 200 colleges and universities. It has built up this system because it cannot accept for its children the so-called neutral education of the state which, until recently, has not permitted religious study to be a part of the curriculum for those desiring it. In the view of the Catholic Church education must include religion if it is to be a complete education for character. Education without character is futile where it is not actually dangerous, even to the state itself. The alarming increase in juvenile delinquency in America today is in considerable part due to such an amoral education. Attempts by several thousand American communities to bring some religious training into the public school system through so-called "released time" in which the student, if he so desires, attends religious classes conducted by a religious leader of his faith, is an attempt to remedy this dangerous condition. It is also an admission of the soundness of the position of the Catholic Church. Released time for religion is at best only a poor substitute since religion should permeate the whole educational system as it should permeate life itself. In its educational system, the Church has always sought to cultivate the arts, both useful and fine arts. Many of them have had their origin in the Church's service. Beauty has ever been the ally of the Church in her teaching mission. Yet the Church does not accept .the absolute autonomy of the arts. Art works are the product of the virtue of art in the practical intellect of man. By that virtue man has the right conception of the way to make a particular thing. Art's end is the making of a thing. In such making it is autonomous. But it must come under the dominion of prudence, as do the other virtues, since prudence is the right understanding and use of the means necessary to attain man's own end. The end of the worker is superior to the end of the work wherever the two may come into conflict. In America the effective work of the Catholic Legion of Decency for the recognition, by Catholics, of the fundamental moral principles in motion pictures is an example of such a philosophy of art. Today the educational system of the Church on its higher levels is becoming increasingly proficient in scientific research and philosophical and theological inquiry. The revival of the philosophy and theology of the thirteenth century Dominican of the University of Paris, St. Thomas Aquinas, is bringing about a far more penetrating understanding of the timeless character of the Angelic Doctor's thought and the service it can perform in solving the difficult problems of our own day. The Church has at its service a host of profound scholars in every field of intellectual endeavor.

If there is one trend that may be selected as particularly characterizing Catholicism of today it is the entrance again of the Catholic layman more fully into his traditional place in every phase of work of the Church. This movement, known as Catholic Action, is officially defined as "the participation of the laity in the Apostolate of the hierarchy." In their attempt to destroy the Catholic Church the so-called reformers of the sixteenth century knew that they must first destroy the Church's priesthood. Hence, they denied the Sacrament of Holy Orders which gave the priest his distinct place in the Church, as the Mystical Body of Christ. The reformers insisted on only "the priesthood of all true believers" which was designed to break down the distinction of place between priest and people. The Church in denouncing such a heresy and insisting on Holy Orders, did not in any way wish to deny what the great theologian St. Thomas Aquinas had long ago proclaimed; namely, that every baptized Christian, by Baptism, assumes a participation in the priesthood of Jesus Christ, whereby he becomes distinct from the pagan world, another Christ, and a co-offerer with Christ in the offering of his Redeemer to God in the Eucharistic Sacrifice of the Mass. But this in no way sets aside the necessity of the priesthood of Holy Orders which Christ Himself ordained as the means whereby the Eucharistic Sacrifice should be constantly renewed and likewise providing the means whereby all the baptized might be able to fulfill their supreme religious duty. The proper understanding of the priesthood of all true believers does not, in any way, preclude the separate priesthood of the priest in Holy Orders. Today, the religious attack upon the Church has largely ceased and the attack is transferred to other fronts. After four hundred years of a state of siege, the Church now resumes within itself the fullness of Catholic life for both laity and clergy. Catholic Action in every country in the world is changing the layman from a passive spectator into an active participant in all the Church's far-flung activities in accordance with his proper sacramentally established position in the Church. The layman's Catholicism is becoming truly what it should be, his very way of life. It is one of the most evident signs of the Church's divine vitality. Despite persecution and restriction by hostile governments, despite constant attacks and misrepresentations of every kind, the Catholic Church of today is the most influential religious influence in the contemporary world working for the sanctification and salvation of man. Refusing to accept the clear evidence of the divine source of the Catholic Church's strength, its enemies accuse it of being a political institution while they themselves are really using that political power, as their only real instrument, wherever they can do so. The Church of Christ remembers its Founder's prophecy of its persecution even as He was persecuted, and also His promise which is being continually fulfilled: "The gates of hell shall not prevail against Thee. . . . Behold I am with Thee all days even to the consummation of the world."

BIBLIOGRAPHY

Popular Selected Bibliography (English Titles Only)

St. Thomas Aquinas, *Summa Theologica*. Translation by Dominican Fathers of the English Province (Benziger Brothers, New York, 1920–1937).

Donald Atwater (Ed.), *Catholic Dictionary* (1931).

Pierre Battifol, *Primitive Catholicism*. Translation by H. C. Brianceau (1911).

Bible (Douay Version) (Baltimore, no date).

Lord Clonmore, *Pope Pius XI and Peace* (1938).

Ralph Adam Cram, *The Catholic Church and Art* (1930).

Christopher Dawson, *Religion and the Modern State* (1935).

Gerard Ellard, *Men at Work at Worship* (1941).

Joseph C. Fenton, *The Theology of Prayer* (Milwaukee, 1939).

Joseph H. Fichter, *Christianity, An Outline of Dogmatic Theology for Laymen.* Translation by Hugh Pope (St. Louis, 1940).

Cardinal Peter Gaspari, *Catholic Catechism* (1932).

Edwin Healy, *Moral Guidance* (Chicago, 1941).

Chas. G. Herbermann and Others (Editors), *The Catholic Encyclopedia* (Encyclopedia Press, 1913).

Cuthbert Lattey (Ed.), *The Church: Catholic Studies at Cambridge* (Cambridge University Press, 1928).

LEO XIII, *Great Encyclicals of Leo XIII* (1913).

JACQUES MARITAIN, *The Things That Are Not Caesar's* (1939).

———, *Art and Scholasticism*. Translated by J. F. Scanlan (1930).

MCCORMICK–CASSIDY, *A History of Education* (Washington, 1946).

JOSEPH MCSORLEY, *An Outline History of the Church by Centuries* (1943).

National Office of the Society for the Propagation of the Faith, *Mission Apostolate: The Story of Mission Activity of the Roman Catholic Church* (National Office, New York, 1942).

BERNARD J. OTTEN, *A Manual of the History of Dogmas* (St. Louis, 1907).

PIUS PARSH, *The Liturgy of the Mass*. Translation by Frederick C. Eckhoff (St. Louis, 1936).

ANTON C. PEGIS, *Basic Writings of St. Thomas Aquinas* (1945).

R. P. PHILLIPS, *Modern Thomistic Philosophy* (London, 1935).

PIUS XI, *Encyclicals of Pius XI*. Translations by James H. Ryan (St. Louis, 1927).

RAOUL PLUS, *Progress in Divine Union* (1941).

HUGH POPE, *Catholic Student's Aids to the Study of the Bible* (3 vols., 1926 to 1938).

Raccolta, A Collection of Indulgenced Prayers. Translation by Christopher and Spence (1943).

THOMAS SLATER, *A Short History of Moral Theology* (1909).

———, *Manual of Moral Theology* (1907).

JOHN F. SULLIVAN, *The Externals of the Catholic Church, Her Government, Ceremonials, Festivals, Sacramentals and Devotions* (1918).

STANILAUS WOYWOOD, *The New Canon Law* (1918).

SHINTŌ

The present confused situation in Japan has made it difficult to ascertain the course of events in her changing religious culture. No one is better informed about her own indigenous religious ideology and practices than is Dr. Daniel C. Holtom who has given to them a life-long period of study and service. An American scholar of note with whom correspondence was had in seeking a contribution on the characteristically Japanese religion for this volume has paid Dr. Holtom this tribute: "He is perhaps the world's foremost expert on Shintō."

Dr. Holtom was professor of modern languages in Tokyo Gakuin from 1910 until 1915; a professor of church history at the Japanese Baptist Theological Seminary in Tokyo the following ten years. After serving one year as visiting professor of church history at the University of Chicago he returned to Japan as educator for fourteen more years, ten as professor of church history and the history of religions and dean of the theological department at Kwanto Gakuin, Yokohoma and four as professor in the Theological School of Aoyama Gakuin, Tokyo—until 1940, teaching church history and the history of religions.

He was born in Jackson, Michigan, in 1884. At both Kalamazoo College and the University of Chicago he took his bachelor's degrees. His B.D. degree he took at Newton Theological Seminary and his Ph.D. at the University of Chicago (1919). Honorary doctorates in divinity were conferred upon him by his alma mater in Michigan and by Brown University. Besides holding from time to time important lectureships (including the Haskell at Chicago and the Rauschenbusch at Rochester) and serving academic organizations (including trusteeship at Kwanto Gakuin) he has written many articles and books dealing with Japanese and Oriental culture. Among his volumes (not listed in the bibliography) are "Political Philosophy of Modern Shintō (1922); "The Japanese Enthronement Ceremonies" (1928) and editor of "The Christian Movement in Japan" (1922–24) and "Transactions of the Asiatic Society of Japan" (1923–25; 1926–28). To the "Encyclopedia of Religion", recently issued, he contributed the major articles dealing with Japanese religions.

Editor

SHINTŌ

DANIEL CLARENCE HOLTOM

Shintō, or *Shindō,* is the Sino-Japanese reading of two ideograms that are rendered into pure Japanese by the term, *Kami-no-Michi,* meaning "The Way of the Kami," or "The Way of the Gods." Shintō thus signifies the characteristic cult practices and beliefs, relating for the most part to the worship of the indigenous Japanese deities, whereby the Japanese people have celebrated, dramatized, interpreted and supported the chief values of their group life.

Kami in its original meaning is practically identical with *mana,* the name adopted by science from the language of the Melanesians to indicate the occult force which pre-literate man found emanating from objects and experiences that aroused in him emotions of wonder and awe. When authentic gods and goddesses appeared in early Japanese religion they were identified by the simple device of prefixing to the word *kami* descriptive titles showing in each case something of the function of the deity; that is, the deity was named by indicating some special manifestation of *kami.* Thus the sun goddess was "The Heaven-shining Great *Kami,*" the storm god was "The Violent Male *Kami*" and so on throughout the entire pantheon.

The term Shintō in its proper historical usage does not carry us back to the earliest manifestations of the Japanese national religion. The word does not appear in the classical literature until the latter part of the sixth century of the Western Era, while the organized religious cultus which it later came to designate is approximately as old as Christianity. In its more remote stages Shintō as a system appears to have been nameless. The term came into existence after the introduction of Buddhism into Japan and was evidently created in order to distinguish the original Japanese religion from the Way of the Buddha. It is significant that the earliest studies of Shintō were made by Buddhist scholars.

Modern Shintō has flowed in two main streams. One of them—

until disestablished from its special position as the state religion by order of the Supreme Commander of the Allied Powers in Tokyo on December 15, 1945—held important relations with the official organization of the national life. Prior to disestablishment this branch of the indigenous religion was called State (*Kokka*) Shintō, sometimes Shrine (*Jinja*) Shintō because of having its ritualistic center in the shrines or *jinja*. The latter designation is still appropriate even after the great change in fortune that has come to it following Japan's military defeat in World War II. The term National Shintō is also permissible inasmuch as Shintō, though abolished as the state religion, still exists as a national faith.

The main effects of the disestablishment of the state religion were: to release the nation from all taxation, direct or indirect, for the official support of Shintō, to exclude all participation by government agents in their official capacities in the ceremonies of the shrines, to prohibit all sponsorship and dissemination of Shintō by government agencies and officials and to close the schools to all Shintō propaganda. The requirement of obeisance before the altars of the national deities as a token of patriotic conformity was removed and participation in the rites of the former state cult was put on a purely voluntary basis. Genuine religious liberty thus came to Japan for the first time in her modern history.

Two weeks after the disestablishment of State Shintō the emperor issued a rescript renouncing his claims to divinity. In this epoch-making pronouncement he declared that the ties between the throne and the people rested on mutual trust and affection and not on the false conception that the emperor was divine. This cleared away at a stroke a whole jungle of medievalism that had formerly entangled Japanese life and made it henceforth impossible to maintain the claim that previously was the foundation of the political structure, that the emperor's right to rule was a sacred trust inherited from the divine ancestors and in no wise dependent on the will of the people.

The other great branch of the national faith is called Sectarian (*Shūha*) Shintō. It has always depended on the voluntary support of adherents for institutional maintenance and propaganda. Both branches—the earlier state cultus and the sectarian form—have received influences from the parent stream of the ancient religion, the former more directly and, on the whole, in more unmixed character than the latter. Modern exponents of Shrine Shintō generally insist that the ceremonies and beliefs connected with their system represent the true and uncontaminated line of pure Shintō, while the sectarian form has been more or less modified by foreign infiltrations and the contributions of founders and other teachers. On the other hand, adherents of the sects have occasionally declared that they alone preserve the true and original Shintō and that the former state cultus may not inexactly be described as another sect, one that was once officially sponsored and urged on the nation as a whole by all the resources of the government. Certainly the effect of the directive of disestablishment has been to reduce Shrine Shintō to a completely sectarian status.

The Shintō of the people exists in the form of thirteen officially recognized sects and numerous sub-sects. The thirteen sects are *Shintō Honkyoku* ("Main Bureau Shintō," sometimes also called *Shintō Kyō* or "Shintō Teaching"), *Shinri Kyō* ("Divine Reason Teaching"), *Taisha Kyō* ("Great Shrine Teaching," after the great shrine of the sect at Izumo), *Shūsei Ha* ("Society for Improvement and Consolidation"), *Taisei Kyō* ("Great Accomplishment Teaching"), *Jikkō Kyō* ("Practical Conduct Teaching"), *Fusō Kyō* (from Fusō, a poetical name for Japan), *Mitake Kyō* ("Great Mountain Teaching," after the sacred peak of Ontake), *Shinshū Kyō* ("Divine Learning Teaching"), *Misogi Kyō* ("Purification Teaching"), *Kurozumi Kyō* (after the name of the founder, Kurozumi Munetada), *Konkō Kyō* ("The Teaching of the Glory of the Unifying God"), and *Tenri Kyō* ("Heavenly Reason Teaching").

The statistics for all sects combined show a total of 18,000,000 adherents, 121,000 priests and teachers and 16,000 churches. The former Shintō of the state did not publish any statistics of adherents, since theoretically all Japanese subjects were included. Shrine Shintō maintains 110,500 shrines, large and small, and 15,800 priests.

The thirteen sects are for the most part the result of the labors of historical founders, organizers and teachers who have systematized special forms of doctrine and ritual and propagated these for the purpose of creating followings and thereby benefiting the individual and the community. This statement is not exclusively true, since at least three of the sects announce that they are without personal founders and say that they merely expound the orthodox Shintō inheritance. Most of the sects represent movements that came into existence in the Meiji Era (1868–1912); in certain cases, however, the foundations date from earlier periods of Japanese history.

Areas of doctrinal and ceremonial emphasis in the sects vary greatly. Some are devoted to the perpetuation of mountain worship mixed with primitive rites of spirit possession; some stress a Confucian heritage; some, ancient purification rites; some, the classical forms of Old Shintō while the influence of others lies in faith healing.

The former state cultus opened its modern career in 1868 when the classical revival that had made vigorous progress in the latter part of the Tokugawa Era (1603–1868) came to fruition in the establishment of "Pure Shintō" as the state religion. A definition of relations with popular Shintō movements soon became imperative and beginning with the opening of the Meiji Era and culminating in the eighties of the last century the government took steps to make clearly drawn administrative distinctions between the rapidly growing sects and the official system centering in the shrines. Regulations were set up under which all the recognized institutions of the state were to reserve to themselves the title of *Jinja* or *Jinsha* ("God House"), while, in contradistinction, the institutions of the sects were to be called *Kyōkai* ("Churches") and classified as ordinary religion along with Buddhism and Christianity. After the promulgation of the Constitution of 1889, guaranteeing a form of religious liberty to all subjects, government officials, supported by various scholars and writers, took much pains to propagate the idea that State Shintō was not a religion, notwithstanding the fact that another group, including Japanese Shintoists of the first rank, was equally emphatic in insisting that State Shintō was *de facto,* if not *de jure,* a genuine religion. The main cause of difference of opinion at this point lay in the relative weight given to governmental expediency in the matter of classification. The purpose of the authorities in this was to set up an administrative control which made it impossible for a subject to repudiate State Shintō on religious grounds.

The situation was not clarified in the interests of genuine freedom of private religious belief until the state religion was disestablished in December of 1945 and until a new Constitution, promulgated on November third, 1946—to take effect six months later—removed completely the old supernatural sanctions of the state and gave all subjects full protection in religious liberty.

The sects, like all recognized religious bodies, have their own independent organizations, and possess legal properties that are almost exclusively distinct from those of the shrines. In general they do not make use of the latter as meeting places for sectarian purposes. They have their own churches. Prior to disestablishment, the shrines received supervision and a measure of support from village, district, municipal, prefectural, or national governments, depending on the rank of the shrine. Other and more extensive sources of revenue still continue even after disestablishment—income from shrine properties, voluntary offerings and subscriptions, earnings from the sale of charms and talismans, and fees for divination and exorcism. Both the sects and Shrine Shintō now carry on voluntary, non-official religious propaganda. A considerable portion of the resources of the former have gone into the maintenance of schools, kindergartens, social welfare activities, and different kinds of organizations for young people and adults, as well as extensive agencies for literary propaganda. Similar activity from the side of Shrine Shintō may now be expected.

Throughout the modern period, State Shintō found its major function in the celebration of rites considered appropriate to the deepening of national sentiment. In its traditional aspects the central element of shrine ceremonies has always been the reading, on the part of the priests, of ritualistic prayers (*norito*) before the altars of the gods, in which supplication is made for good crops, peaceful homes, prosperous occupations, success in war, stability of government, security in the food supply, and long and majestic reign on the part of the emperor. This activity may be expected to continue—directed away from the support of militarism and imperial absolutism to the peaceful reconstruction and development of the nation.

The deities or *kami* honored in Shrine Shintō are of multiform origin. They include numerous primitive nature forces, interpreted as "ancestors," the spirits of a limited number of emperors, and the spirits of heroes who have given their lives in the service of nation and throne. Taking the sects as a whole, it may be said that they have included in their god-world the entire pantheon of Shrine Shintō and have added certain deifications of their own, notably the spirits of founders.

The most noteworthy theological movement in contemporary Shintō, manifested especially in the sects but appearing also in Shrine Shintō, is a trend toward integration in terms either of a unitary pantheistic background or of a fundamental monotheism. Both Buddhist and Christian influences are manifested here. The numerous deities of Shintō polytheism are interpreted as attributes of a monist absolute that is spiritual in essence.

Throughout most of the modern period Shrine Shintō was managed by a special Bureau of Shrines in the Department of Home Affairs, while Sectarian Shintō, along with other recognized religions was controlled by a Bureau of Religions in the Department of Education. In the spring of 1946 the Religious Corporations Ordinances that had gone into effect in 1940 were amended so as to be applicable to Shintō shrines. This meant the perfection of legal and organizational arrangements that would accord to the former state religion exactly the same kind of treatment as that given every other religious body.

BIBLIOGRAPHY

M. ANESAKI, *The Religious Life of the Japanese People* (Tokyo, 1938).

———, *History of Japanese Religion* (London, 1930).

W. G. ASTON, *Shintō: The Way of the Gods* (London, 1905).

———, Eng. Trans. of *Nihongi, Chronicles of Japan from the Earliest Times to A.D. 697*, 2 vols. (London, 1896).

ROBERT O. BALLOU, *Shintō: The Unconquered Enemy* (New York, 1945).

B. H. CHAMBERLAIN, Eng. Trans. of *The Kojiki or Record of Ancient Matters*, 2nd ed. (Kobe, 1932).

TASUKU HARADA, *The Faith of Japan* (New York, 1907).

D. C. HOLTOM, *The National Faith of Japan* (London, 1938).

———, *Modern Japan and Shintō Nationalism* (Chicago, 1943).

———, "The Meaning of Kami," *Monumenta Nipponica*, Vol. III, nos. 1 and 2, Vol. IV, no. 2 (Tokyo, Sophia University, 1940–1941).

GENCHI KATO, *A Study of Shintō: The Religion of the Japanese Nation* (Tokyo, 1926).

GEORG SCHURHAMMER, *Shin-Tō, der Weg der Götter in Japan* (Bonn, 1923).

ISLAM

Salma Bishlawy, a graduate student in philosophy at the University of Chicago, is, at the moment, continuing the residence requirements leading to the doctorate. In 1945 she was awarded her master's degree by the university in its department of Oriental languages and literature, after the presentation of her thesis entitled "The Book of Science by Ghazali". Her work consisted in a translation of a portion of this difficult Arabic book and a critical estimate of the philosophy of Islam's great medieval theologian.

Reared in the Islamic faith and still professing it, she is the daughter of parents who are cultural leaders among her own people. Her mother has for many years occupied the public platform as an accomplished singer and her father is engaged in literary work as editor of the magazine called "Abu Naddara." She was born in Cairo, Egypt, in 1921. After attending her native schools and also a conservative Presbyterian missionary school, she came to America in 1939 to finish her formal education. She planned a career, first in music and then in medicine and finally discovered to her own delight that philosophy was her really supreme interest. With a major in that subject, she was graduated from the College of Wooster, B. A., 1942. Thereupon she accepted a scholarship for advanced studies offered her by the Oriental Institute of Chicago. During the period of the war, she worked in the linguistic division of the war department for the United States government.

Her own government has granted her a government scholarship to study for her doctorate with the view of teaching and doing research in her native country. She is preparing to make Moslem philosophy the field of her specialty.

It need hardly be said that Miss Bishlawy is eminently qualified by background, training, conviction and linguistic attainments to contribute the essay on the Islamic faith for this book.

Editor

ISLAM

SALMA BISHLAWY

FEW RELIGIONS, if any, have been as badly represented and widely misunderstood in the Western world as Islam,* and that, despite the fact that it claims for its adherents about one-eighth of the world's population, over 250,000,000, and extends from Morocco to Zanzibar, from Sierra Leone to China, from the Balkans to the Philippines. Besides the nations of the Near East where the population is predominantly Mohammedan, the ninety millions in India and the millions in China and Russia, there are communities of Muslims in Lithuania, the Cape Colony, West India Islands, British Dutch Guiana, England, Australia, Japan, and the United States.

No less misrepresented has been the founder of Islam himself. Although recent biographies have been more objective and less polemical in character, the former popular conceptions have tended to carry over a partially distorted and partly inadequate picture of the prophet and his religion; mainly, that he was a sensuous voluptuary who propagated a faith in which the chief dramatic feature is allowing the male several wives.

In order to understand the influences operating upon the inception of this great world religion a brief survey of Pre-Islamic Arabia is necessary.

Pre-Islamic Arabia

Roughly speaking the Arabs of this period can be classed in two major groups: nomadic Bedouins and city dwellers with intermediate stages of semi-urbanity and semi-nomadism. The nomad, with his cultural isolation, his economically necessary raids on more prosperous neighbors, his extreme individualism, his indifference

* Meaning submission or surrender to the will of God.

toward organized religion, his chauvinistic attachment to his clan
or tribe, his democratic feeling in his own milieu coupled with his
aristocratic feeling toward the rest of creation, is essentially the same
type now that he was centuries before Islam, a type which constituted the majority of the population of North Arabia. His history,
in the main, was one of blood feuds, guerrilla warfare, tribal rivalries
and disputes over pasture lands, springs, and cattle. Among his
traditional practices were: unrestricted polygamy in which the
marital tie was quite easily severed by either party, and female in-
fanticide, an abominable practice arising from an exaggerated sense
of pride and also from economic want.

Among the urban population of al-Hijaz (the region which
stands between the Najd and the coastal lowlands of Tihamah, the
land which was to be the cradle of another world religion) the worship of the three goddesses Al-Lat, Al-Uzza and Manah was widespread. Mecca, the principal city of Hijaz, and the heart of its commercial empire, was not the exclusive domain of one religion, as it
is now, but a pagan center boasting of its sacred black stone and
attracting a multitude of pilgrims every year. Through its trade it
felt intellectual, religious and cultural influences of Byzantia, Syria,
Persia, and Abyssinia. The monotheistic ideal was not strange to
it since Christian and Jewish settlements had been in Arabia for
centuries. But neither religion had ever established a strong foothold
in the Arabian peninsula as a whole.

Muhammad

Muhammad was born to the clan of Banu Hashim, of the leading Meccan tribe of Quraish around 570 A.D. Orphaned early in
life, he was first brought up by his grandfather and upon the latter's
death was entrusted to his paternal uncle, Abū Tālib, a man of
modest means. Little is known of Muhammad's early life aside from
the fact that he was a caravan conductor until his marriage to his
employer, Khadījah, a wealthy widow fifteen years his senior and a
woman of great character. This union which came when he was
about twenty-five years of age, brought him freedom from economic
care and enabled him to pursue his spiritual inclinations.

According to Muslim tradition, Muhammad, who had periodically sought solitude for his meditation, received his divine call (610 A.D.) in a cave outside Mecca.

"Recite thou in the name of thy Lord who created" *(Qur'ān* 96:5). Like the Old Testament prophets an overwhelming desire to proclaim to his countrymen his revelations overtook him. Fired by his vision he began to preach the Unity of God, the Creator, His omnipotence, the rewards of the believers in paradise and the punishment of the wicked in Hell. His ideas were largely the result of the impression religious and moral concepts of both Judaism and Christianity had made upon him. In the main, there were three chief features of his teaching upon which he laid particular emphasis: the Unity of God, the moral responsibility of man toward God, and the judgment awaiting mankind on the day of resurrection.

At first the powerful group that were the custodians of the pagan shrine, and for whom such doctrines were detrimental to their vested interests, met the new Prophet with ridicule and derision. In time, as more converts to the new faith were won, the persecution took a more severe turn and forced Muhammad to advise a number of his followers to seek refuge in Christian Abyssinia. The Prophet continued to preach, exhort and threaten, despite all kinds of abuse and discouragement. Meanwhile his fame spread to neighboring tribes and cities. About 620 A.D. he was invited to make Yathrib (later called Medina) his home and to mediate in the suicidal feud between the Aws and Khazraj tribes, which was fast depleting their ranks. They promised him and his Meccan followers protection. The Prophet accepted, and two years later, after he had arranged for his Meccan followers to precede, he followed them and arrived in Medina on September 24, 622, the official day of the beginning of the Muslim era.

For the next ten years Muhammad ruled in this city as a Prince-Prophet. The Mediniese were more interested in a political leader than in a religious figure and they found in him besides an inspired Prophet, a brilliant political genius. Having lost Khadijah three years before his flight to Medina he now acquired a number of wives; some for cementing political alliances and acquiring greater prestige, and others for their beauty or charm. By far his favorite among his wives was Aisha, the daughter of his friend and loyal supporter, Abū-Bakr. Muhammad had the good fortune to have chosen loyal women who contributed a great deal to his success but who were also human enough to be troublesome in their jealous rivalries for his affection.

As legislator, Muhammad enacted the social and political ordinance of the new Muslim theocracy dealing with marriage, divorce, fasting, almsgiving, treatment of slaves, prisoners of war and enemies. It was also during this period that the Prophet broke off with the Jews who had attacked and ridiculed him. At first he seems to have tried to establish an alliance with the Jews in Medina. He included several features of their worship such as the instituting of the 10th Muharran as a fast day resembling the fast of the Day of Atonement on the 10th of Tishri, the introduction of the midday prayer and the purification ritual before the prayer—just to cite a few instances. However, it soon became quite apparent that compromise with the Jews was becoming increasingly impossible as they heaped ridicule upon him for his reproduction of Old Testament stories. This brought about a difficult situation. All along Muhammad had simply claimed that his revelation confirmed the Jewish and Christian scriptures. Instinctively he took over elements from the older religions and perpetuated them in his teaching, even though his sources were in the main apocryphal and heretical. The doctrine of the Logos can be easily traced in the Qur'ān, III:4 and IV:169. In his Christology Muhammad accepted the doctrine of the virgin-birth, the miracles of healing the sick, raising of the dead and the ascension. He rejected the suffering of Christ on the cross and vigorously denied the idea of Jesus being the son of God or that he ever made such a claim for himself.

Muhammad now accused both Jews and Christians of falsifying their scripture, and proceeded to Arabicize Islam. Friday was substituted for the Sabbath, the direction of prayer was changed from Jerusalem to Mecca, the pilgrimage to the Ka'ba was included in Islam and the kissing of the Black Stone was permitted. Muhammad during this period led several battles against the Meccans and their mercenaries, but it was not until 630 A.D. that the complete conquest of Mecca was accomplished. The pagan idols were utterly demolished, but the inhabitants were treated very generously. Now one tribe after another, from all corners of Arabia, flocked to his banner. A year later he headed the farewell pilgrimage to Mecca and there gave his last sermon where he substituted the most vital bond of Arab relationship, that of tribal kinship, with the brother-hood of Islam. His life ended suddenly after a short illness on June 8, 632 A.D.

Arabia after its long strife and disunity had finally brought forth a man who aroused the religious feeling of his countrymen and laid down for them a socio-economic and moral code which not only satisfied them but served as a foundation for an intense and highly productive intellectual activity for other people who already could pride themselves on an old and venerable civilization. Muhammad had never claimed divine origin nor did he want to be regarded as different from other men. He did not claim that he could perform miracles and frequently admitted that he was not free from sin. However, his conviction was unshakable that God had selected and privileged him to preach his will to the Arabs. It was this firm belief in the divinity of his message that conquered the religiously indifferent Arab and made him a fanatical follower of his call.

After Muhammad's Death

Shock and confusion fell upon the ranks of the faithful. Muham-mad had not left a male heir or appointed a successor. In his capacity as Prophet, no one could possibly succeed him. But there were his other functions as Commander of the Faithful to fill. Sev-eral parties arose, each claiming that the successor (caliph) should be one from their ranks. Finally, 'Umar ibn-al-Khattāb, an intimate friend of the Prophet and a great figure of early Islam, gave the oath of allegiance to Abū Bakr, the Prophet's best friend and father of his favorite wife, Aisha, and was followed in this act by the assembled chiefs.

Abū Bakr became, then, the first of the Four Orthodox Caliphs, all of whom were friends of the Prophet. The last of them was his cousin and the husband of his only surviving daughter, Fatima. Their reign, which lasted for the next thirty years, was first occupied with the secession wars, which were fought to bring back into the fold tribes which had committed apostasy. Soon these campaigns gather-ing momentum led to others which brought the whole of the Arabian peninsula under the sway of Islam. Now there was a new outlet for the fighting spirit of the Arab tribes, who were now forbidden to en-gage in fratricidal wars by the new religion and forced by economic necessity to expand outside the Arabian peninsula. This led to the conquest and colonization of Syria, Iraq, Persia, Egypt, and Tripolis. Shortly after the establishing of this vast empire, Islam was plunged into civil war on the question of the Caliphate. 'Ali's election to the office was contested by Mu'awiyah, the governor of Syria.

'Ali was eventually murdered by an assassin's dagger and Mu'awiyah succeeded to the Caliphate, which remained in the Ummayad's hands for the next 90 years (661–750 A.D.). The Ummayad dynasty was one which by no means considered religion as the predominant passion in life. Its rule had a secular character; hence their unpopularity with Muslim historians. However, they produced some very excellent rulers, under whose hands the Muslim empire reached its greatest expansion, extending from the Pyrenees to the Indies and the confines of China, and from the Aral Sea to the upper cataracts of the Nile. Nevertheless, their home rule was disturbed now and then by Shi'ite uprisings, who held that the Caliphate should have remained in the house of the Prophet from the beginning, that 'Ali and his descendants should have assumed the office immediately after the Prophet's death. All other Caliphs they regarded as usurpers. Their malcontent, coupled with that of the Persian Muslims who loathed the Ummayads, gave the 'Abbāssids, descendants of the Prophet's uncle 'Abbās, a chance to head the movement and use it for its own ends, the overthrow of the Ummayads and the practical extermination of almost all of them.

The 'Abbāssid Dynasty (750–1258 A.D.).

The new dynasty, whether or not it was actually more religious than the former, at least gave the appearance of piety. Although this dynasty enjoyed the longest reign of any in Islam, its actual rule ceased after the middle of the ninth century and the power resided in the hands of Persians at first and later in the hands of Turkish sultan dynasties. The predominantly Arab character of the Ummayad rule gave way to the infiltration of various foreign elements under the 'Abbāssids. Persian, Turkish, Armenian, Greek, and Slavic slaves swelled the courts. This was also the age of great learning. Scholars, artists, singers, and poets enjoyed generous patronage. Science and the fine arts flourished. The Golden Age of Islam was reached with the reign of Harūm al Rashīd (786–809 A.D.) and its magnificent splendor. Soon after reaching its peak the empire began slowly to collapse; several independent dynasties sprang up; large provinces became independent and their rulers accepted the caliph's nomination as a mere formality. Rival caliphates were temporarily established by the Ummayads in Spain (756–1031 A.D.) and the Fātimids in Egypt (909–1171 A.D.) and the 'Abbāssid caliphs themselves became little more than mere puppets in the hands of their Turkish deputies. The Mongol storm which dealt the final blow came with the sack of Baghdad in 1258 A.D. The majority of the population, including the caliph and his family, was wiped out of existence.

After Hulagu had finished with Baghdad, he led his Mongol hordes westward, where he was checked by the Egyptian Mamelukes and forced to retire to Persia. Fifty years later the Mongols embraced Islam and made it the state religion, one of the most magnificent victories of Islam and one of the many instances where the religion triumphed when the force of arms of its adherents had become impotent. Later, one of their descendants, Bābur, founded a great Muslim empire in India. However, it was not the Mongols who brought back to Islam its military glory, but the Ottoman Turks, the last Muslim dynasty to hold the Caliphate.

Although the founder of the Ottomans, 'Othmān, established the dynasty in 1295 it was only two centuries later that Sultan Selims assumed the Caliphate after his conquest of Egypt. It continued in his line until 1924 when it was abolished and a Turkish Republic was established in its stead.

The Tenets of Islam and Its Prescribed Duties

Belief in God, in His Angels, His divine Books, His Messengers, in Muhammad as the last of His Prophets, and in the Judgment Day—these are the tenets which constitute the articles of faith of Islam.

The only unpardonable sin is "shirk" or the joining of other Gods to the One Allah. Islam maintains an uncompromising monotheism. The practical religious duties incumbent on each believer are:

1. The profession of faith (*shahādah*) which is summed up in the formula "there is no God but Allah; Muhammad is the Messenger of Allah." Upon conversion to Islam, the new believer is required to pronounce the formula once and hence becomes automatically a member of the Faith. There is no other ceremony involved.

2. Ritual prayer (*salat*) five times a day with the believer facing the direction of Mecca. The worshipper must be in a state of ceremonial purity and must use the Arabic language as his medium. The prayer consists always of the Fātihah (the Muslim equivalent of the *paternoster*) and additional phrases of the Glorification of God, combined with genuflexions and prostrations. The Friday noon prayer is the only public prayer obligatory for all adult males. An address is usually delivered during this service by the leader of the Prayer, the *Imām*.

3. The alms-tax (*zakāt*) was originally a voluntary act but it soon evolved into an obligatory tax on property. The money thus collected was used for the support of the poor, the building of mosques and for expenses incurred in the administration of the Muslim empire. With the disruption of the purely Muslim state, the *zakāt* became once more a voluntary gift left to the believer's conscience.

4. Fasting during the month of Ramadan. During this month, in which the *Qur'ān* was first revealed, food and drink are abstained from, from dawn till sunset. The occurrence of Ramadan at times during the summer months in hot countries makes this duty a particularly rigorous one.

5. The pilgrimage (*hajj*). This duty is incumbent on every Muslim at least once in his lifetime, provided he is physically and economically able to perform it.

The pilgrim before entering the holy precincts wears a white seamless garment. He then performs the seven circumambulations of the Ka'bah, the seven-fold course between a Safa mound and the Marwah eminence, the march to 'Arafah and the halts at the two sanctuaries of al-Muzdalifa and Mina, the stone-throwing ceremony at Jamrat al-'Aqabah ending with the sacrifice at Mina of a camel, sheep or some other horned domestic animal on the tenth of the Muslim month of Dhū'l Hijah. With the discarding of the pilgrim garment, the secular state is once more resumed.

This ceremony is the most unifying influence in Islam. Hundreds of thousands of Muslims, rich and poor, Arabs, Turks, Persians, Berbers, Negroes, Chinese Malayans, and other nationals from all walks of life, meet on common ground and are impressed with their equality before God. It is one of the major practical influences in tearing down the barriers of race, color and nationality within the world of Islam.

The duty of Holy War *(jihād)* so much emphasized in early Islam and raised to the status of a sixth pillar by one Muslim sect, the Kharjites, has of late found little support in the Muslim world, owing to the complexity of Muslim political entities and the far-reaching extent of Islam. The last call to the Jihād was issued by the Ottoman Caliph, Muhammad Rashād in 1914 and proved to be a complete failure.

The Modern Reform Movement in Islam

The modern reform movement in Islam was given its initial impulse by the famous exponent of Pan-Islamism, Jamāl al-Dīn al-Afghanī.

Jamāl-al-Dīn was born in 1839 in Afghanistan. When he was eighteen, he had become highly familiar with almost the whole range of Muslim sciences, of Muslim history, theology, logic, philosophy, physics, metaphysics, mathematics, astronomy, Arabic grammar, philology and others. He then went to India to acquaint himself with the European sciences and their techniques.

By his brilliance he had become prime minister of Afghanistan at the age of twenty-seven, but soon after he had to flee the country when the king was deposed. He went to Constantinople where he was acclaimed and honored as a great Islamic figure but again political power manipulation made his stay impossible and he was asked to leave the country.

Complying with the order, Jamāl left for Egypt, arriving there March 22, 1871. The Egyptian Government was so pleased to have him that they conferred upon him a monthly stipend as a token of recognition. Eager students flocked around him and he lectured to them on theology, philosophy, jurisprudence, astronomy and mysticism. He also, as was always his wont, plunged into Egyptian political affairs. He minced no words in expressing his anti-British sentiment and did his utmost to warn the country of the dangers of foreign intervention.

During the eight years he pursued this kind of life in Egypt, he aroused the oppositions of two people in particular, the conservative theologians who distrusted his liberal views and his revival of the study of philosophy, and British officialdom who did not appreciate his political agitation. When the Khedive Isma 'il Pasha was deposed and his son Tewfik took his place, Jamāl's enemies triumphed, for a Khedival decree ordered his expulsion from the country.

Again Jamāl went to India and there he wrote his only lengthy work, the *Refutation of the Materialists,* an apologetic of Islam against modern attacks. Later he went to London for a few days and followed it by Paris where he stayed three years.

During his stay in Paris he was joined in 1884 by his friend and disciple, Muhammad 'Abduh, exiled from Egypt for political reasons. They now began publishing an Arabic weekly called *Al- 'Urwah al-Wuthkah* or "The Indissoluble Bond." Its editorial policy was directed to arouse the Muslim people to form a united front against Western aggression and exploitation. The paper had the brief existence of eighteen issues. Great Britain banned it from Egypt and India. But despite all that, the paper in its short existence awoke the national spirit of slumbering Muslim nations.

Now Jamāl, after a brief visit to London, went to Russia, where he received a very warm reception. He remained there for the next four years. In 1889, while in Munich, the Shah of Persia urged him strongly to become his prime minister. Jamāl accepted and was received by the people as their one hope for the improvement of the country. But again his political success was undermined by the jealousy of the Shah who finally drove him out of the country. His remaining years were spent in Constantinople where he died in 1897 from cancer of the jaw.

The influence of this great personality was felt in all Muslim countries and his political agitation was responsible for practically every national movement in the modern Near East. His aim was the unification of all Muslims under one government, over which the Caliph would rule. Foreign domination in Muslim states was contributing to their decadence and no reform or adjustment to modern conditions was possible before freedom could be achieved. Islam, to him, was quite capable of doing its own housecleaning and adapting itself to the changing world.

That Jamāl should choose the means of political revolution to achieve his ends was quite consonant with his fiery and restless temperament. Slow evolution and education took too much time. "Wherever he went," says Michel in his biography of Shaihh Muhammad 'Abduh, "he left behind him a hot-bed of contention, and it can be said without exaggeration, that all the movements of national emancipation, of reaction against European enterprise, which we have been witnessing in the Orient for a score of years, have their origin directly in his propaganda."

Muhammad 'Abduh

Muhammad 'Abduh, friend and disciple of Jamāl-al-Dīn was to carry out many of the public reforms Jamāl had preached. He was born of a peasant family in 1849. As a youth he attended al-Azhar University, which is really a seminary specializing in the Muslim sciences rather than a university in the Western sense of the word. He became attached to Sufism during that time and drifted more and more into its practices until Jamāl-al-Dīn al-Afghanī rescued him from what was becoming too great an involvement. Muhammad studied regularly with Jamāl and began opening his eyes to a new world, one of Western scientific thought. Jamāl also trained him along with some other students in the art of writing for the press.

Soon after Muhammad 'Abduh received his degree of " 'ālim" from al-Azhar he came back to the same school as a teacher. When Tewfīk took over the reigns of government he ejected Jamāl from the country and forced Muhammad 'Abduh into retirement. But when the liberal prime minister Riad Pasha, who had been out of the country, returned, he appointed 'Abduh chief editor of the journal *The Egyptian Events,* official organ of the government. This gave 'Abduh an excellent chance to spread his views on reform of morals and customs in Egypt. He continued to do so until the 'Arabī uprising, the military part of the national movement, suffered its great defeat. All the nationalist leaders, Muhammad 'Abduh included, were arrested and exiled from the country for three years and three months. It was during that exile that he joined Jamāl in

Paris and helped him edit the famous "Indissoluable Bond." Later he had the opportunity to travel in Syria and other Muslim countries where he got first-hand information of their conditions. He was appalled at the ignorance of Islam displayed and the resultant decay of morals throughout the Muslim Empire.

When Muhammad 'Abduh returned to Egypt, he was received with great esteem by the Egyptian people who appreciated his efforts on their behalf. In every position he occupied in this last phase of his life (1888–1905), he endeavored to press forward his public reforms in almost every field where he thought them necessary.

In 1899 he occupied the highest position a Muslim jurist can aspire to, that of *mufti,* or supreme official interpreter of the canon law of Islam for Egypt. His decision on legal matters, referred to him, were final. Shortly following his appointment as *mufti,* he also became a member of the Legislative Council. Six years later the entire country was to mourn the loss of its great reformer, who died after a few days illness on July 11, 1905.

The reform of Islam was the central theme of Muhammad 'Abduh's life. Thoroughgoing reform of the entire system was in his opinion the only way for Islam to prove its inherent adaptability to modern conditions. He believed that Islam should be purified of all accretions and freed from all divisions by a return to the original form. He claimed that there was no essential conflict between science and religion, that the spirit of the true Islam was tolerant of all scientific investigation and he encouraged Muslims to take up the study of the physical sciences and equal the Western World in its achievement.

'Abduh excited the opposition of the orthodox theologians when he fought against *Taqlid,* blind acceptance of belief on the authority of others, that reason should sit in judgment upon religion and insisted on the right of independent investigation to form one's opinion on any matter of religion.

'Abduh's fame and influence were not confined to Egypt but among Muslims all over the world. As one of the leading Muslim figures of the last century he left his mark upon his age and as a great compatriot and reformer "he set in motion influences which outlived him," and are operating to the present day in Egypt and other Muslim countries.

The Qur'ān

During the reign of 'Uthmān ibn 'Affān, the third Muslim Caliph, quarrels broke out centering upon the authenticity of the various readings in the current copies of the *Qur'ān*. 'Uthmān realized the danger of such disputes and the desirability of a universally binding text. He appointed Zaid ibn Thabit, the Prophet's former secretary, who had made a former collection of the *Qur'ānic* verses, to head the committee on revision. The committee presided over by Zaid studied all copies available and prepared an edition which was canonized. All other copies were destroyed. That the text contained none but genuine material is attested by the fact that no opposition was placed by any party against it, although there were people still living who knew and heard the *Qur'ān* from the Prophet directly and many among those were men who had objected to 'Uthmān's policies in other respects and fought him on the slightest provocation.

It is the Orthodox Muslim view that the *Qur'ān* is the word of God transmitted to Muhammad through the Angel Gabriel from an archtype preserved in heaven. Hence it is eternal and uncreated. It is also considered the most perfect model of the Arabic language.

The contents of the *Qur'ān* are highly varied. Histories of saints and of former prophets are recounted so as to show how the righteous get their just deserts and how the wicked are damned. The Old Testament characters who figure prominently in the *Qur'ān* are Adam, Noah, Abraham, Ishmael, Lot, Joseph, Moses, Saul, David, Solomon, Jonah and Job; while of the New Testament only Zachariah, John the Baptist, Jesus and Mary are emphasized. There are also other *Qur'ānic* figures of purely Arabic origin.

The substance of the material indicates parallelism with accounts in the apocryphal Gospels, the Mishna, the Aggada, the Midrash and other non-canonical Jewish works. Several passages dealing with the theological reflections, moral exhortations and a great system of ceremonial and civil laws are laid down forming the core of Muslim canon law. The arrangement of the *Qur'ānic* material was arbitrary and mechanical. The longest *sūras* were placed first and the shorter ones toward the end.

The word *Qur'ān* translated means recitation and the book's real beauty actually is revealed by its being read aloud. With its specific intonation and traditional melodiousness this has become an artistic performance of Muslim professional reciters. Highly illuminating commentaries in many *Qur'ānic* editions take up more space than the *sūras* themselves. The commentaries are usually grouped around the *Qur'ānic* writing as a framework of smaller print. In writing and lettering, invention of beautiful ornamentations and the production of highly decorative volumes Muslim artists have found an outlet for their creative drive which otherwise was blocked in the Mohammedan world in which the illustrative and plastic arts are not allowed.

The *Qur'ān* has been translated into forty languages and is considered the most widely read book ever written. Since it is the text from which Muslims all over the world have to study the Arabic language, the religious and literary influence of this one book could hardly be overestimated. For besides being the religious and ethical manual by which millions of Muslims are guided, it is the only reason why the Arabic dialects have not become distinct languages and why, although the Syrian may find it difficult to understand the Moroccan's spoken idiom, he has no trouble reading the written Arabic since the latter is modelled upon the *Qur'ān*.

Muslim Sects

The two main sects in Islam are the Sunnī and the Shī'ites. The former is by far the larger majority; the latter does not exceed nine per cent of all Muslims. The Shī'ites and their various subsects are found mainly concentrated in Iran and to some extent in India where the followers of Agha Khan, the Isma'ilies, attract the attention of the Western observer by their pompous ceremonial where for charitable purposes the Agha Khan's weight was recently equaled with precious stones.

In contrast to the Sunnī who recognize no figure comparable to Muhammad, some Shī'ite groups venerate 'Alī, Muhammad's cousin and son-in-law, as of divine origin and claim that Gabriel in his call had mistaken Muhammad for 'Alī. Briefly it can be said that the Shī'ite split occurred shortly after Muhammad's death. The followers of this separatistic movement adhered to 'Alī's sons Hasan and Hussein and their direct descendants, the Imans. According to the one Shī'ite group, the Twelvers, the 12th successor of

Alī, the Mahdī is believed not to have died but may appear any time to reunite and revitalize and conquer the world.

The Sunnī have shown relative unity in their main beliefs even though mystical elements, a few centuries after Muhammad, gained entrance into the rationalistic theology of Islam. Subsequently, we find development of pious fraternal organizations and worship of saint-like figures which heretofore were rejected as idolatrous. On the other hand, puritanical and orthodox movements such as the Wahhabi movement in Saudi Arabia have been attracting the attention of the world at large due to the discovery of the rich sea of oil upon which this country floats.

Contribution of Islam to Religious Thought and Practice

According to our historical knowledge, Muhammad has modified his concept of the monotheistic convictions according to the specific emotional needs of the Arabic people. Nevertheless, he was carried by the firm conviction that his revelation of God was the true God of Abraham undistorted and undiluted by faulty tradition. Although he meant to be the Prophet through whom God had spoken to the Arabic people, the character of his teaching proved to be akin to the spiritual needs of many nations which lay beyond the border of the Prophet's homeland and quite different as to historical tradition and racial descent.

It has been pointed out by scholars of many faiths that Islam has found its success by its great realism as to human nature. Its ethical teachings are not transformed into rigid demands interfering with the biological needs of human existence. The divine laws are not zealously surrounded by narrow barriers of continuous ritual. God's character is not presented by mystical and secretive allusions. No original sin and self-sacrificial purifications interfere with the positivism of the Muslim's attitude towards God. God is merciful and compassionate. He needs no interpretation by priest appointed by Him or devoted exclusively to the performance of religious rituals. No theological hierarchy interferes with the immediacy of the individual's worship and his communication with his creator.

Islam can boast of being thoroughly practical. It makes no

demands upon its adherents which require explaining away because of their impossibility, none that cannot be fulfilled. It is too realistic to call the poor happy in their need. It may pronounce worldly things as vain but in doing so it does not neglect to take account of human needs and desires and provides for them with laws concerning property and goods.

The simplicity of the creed together with unelaborate but still all-pervading ceremonial of worship which keeps a constant unifying bond within the believers has proved to be of equal appeal to the primitive nomad as well as the sophisticated scholar.

Is Islam a Missionary Religion?

Students of Islam have held quite controversial views about the basic missionary attitudes in Islam. On both sides, chapter and verse are cited from the *Qur'ān* favoring the pros and cons of this question. But the attitude of the Muslim himself and what has been undertaken in missionary activity and still is should speak more eloquently.

It is a contention of the average Muslim that Muhammad topping the list of prophets had to proclaim the ultimate truth of God; that therefore related religions by previous law-givers have become obsolete and subsequently everyone should be encompassed by the Islamic Faith. Actually, the history of Islam shows that missionary activities have not necessarily coincided with military conquests of the Islamic Empire. The popular misconception of the Muslim warrior, advancing with sword in one hand and the *Qur'ān* in the other, is a distortion of the facts. The *Qur'ān* forbids forced conversion. On the other hand, economic considerations do not favor wholesale conversions for the tribute paid by non-Muslims filled the Muslim treasury.

The expansion of Islam took an unforeseen turn when the Arab people, unified by their religion, experienced a national and cultural renaissance with subsequent mobilization of heretofore internally absorbed energies.

It is interesting to note that Islam knew no organized mission until very recent times. Proselytizing was usually carried out by individual Moslems who in their peaceful activities as merchants came in contact with people of various religions. The Muslim communities in China and especially in Japan testify to this phenomenon.

The history of Islam plainly shows that, on the whole, tolerance was practiced toward non-Muslim communities and there are many instances where both Christians and Jews occupied important positions in the courts of the caliphs.

A Concluding Estimate

Historical evolution of the last century has placed previously powerful Islamic nations into a state of cultural stagnation which only recently has been interrupted by revolutionary modernizations with subsequent revitalization of all cultural efforts. Consequently the religious faith of these countries and its inherent strength were little felt by other nations. If, however, we try to visualize how, in centuries past, Islam was strong and ruled the center of the known world, that an era of highest civilization had developed and was maintained in spite of the medieval darkness in which the surrounding world was kept—we may conclude that this religion can offer a spiritual framework for enormous economic, scientific, aesthetic, and social progress.

The Mediterranean countries in the hands of Islamic rulers experienced a renaissance in which science and the arts flourished in a measure heretofore not surpassed since the time of the Hellenic prime. This was centuries before the European Renaissance broke the long cultural winter that has beleaguered Europe since the fall of the West Roman Empire.

Other Islamic countries enjoyed national security; the spirit of the religion allowed people of all faiths to maintain their individual beliefs and encouraged them to contribute in their own fashion to the cultural commonwealth of the country. It is a well-known fact that the highest flowering of exilic Judaism developed in Spain under the auspices of the Muslim Ummayads.

During the reign of the 'Abbāssid scholars were encouraged to translate and preserve for posterity the knowledge of the classics which had become inaccessible to a medievally dogmatic Europe. There is all reason to believe that when the Islamic world is once more nationally secure it will fertilize and strengthen human efforts toward progress.

A contribution that Islam even now can show us is the proud fact of its completely unprejudiced attitude towards race distinction. Our century polluted by pseudo-biological race-discriminations may very well face on this score one of the most destructive ideological developments that our world has ever encountered. It is true that all progressive religions of our time have been actively fighting against this dissociative process. However, in the Islamic world alone, racial equality has been practiced and maintained for centuries. It is entirely incredible to a Muslim that a brother in faith should be denied entrance to his mosque because of a swarthier shade of skin. Within the Brotherhood of Islam and in the sight of God we all stand equal and nothing can raise us to greater stature other than our right actions and our goodness.

BIBLIOGRAPHY

PHILIP K. HITTI, *History of the Arabs*, 3rd ed., revised (London, 1943).

T. W. ARNOLD, *The Preaching of Islam* (New York, 1913).

THOMAS ARNOLD AND ALFRED GUILLAUME, *The Legacy of Islam* (Oxford, 1931).

C. D. ADAMS, *Islam and Modernism in Egypt* (London, Oxford, 1933).

THE EASTERN ORTHODOX
CHURCH

George Fedotov was born in Jaratov, Russia, in 1886. He graduated from the University of St. Petersburg (now Leningrad) having spent two years in study in Germany. He holds the degree of Magistrant of General History (which corresponds to the American doctorate). From 1916 to 1922 he taught the history of the Middle Ages at the Universities of Petrograd and Jaratov with the rank of professor. He lived in Russia for seven years after the Revolution but was forced to leave the University because of the demands of his conscience to write and to speak freely. In 1925 he left his native land and found for himself an academic chair in the Orthodox Theological Institute in Paris where he remained for fifteen years teaching Church History. During this period he published many books, pamphlets and essays on subjects relating to Russian religious history, Christian sociology and on politics. A Christian socialist and liberal, he became interested in the Christian ecumenical movement, particularly hopeful of a rapprochement between the church of his heritage and the Anglican church.

Upon Hitler's invasion of France in 1940, he left for the United States where he arrived the following year, his emigration full of adventure. He is now professor at the Russian Theological Seminary of St. Vladimir in New York. In press is the first volume of his new work on "The History of the Russian Religious Mind" which is to appear under the imprint of the Harvard University Press and for the continuation of which he was granted in 1945 a Guggenheim fellowship. His other publications are: "The Treasury of the Russian Spirituality," an anthology in process of publication; "The Russian Church since the Revolution" (London, 1928); and articles dealing with Russia's religious situation, the Orthodox Church, etc., in magazines here and abroad.

Editor

THE EASTERN ORTHODOX CHURCH

GEORGE PETROVICH FEDOTOV

THE NAMES under which this Christian confession is known vary within as well as outside its body. The members of this Church call it simply Orthodox, although the designations of Greek-Catholic, Greek-Russian or Eastern Orthodox are also common. For the western world the name of Orthodox sounds ambiguous inasmuch as every denomination has claims to orthodoxy. On the other hand, the usual short designation of the Eastern Church is inexact. The Christian East embraces, besides the Orthodox, many heterodox denominations (as Monophysites and Nestorians) as well as the "Uniates" of the Roman allegiance who are not in communion with one another.

In the self-consciousness of the Orthodox Church it is the only true Church of God, founded by Jesus Christ and preserving faithfully the traditions of the apostolic and ancient undivided Church. The modern Orthodox theologians are not unanimous as to the question to what degree other Christian denominations possess the character and enjoy the grace inherent to the Church of God. But they consider them as deviations from the only true Church which is the Orthodox one.

Historically, all existing branches of the Eastern Orthodox Church can be described as the inheritors or daughter churches of the Church of the Byzantine Empire which itself is a direct continuation of the ancient Church within the Roman Empire as expressed in its Eastern, Greek-speaking and Hellenistic minded parts. Until the eleventh century the Orthodox or Catholic Church (as different from separated sects) was undivided. It included all nations brought up in the traditions of the Hellenistic-Roman culture. The ever growing tension between the Greek and Latin provinces of the Christian world, after many temporary schisms, i.e., breaks of ecclesiastical communion, ended in the final separation of 1054.

For many centuries all Orthodox Christians of the East were citizens of the same Byzantine Orthodox state which called itself the Roman. Outside the state frontiers in the provinces conquered in the seventh century by the Arabs, lived mostly the heterodox. The only exception was small Georgia, the independent nation in the Caucasus, converted to Christianity in the fourth century, which never belonged to the Empire. One church—one state, was the principle of the Byzantine patriotism as well as its piety; both were universalist and theocratic but in a sense different from Roman Catholicism.

Since the eighth century, however, the conversion of the Southern and Eastern Slavs, Bulgarians, Serbs, Russians, to Christianity by Greek missionaries and in Greek ritual forms, created many national Orthodox churches striving for independence and really achieving it. The fall of Constantinople in 1453 brought all the Orthodox nations in the Balkans under the Turkish rule and, through the politics of Sultans, under the spiritual and even civil administration of the Greek patriarch of Constantinople. For some centuries the role of Byzantium as the only Orthodox state was claimed by Muscovite Russia. But in the nineteenth century, the gradual liberation of Balkan Christians (Greeks, Serbs, Bulgarians and Rumanians) from Turkish domination created a new ecclesiastical situation: the coexistence of many independent national Orthodox states and, consequently, national churches.

At present, in its structure, the Orthodox Church is a free federation of independent (autocephalous) and half-independent (autonomous) local churches united by common creeds, common liturgy and common theological and spiritual traditions. No common organ of administration exists. Two different canonical principles are laid at the base of the ecclesiastical structure. The ancient Church knew only territorial divisions, corresponding mainly to the administrative divisions of the Roman Empire. Five patriarchates were not independent while standing under the general or oecumenical Councils on the one hand and under the Imperial Government on the other. Nowadays four ancient patriarchs, after the separation from the Roman Pope, are heads of so many autocephalous Churches, those of Constantinople, Alexandria, Antioch and Jerusalem. To them must be added, as historical survivals, the two small but autocephalous Churches of Cyprus and Mount Sinai, both under their respective Archbishops, the second consisting of a famous monastery only. All these ancient Churches are Greek in liturgical language with the exception of Antioch whose Patriarch, residing in Damascus, since recent time is elected by the predominant Arabian population. Some of these patriarchates count a few thousand people, less than an average bishopric. Their very existence and the great reverence bestowed upon them by the whole Orthodox world is due to the power of tradition.

More important in number and cultural achievements are younger national autocephalous churches: Georgia, Russia, Bulgaria, Serbia (or Yugoslavia), Rumania and Greece. The latter embraces the Orthodox population of the Greek State (Hellas) only, excluding the inhabitants of ancient patriarchates outside Greece.

In many countries where the Orthodox minority lives among the heterodox population, or on mission fields, the churches enjoy only the status of autonomy under the supremacy, sometimes nominal or only liturgical, of their mother churches by which they have been founded. Their number considerably increased since the Russian Revolution when several western provinces of Russia were built into independent states.

These are the autonomous Orthodox Churches, or at least, these Churches existed between the first and the second World Wars: Finland, Estonia, Latvia, Lithuania, Poland, Czecho-Slovakia, Albania. Missionary autonomous churches founded from Russia exist in China, Manchukuo and Japan. In America where the missionary Russian Church was founded at the end of the eighteenth century (1794) different Orthodox nationalities have, at present, their own national Churches dependent, in different degrees of autonomy, on their mother Churches in Europe (Russia, Ukraine, Greece, Rumania, Yugoslavia, Syria).

As the political map of Eastern Europe is rapidly changing in the last decades, the number and status of autonomous Orthodox Churches is also in continuous swing. Under favorable constellation they aspire to autocephaly which was attained in 1924 by Poland with her 3,000,000 of Orthodox population. Upon the political catastrophe of the recent occupation by Russia of the whole of

Eastern Europe some of them lose even the autonomous status which they enjoyed before.*

Even as it is not easy to determine the number of independent Orthodox Churches so is it difficult to determine the general number of believers. The USSR which contains the overwhelmingly largest Orthodox population admits of no religious statistics. Before the Revolution, Russia counted officially about 100 million of the Orthodox. On this basis, the whole Orthodox world could be calculated at about 130 millions. How many Russians have abandoned their religion as a result of persecutions and antireligious education—one third or one half of the population—is a matter of conjecture.

All the autocephalous Churches acknowledge, in principle, only one supreme instance over them: The Oecumenical Council which in the Orthodox theology occupies the same place as the Pope in the Roman Church, endowed with the *charism* of infallibility. But no Oecumenical Council has convened since the eighth century (787). Only seven oecumenical councils are accepted by the Eastern Orthodox Church, as a matter of fact and not of principle. The notion of an Oecumenical Council itself is far from clear. It is not entirely dependent on the universal character of attendance, because there are known heretical councils assembling under exactly the same conditions as the Orthodox ones. Modern theology postulates the general acceptance by the Church of a Council's decision as the condition of its oecumenicity.

In recent times the need of convening a new oecumenical Council is felt by many theologians and prelates. In the 1920's the Patriarch of Constantinople, who bears the title of the Oecumenical Patriarch and is considered as the *primus inter pares* in the Orthodox world, took upon himself some measures for the preparation of such a Council. Yet this action came to nothing mainly because of political obstacles. The absence of the Russian Church, the greatest Orthodox body, from all international fields during some thirty years of the Communist regime was paralyzing all inter-Orthodox intercourse.

In the absence of common Government the national Churches

---

* The Church of Georgia had lost her autocephaly since the incorporation of the country into the Russian Empire (1802) but recovered it after the Revolution of 1917.

possess a common book of Church laws or canons—in Greek the *Pedalion*. Yet it is not a *Corpus juris,* a Code of valid norms, but a collection of Canonical documents of the ancient Church. In spite of the veneration with which the Canon Law is held, many, if not most, of its norms are long out of use, and the life of the Church is regulated not so much by the ancient canons as by national traditions and the State ordinances.

Indeed, the close connection of the Church with national state and national life is one of the characteristics of the Eastern Church. In Byzantium and in ancient Russia the connection took the form of a theocracy. In theory, Church and State lived in "symphony," that is, in harmony with one another; in fact, the State was a predominant power. The person of the Emperor was sacred and he was guardian of Orthodoxy and Church order. He appointed patriarchs through the councils and often deposed them; with their assistance he ruled over the Church as he ruled over the State. He interfered with dogmatic matters as well as with matters of canon, and his edicts (*novellae*) were accepted into Canon Law on the same footing as the canons of the Councils. The term of Caesaropapism which is often applied to the Byzantine-Russian Church order is perhaps too strong. The Emperor never occupied in the Eastern Church the same high position as the Pope in the West. His infallibility was out of the question. The voices of opposition against the Emperor's interference with ecclesiastical affairs were never quite silenced. And thus the downfall of the Imperial power, at first of Byzantium (1453), and lately in Russia (1917), though borne with uneasiness and regret, did not mean a serious upheaval in the constitution of the Church. In the eyes of many canonists it opened the prospect to the restoration of the freedom of the Church and a true canonical order.

In modern Orthodox nations, the Church lives in various relations, mostly close, with the State. Either friendly or hostile, these relations are far from the medieval theocracy. Beyond those Byzantine centuries, the canonical thought turns readily to the ideals of the ancient and even early apostolic Church. In terms of political theory the present constitutions of national Churches represent varieties of aristocratic and democratic elements in their blending. Aristocracy is represented by bishops, all chosen from the monks; democracy, by laymen. The middle clergy, priests and deacons, have relatively less influence. As a married order the clergy is not too strongly differentiated from the laity as in the Roman Church. There is no sharp division between the "teaching" Church and the flock. The ideal forms of the Church organizations presuppose a collective or corporate participation of all the members in the parish (Parish Assembly), the diocese (Diocesan Assembly) and in the national Church (National Council). In some of these phases, the democracy of laymen is predominant, in none is it absent. At the head of national Churches stand either patriarchs, of modern titles, as in Russia, Yugoslavia, Rumania, Georgia, or Synods or small bodies of bishops (Greece, Bulgaria, pre-revolutionary Russia). Even in patriarchal churches Synods assist the ruling hierarch and limit his power. The synodal system was invented in Russia by Peter the Great (1721), after the Western Protestant pattern. The tsars ruled over the Church through the synod of bishops who were appointed by them. But the same form was adopted by modern Greece and proved to be capable of becoming the organ of self-government of the Church.

It can be safely stated that canonical forms of life in the Orthodox Church are, at present, in a transitional stage. Rejecting the monarchical absolutism of both the Popes and the Emperors, the Church is seeking for the balance in the coöperation of clergy and laity. The bishops represent the unchanging element of the apostolic tradition; the laity, or the "ecclesiastical people," are regarded now as the guardians of the same tradition, taking the place of the Byzantine Caesars.

The Eastern Church did not know the Reformation. But it can also be stated that it did not know the Middle Ages either, as a particular and creative period of history which gave, in scholastic philosophy and sacramental development, a new shape to Western Catholic Christianity. No clear-cut lines divide the Byzantine Church from that of the ancient fathers as well as from that of modern times. In the eyes of many, the patristic age was never outlived in the East: some Orthodox theologians in the nineteenth century were wont to write in the framework of ideas and even in the style of the ancient fathers. And yet, this estimation would be inexact. In the last three or four centuries an enormous mass of modern theological, philosophical and scientific ideas from the West was absorbed, though not without a struggle, by the Eastern Church. These ideas fell fructifying, directly on patristic soil. Only indirectly, together with the products of modern theology, did the doctrines of the Catholic Middle Ages or of the Protestant Reformation find a partial reception into the bulk of Eastern patristic thought. St. Augustine and Thomas Aquinas, Luther and even Calvin are reflected in the Orthodox systems which are intended to oppose them.

In this clash and fusion of ancient and modern ideas, where is the criterion of Orthodoxy? The Holy Scripture is not considered a sufficient rule of faith. The Holy tradition, on the other hand, assumes a greater importance than in the Roman Church because of the lesser significance attributed to the authority of the governing Church. The authority of the Church is not seldom proclaimed as the supreme source of truth. But there is no infallible organ of this authority in the East, whether a monarchical or collective one. And thus the faithful are obliged to seek for this authority (or "the voice of the Church") in tradition. The times are past when tradition was considered stable and unchanging since the apostolic age including all details of liturgical and canonical order. At present, tradition is considered by enlightened theologians as "living," that is, ever moving and enriching itself in the collective experience of the Church. This conception opens the door to considerable amount of freedom. Yet, in distinction from the Protestant notion of freedom, in the sense of religious individualism, the Orthodox freedom has this differentiating note: it must be rooted in tradition, in its spirit, if not in its letter, and be exercised in the common life, in the common liturgical and sacramental experience of the Church. This is the meaning of the famous idea of *Sobornost'* (the Slavic word for catholicity), as the synthesis of ecclesiastical corporate life and personal freedom, formulated by Khomiakov and retained after him by all Russian theological schools. A very small part of the Church tradition is fixed in the dogmatic definitions of the seven oecumenical councils. It is the "infallible" part of it, never questioned. Indeed, there is no "liberal" current in modern Orthodox theology which denies the whole or the part of the dogmatic tradition as formulated by the ancient Church. Besides this comparatively limited circle of dogmatic truths there is a larger circle of dogmas and doctrines taught by the Church and accepted by all the Orthodox world: the veneration of the Holy Virgin and the Saints, the doctrine and practice of Sacraments and "Sacramentalia" and so on. Here a greater freedom of interpretation is admitted, provided it is faithful to liturgical fundamentals.

In the sixteenth-seventeenth centuries there were many attempts to fix the unwritten dogmatic tradition by strict and binding definitions, after the pattern of the Reformation and the Roman Church. They resulted in several "Orthodox Confessions" issued either by private theologians (Patriarch Dositheus of Jerusalem, Metropolitan Peter Mohila of Kiev) or the local councils (Jassy, 1643; Jerusalem, 1672). For a period of time these confessions were accepted as the norms of dogmatic creeds, in spite of their contradicting one another on some points. Nowadays they are seldom read and studied; nobody attributes infallible authority to them.

The same must be said of all catechisms used by national and local Churches. The excellent catechism of Metropolitan Philaret of Moscow, as well as the Dogmatic Theology of Macarius of Moscow, which were highly appreciated for two or three generations not only in the Russian Church, were severely criticized by recent theologians, both of liberal and even of conservative trend.

Thus the theology of the Orthodox church, on the whole, is more traditional and less definite than that of the Roman Church. It reproaches her Western separated sister for many dogmatic innovations of medieval and modern times. Among them the additional clause of *filioque* in the Nicene Creed and the corresponding Augustinian theology of the procession of the Holy Spirit were long considered as the main dogmatic errors. Incidentally, Protestants reciting the creed in the same Western form fall under the same censure. Nowadays, in the Russian School (Bolotov, Bulgakov) the bearing of the age-old *filioque* controversy is much lessened. It has been recognized, though by far not universally, that there was this diversity of opinions among the fathers of the ancient Church on this matter as well as the absence of an authoritative definition of any General Council of the undivided Church.

The other Roman dogmas arousing the protest of the Eastern Church are: the doctrines of Purgatory, of the Immaculate Conception and of the Infallibility of the Pope. The most heavily weighing and really fatal for the prospects of reunion is the last dogma. Since the Vaticanum (1870) the issue in question is not the primacy of the Roman See or its administrative competence in the Church but the dogma of the Church itself as the mystical body of Christ. The absence of any earthly head of the Church, the necessity of corporate oecumenical action in finding the truth is mystically essential for the Orthodox consciousness.

Besides these dogmatic tenets the Orthodox are generally repulsed by what they call the "juridical spirit" of the Roman Church which finds its expression in a too logical elaborateness of the dogmatic and sacramental system. The Orthodox prefer to leave its veil to the divine mysteries, to let them only be translucent instead of being grasped in logical notions. The reaction against scholasticism goes so far in our days that the modern mystical school of theology (Florensky, Bulgakov) deny in principle the validity of logical rules or laws in respect to the divine world and positively revel in contradictory judgments, under the name of "antinomies" and "aporias."

In past centuries, however, Orthodox theology paid, not to its benefit perhaps, a large tribute to Western scholasticism in both its varieties: Catholic and Protestant.

Beyond the dogmatic divergences of Eastern and Western Catholicism, in the very common dogmatic treasure of the ancient Church, there were and still are the differences of accent, of spiritual interest which are of higher bearing for religious and cultural life than the famous *filioque* clause. The theology of the East always was theocentric; the nature of God was the main object of dogmatic interest: Trinitarian and Christological controversies agitated deeply the Greek world. Latin Christianity was interested more in man and the conditions of his salvation (Christian anthropology). The problems of original sin, of man's freedom and divine grace, of redemption by Christ and the nature of the Church were the main objects of concern for St. Augustine as well as for the Reformers of modern times. For the Eastern Church these problems belong, even at present, not to the sphere of dogma but to that of theological speculation.

The second distinctive feature lies in Christology and corresponds to the diversity of theological approach of St. Cyril of Alexandria and Pope Leo the Great in the fifth century. Cyril and the whole Byzantine Church were more interested in the divinity of our Lord than in His humanity. The Eastern Church stood in awe and amazement before the ineffable mystery—God in human flesh. To consider the human soul of the Savior, to seek a psychological approach to His person seemed impious to it. It did not concentrate the religious attention, as much as the Western Church did, upon the sufferings of Golgotha. The Eastern crucifix shuns the realistic reproduction of human pains. The devotion to the man Jesus of Western Middle Ages was strange to the East as well as the Christian humanism grown up on its base.

All this greatly changed, however, in modern times. The limited reception of Augustinianism and the full assimilation of the dogma of God-manhood in Christ were gradually and almost unconsciously accomplished upon contact with Western theology. The modern Orthodox catechisms in their structure are nearer the Western type originating in Abailard than the catechism of St. John of Damascus (eighth century). For a long time it was said and believed that Orthodoxy is a true balance, a middle way between Roman Catholicism and Protestantism. It is not the outlook of recent theological thought, especially Russian. In searching for its own heritage, in a closer study of the Greek Fathers it rediscovers the problems (trinitarian, cosmological, sacramental) that lead it again from Western theology into its own half-forgotten past.

The unbroken link of the Orthodox tradition is seen more clearly in its liturgy than in its theological development. The Eastern Church is often defined as the praying church. Its liturgy is, without comparison, richer than the Roman, though it consists of essentially the same daily acts of worship: the Mass, Matins, Vespers and the Canonic Hours. The richer development is achieved by means of Greek rhetoric which attains sometimes, with a few Byzantine hymnographs, to a true poetic height; on the other hand, poetry is fused here with Greek theological thought, a highly intellectual poetry which, by itself, represents a mine of theological doctrine. In analyzing the constituent elements of the Eastern liturgical style one finds the Biblical word undergoing the influence of the Hellenistic mysteries and, later on, of the Byzantine palace. The latter is responsible for the general impression of gorgeous beauty which finds also its expression in liturgical vestments and general ornamentation of the temple. Gold is the favorite color. Many rites reproduce ceremonies of the Imperial Palace. The Mass in its threefold form of Constantinople's Church has a more dramatic character than in Rome. Its action represents symbolically the life of Christ from the beginning of his preaching until the ascension into heaven. The mysterious significance of the Holy Eucharist is underlined by concealing the Sacramental act itself from the laity; it is achieved by pronouncing silently the prayers of the liturgical canon as well as by the high wall which separates the sanctuary from the nave of the temple. The invisibility of the "terrible mysteries of Christ" is compensated by the abundance of icons covering completely the partition wall of the sanctuary and most of the temple walls. Candles and colored lamps are burning before them. This is specifically the laymen's participation of the holy. For his devotions also serve the ever returning litanies said by the deacon as well as the hymns sung by the choir which represent, in principle, the "people."

The separation of the mysterious part of the priest from the simultaneous part of the laymen favors personal prayers. Everyone brings to the church his personal griefs and woes and effuses his heart before his beloved icon. Although the original Greek of the liturgy yielded in the later converted countries to national idioms, the liturgical languages (old Greek, Old Slavonic) became very remote from modern spoken ones. It is not easy for a not specially trained layman to follow the common liturgy. The extreme length of the services makes it practically impossible for an average layman to attend them all and to stand in the church (the regular position at praying) for their entire duration. The people come and go during the service as they please. This also accounts for an individual character of prayer within the common liturgical frame.

The length of the services is explained by their monastic origin. Developed in great monastic centers (Studion in Constantinople, St. Sabbas in Palestine), where prayers were destined to occupy the greater part of the day and night, the monastic liturgy, in the course of time, evicted the ancient, much shorter patterns of Patriarchal and Episcopal churches. At present the full extent of services is observed only in a few big monasteries; everywhere else those services which amaze a stranger by their length offer but an abridgment of the regular text.

The number of sacraments was fixed at seven only in the seventeenth century under the Roman influence. Various sacramental actions were and still are considered by many as true sacraments, for example, monastic consecration (tonsure) and the anointing of the tzar. The rich development of the "Sacramentalia" like the blessing of water, fruits, fields and houses is one of the outstanding marks of the Eastern Church, bringing it near the simple folk, their professional and especially their agricultural life. Like the Western Church in the Middle Ages, the Church of the East incorporated and Christianized some innocuous survivals of paganism, blending them with the popular forms of the cults of the saints and the festival calendar of the ecclesiastical year.

The married clergy shares with the people their familial, economic and national concerns. Yet, its influence is counter-balanced by that of the monastic order, as popular ritualism by latent sacramental mysticism. In the past, the influence of the monastic clergy was, perhaps, much stronger than in the West. Only a monk was considered a perfect Christian. In the Middle Ages he used to be the exclusive or preferred confessor of the laity. In practice, if not in canon law, the bishops still are chosen only among the monks, which creates, perhaps, a greater distance between the high and middle clergy than between clergy and laity.

The Christian East was the motherland of monastic life. The writings of the ancient ascetic fathers constitute a huge library still inspiring spiritual life, especially in the form of a vast anthology called in Greek *Philocalia*. The Eastern monks do not form various orders, differentiating after the spiritual and social callings. They all wear the same black cassock but it is incorrect to say, as often is done, that they all live after the rule of Saint Basil. There is no such rule at all. But it is true that in the ascetic corpus of Saint Basil's writings, Greek monasticism found its main practical directive. The greater monasteries of Byzantium (Studion, St. Athanasius in Athos and others) had their own particular rules radiating very far. The rule of Studion, for instance, was accepted in ancient times as a norm for all of Russia. Yet, now as ever, there are many particularities among the cloisters even of the same country concerning mainly the strictness of community life and individual property.

The common feature of Eastern monasticism is its orientation to praying, especially to liturgical life. Monastic order is the spiritual army of the Church praying for the world. Cultural and social work stands far behind. This was the general state of Byzantium and obtains now everywhere, although in ancient Russia monasticism was nearer the Western pattern by taking a very active part in social and cultural life.

It is commonly believed that mysticism represents a particular mark of Eastern monasticism. The Church of Maria has often been opposed to the Western Martha. This statement is not true if weighed against the flowering of mystical life in the medieval and modern Roman Church. Praying is not contemplation. The contemplative life with special mystical forms of prayers has always existed within Eastern monasticism but as a particular school. Originating in Egypt, it was revived in Byzantium, in the 10th–11th centuries, achieving its climax in the fourteenth. In Russia the mystical current came into being at about the same time, in the 14th–15th centuries. Destroyed violently by the Muscovite Church it was revived in nineteenth century Russia. In Greece, Mt. Athos has been its center until very recent times. The great names of Eastern mysticism are: St. Isaac the Syrian, Symeon the New Theologian, Gregory the Sinaitas; in Russia Saint Nilus Sorsky and Saint Seraphim of Sarov.

Mysticism of every type is aiming at the immediate and closest union with God to the extent of a temporary loss of individual consciousness. Western doctrine, as well as the practice of mysticism since St. Augustine is based upon the Platonic idea of divine love, the Eastern upon that of divine knowledge. Eastern intellectualism versus Western emotionalism was the specific difference. "Soberness", purity from images, "quiet" (*Hesychia*) are the means and technical terms of Eastern spirituality. Since the tenth century a technical instrument for mystical states was invented (or perhaps came to the surface). It is the continuous repeating, vocal and then voiceless, of the so called "prayer of Jesus," a short formula of seven or eight words, under the corresponding regulation of breathing and beatings of the heart. The latter practice was supposed, not unreasonably, to have been derived from India. At present, Eastern monasticism, in most of the Orthodox countries, appears in a state of decadence. In some places it became purely nominal. In Russia it was violently destroyed since the Revolution. Nevertheless, the monastic ideal did not perish. Its sway is even extremely strong among the Orthodox youth in Russia in the secret forms within the USSR and openly in exile. Its attraction is particularly felt among the religious intelligentsia.

After the fall of Byzantium and the free Slavic principalities in the Balkans, during centuries of oppressive Turkish yoke, the cultural level of the Orthodox nations became extremely low. It was the same in Russia under the Mongolian conquest (thirteenth-fifteenth centuries) and the Muscovite Tzardom. The consequences of this agelong retrogression are not yet outlived. The Orthodox masses which were the stronghold of religion as well as of national patriotism live still in a half medieval world outlook. The intelligentsia of these countries, repulsed by these conditions, is more estranged from, or even hostile to religion than the educated society in Protestant countries. Yet, the revival of Orthodox culture has been going on for the last two centuries. In Imperial Russia four so-called "Theological Academies" functioned with the curricula and level of studies not unlike the theological faculties of European universities.

They were handicapped by a severe censorship which was particularly oppressive in the field of Biblical studies. But in all types of historical theology Russia possessed very distinguished scholars.

A theological faculty at the University of Athens counts many scholars of world reputation.

Although the bulk of the Orthodox clergy is graduated from Seminaries with only middle (American High School) education, in Rumania the majority of the clergy come from universities. Theological faculties exist also in Belgrade (Yugoslavia) and Sophia (Bulgaria).

A peculiar feature of the Orthodox theological school is the eminent part which lay professors have in teaching.

Still more promising is the process of the intelligentsia's return to religion. The most dramatic and culturally the most fruitful has been going on in Russia. Upon the background of prevailing positivism and atheism a group of thinkers brought up in the school of German idealistic philosophy of Schelling and Hegel began the revaluation of the generally despised religious and national tradition of popular Orthodoxy. They were called, most inexactly, "Slavophiles." The brothers Kireievsky were their initiators in the 20's of the nineteenth century, A. Khomiakov in the 40's was their theological prophet. The movement, as a whole, was one of the offsprings of Western romanticism on Russian soil. The Slavophiles stood for the values of heart, for irrational intuition, for freedom in corporate life (*Sobornost'*) against rationalism, authoritarianism and individualism of both the Roman Catholic and the Protestant world.

Classical Russian literature of the nineteenth century was imbued with Christian ethos more than any other modern literature; it always had a moralistic character—that of self-examination, a fiery compassion for the sufferings of oppressed people, a judgment over cultural values in the name of the Absolute. Two religious geniuses, Tolstoy and Dostoievsky, most unlike and even antagonistic to each other, represented an explosion of gigantic religious powers slumbering in the depth of the national soul.

Vladimir Soloviov (d. 1900), a philosopher and lay theologian, worked out an elegant and all-embracing system which, on the basis of Christian dogma, construed the meaning of history and culture. To this dogma he added his own intuition of the "Sophia" (Divine Wisdom) as the personal principle of cosmology uniting the divine and the created world. The Sophia's gnostic theme was bequeathed by Soloviov to the school of modern Russian theology (Florensky and Bulgakov). Soloviov had a majestic dream of a "free theocracy" and new era of a united, creative Christendom. The disillusionment of this ideal ended in his apocalyptic vision of the near coming of the Antichrist and the close of human history.

The disciples of Vladimir Soloviov passing through a mighty esthetic and mystical movement of Russian symbolism tried a new theological interpretation of the ecclesiology and the sacramental and liturgical life of the Church. The resurrection of the mystic Byzantine fathers, strangely enough, was the result of this movement which is still rejected by many on the ground of its modernism. However questionable this theology must be or appear, Russian theology has already its word to say to oecumenical Christianity. It is beginning to influence Western thought. Still greater is the religious import of the secular "fictional" literature.

It is too early yet to draw the balance of the Russian revolution upon the religious life. Scores of millions were lost to the Christian faith, either frightened by three decades of persecution or seduced by a new atheistic culture propagated by a totalitarian state. The Church paid dearly for its too close connection with the monarchy and for its unpreparedness in carrying out a rational apology with the weapons of modern science. But, on the other hand, under the menace of death and sufferings, a small minority revived their faith and made it pure and flaming like that of the early Christians. The Russian Church had thousands of martyrs and perhaps millions of confessors, some still languishing in concentration camps for their Christian convictions. During the second World War, the state, threatened by a deadly danger, made an appeal to the clergy and, for a factual freedom of cult, made it the instrument of the Government's politics within and without Russia. The new temptation is the prospect of the restoration of the Established Church within the framework of an atheistic state. Whether this unnatural marriage will succeed the future will show. In our hopes and expectations we must not lose from memory the underground church of the martyrs as expiating the sins of the opportunist hierarchs.

A place apart belongs to N. A. Berdiaev, an original thinker, a free philosopher, non-theologian who combines in his thought many Western (Jacob Boehme, Marx, Nietzsche) as well as Russian (Khomianov, Tolstoy) influences. His own theme is anthropological: the defence of man as a free and creative being. Yet, the influence of Berdiaev's ideas is much stronger in the foreign world than within Russian Orthodoxy where ecclesiastical Byzantinism is now prevailing.

Orthodoxy is not worn out and decadent as many believe. In other countries besides Russia there are, or were before the war, spiritual popular movements aiming at a revival of religious life and its social implications. Such is the movement called "Zoe" (life) in Greece, and the analogous movement in Yugoslavia. Now, with Russian occupation, the Churches of Yugoslavia and Bulgaria, in their turn, enter a period of martyrdom and acute anti-religious propaganda. The whole Orthodox world stands on trial. In blood and tears the renovation of the oldest stem of Christianity is proceeding.

Just at the critical time, the Orthodox Church stepped out of its age-long isolation into the oecumenical intercourse with other branches of Christendom. The isolation was partly conditioned by historical destinies; partly it was the outcome of self-sufficiency, due to the consciousness of the fullness of spiritual possessions. Lacking entirely the spirit of proselytism, characteristic of the Roman Church, the Eastern Church was rather indifferent to the fate of other non-Orthodox brothers. The tragic experience of the past embittered it against the Roman Church from which it had often had to defend itself. In Greece it was the aggression of the crusades, in Russia the threat from Poland; in both cases religion and politics were closely interwoven. As a particular form of Roman aggression were felt the continuous attempts at reunion in the form of splits and schisms, rending off from the national Orthodox Churches small bodies which accepted the supremacy of the Pope and Roman dogmas while preserving Eastern rites. The so-called Uniates or the Catholics of the Eastern rite create, in fact, the highest barrier for any rapprochement between the two branches of the Catholic Church. Towards Protestants, in spite of a wide dogmatic distance, there is no such bitterness. A practical cooperation with Protestants on a friendly basis is going on very easily. It is supported by a sincere esteem for the ethical energies of Protestantism and its social and scientific achievements. In the last fields the Orthodox are ready to learn from their Western brothers up to a certain dogmatic and sacramental limit. Thus it happened that from the very beginning of the oecumenical movement, after the first World War, the Orthodox bishops and theologians took an active part in it. They were present at all oecumenical gatherings from Stockholm in 1925 up to Oxford and Edinburgh in 1937; they joined the organizations created by them, such as the "Life and Work," the "Faith and Order" and since 1937, the World Council of Churches. Some national and local Orthodox Churches are represented officially, through their bishops, but the great Russian Church, cut off since the Revolution from the outside world, found its voice only through Russian theologians in emigration. Their main theological center is the Theological Institute in Paris, whose professors do most of the Orthodox oecumenical work. This work, as yet, is not backed by broad popular masses; it is due to the initiative of an enlightened minority which is met at times by the suspicions of the conservatives. But the beginnings of a common work are laid. Especially intimate, going even into the liturgical sphere, are the relations with the Anglican or Episcopalian Churches. There were even created special bodies for the rapprochement of the two respective Churches. After the old Anglican and Eastern Church Association founded in 1864, a young active brotherhood was created in 1927, under the name of the Fellowship of St. Alban and St. Sergius with now about 1,000 members, having yearly conferences and a magazine called *Sobornost'*.

In the voluntary absence of the Roman Church, the Orthodox represents within the oecumenical movement the catholic type of Christianity. They bring to the Protestant world a new, indeed the most ancient experience of dogmatic sacramental Christianity. Besides a general Catholic background they offer their own particular contribution: an inheritance of the mystical Greek fathers and the visions of modern Russian thought. The exchange of ideas between

East and West is free from the bitterness of traditional theological polemics and is being worked out on the basis of the give-and-take principle. That is why the influence of a small group of Orthodox theologians in this movement is quite incommensurable with their number or even their official status. They represent numerically the third part of the Christian world, spiritually—the whole of the Christian East.

BIBLIOGRAPHY

N. S. Arseniev, *Mysticism and the Eastern Church* (London, 1926).

S. Bulgakov, *The Orthodox Church* (London, 1935).

G. Fedotov, *Russian Religious Mind* (Harvard Univ. Press, 1946).

A. Fortescue, *The Orthodox Eastern Church* (London, 1908).

Fr. Heiler, *Urkirche und Ostkirche* (Muenchen, 1937).

B. J. Kidd, *The Churches of Eastern Christendom* (London, 1927).

An. Le Roy-Beaulieu, *The Empire of the Tsars,* Vol. 3 (New York, 1903).

J. M. Neale, *History of the Holy Eastern Church,* 2 vols. (London, 1850).

Orthodox Spirituality, by an Orthodox monk (London, Soc. Promoting Christian Knowledge, 1945).

S. Zankov, *The Eastern Orthodox Church* (London, 1929).

N. Zernov, *The Church of the Eastern Christians* (London, 1944).

———, *The Russians and Their Church* (London, 1945).

SIKHISM

Writing of the Sikhs as she has come to know many of them personally, Mrs. Boulter portrays these people as sturdy, fearless, honest, full of humor, loving, kindly and charitable. "I honestly do not know any group of people who stand the test of long and close association so well as these do, nor any who live up to their beliefs so well," she has written the editor.

This article was written in consultation with Dr. Anup Singh, a Sikh, born near Amritsar, India. Dr. Singh (M.A. and Ph.D., Harvard) is the Watumull Professor of Oriental Philosophy and Ancient and Medieval History of India at the American University, Washington, D. C., secretary of the National Committee for India's Freedom and editor of the "Voice of India." Mrs. Boulter was the first American member of the India League of America (founded, 1937) and served on its executive committee and as research assistant and assistant editor of the League's bulletin "India Today" of which Dr. Singh was the editor.

Born in New York City, in 1892, Mrs. Boulter received her early education at the hands of governesses and tutors, with special study later in Paris. Her many articles on India have appeared in such magazines as the "Modern Review" (Calcutta), the "Hindustan Times" (Delhi), "Bombay Chronicle" (Bombay), "Unity" and "Asia Magazine." Her book on India was published in 1944, a part of the United Nations' Series. She has wide acquaintance in India among those who are re-making its history; she writes Gurumukhi script and understands both Hindi and Punjabi. A lecturer, she has appeared frequently on school, college and club platforms.

As this book goes to press, she is on her way for a year's sojourn among her Indian friends to gather material for further literary work.

Editor

SIKHISM

HILDA WIERUM BOULTER[1]

"If a man loves to see God, what cares he for Salvation or Paradise?"

Guru Nanak[2]

"Sagal Dharam men grist pardhan hai."
"Of all ways of life, that of the householder is supreme."

Guru Gobind Singh

In these two sayings lie the fundamentals of Sikhism as a faith, and through their logical extension and practical application was evolved Sikhism as a way of life.

The Faith

Sikhism is the outgrowth of the teachings of Nanak, a Khatri[3] Hindu born at Talwandi, a small village close to Lahore in the Punjab, in the year 1469. Nanak was himself influenced by Kabir, a Muslim poet who taught through his poems the Union of Man with God, the Islamic doctrine of the Oneness of God, and the unimportance of creed and dogma. Nanak, born a Hindu, accepted these ideas which were largely derived from Islam, but from Hinduism kept many other ideas, including the doctrine of reincarnation which is quite foreign to Islam. The chain of births, said he, can be broken by Love and good deeds. Salvation (*mukati*) should be sought in works performed for love of God, rather than in any mystic ecstasy of faith. "For your good actions may procure for you a better birth, but emancipation is from Grace alone," sang Guru Nanak. To which Guru Arjun added: "Without pleasing

---

[1] In consultation with Dr. Anup Singh.
[2] *Guru* means Teacher; *Sikh* means Disciple.
[3] A caste name denoting one above the *Jat* farmer but below the *Kshatrya*, or warrior.

God all actions are worthless. . . . Serve your God and remember Him, leaving all your pride of self." And Sikhism makes it clear that good actions must be inspired *not by any desire for salvation,* but from *an intense and selfless desire to please God,* and to serve one's fellow men.

Like Buddha and Jesus, Nanak was a reformer who had no intention of founding a new religion. He sought to correct the over-emphasis which Hinduism had laid on renunciation, to do away with the formalism which by his time had fettered the true spirit of Hinduism, and to bring in the fresh spirit of Islam with its pure monotheism and its democracy.

Sikhism combines the Aryan idea of Immanence with the Semitic idea of Transcendence. Thus Guru Nanak: "We should worship the Name, believe in the Name, which is ever, and ever the same and true." God is known as *Ek-Unkar* (One God), *Sat Nam* (True Name), *Akal-Murat* (Endless Being), *Ajuni-sen-bhin* (The Un-created One). Before there was any creation God Was—absolutely, living in Himself alone. "When God was Himself self-created, there was none else; He took counsel and advice with Himself; What He did came to pass. Then there was no heaven, or hell, or the three-regional world. There was only the Formless One Himself; creation was not then." (*Guru Amar Das*). But, being thus self-created, and being then manifest as The Name, in order to realize Himself, God made Nature, wherein He has His seat and "is diffused every-where in all directions in the form of Love." (*Guru Gobind Singh*).

"Why dost thou go to the forest in search of God?
He lives in all, is yet ever distinct; He abides with thee too.
As fragrance dwells in a flower, or reflection in a mirror,
So does God dwell inside everything;
Seek Him therefore in the heart." (*Guru Tegh Bahadur*)

God is "the indweller of Nature," filling all things. But Nanak em-phasized also the reality of the Universe. For, since the Universe is rooted in God, containing God, and contained by God, who is real, the Universe also is real. Its reality, however, is not of itself, but derived from God's presence in it. God's Will is both above Nature and working with Nature. God is indivisibly One, and both *in all else,* and *above all else.* Above all manifestations such as Brahma, Shiva, Vishnu—the Hindu names for personifications of different aspects of God—and Krishna, a manifestation of God in human form, but with divine attributes. Furthermore, God is not the tribal God of a Chosen People. He is the "dispenser of life Universal." He is to be realized not through theories or knowledge, or even through any meritorious action performed *for the reward,* but through love and faith. Man should sing His praises and meditate upon His Name *while living a life of active service in this world.*

Man has been born before and inherits the personal past of his previous incarnations. He also inherits the past of his family and race. These family and racial inheritances help to mould his nature, just as his personal past, his acquired tendencies, help to determine his conduct in this life. But this does not mean that man is the helpless creation of an Arbitrary Supreme Being, with every thought and action predetermined by a combination of the Will of an Arbitrary God, plus his own conduct in past lives and those tendencies inherited from his ancestors. For man has his own will, by which he can modify both inherited and acquired tendencies, and determine his own conduct. Yet man has neither strength nor existence without God, and though he may decide *of his own will to run counter to God's will, he cannot escape the rule of God's will.* Man's ego is given him by God, and according to whether man subjects— *of his own free will*—his ego to the Will of God, or—*also of his own free will*—does not so subject it, that ego is either a blessing or a curse. The strength to make the right choice is not in man of himself, but comes also through the Will of God. But man can overcome his own inherent weakness by reinforcing himself through the personality of the Guru.

The Guru of the Sikh, however, though perfect and sinless, is not divine. Whereas Christianity as it now exists offers to imperfect man a model not only perfect and sinless, but *divine* and therefore impossible of perfect imitation by imperfect human beings, Sikhism offers man a way of life and a model *subject to the same nature as himself,* one who has himself fought sin and overcome it. Through his personal devotion to the Guru, man offers his love and devotion to the Impersonal Formless God. This may be compared to the Catholic's devotion to the saint through whose intercession he approaches God, but the analogy is not perfect. For the great difference is that the Sikh is not asking the Guru to intercede for him; his devotion is without fear. And the Sikh loves selflessly, not for the reward.

Sikhism, unlike both Christianity and Islam, looks to no decisive Day of Judgement with eternal reward or punishment, but rather to the continued development of the soul through countless births—as in Hinduism, until it becomes at last ready for absorption in the Infinite Soul. But this salvation of the Sikh, like *Nirvana* of the Hindu and Buddhist, is not annihilation, for as the drop of water becomes one with the ocean into which it falls, *yet is still there,* so is the soul of man to be one with the Divine Soul, *without being destroyed or itself coming to an end.*

Sikhism is essentially character training; actually Nanak and the nine other Gurus personally supervised the character training of a whole people. There are five enemies within man which he must conquer to achieve spiritual purification: *Kam*—Lust, *Karodh*—Anger, *Lobh*—Greed, *Muh*—Attachment to things of this world, *Hankar*—False Pride. "*Man jite jagjit.*" "He who conquers his mind, conquers the world." It is for this conquest of the mind that teachings of the Gurus and the discipline of Sikhism is intended.

Guru Gobind Singh, 10th and last Guru, ordained that after him the Guru of the Sikhs should be the *Granth* (The Book—see later) and the Assembly of the Sikhs. (See later.) Thus Sikhism today, as always, is a combination of a working democracy and a theocracy. For the Spirit of Nanak as the Guru through whom the Sikh approaches God, *was* in all the Gurus, and *is now* in the Guru *Granth Sahib*—the Noble Book. The Guru *Granth Sahib* is the *spiritual ruler* of the Sikhs. The *Panth,* or Assembly, deriving its strength through the spiritual union between the Sikhs and the Guru —and through the Guru with God, makes decisions on temporal matters. Decisions on very serious subjects taken by the *Khalsa Panth* are called *Gurumattas*—decision of the Guru. For the *Khalsa Panth* is the embodiment of the Guru, just as the Guru *Granth Sahib* is the embodiment of the teachings of the Gurus.

The idea of service, what we now call social service, was one of Nanak's own contributions to Sikhism. The Sikh is sworn to the protection of the poor and the weak. The Sikh is enjoined to share what he has with the needy. Sikhs are brothers—they call each other

Bhai, Brother. Equality between man and man is stressed. Guru Gobind Singh said: "Recognizing all human nature as one," and, "All men are the same, although they appear different under different influences." Equality between the sexes was also stressed. Said Guru Nanak of women: "How can they be inferior when they give birth to the greatest men?" and Guru Har Gobind called woman "the conscience of Man."

Thus the Sikh believes in the One-ness of God and the Brotherhood of Man. He is to lead a healthy, normal life, serving his fellow man, and worshipping God through the True Guru. *"Hasandian, kalandian, panandian, matedendian, Viche hoi mukat pura satgur bhetiye puri hoi jugat."* "Let the True Guru be followed, let the right attitude of mind be maintained, and in laughing, eating, drinking and playing—in all these may salvation be found," said Guru Arjun Dev. Throughout, the accent is on truth. The True Guru, the true life, is the normal life lived according to the True Will of God and with True Love of God. The Sikh's greeting to his fellow Sikh is *Sat Siri Akal*—Truth is Eternal!

Up to the time of the 5th Guru the emphasis was on pacifism, following the good old Hindu tradition. But persecution overcame pacifism. When there is an organized attack on truth, it must be defended by all means. But the sword of the Sikh is only to be drawn in a just and unselfish cause. It is not for aggression or conquest. The Sikh is the Soldier of God in the Service of Righteousness.

Sikhism as it exists and is practised today by about 6 million Sikhs in India and elsewhere, still contains the original doctrines propounded by Guru Nanak, but added to the original, basic ideas are the contributions of the other nine Gurus, plus the accretions which came from the impact of historical events. Geography, and the history and politics of India from the fifteenth century to the present time, have had their share in giving to Sikhism its peculiar characteristics; and no study of this faith can be complete without including some reference to these contributing forces.

Nanak found his original followers largely in the Punjab, and it is still the centre of Sikhism today. Punjab (from *paunch,* five, and *ab,* water) means the Land of the Five Rivers. Here is a land watered not only by the five rivers of the Indus system, but, even in Guru Nanak's time, by an irrigation system based on those five rivers, and consequently a fertile land, yielding a variety of crops—

from rice, sugar-cane and cotton, to wheat. The population, largely agricultural by occupation, is of many racial strains. There are traces of Persian, Scythian and Greek.[4] There are pure Rajputs and many whose Rajput blood is diluted in various ways. There are Muslims from Afghanistan, and descendants of the Muslims of former days who came from that same region. For the Punjab is not only the Granary of India, but also its Threshold for those invaders who came down through the Northern Passes. And, since the first Aryans came to India, every invasion has left its traces in the Punjab. The resulting population has always been sturdy and of necessity inured to warfare. Ordinarily peaceful, law-abiding, industrious farmers, the Punjabis are when need arises mighty warriors. And of the Punjabis the Sikhs are the most closely knit group. Organization has from the very earliest days been a strong point among the Sikhs. Nanak, wherever he went, left behind him a *Sangat*—congregation. He refused to work miracles in the ordinary sense of the word, but actually did perform a very great miracle by laying the foundations of such a closely bound, well disciplined group drawn from a population by no means homogeneous— foundations so firm that to this day the Sikhs are a strongly organized community. Soon after Nanak's death there were in the Punjab 22 *manjis,* or dioceses, and 52 *pirahs,* parishes—to use the most closely corresponding English terms. Missionary work was regular, but whereas Nanak himself had wandered all over India, after his time Sikhism tended to concentrate itself in the Punjab proper. It was partly at least because of the organization of the Sikhs, which made of them a political force, that the Moghul Emperors turned against the Sikhs and from the time of Tegh Bahadur until about 1763 persecuted them so terribly. And, as we shall see, from this very persecution grew a yet stronger organization of the Sikhs.

The Founder—Fact and Fancy

Nanak's personal history as it is told today is a curious mixture of fact and legend. But the character of the legends tells us something in itself, and, of course, every legend has some sort of basis

[4] The very common Punjabi name *Sikander* is a corruption of Alexander, from Alexander the Great who once conquered the region.

of fact. We do know where and when Nanak was born. We do know that his father was the village clerk. It is *said* that Nanak was a pious, reflective child and that he studied both the *Q'ran* and the *Shastras* at an early age. Considering his later preoccupation with religion, these bits of information seem likely to be true. It is also said that when still a little boy he astonished his teacher by asking for the hidden meaning of the letter *Alif*—A, which in the Persian and the Arabic script is a single, straight vertical stroke (I) and is supposed to denote the Unity of God. This, though possible, is less probable. The parallel between this story of Nanak and that of Jesus at the age of 12 confounding the teachers in the Temple at Jerusalem is obvious, and interesting.

We know that Nanak was married and that he had two sons. Tradition says that he was married "between the ages of 14 and 19 but that he showed little affection for his wife" and was restless and unhappy. This may well be true, for an arranged marriage of a fairly young boy—and Indian marriages were and still are usually arranged—might well be less than happy. A legend has it that when put in charge of his brother-in-law's grain shop, he gave all the stores away in charity—yet they were always miraculously replenished. Some time after his marriage he left his home and wandered around India in traditional fashion in search of Wisdom and Truth. It is said that he even went out of India, and tradition has him make pilgrimage to Mecca—though he was a Hindu. While at Mecca, Nanak is said to have lain down to sleep with his feet turned toward the *Q'aaba*—a deadly insult which brought down upon him the wrath of the Mullahs. "How dare you turn your *feet* towards God?" they shouted. Nanak replied "Show me where God is *not,* and I will turn my feet towards *that* place." The stories and legends of Nanak are legion, but the most beautiful of all concerns his death. After he died, both Hindus and Muslims claimed him as their own saint, and struggled over his body—whether it should be burned according to Hindu custom, or buried according to Muslim usage. Someone lifted the sheet that covered the Guru's body—and lo, there was only a heap of fragrant roses! [5] The *fact* behind this lovely legend is that among Nanak's earliest followers were Muslims—although Nanak was a Hindu.

[5] This same story is also told of the Muslim poet Kabir.

Nanak's Successors [6]

Guru, or as he is also known, *Baba* (father), Nanak had two sons, but to succeed him as Guru he chose one of his disciples. It was to be a spiritual, not dynastic, succession. Nanak's choice was Lahna, a man whose devotion and saintliness Nanak had proved by many tests during the years when they had wandered together. After proving Lahna Nanak renamed him *Angad* (meaning One Body—signifying that Angad was now one with the Guru), and he is known as *Guru Angad* (1538–1552). According to some, Guru Angad invented a special script and called it the *Guru-mukhi* (from the mouth of the Guru), and according to others he merely re-arranged an already existing script of that name. In any case, it was designed for the special purpose of writing down Nanak's hymns and sayings. All sacred Hindu literature is written in Sanskrit—already in Nanak's time a language for scholars only, and Muslim sacred writings are either in Arabic or Persian—also languages for the learned. Nanak had composed his hymns in Punjabi, the common speech of the people of the Punjab, and Sikh Scriptures are accordingly in Punjabi, written with Angad's script—the Guru-mukhi. To Nanak's sayings and hymns, Guru Angad added some of his own devotional observations.

Amar Das (1552–1574) is noted for his humility, and this quality is stressed in his teachings. Amar Das was the first Guru to lay down a formal rule prohibiting *Sati*,[7] though Nanak, informally at least, had also forbidden the practice of self-immolation of widows and had even encouraged remarriage for them. Amar Das said: "The true Sati is she whom grief, not flame, consumes, and the afflicted should seek consolation with the Lord." In passing, it is interesting to note that besides this prohibition of Guru Amar Das, laws against *Sati* were passed by the Moghul Emperors Akbar and Jehangir, thus by many years anticipating those passed by the British.

Ram Das (1574–1581) was the son-in-law of Guru Amar Das.

---

[6] The dates are of *Guruship*, not of birth and death. On some of these dates authorities are divided. I have given them according to *Sikh* authority, and have noted where Robert Ernest Hume disagrees in his *The World's Living Religions*.

[7] Self-immolation of widows.

Guru Ram Das was greatly esteemed by the Emperor Akbar and obtained from the liberal-minded Akbar a grant of land on which he started the building of a temple, called the *Har-Mandir*— Temple of God. Since there was connected with the temple a small pool, Ram Das named the place *Amritsar*, or Water of Immortality. It became the centre of Sikhism, and still remains so.

Arjun Dev (1581–1606) was the son of Ram Das. Hitherto no son had succeeded his father as Guru, but from now on the Guruship became hereditary. Guru Arjun Dev added to and completed the Temple (the Punjabi word is *Gurudwara*, literally the doorway, *dwara* to the Guru) which his father had started, and enlarged the sacred pool.[8] But more than completing the Temple Guru Arjun's really great work was the collecting and arranging the hymns and sayings of all the previous Gurus, his own writings, and some of the writings of certain Hindu and Muslim saints and other worthy persons. The resulting compilation is the *Granth*, the *Book*, the Sikh Scripture. It was later called the *Adi Granth*—First Book, to distinguish it from the Granth compiled in the name of Guru Gobind Singh. The *Granth Sahib*—Noble Book, as the Sikh Scriptures are now known—is the only example of a Holy Scripture including writings and teachings from other religions.

Thus under Guru Arjun Dev the Sikhs acquired a Sacred City and a Sacred Scripture. Under Arjun also was started the practice of making pilgrimages to Amritsar. Sikhism was spreading very rapidly, for it offered to converts not only a means of salvation, but a way to escape from the bonds of caste. It was becoming somewhat codified, and each succeeding Guru added to the code and to the organizational side of what was now really a new religion.

Guru Arjun encouraged "foreign" trade, and to this end sent his agents outside the Punjab. He also took part in the politics of the Moghul Empire, siding with Khusru, son of Jehangir, when he rebelled against his Imperial father. Arjun was imprisoned by

---

[8] The present Golden Temple of Amritsar which stands in the centre of the sacred Lake is not the original building. Arjun's temple was destroyed in 1761 by Ahmad Shah of Persia, who piled the heads of slain Sikh devotees in the ruins of the Temple. Rajah Ranjit Singh, after he came to power in the early 1800's, restored and enlarged the Temple. As a measure of retribution, Ranjit Singh made use of materials from various famous Muslim buildings in the vicinity to rebuild the Sikh Temple—the *Darbar Sahib*, the Noble, or Great, Audience Hall, or House, in other words, God's House or Audience Chamber.

the Emperor, but there is reason to believe that Jehangir was influenced by Chandu Shah, financial administrator—or as we should now say, minister, of the Province of Lahore. Arjun had refused to betroth his son to Chandu Shah's daughter—which shows clearly to what a position of importance the Sikh Gurus had by that time arisen. Arjun did not remain forever in prison, however, for Jehangir, convinced that he was a saint, released him. The Guru died soon after his release—no doubt as a result of his imprisonment—but Sikh tradition has it that he obtained permission from his captors to bathe in the river Ravi—and *vanished*—though the river at that spot was but a shallow stream, and Guru Arjun under close guard at the time!

Har Gobind (1606–1645, or 1638 according to Hume). Under this Guru the separation of Sikhs from Hindus which had been gradually going on was completed. From the very beginning Sikhs had been warned against the dangers inherent in asceticism, and had held up to them the ideal of a *normal* life lived in a spirit of devotion. Now they began to eat meat, and, for reasons of health, to abjure the use of intoxicants and tobacco. Under Guru Har Gobind for the first time the Sikhs were forced to take up the sword. For not only had Sikhism become a recognizably distinct religion, but the Sikhs had begun to assume almost national character. And it was in this character that under Har Gobind Sikhs more than once engaged in battle with the troops of Jehangir. At one time Har Gobind was taken prisoner by Jehangir and held in the fort at Gwalior. The Sikhs in huge crowds flocked to Gwalior and bowed before the walls of the fort where their Guru was imprisoned. Jehangir, inspired perhaps as much by superstition and fear as by love of justice, released the Guru. Guru Har Gobind, after a career which involved him and his followers over and over again with the Moghul Emperor, finally died quite peacefully. Many of his followers wished to immolate themselves on his funeral pyre, but were restrained by the new Guru. Guru Har Gobind left the Sikhs well on the way to being a State within the State—a fact which contributed considerably to the persecution which from now on they underwent at the hands of the Moghul rulers.

Har Rai (1645–1662 or, according to Hume, 1638–1660). Neither Guru Har Gobind nor Guru Har Rai left any hymns. They used the *Granth Sahib* as their means of instructing their followers without adding to it. Although they were primarily the teachers and leaders of a religious group, their history is more like that of national leaders and is secular in character. But this very fact was having its influence on Sikhism, and was preparing the way for the great additions to Sikhism made later by Guru Gobind Singh.

Har Krishan (1662–1664),[9] younger son of Guru Har Rai, was only five years old when he became Guru. He died of smallpox at the age of seven. Upon his deathbed the boy Guru indicated that the new Guru would be found in a certain village.

Tegh Bahadur (1664–1675), son of Guru Har Gobind and great-uncle of Guru Har Krishan, was at the latter's death already well past middle age. He was living in the designated village, and was finally persuaded to come out of his retirement and assume the Guruship. Guru Tegh Bahadur was by nature a gentle, quiet man, but he had tremendous courage. Aurungzeb, the Emperor, was a fanatic, a bitter religious zealot, whose goal was the conversion, by force if necessary, of all his subjects to Islam. The Sikhs were by this time a very well organized group, and their faith was even stronger than their organization. They steadfastly resisted all attempts at conversion, and in consequence were the special objects of the fierce and terrible persecution instituted by Aurungzeb. Guru Tegh Bahadur, however, was able to make converts to Sikhism even in the midst of this persecution—a tribute not only to his own powers of persuasion, but to the inherent spiritual force and vitality of Sikhism. Aurungzeb, thoroughly angered by the stubborn resistance of the Sikhs, ordered the Guru to Delhi. Tegh Bahadur was fully aware of his danger, yet determined to face the Emperor and "bear witness to the Truth" in his very presence. But on the way to Delhi he provided for a successor by conferring "the sword of leadership" upon his fifteen year old son Gobind Singh. Tegh Bahadur's fears were justified. In 1675 he was beheaded by Aurungzeb, thus becoming a martyr. Tegh Bahadur was almost more of a king than a religious leader.

The Tenth Guru and the Khalsa

Guru Gobind Singh (1675–1708). After Nanak himself, Guru Gobind Singh, tenth and last of the Sikh Gurus, is the most famous.

---

[9] Hume gives 1660–1664. But this gives Har Krishan *four* years as Guru, which is contrary to various other authorities.

Assuming the leadership as a mere youth, at the beginning of a period of the most horrible persecution, Guru Gobind Singh was obliged to turn his religious following into an army. The disciples were trained in the use of arms and enrolled as soldiers. The Sikh women also learned the use of arms, and on many occasions fought side by side with the men.

But Guru Gobind Singh did not concentrate entirely upon military training. There was a great revival of religious fervor, and the Sikhs would gather in huge crowds to sing hymns, listen to preaching, and to offer congregational prayers. New converts were drawn in from every caste, including those beneath all castes. There was an extraordinary loyalty among the Sikhs, at this time especially. It is from the days of persecution that began during the life of Guru Gobind Singh that the insistence upon beard, long hair and turban dates. Uncut hair and beard have always been considered marks of saintliness in the East and Near East. The Sikhs, who strove for saintliness, usually wore their hair long and their beards untrimmed. The turban was a common form of head-dress in India; the Sikhs merely tied theirs in a distinctive way. But soon after Aurungzeb began his ferocious campaign against the Sikhs a price was set on the head of a Sikh. It thereupon became a point of honor to keep the long hair and untrimmed beard by which the Sikh could easily be recognized. Even today cutting the hair and shaving the beard are frowned upon by orthodox Sikhs. As time went on and the persecution became more strenuous, the Sikhs were forbidden to enter the towns and were obliged to roam in *jathas* (bands) in the deserts of Rajputana or in the forests of the northern Punjab. But this was much later.

Guru Gobind Singh led the Sikhs as their general in the struggle against the Moghul Emperor. It was after the Sikhs had suffered a bad defeat that the Guru founded the *Khalsa*—the Brotherhood of the Pure—with its magnificent rule which was to give the Sikhs the strength they needed then in order to survive persecution, and which is still a living force making the Sikh Community itself a force to be reckoned with in India today. This institution of the *Khalsa* is Guru Gobind Singh's great contribution to Sikhism. At its beginning it was more or less what we would today call an "underground movement"—but with the enormous added strength of a religious revival.

As the defeated Sikhs clustered around their leader, the Guru called for five volunteers willing to lay down their lives for him. One at a time five Sikhs at the Guru's bidding entered his tent, and after each had disappeared Gobind Singh stepped forth alone holding in his hand his sword dripping with blood. Yet not one of the five shrank from the ordeal. After the fifth had disappeared the Guru called on them to come forth, and the awed beholders saw the five emerge alive—and were told that the blood was from a newly slain goat. Next Guru Gobind Singh poured water into an iron vessel, sweetened it to typify the affection between Sikhs, and stirred it with his sword. He then sprinkled five times each one of the chosen five with the sweetened water, saying as he did so *"Wahiguruji ka Khalsa, Siri Wahiguruji ki fateh"*—"The Khalsa belongs to the Guru, and the Victory is to the Guru," and each repeated it after him. He then asked these five, known henceforth as the *Paunch Pyare*—the five Beloved or Chosen Ones—to baptize him in order to demonstrate the unity and interdependence of Guru and disciples. All the Sikhs then present thereupon received baptism (*Amrit*), and afterwards the Guru gave them the new name *Singh*—a Rajput name meaning Lion. And to this day every baptized Sikh is a Singh, and the ceremony of baptism,[10] performed by five Sikhs who have never broken the Rule, is still the same as originally instituted by Guru Gobind Singh.

After that first baptismal ceremony all present partook of the common food. This practice of eating from the same dish had been started by Guru Nanak as the most practical method of breaking the caste rules, but from now on it became a communion. The food of the communion is always the same dish—a sort of pudding made of wheat flour, sugar, butter and water and probably chosen as a ceremonial food because it is a sweet known all over India. When made ceremonially for temple use by the Sikhs it is cooked in an iron vessel and stirred with a sword. It is dispensed at the close of every service in a Sikh Temple, and must be eaten then and there. It is called by the Sikhs *Kara Prasad,* Holy Food.

Guru Gobind Singh laid down for his followers a daily routine: Rise at 3 A.M., bathe in cold water, meditate on the Name of God, recite certain prayers. In the evening other prayers are recited in-

[10] Both boys and girls are baptized, usually between the ages of 8 and 15. Both select new first names to which the boys add *Singh*, and the girls *Kaur*.

cluding six stanzas from the *Anand*—or blessings; and before going to bed the Sikh recites certain special prayers called *Sohila*—from the verb *sohna*, to sleep. He further ordained for the Sikhs five distinguishing marks, called the five K's because the Punjabi words all begin with K. These are: *Kangha*—a comb of steel, a simple necessity for keeping hair and beard clean and tidy; *Kara*—an iron bracelet worn on the right wrist as a sign both of sternness and restraint; *Kesh*—long hair, symbol of saintliness; *Kirpan*—the sword, instrument of defense and emblem of power and dignity; *Kuch*—shorts, which ensured briskness in action. Guru Gobind Singh prohibited pilgrimages (for reasons of health, having apparently noticed that they produced epidemics) and *Sati*. He also strictly reinforced the prohibition against tobacco and intoxicants of any sort. Meat might be eaten, but the animal must be killed by a Sikh with one blow of his sword, not slowly bled to death according to Muslim custom. He also wrote the *Granth of the 10th Guru* which assumed supplementary authority with the original or *Adi Granth*.

Thus was the *Khalsa* founded and given a set of rules which made for both democracy and health among its members. After the death of Guru Gobind Singh the methods of making community decisions were worked out—but all the later rules are but the natural additions made necessary by the evolution of the community as it grew in size and strength. It is said that Guru Gobind Singh's motives for ending the personal Guruship were mixed. He felt that a personal Guru was no longer needed as the *Granth* contained all that was necessary for the spiritual guidance of the Sikhs, and he also saw the dangers inherent in a dynastic leadership—that the secular interests of the ruler might in time eclipse the spiritual interests of the people. If so, his judgment was correct. For after Ranjit Singh established a secular Empire, some of the Sikhs became proud, rich and luxurious, and forsaking their stern simplicity of life, lost some of their former strength—thus contributing to their defeat by the British. Even so, enough of the old sturdy qualities was left to make the Two Sikh Wars a bitter struggle in which the Sikhs very nearly won.

Guru Gobind Singh lost four of his sons—two slain in battle and two as martyrs, walled up alive in a dungeon by order of Aurungzeb because they refused to accept Islam. When told of their deaths, Gobind Singh exclaimed: "What does it matter if these four died, if by their deaths all these other thousands of my sons shall live!"

In 1708 Guru Gobind Singh died, having first declared that there should be no more Gurus. From thenceforth the *Khalsa* and the *Granth Sahib* should be the Guru, and by "diligently searching the hymns of the sacred book" the spirit of the Guru would be found.

Sikhism as it exists today is as much the product of Guru Gobind Singh as of Guru Nanak. One could diagram Sikhism, roughly of course, as follows:

Nanak	Gobind Singh
Sat Nam (True Name)	*Seva* (Service-groups)
Meditation	Organization
Devotion	Social Service

Pertinence of Sikhism Today

The particular features of Sikhism which should recommend themselves for consideration today are: the equality and democracy of the Sikhs. Even Rajah Ranjit Singh, ruler of an Empire which took in the Punjab, plus what is now the state of Kashmir and Jammu, was made to stand among the shoes at the entrance to the Gurudwara as punishment for conduct unbecoming a Sikh. Since shoes in the Orient are considered unclean (that is why they are shed at the entrance to temples and mosques) this was the most humiliating punishment that could be ordered. This tradition of equality and democracy is just as strong today among the Sikhs as it was during the days of Ranjit Singh. The *Khalsa* rules through a system of representatives—the whole *Panth* (Sikh community—as a *congregation*) would be too unwieldy. Before the chosen delegates may even consider a decision they must swear that they are one in the Guru, that there is no unfriendliness among them. A practice that might be adopted for use in international deliberations today with considerable profit! In Sikh temples the *Granth* is paid the highest respect, and this was true even during the lives of the Gurus, for they sat lower than the *Granth*. This is personal humility, and the subjection of the individual to the *spirit* of the Com-

munity. Sikhism puts Truth, Good Behavior, Moral Courage before .
everything. It enjoins personal purity, charity and equality among
its followers. It is open to anyone, man or woman, from any part
of the earth, who will accept baptism and follow the rules laid down
for Sikhs. And for those who fall by the way, whether born in the
faith or converts, there is always open confession, forgiveness and
re-baptism.

Since Guru Gobind Singh

After the death of Guru Gobind Singh while the *Khalsa* and the
Granth constituted the Guru, it was deemed necessary to have some
personal leaders. Sikhs of proven quality were therefore chosen as
leaders, and were called *Sirdars*[11] (sometimes spelled *Sardars*). It
was not intended that the title should be hereditary, but it has
become so. Time has made the organization slightly more formal
and, one might almost say, complex than it was originally. But
these are natural changes. The spirit remains the same.

The memory of Muslim persecution caused the Sikhs, generally
speaking (there were numerous exceptions), to stand by the British
during the Indian Mutiny of 1857. Actually it was because they
"preferred the devil they did not know to the devil they did know"—
but there are many in India who do not understand that, and as a
result the Sikhs became somewhat isolated. British policy towards
them after the Mutiny, as well as their own fighting tradition, has
led many Sikhs to join the British Indian Army and the Police Force
of India. But after Mahatma Gandhi took over the leadership of
the Indian National Movement in 1919 and began his Non-Violent
Revolution, more and more Sikhs have joined the Indian National
Congress, and have gone back to the pacifism originally preached
by Guru Nanak—with certain mental reservations, however, since
both pacifism and militarism belong to their tradition. The Sikhs
are pretty well concentrated in the key province of the Punjab,
which gives the close and solid Sikh minority—only about 6,000,000
strong in the whole country—very great political importance.

Sikhs are to be found in many places outside of India. Wherever
there is a large group of Sikhs there is a *Gurudwara* (Temple) and
a branch of the *Khalsa*. At the *Gurudwara* anyone, of any race or

[11] Sirdar: The one at the head—from *Sir,* head; therefore, leader.

creed, can obtain hospitality. He may sleep there, and use the common kitchen to prepare his food. For the Sikhs hold fast to their ideal of service, and no good Sikh turns down a request for help. The congregation still decides major issues. This is true not only in India, but wherever there are Sikhs—in Shanghai, Hong Kong, Singapore and London, just as in Amritsar. In Vancouver and Victoria, British Columbia—where about 2,000 Sikhs live, and in Stockton, California—centre for the approximately 2,000 Sikhs of California, the *Gurudwara* and the *Khalsa* occupy the same place in the lives of the Sikhs as they do in the Punjab.

The Sikh still shows his devotion to God, the Eternal True Name, by living a normal, healthy, useful and good life. Though there are still certain forms and external symbols—as the long hair, beard and steel bracelet of the orthodox Sikh—these are recognized as being only symbols. The accent is still on Truth, on the Spirit of Devotion that inspires the good life—not on any forms. Wherever there are Sikhs there are living testimonials to the nobility of the doctrines originally preached by Guru Nanak, and to the enduring strength of the Brotherhood of the Pure founded by Guru Gobind Singh. These people praise God in work and play, and help the poor and weak. Sikhism is a strong, vital, living faith, because it has a certain *human warmth* as well as high ethics and true spirituality, and because it is of *practical value* to human beings.

BIBLIOGRAPHY

TEJA SINGH, *Sikhism*.
J. D. CUNNINGHAM, *History of the Sikhs* (1918).
M. A. MACAULIFFE, *The Sikh Religion* (1909), 6 vols.
RATTIGAN, *History of the Sikhs*.
JOHN CLARK ARCHER, *The Sikhs* (1946).
ROBERT ERNEST HUME, *The World's Living Religions*.
DOROTHY FIELD, *The Religion of the Sikhs* (London, 1914).
SADDHU SINGH DHAMI, *The Sikhs* (1943)—a brief but excellent pamphlet (Published by the Sikhs of British Columbia, Canada).
M. A. MACAULIFFE's translation of the *Granth Sahib*.

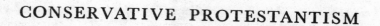
CONSERVATIVE PROTESTANTISM

Born in Melbourne, Australia in 1893, Andrew Rule did his college work at the University of New Zealand (B.A., 1915, M.A., 1916), coming to the United States in 1916. He attended Princeton Theological Seminary where he was awarded a fellowship in apologetics and in 1919 his B.D. degree. Further studies were pursued at Bonn, Germany, and at the University of Edinburgh in Scotland from which institution he was given his Ph.D. degree in 1923 with his thesis on "The Theistic Philosophy of Hermann Lotze." He taught philosophy at Friends University in Wichita, Kansas, and at Illinois College in Jacksonville, Illinois, until his call to become professor of Church History and Apologetics at the Louisville Presbyterian Seminary, Louisville, Kentucky, in 1927. He holds life membership as associate of the Victoria Institute.

Numerous articles on Presbyterian doctrine and polity, including the main article on the "Presbyterian Church" were contributed by him to the recently issued "Encyclopedia of Religion." The conservatism he represents is characterized by breadth and tolerance, always the marks of a scholar. He would be glad to accept, it seems certain, the designation of Calvinism as undergirding his type of conservative faith while at the same time would repudiate association with those whose imprisoned conservatism is designated as Fundamentalism.

Editor

CONSERVATIVE PROTESTANTISM

CONSERVATIVE PROTESTANTISM belongs to and claims to be an authentic, or *the* authentic, form of Christianity. The name "Protestant" derives historically from a formal protest lodged by the evangelical, Lutheran princes against certain actions taken, under strong Roman Catholic pressure, by the Diet of Spires, in 1529. But both the connotation and the denotation of the term have been widened immensely, and, in the process, the edges of its meaning have become ragged. The suggestion of a protest against certain of the doctrines and practices of Roman Catholicism has never been lost, though this element in its meaning varies in prominence and intensity with time and place. In America, for example, it is more prominent in the South and Southwest than in other parts of the country; and, largely latent in the North and East for a considerable time, it has lately been rising into prominence, along with an effort, which is by no means a novelty, to find at least a friendly *modus vivendi* with the Roman Catholic Church.,

But it is only in special situations that the movement called Protestant has had the negative character which the name implies. From first to last, it has been a triumphant, positive affirmation of Christian truth, by ecclesiastical organizations with an affirmative program looking towards a world-wide goal. Once more, the prominence and intensity of this characteristic varies with time, and place, and circumstance; but it has never been lost or repudiated; and, of course, it places Protestantism in a relation of rivalry with other forms of Christianity, with the non-Christian religions, and with every form of secularism and non-belief. This rivalry involves the elaboration, propagation, and defense of a theology which, though it is marked by quite sharp divergences, is also conscious of its unity of interest, of basic religious point of view, and of fundamental philosophy, in relation to the rivals mentioned

215

above. It involves also the active efforts of ecclesiastical organizations which may be, in relation to one another, independent to the point of hostility, but which are clearly aware of their common interest in relation to the common rivals. It still remains true, however, that the negative characteristic of rivalry is not the basic characteristic of Protestantism, but is a consequence of its positive view of God and the world. And it is this positive view that is meant when we speak of Protestant theology or Protestant religion or Protestant Christianity. Conservative Protestants, at least, are convinced that this is the authentic form of Christianity and the only hope for time and for eternity.

But the term "Protestant" has been widened in denotation as well, to include many denominations in addition to the original Lutherans. It is not necessary to enumerate them. There is a general consensus of opinion on that point, though, with regard to some denominations, that opinion is either unformed or unclear or disputed. For example, it seems to be unformed with regard to some of the modern American "sects"; it is unclear in its classification of the Unitarians; and, though most people would probably include the Baptists as Protestants, many of the latter, because of the term's implication of a historical connection with the Reformation, reject such a classification. However, the term "Protestant" is sufficiently clear in its denotation as to call for no further definition at this point.

The term "conservative" in our title serves to mark off a group of Protestants, which may be found represented in all the Protestant denominations, from certain other groups which are similarly distributed. Opinions differ as to the number of the other groups, but we propose to distinguish three—the Fundamentalists, the Liberals, and the Modernists. In the heat and the sinuosity of controversy, all of these terms have tended to become epithets of approbation to those who claim them, and of reprobation to those who reject them, until they serve often as little better than triggers to release emotional responses which decrease in clarity and fairness as they increase in intensity. We shall endeavor to employ them merely as descriptive terms, giving them each a meaning which, we trust, will be acceptable to those who claim them. It should not be difficult thus to define or describe the systems involved; but the classification of individuals in terms of these systems is a very different matter. We shall not attempt it. And so we are not in a position to furnish statistics of the various groups beyond hazarding the guess that the great majority of modern Protestants really fall within the conservative group, though many of them are more or less consciously affected by the propaganda of one or another of the other groups. That is to say, they really are conservatives, but they are partly inclined towards fundamentalism, or modernism, or liberalism, or are so confused by the rival propagandas that they know not where they stand. The fundamentalists, liberals and modernists, in other words, seem to us to be minority groups within Protestantism.

The term "conservative" serves admirably to express the fact that the Protestants who are thus described are clearly conscious of, and prize highly, their historical continuity with the Christian tradition. They see Christian history as, among other things, a process of exploring the essential nature and the wider implications of a redemptive truth "once for all given to the saints." They are convinced that, in the creative period which ended with the death of Augustine, the Church was, in its major decisions as to doctrine, guided aright by the Holy Spirit as it rejected heresies and formulated its creeds. They affirm that the progress was resumed by the great reformers of the sixteenth century and that the resulting creeds of the seventeenth century were essentially correct formulations of Christian doctrine. They freely acknowledge that all human counsels may err and have erred; and so they do not elevate these creeds to the position of primacy over the Scriptures, nor do they employ them to rule out new insights. But the system of truth which appears in this historical development and, with greater or less adequacy, in all of these creeds is, in the judgment of conservatives, sound Christianity. In confronting other teaching, these creeds are employed, not as shackles, but as guides; and any teaching which departs radically, or seems to do so, is regarded with strong suspicion or is rejected. That is the attitude and conviction which the term "conservative" is intended to express, and, when so understood, it is a good adjective.

But, from another point of view, this term may seem to carry implications which the true conservative would unhesitatingly and most emphatically reject. It may seem to imply, and the charge has often been made, that conservatives employ a chronological appeal to the past as a final and decisive criterion in deciding questions of validity. They are thought to reject the new because it is new, and to accept the old because it is old. Now, it is true that a man who has intelligently accepted the conservative position approaches the new with a great deal more caution than he now displays towards the historic creeds. The reason, however, is a practical one merely. He has already examined the historic creeds, applying to them, not chronological tests, but the tests appropriate to questions of validity; and his mind has been satisfied by the result. Also, he is aware that these creeds have long been subject to the stern testing of the historical process, and have met that test. The new, on the other hand, has not yet been subjected to such a personal or historical examination. He therefore approaches it hopefully but cautiously. He is cautious towards the new, also, because he observes that much of it represents hasty inference from the newest hypotheses of experts in fields that are not primarily religious or theological, and that pride themselves in the mutability of their doctrines. With regard to this kind of novelty, the conservative would rather wait and see. But the conservative is not opposed to the new on account of its novelty; he approaches it hopefully. And he is not attached to the old because it is old. He trusts it because it has been well tested and revealed to be good; but he hopes for something even better, and he is prepared to change when appropriate evidence shows the way.

In the writings of the Liberals or Modernists, a picture keeps bobbing up of a most unattractive person, called a Fundamentalist. Studied dispassionately, it looks like a figment of the propagandist imagination—a "straw-man" so created that it may easily be demolished, thus fostering the illusion that all opposition has been destroyed—a caricature formed, by misunderstanding and (probably unconscious) misrepresentation, out of materials garnered from the more rigid and bellicose of the conservatives. This impression is supported by the fact that these writers commonly imply, if they do not explicitly assert, that this is an authentic picture of the opponents, who are all lumped together as Fundamentalists. Occasionally, also, the label "conservative" is attached to the same picture. Possibly a conservative is allowing the wish to be father to the thought when he hesitates to believe that all opponents of Liberalism are as ignorant, as inflexible, as close-minded, and as ugly in spirit as they are thus represented; or, in fact, that such persons, if any exist, are confined to only one theological party. One fact, however, is quite certain. If such persons are to be found among the opponents of Liberalism, they are not representative of the conservatism which we are endeavoring to characterize. For these alleged Fundamentalists, so we are told, are attached to the old because it is old, and have their minds closed towards anything new simply because it is new. They are hostile to science, because, in their attachment to old formulae, they are afraid of the truth. Their attitude towards anything new is "yes, but . . ." The true conservative, as we have stated, refuses to submit questions of validity to chronological tests. He is not afraid of the truth, and that is the very reason for his confidence in older statements that have been quite well verified in human experience, and his friendly caution towards novelties. Because of his love for truth he is hopeful of strangers; but he requires them to present adequate and appropriate credentials before he will admit them to the household of truth; and he does not accept mere novelty, or capacity to intrigue and startle, as appropriate credentials. Nor is he unwilling to re-examine and, if necessary, expel any previously admitted member of the household when tested evidence and sound reason require, in spite of a certain reluctance born of affection.

The writers who are properly called Modernists also employ chronological criteria in determining questions of validity. Assuming the optimistic form of evolution, they take it for granted that the basic insights of the contemporary culture are truer than anything previously known and the most reliable guides to further investigation. Since the Modernism that is best known at present is the nineteenth century form, also called Liberalism, it is usual to identify the two; but, when the two terms are strictly defined, Liberalism is not necessarily, and is not now, Modernism, and Modernism is not necessarily Liberalism. If the basic thought-trends of a certain era happened to possess a certain character, the Modernism of that era could agree, in its affirmations, point for point, with those of conservatism. But even if that did occur, one basic point of difference would still distinguish the two. Modernism would make those affirmations for a chronological reason, because, in short, they were "up-to-date"; conservatism would make them for a very different reason, which we hope to make clear presently.

For the moment we will merely say that, in contrast with alleged Fundamentalism and with Modernism, conservatism rests on belief in a supernaturally given and supernaturally received revelation, coming into the historical process from One that dwelleth in eternity—coming, therefore, to every age, past, present and prospective, to commend and sustain and develop its values and to judge its errors and deficiencies. The ultimate appeal of conservatism is to that eternal truth; and any use which it may make of chronological considerations is subordinate and merely practical. This brings us to a consideration of the subject of revelation.

In the present state of theological discussion, probably no doctrine more insistently demands, or would more richly reward, a sound and, above all, a comprehensive reconsideration than this. During the past century and a half, much useful work has been done; but each of the various theological schools has been vigorously pursuing its own partial insight or emphasis, with a negative attitude towards the equally useful and partial approaches of the others. And this negative attitude has introduced narrowness and error into the doctrines of the several schools, and confusion into the discussion as a whole. The time seems ripe for comprehensive evaluation, and for integration of valid results. The conservative is fairly sure that, when this task has been accomplished, the resulting doctrine of revelation will be his own, extended and enriched perhaps but not radically changed.

The conservative has always maintained that revelation involves a supernatural incursion from eternity into time; and so he is prepared to look hopefully to the Barthian emphasis on that point. Two things, however, seem to be defective in the Barthian presentation of this truth. On the one hand, in their violent reaction against the immanentism and psychologism of Liberal doctrine, the Barthians have adopted a transcendentism which is as one-sided as the Liberal immanentism. The truth seems to lie, not halfway between the two, nor in a simple addition of the two, but in a higher synthesis; and the conservative feels that he knows what that synthesis is. On the other hand, in their attitude to the Scriptures, the Barthians have uncritically adopted too many of the results of a Criticism which was based on the very principles which, in their theology, the Barthians have rejected. Many of these critical results, so the conservative is assured, are really speculative implications of the principles of Naturalistic Humanism and not inductions from empirically tested facts. Once the Barthians—and the Realists also—discover that truth, the ground will have been cleared for a great advance.

Conservatives have always known that, though the revelation comes out of eternity, it comes into, and becomes a part of, the historical process. They, therefore, look hopefully to Troeltsch and his school, to the Social Theologians, and to those neo-Orthodox theologians who have rediscovered the importance of history. But the Social Theologians, in their desire to be simply scientific and to eschew all philosophy, deprived themselves of the power to evaluate, except in so far as they surreptitiously introduced a philosophy. And when they did that, it was an inadequate, naturalistic Instrumentalism to which they turned. Troeltsch and many of the neo-Orthodox more openly employ a philosophy, but it, too, is unduly naturalistic; and many of the neo-Orthodox narrow their consideration of revelation by confining it to divine acts and excluding divine statements. Conservatives are assured that, in germ at least, they have the truth of this matter and can readily incorporate whatever values may be contained in the teachings of these historical schools.

Conservatives, except where their thinking has been unduly influenced by a "low" conception of the Church, coming out of the English dissenting tradition and out of the "social contract" theory of the eighteenth century, have always recognized the function of the Church in relation to revelation. They have valued the Catholic emphasis on this function, but found it vitiated by a false doctrine of the nature of the Church. They value the modern Protestant emphasis on the Church, but feel that the doctrine of the Church with which it operates is still embryonic and confused. They even see an element of truth in the Liberal contention that it was the Church which created the Scriptures, rather than the Scriptures the Church; though they also detect, and have the answer for, the serious error in that doctrine.

Conservatives have always known that revelation cannot be a completed act until it is appropriated by the human mind, and that, from this point of view, revelation must be a continuing process. They are prepared, therefore, to welcome and make use of any real values that come out of the intense concentration of the Liberals on the psychology of revelation, though they must also insist that this can never be more than a partial treatment of "subjective revelation"; and they are ready to profit by the Liberal contention that, in some sense, revelation is still going on.

Conservatives, finally, have always known that revelation is not confined to the "supernatural revelation" that came through the Hebrew-Christian tradition. They are, therefore, prepared to agree with the Liberals as to the value of Comparative Religions, and to profit from such studies. But they do not rely to nearly the same extent on these studies, and they avoid the naturalism which has thus crept into Liberalism, or been reinforced in it thereby.

If these claims for conservatism are valid, then it must be the basic point of view which preserves, or can contain, the values of the other emphases, while avoiding and correcting their limitations and mistakes. A detailed exposition of the conservative view of revelation would be too lengthy for this brief discussion; but a germinal statement may be sufficient for our purpose.

The doctrine of revelation presupposes belief in a personal God, the creator and providential sustainer and governor of all, Who has willed to bring His human children into a relation of fellowship with Himself, and Who, to that end, has taken the initiative in making known to them enough of His Nature and purpose and of their need and the remedy. Such revelation involves the divine self-communication and a human appropriation. The former is called Objective, and the latter Subjective, Revelation. Since, as the conservative neither forgets nor denies, it takes both to complete an act of revelation, neither alone should, in strict accuracy, be called revelation. But these terms are convenient; they need not occasion confusion; and they are employed for lack of better terms.

As Creator and Providential Governor, God may be known inferentially through a study of the works of His hand; and, though they have purposes and rights of their own, all the sciences, natural, normative, historical and psychological, together with the whole range of the arts, may be considered as contributory to such a study. They make their contribution, not directly, but through philosophy. Such a study is known as Natural Theology, and the process wherein God thus makes Himself known is called the Natural Objective Revelation.

But, as Father, God never intended that His approach to His

children, and their approach to Him, should be confined to such indirect and uncertain inference. From the beginning, He has come to them directly and personally—that is to say, supernaturally—as historical occasion warranted and as they, or some of them, were prepared and able to receive such an approach. In the fullness of the times, He came in the Person of His Son, the Second Person of the eternal Trinity, Who was able to say, "He that hath seen me hath seen the Father." This Supernatural Objective Revelation may not have been confined to the Hebrew-Christian tradition, but it found its clearest and final and normative realization in that tradition. It was embodied in the whole prophetic, priestly, kingly dispensation of the Old Testament, and found its culmination in the life and words and death and resurrection of Jesus Christ. Certain people, the prophets and the apostles, were chosen by God and uniquely prepared to receive and to transmit this revelation, and such of their writings as have come down to us constitute, in the original autographs, the inspired and authoritative Scriptures.

The terms "natural" and "supernatural" as thus employed offer plenty of scope for the cavilling of a subtle and pedantic mind; but they are convenient and clear enough in their meaning and application for practical purposes, at least until someone can suggest better terms.

In dealing with Subjective Revelation, the conservative is happy to receive all the light which psychology has thrown, or may yet throw, on the process. But he insists that, just as in Objective Revelation God did not confine His approach to the "natural," so in Subjective Revelation there is, and must be, a "supernatural" aspect. Before either the Natural or the Supernatural Objective Revelation can come home to a human personality in such fashion as to lead to that self-commitment wherein salvation consists, there must be an operation of God, the Holy Spirit, renewing the spirit in regeneration, illuminating the mind, and moving the will to conversion.

The conservative is convinced that the Supernatural Objective Revelation ceased, at least until the Second Coming, with the ascension of Christ; and that its authoritative interpretation and transmission ceased with the death of the Apostle John. But he thankfully acknowledges that, in so far as this is a developing world, the Natural Objective Revelation is still going on, and that the whole process of Subjective Revelation, natural and supernatural, is continuing and will continue.

It remains to define certain aspects of conservatism by means of its relations with Liberalism. It may be acknowledged that, by the end of the eighteenth century, the alleged expositions of Protestant orthodoxy had become extremely unsatisfactory. They were "wooden" and dry, and the breathing of a new life was sadly needed. They followed the leading of human logic to an extent, and with an arrogant confidence, which made a drastic lesson in humility a historical necessity. The doctrine of God which controlled their thinking had become so abstract and one-sided that they were led to emphasize the depravity of man to the neglect of man's greatness, and the regeneration of the individual to the neglect of the social results which should follow from such regeneration. A new beginning was certainly called for. It should have been a recovery of full-blooded conservatism through a return to a Christ-like conception of God. Unfortunately, what we received instead was Liberalism.

The Liberals took hold of their problem by emphasizing the greatness of man, and making that the controlling idea. True conservatism has a doctrine of the greatness of man. It is based on a gloriously wonderful divine love and purpose, and so it is a sounder and more brilliant greatness than the best that Liberalism was ever able to achieve. For the Liberals turned, not always consciously perhaps, to naturalistic humanism for their doctrine. Such a doctrine, as naturalistic, is bound to be an unassimilable alien in any true religion, especially in such a supernaturalistic religion as Christianity. And, coming from that strangely jumbled mixture of the glorious and the horrible which is the historical record, it was bound to become unduly romantic in its picture of human greatness and unrealistic in its reluctant acknowledgment of human depravity. As a result, the social gospel based upon it was bound to be superficial. The conservative is not surprised that Liberalism was unable to sustain the shock of the history of the past twenty-five years. He welcomes the willingness of the Realists to look the "dark" facts in the face; but he fears their program to "begin with" such facts. There is too much danger of an ultimate pessimism in such a program.

Why not begin, where any religion must centre and where any sound philosophy or theology must logically begin, with a truly sound doctrine of God—that is to say, with the God and Father of our Lord, Jesus Christ? Deriving it primarily by exegesis from the Scriptures, why not enrich our appreciation of it with all the values that come from the widest possible study of the natural revelation? From that will come a sound understanding of the way of salvation for the individual; and he will be discovered to be, not only an individual, but an essentially social individual. This social individual will appear in all his true greatness and in his desperate depravity, and the superindividual forces of goodness and of evil will be made clear. From this may come a social gospel which is comprehensive and realistic; and social programs that are alluring enough to fire the imagination of the romantic and practical enough to win the allegiance of the hard-headed. This is the message of Protestant conservatism for our day, and for every day.

BIBLIOGRAPHY

The best exposition of the spirit and convictions of Protestant Conservatism is *The Selected Writings of Benjamin Breckinridge Warfield,* 10 vols. (1927) etc.

For an exposition of the basic spirit of Liberalism, see *"Yes, But—,"* by Willard L. Sperry (1931).

A more detailed analysis is D. S. Robinson's *The God of the Liberal Christian* (1926).

For defence of a more conservative view, see J. G. Machen, *Christianity and Liberalism* (1923); and *The Nature and Destiny of Man,* by Reinhold Niebuhr (1943).

THE SOCIETY OF FRIENDS

The fame of "Pendle Hill," a center for religious and social study maintained by members of the Society of Friends at Wallingford, Pennsylvania, is growing. Students from far and near gather at this quiet spot for study and religious discussion. The director of this School for Religious and Social Study is Howard H. Brinton, author of this essay on the religion of the Quakers.

Born at West Chester, Pennsylvania, in 1884 Dr. Brinton took his bachelor's and master's degrees at Haverford College, another master's degree at Harvard and his Ph.D. degree at the University of California (1925). He has been on the faculty of several academic institutions: at the Friends Boarding School in Barnesville, Ohio, Pickering College in Ontario, Guilford College in North Carolina, Earlham College and at Mills College, teaching subjects ranging from mathematics and physics to religion and serving as administrative officer. Besides he has held a number of lectureships in colleges both in England and America. The Society of Friends continues to call upon his time in extensive committee work. His services to his group have included directing publicity work for the American Friends Service Committee and director of child feeding in the plebiscite area in Upper Silesia after World War I.

Other of his published writings (not including those listed in the bibliography to the article) are: "Vocal Ministry and Quaker Worship" (1929); "The Mystic Will" (philosophy of Jacob Boehme) (1930); "A Religious Solution to the Social Problem" (1934); "Sources of the Quaker Peace Testimony" (1941); "Critique by Eternity" (1943); and editor and contributor to two volumes of studies: "Children of Light" (1938) and "Byways in Quaker History" (1944).

Editor

THE SOCIETY OF FRIENDS

HOWARD HAINES BRINTON

Distinguishing Principles. The Society of Friends formed the extreme left wing of the English Reformation. Originating in the middle of the seventeenth century, it was a significant part of the religious revolution which accompanied the political revolution under Cromwell. But the Quakers' true religious ancestry can best be traced, not so much to early Puritanism as to the pre-Reformation mystical sects on the continent of Europe. The Society of Friends should be classified as neither Catholic nor Protestant, but as a third form of Christianity.

The so-called "purification" of Roman Catholicism, begun by the early Puritans, reached its culmination in the Quakers, who made radical efforts to eliminate all the religious practices which they believed had originated since New Testament times. But Quakerism resulted from something more than this process of subtraction. It revived a doctrine, central in the experience of the early Christian church. This was the belief that the Spirit would be poured out upon the congregation ready to receive it. This Spirit, or "that of God in every man," or Christ within, or the Seed of the Kingdom, or the Inward Light, to use some of the many names which the Quakers applied to the Divine Presence in the midst of the worshiping group, unites all the members into a single organic whole, the body of Christ. The individual experience of inward oneness with an invisible Reality is also an experience of the mystical union of individuals with one another. The meeting for worship, in which the Divine Presence is realized through silent communion with God and man, is the most distinctive and perhaps the only distinctive contribution of the Society of Friends to Christian practice. The Quaker Meeting, in this respect, is closer to the altar-centered worship of Catholicism than to the sermon-centered worship of Protestantism.

Second in importance to group-centered inspiration and subordinate to it is individual inspiration. The claim of the early Quakers that they were inspired in the same way, though not to the same degree, as were the prophets and apostles who wrote the Bible, brought them into sharp conflict with the Puritans who had substituted the authority of the Bible for the authority of the Church. To the Quakers, the Bible is *a* word of God, but not *the* Word of God. Since the Bible came from the same Divine Source as does all true inward inspiration, it is a valuable and necessary check on the authenticity of such inspiration. The Light Within is superhuman and no part of man as such, but when unresisted it can permeate and transform man's reason and his conscience. This Light is a source of religious and moral truth, of power to conform to this truth, and of unity not only within the group, but eventually with all men everywhere. Since this Light of Truth is not divided but exists whole in every man, the nearer men come to it the nearer they come to one another.

The implications of these doctrines were revolutionary. In congregational worship no leadership of priest or pastor was necessary. Anyone in the worshiping group might become a vehicle of vocal ministry whose primary function was not so much instruction in belief and in behavior as spiritual guidance in prayer, meditation and worship. There could be no pre-arrangement. To inward baptism of the Spirit and inward communion with God, outward ordinances could add nothing. For this reason, they were given up. There could be no formal singing of hymns, or repeating of prayers, or even reading of Scripture, as few could sincerely put in their own mouths the words of another. Since the Divine Light was in all, there must be complete equality in the meeting: equality of men and women, servants and masters, educated and uneducated.

Because this Light is continually capable of revealing new and living truth, the Friends possess no written statement of belief which has the authority of a creed. But the test of truth is not wholly subjective. There is an objective test in the teachings and work of the historical Christ, as interpreted and vitalized by the Christ Within. The Quakers consider themselves Christians, not simply mystics. The early Friends agreed to much of the Christian theology generally accepted at the time, but they objected to the doctrines of imputed sin and imputed righteousness; they held to the possibility of perfection and complete freedom from sin in this life, and they declared that, since the Light "lighteth every man that cometh into the world," all men, including the ancients and heathens who had never heard of Christ, could be saved if they lived up to the measure of the Light given them.

The group which worships together meets also from time to time, usually monthly, to transact the business of the church. A clerk is appointed to record decisions. Votes are not taken, because all decisions should be reached on a basis of unanimity. Exceptions to this principle sometimes occur, as the degree of unity required depends on the character and urgency of the question. The search for unity succeeds in proportion as the process of attaining unity becomes a religious exercise.

A group of Monthly Meetings combines to form a Quarterly Meeting, and a group of Quarterly Meetings combines to form a Yearly Meeting. The larger meetings do not exist to exert authority over their constituent parts, but to engage in larger undertakings. There is no delegated authority.

The social doctrines of the Society of Friends are derivatives of their religious doctrines. Disobedience to the Light results in inner conflict, but obedience results in peace and serenity of mind. An act is good which creates inward peace, regardless of apparent or immediate outward consequences. Quaker pacifism is not derived primarily from the New Testament nor from facts showing the futility of war, though both these types of arguments are sometimes referred to. The consistent Quaker refuses to fight because, if he fights, the Light in his conscience will give him no peace. War is wrong, not so much because of the physical damage it causes as because of the spiritual damage done to those who participate in it. This doctrine does not entirely eliminate the use of force in the enforcement of law, provided that force is used lovingly and impartially for the good of all concerned. That Quaker pacifism is a fruitful doctrine in the general field of human experience is shown by the fact that it made Quakers pioneers in prison reform, and in the use of non-violent methods in institutions for the mentally ill. After every war within the past three centuries, the Quakers have engaged in rehabilitation, not only to repair physical destruction, but primarily to remedy the spiritual damage caused by hatred and acts of vengeance.

The equalitarian doctrines of the Quakers brought upon them severe persecution by persons who wished to safeguard their status as superiors. The use of the familiar "thou" instead of the then complimentary "you," the elimination of all flattering titles, including mister and mistress, the refusal to remove the hat or bow the knee in salutation, appeared like rudeness to their contemporaries, but the Quaker insistence was intended to stress the doctrine that all men are worthy of equal respect. The Quaker doctrine of simplicity called for avoidance of all superfluity "in dress, speech and behavior." In dress, this resulted for a century and a half in the adoption of a standardized pattern, the object of which was to avoid being victimized by changes in fashion. In speech, it resulted in an extreme endeavor to stick to the simple truth without verbal adornment. Related to this was a practice which resulted in great suffering, the refusal to take a judicial oath. The oath was objected to as recognizing a double standard of truth telling. The old testimony, now happily abandoned, against several forms of art, such as music, the theatre and fiction, came partly from viewing them as untruthful, and partly as superfluities which might distract attention from more important things, rather than from the Puritan belief that they were carnal pleasures, wrong in themselves.

Of great historical importance was the doctrine of religious liberty on behalf of which the Quakers suffered severe penalties as law-breakers for many years. In America, there was no persecution for religious belief in colonies controlled politically by the Quakers,— Pennsylvania, New Jersey, Delaware, Rhode Island, and for a short time, North Carolina. These were, also, the only colonies which had no state-supported church.

History. The history of the Society of Friends may be divided into four periods as follows: (1) the apostolic age, 1650–1700, (2) the age of conservation and cultural creativeness, 1700–1800, (3) the age of conflict and decline, 1800–1900, and (4) the modern period, 1900– . These dates are approximate. Changes took place in different areas at different times.

1. In the apostolic or heroic age in the later seventeenth century, the first Quakers set out, not to found a sect but to bring all Christianity back to what they believed was its primitive state. In 1647, George Fox at the age of 23 discovered "experimentally," as he said, the Christ Within. He soon found other persons who had

similar experience. After 1652, under Fox's leadership, the movement grew rapidly. In spite of violent opposition and persecution, it spread to all parts of England. Fervent Quaker preachers could be found everywhere. They proclaimed their message in the market place, in the fields, in taverns or quiet homes. After the fashion of those days, they even interrupted the minister in the pulpit. Soon they appeared and made converts in various parts of Europe and in all the American colonies. The Quaker invasion of New England is a dramatic story. The Puritans used every device, including hanging, to keep them out, but to no avail. The severest persecution took place in England between 1662 and the Act of Toleration in 1689, during which time there were many thousands of Quakers in prison. More than four hundred died in jail.

2. With the end of persecution, the Quakers emerged as a respectable sect, though losses through fines continued for some time to be heavy because of refusal to pay tithes to the Established Church. To many who had lost all their property in the struggle, the New World became a haven of refuge. The Baptist colony of Rhode Island, holding to religious liberty, received so many Quakers that they controlled its affairs politically until the Revolution. New Jersey was purchased in 1674 and colonized, and Penn received Pennsylvania in 1681, giving it the most liberal charter of its time. For seventy-five years, the Quakers ruled Pennsylvania, resigning their control because their refusal to support the French and Indian War would mean the loss of the charter of the commonwealth. During their rule, they were wholly successful in maintaining peace with the Indians.

In the eighteenth century, the old missionary fervor disappeared, but there continued to be a powerful non-professional itinerant ministry. The society not only held its own numerically, but gradually increased. A written discipline was developed and strictly enforced. This sharply defined the Quaker way of life, which became a genuine cultural pattern distinct from that around it. In this century, largely under the leadership of John Woolman, members of the Society of Friends freed their slaves. As a result of the struggle over slavery, most Friends in Virginia and the Carolinas after 1800 migrated to the old Northwest.

3. The synthesis of mystical inwardness and evangelical outwardness was a source of strength to early Quakerism. At the beginning

of the nineteenth century, the evangelical elements were accentuated by the influence of the Wesleyan revival and the original synthesis was weakened. In England, there were tensions but no important separations occurred. English Quakers were busy in an effort to abolish the slave trade, to reform prisons and to carry out works of philanthropy. Numbers and spiritual vitality declined, although there was toward the end of the century an awakened intellectual interest in Quaker history and thought.

American Quakerism in the nineteenth century was torn by divisions. The most important of these occurred in 1827, when the elders of Philadelphia forbade the preaching of Elias Hicks, a prominent minister from Long Island. Hicks was a pure mystic, to whom historical Christianity meant little. Those who sided with him claimed that the separation was caused solely by an undue exercise of authority against an approved minister, while their opponents, the so-called Orthodox, claimed that the tension was due to the denial by Hicks of the divinity of Christ. As the country Friends were mainly followers of Hicks, we have here an example of the long-brewing rebellion of the country against the growing domination of the city. This separation spread from Philadelphia to other Yearly Meetings.

In 1845, a new separation began in New England. John Wilbur accused Joseph John Gurney, a prominent English Friend then travelling in America, of subordinating the inward work of the Spirit to the Bible and the historical events at the rise of Christianity. The resulting separation between the Wilburites and the Gurneyites, like the earlier separation, was a cleavage between the mystical and evangelical trends. Wilbur stood midway between the ultra-mysticism of Hicks and the ultra-evangelical doctrines of Gurney. This separation also spread to various parts of the Society. Philadelphia Yearly Meeting, Orthodox, recognized the Wilburite Yearly Meeting in Ohio, but eventually gave up official correspondence with all groups in order to appease its own small Gurneyite minority.

The differences between the Wilburite or Conservative Friends and the evangelical Gurneyites were widened by the great religious revival which followed the Civil War. The fervor of this movement stirred many Christian churches, including the Gurneyite meetings. A type of travelling evangelist new to the Society of Friends began about 1868 to use revivalistic methods in Quaker meetings. Many converts remained unconvinced of Quaker practices in general, and in particular of the Quaker way of worship. As a result a majority of the meetings throughout the West, New England, and the South changed their way of worship to a programmed service of the usual Protestant type, conducted by a professional pastor. These groups usually call themselves "The Friends Church," as distinguished from "The Society of Friends."

From the beginning, Friends emphasized the need for education of all their members, but as compared with the Puritans, they were slow in creating colleges because they did not feel the need for a trained and scholarly ministry. Also they distrusted the intellectual emphasis which encourages men to rely too much on human wisdom. A life-long self education was stressed by many as the soundest way of making the proper use of spiritual gifts. In the eighteenth century, almost every meeting in America had beside it an elementary day school. In the first half of the nineteenth century, co-educational boarding schools and academies were developed, and in the latter half, nine colleges were established. Throughout this century, Friends were also busily engaged in promoting education among the negroes and Indians. Their greatest single achievement was their work for negro freedmen after the war between the states.

4. The twentieth century finds in America a great variety in faith and practice under the name of "Friends." The chief groups are as follows:

The *Friends General Conference* (or Hicksite) group holds a general conference without legislative authority every two years, and maintains a central office at 1515 Cherry Street, Philadelphia. It is made up of six yearly meetings with a total membership of 17,761. Its chief organ is *The Friends Intelligencer.*

The *Conservative* (or Wilburite) group has no headquarters, though its chief center is the Friends Boarding School at Barnesville, Ohio. It is made up of five yearly meetings, with a membership of about 3,000. As its meetings are mostly rural, it has suffered through migrations to the city. Closely allied to this group is *Philadelphia Yearly Meeting* (Orthodox) with a membership of 5,133 and headquarters at 302 Arch Street, Philadelphia. Its periodical is *The Friend,* published fortnightly.

The most important recent event in Quakerism has been the

spontaneous growth of more than a hundred *Independent Meetings* in all parts of the country whose members are drawn from several branches or from none. These new meetings are all non-pastoral, and held on a basis of silence. Many of them are giving up their independent status to join a larger, regularly constituted body, or in some instances, to avoid partiality, by joining more than one larger body.

The groups listed above adhere to the historical Quaker type of worship based upon silent waiting. Of the groups which generally have, or which include, programmed religious services, the *Five Years Meeting* comprises eleven yearly meetings with a total membership of 69,964. These yearly meetings send delegates to the superior meeting held every five years. The headquarters of the Five Years Meeting is at 101 South Eighth Street, Richmond, Indiana, where its organ, *The American Friend,* is published. It supports missionary work in Africa, Asia and Central America. Many local meetings in the eastern yearly meetings of this group are of the non-pastoral type.

A group of four *independent pastoral yearly meetings,* Ohio, Kansas, Oregon, and Central in Indiana, hold a more pronounced evangelical theology and make a wider use of revivalistic methods, often approximating the Pentecostal or Holiness type. They have a total membership of 18,262. Their chief organ is *The Evangelical Friend.* Foreign missions are a primary interest of this group.

In general and cutting across the old distinctions which are ceasing to have their former importance, the Society of Friends in America today may be divided into three approximately equal groups: those who adhere to the historical Quaker practice in worship, the pastoral-modernist and the pastoral-fundamentalist. The first is slowly increasing; the second, which contains many community churches, is slowly decreasing; while the fundamentalist groups continue numerically about the same.

Since the Quakers hold to a highly non-authoritarian form of church government, separations among them are not as significant as would otherwise be the case. Unity is rapidly increasing among the various meetings in the eastern United States, where the more conservative tendencies prevail. All branches of the Society in New England have reunited. Many meetings in the New York, Philadelphia and Baltimore areas are affiliated with more than one branch.

The two Philadelphia Yearly Meetings have long shared most of their enterprises, and in 1946 they constituted a General Meeting in which distinctions are eliminated. In 1920, in London, and in 1937 at Swarthmore College, Pennsylvania, conferences were held at which all Quaker bodies in the world were represented.

The Society of Friends in England (London Yearly Meeting) has a present membership of 21,812. Its chief organ is *The Friend*, of London. Its headquarters is Friends House, Euston Road, London. Membership has considerably increased during the past fifty years, furnishing a number of leaders in religion, education, social reform and politics. The resistance to conscription of Quaker pacifists during the First World War, when many went to prison, won a special status for English pacifists during the Second World War. English Friends have engaged in extensive relief work during and after these wars. Closely associated with them in these undertakings is Dublin Yearly Meeting, with a membership of 1,990.

Groups of Friends exist in Australia, China, Denmark, France, Germany, Holland, India, Japan, New Zealand, Norway, Palestine, South Africa, Sweden, and Switzerland. Though small, these bodies exert an influence out of all proportion to their numbers. In Germany and France during the last war, local Friends had an opportunity to perform special services to persons in acute need because of persecution or privation. These groups practice the characteristic Quaker ways.

The best known recent development in American Quakerism is the American Friends Service Committee with headquarters at 20 South 12th Street, Philadelphia. It was organized in 1917 for reconstruction work in France by conscientious objectors to war. Since then, in collaboration with the corresponding but older English committee, it has carried out relief work on a large scale in many countries of Europe and Asia in World Wars I and II. It has also engaged at home in a variety of enterprises including care of refugees, the organization of work camps for college students, promotion of international and interracial understanding and education for peace through institutes and seminars.

The American Friends Fellowship Council and the Friends World Committee for Consultation are two other agencies which represent all branches of Friends. The Fellowship Council looks after new, independent meetings, intervisitation among meetings, and the *Wider Quaker Fellowship,* a group of about 4,000 persons scattered all over the United States who wish some affiliation with the Society of Friends, but who do not desire to join it. The World Committee for Consultation seeks to increase mutual interest and understanding among all groups of Friends in the world through publications, intervisitation and conferences.

The modern member of the Society of Friends is much more keenly aware of the history of his sect, and of the place which it holds among Christian bodies and in world religion than was the Friend of a generation or two ago. This is largely due to the growth of educational conferences, summer schools, study groups and institutions for adult education in religious and social subjects, such as Woodbrooke in England and Pendle Hill in America. Most Friends today attend college. The effect of higher education has frequently been to modify the older type of mysticism, sometimes completely erasing the distinction between mystical and rational insight. As a result, there is now a greater emphasis on the immanence and less emphasis on the transcendence of the Inward Light. There is more dependence on thinking and less on feeling. But the recent growth of new meetings in the neighborhood of colleges and universities does not necessarily mean that Quakerism is becoming a religion for intellectuals. The intellectual often seeks the silence of a Quaker meeting because he feels the necessity of penetrating below the rationalizing surface of his mind to the inner depths of being where the meaning and significance of life can be discovered.

The old tension between mystic and evangelical is replaced in many areas today by a corresponding variance in point of view between a Quakerism which emphasizes the cultivation of the inward life and a humanitarian Quakerism which finds its principal expression in remedial works. The evangelical who stresses an improved status in the world to come is replaced by the exponent of a social gospel who desires to improve conditions in this world. The type of mind is the same, though a shift has taken place from the religious to the secular. Most members of the Society of Friends realize that a synthesis of the way of Mary and the way of Martha is better than is either way alone, though differences of emphasis must continue because of differences of temperament.

The modern Quaker believes that mystical faith can contribute a needed element in religion today. Because it is primarily based on living experience rather than on outward authority, Quakerism is compatible with contemporary science, and has no fear of losing anything through scientific discovery. But modern science has directed its attention to gaining power over the external world. This brings neither peace nor happiness. Peace and order will not come in the outer world until they first come within. Chaos in the world today is a reflection of the inner chaos in the soul of man. Quakerism offers one means for obtaining inward peace and order. In the silence of prayer and worship, enlivened by the united efforts of a group, there comes out of the depths of the soul strength and order which can overcome conflict, unify the inner life and the life of the group, and produce the only kind of peace which can propagate itself in the outer world. The history of the Society of Friends shows that, when the conscience becomes sensitized by such a process, actions tend to follow which are in accordance with the dictates of conscience. For this reason, members of the Society of Friends have become pioneers in such fields as religious liberty, prison reform, the abolition of slavery, the effort to abolish war, the education of negroes and Indians, the treatment of the mentally ill, the equality of the sexes, and a type of religious democracy which developed into political democracy. The present day function of the Society of Friends is to aid all men everywhere to create such a sensitivity of conscience that social pioneering will continue.

BIBLIOGRAPHY

GEORGE FOX, *The Journal of George Fox* (Everyman's Library).
JOHN WOOLMAN, *The Journal of John Woolman* (Whittier edition, Houghton Mifflin).
ROBERT BARCLAY, *Apology for the True Christian Divinity* (Friends Book Committee, Philadelphia).
W. C. BRAITHWAITE, *The Beginnings of Quakerism* (1912).
———, *The Second Period of Quakerism* (1919).
RUFUS M. JONES, *Quakers in the American Colonies* (1923).
———, *The Later Periods of Quakerism* (1921).
———, *The Faith and Practice of the Quakers* (1938).
A. NEAVE BRAYSHAW, *The Quakers, Their Story and Message* (1938).
ELBERT RUSSELL, *The History of Quakerism* (1942).
WILLIAM WISTAR COMFORT, *The Quaker Way of Life* (1942).
ISAAC SHARPLESS, *A Quaker Experiment in Government* (1902).

ALLEN C. THOMAS, *A History of Friends in America* (1905).
MARGARET E. HIRST, *The Quakers in Peace and War* (1923).
AUGUSTE JORNS, *The Quakers as Pioneers in Social Work* (1931).
A. RUTH FRY, *Quaker Ways* (1933).
MARY HOXIE JONES, *Swords into Plowshares* (1937).
HOWARD H. BRINTON, *Creative Worship* (London, 1931).
———, *Quaker Education in Theory and Practice* (1940).
———, *A Guide to Quaker Practice* (1943).

THE CHURCH OF THE
NEW JERUSALEM

The Swedenborgian Church finds itself admirably represented in this volume by William F. Wunsch, one of its distinguished theologians and churchmen of today.

Born at Detroit, Michigan, in 1882, he was educated at the University of Michigan (LL.B., 1906, B.A., 1908) and graduated from the church's own seminary (New-Church Theological School) in 1909. His professional career has been spent in the service of his church: ordained to its ministry in 1909; minister at Bath, Maine, 1909–1912; at Roxbury, Mass., 1912–1916; instructor at his theological alma mater, professor of theology, of Biblical languages and literature and principal, during the years 1909 until 1935; minister, Waltham, Mass., 1919–1935, summer preacher at Little Harbor Chapel, Portsmouth, N. H., since 1927, minister of the Church of the Neighbor, Brooklyn Heights, N. Y., 1935–1943, and minister of the National New Church, Washington, D. C., since 1943. He has served on important boards of the church, its Board of Missions, director of the New-Church Board of Publication, chairman of the Board of Managers, the New-Church Theological School as well as director of the Swedenborg Publishing Association.

Besides serving as editor of the "New-Church Review," 1917–1934, and of "The New Christianity," 1935–1943, he has issued books dealing with matters of the faith of his church: compilations and translations of Swedenborg, "The World Within the Bible" (1929), "A Practical Philosophy of Life" (1937) and two other volumes listed in the article's bibliography.

Editor

THE CHURCH OF THE NEW JERUSALEM

WILLIAM FREDERIC WUNSCH

THE CHURCH of the New Jerusalem, with a constituency chiefly in the United Kingdom and in the United States, but represented also in most parts of the globe, was organized in London, England, in 1787. The Church of the New Jerusalem is the official name. Members refer to it more briefly as the New Church; more generally it is known as the Swedenborgian Church.

In England and Scotland the General Conference of the New Church, organized in 1789 and since 1815 meeting annually, administers the affairs of the church at large. In the United States the General Convention of the New Jerusalem, which also meets annually and has been in existence since 1817, serves the like purpose. In addition to the General Convention there is in the United States the General Church of the New Jerusalem, which has existed as a separate body since 1890, and has headquarters at Bryn Athyn, Pa. There are smaller organizations in Europe and in the Philippines, and a conference in Australia similar to the British Conference.

On the whole the polity of the church is congregational, local churches engaging their ministers and freely conducting their activities. An exception to the polity is found in the General Church of the New Jerusalem, which recognizes three distinct grades in the ministry: minister, pastor and bishop. In the General Convention there are indeed Presiding Ministers in the state or other Associations which directly constitute that body, and these Presiding Ministers are often General Pastors, in whom the power is vested, under Convention or Association, to ordain.

The General Convention, made up of the clergy and of lay delegates from the Associations, meets annually for a week or more to handle the business and the ecclesiastical affairs of the church.

A General Council of the body conducts matters the year around. A Council of Ministers, meeting before Convention, initiates and conducts matters pertaining to the ministry, but its action is usually still to be approved by the general body. Officers of the Convention are a President, Vice-president, Executive Secretary (offices at 815 Boylston St., Boston 16, Mass.), Recording Secretary and Treasurer.

The liturgy of the church, first given form in England, resembles the Episcopalian. The Convention publishes a *Book of Worship,* which offers a standard of services of all kinds, and a hymnal, *The Magnificat,* many hymns in which, music and words, are the composition of members of the church. Both books have been undergoing revision for several years. The Holy Supper is celebrated quarterly in most of the churches. Baptism, which is by sprinkling, is into the name of the Father and of the Son and of the Holy Spirit, and is administered to infant or adult. The rite of confirmation also obtains.

As part of it or affiliated with it, the General Convention gathers about it a number of other bodies. The New-Church Board of Publication is its official publishing arm, issuing not only the *Book of Worship* and the hymnal, but also the official bi-weekly church paper, *The New Church Messenger.* The main publishing house of the church in this country, The Swedenborg Foundation (New York), maintaining translation and publication of Swedenborg's Theological Works, is an independent organization. There are a number of other publishing agencies, putting out either Swedenborg's works, like the Iungerich Trustees (Philadelphia), or periodicals and tracts, like the American New-Church Tract and Publication Society (Philadelphia). Book rooms are maintained in many cities. Besides *The Messenger* there is a quarterly, *The New Christianity,* published independently. The General Church publishes a magazine, *The New-Church Life.* Members of the General Convention and of the General Church share in a Swedenborg Scientific Association, which also publishes a quarterly, *The New Philosophy.* The women of the church are organized in state alliances and a national alliance. The young people have a national league, with a monthly journal.

In the present century the Convention's Board of Home and Foreign Missions has seen its work grow as never before. Missions are prosecuted in western Canada, in the southern states, in the West Indies, in the Guianas, in parts of Europe and in South and West Africa, and in India, Burma, China, the Philippines, and Japan. The practice is to employ native missionaries, who are brought to America for their theological training. In church extension the radio has been more and more largely utilized. A Swedenborg Fellowship carries on much of the broadcasting.

The Convention conducts a Theological School at Cambridge, Mass., to train its ministers, missionaries and also lay-leaders; the General Church has a seminary at Bryn Athyn, Pa., and the British Conference one in Woodford Green, Essex. Having connections with the General Convention are two schools, a preparatory school for girls at Waltham, Mass., and a coeducational junior college at Urbana, O. The Convention owns a national church at Washington, and the General Church has a cathedral at Bryn Athyn, Pa.

Religious education is provided for nationally through the American New-Church Sunday School Association. The Convention has a standing Committee on Education. In touch with the federated theological faculties of Chicago University a Swedenborg Philosophical Centre was organized in 1945 with a home near the University. Summer schools are held annually at Almont, Mich., and Fryeburg, Me.; these, like the Centre at Chicago, are independent organizations.

Not all persons who become interested in the teachings of the New Church by reading Swedenborg associate themselves with the institutions of the church. Church members in the United States and Canada at present number about 5,300 in the Convention, 1,300 in the General Church. There are (in 1946) 77 societies and 66 ministers in the Convention (counting only the ministers active on this continent), and 15 societies and 29 ministers in the General Church (many of these ministers are engaged in that body's comprehensive educational institutions). The world-wide membership of the church may be put conservatively at 12,000.

Two events should be mentioned in an account of the Church of the New Jerusalem in the twentieth century. One is the observance in London in 1910 of the centenary of the Swedenborg Society, the great publishing arm in England. A pronounced interest had arisen among European scientists in Swedenborg's science and philosophy, notably in that production of his earlier period, *The*

Brain. A superb edition of his scientific and philosophical works was edited and issued under the auspices of the Swedish Academy of Sciences and with the help of distinguished scientists in Sweden and elsewhere. An International Congress met July 4–8, attended by four hundred representatives of the church and of the sciences from the United Kingdom, the United States, Canada, Australia, India, France, Germany, Austria, Switzerland, Spain, Holland, Belgium, Sweden and Norway. The King of Sweden was patron, and a member of the Swedish House of Nobles, to which Swedenborg had belonged, was honorary chairman. The Swedish government had also provided a sarcophagus in Upsala Cathedral for the remains of Swedenborg, and took his remains there aboard a Swedish vessel from London, where he had died in 1772.

The other occasion is the celebration in 1938 of the 250th anniversary of Swedenborg's birth, a celebration again attended by scientists and representatives of philosophy as well as of the church. The main observances took place in London and New York, lesser ones in both countries and elsewhere, with unusual newspaper coverage. The Swedish government put out commemorative stamps. Like the London Congress of 1910, the meetings in 1938 were much concerned with the due alliance of science, philosophy and religion.

Besides expanding its missionary work in these decades, the General Convention has shown a growing interest in the social application of Christian principles. The church's especial teachings make much of the unity of the human family, the principle of neighborliness in national and international policy, and the embodying of the spiritual life in the educational, economic and industrial life of society. Committees were named on the Social Aims of the Church and on a Just and Lasting Peace; their reports served for discussion in conferences and forums.

Like other churches, the church found the recruiting of ministers more difficult during and after the world wars. In England and on the European continent, in Japan and in the Philippines, it suffered loss of life and property; London churches suffered heavy property loss, and on the Continent buildings and books were confiscated by the Germans. Besides material rehabilitation, a decline in membership called urgently for attention. Membership figures and the work of the church compared disturbingly with the peak growth in the latter half of the nineteenth century. In those years the contrasting doctrines of the various denominations held public interest, and the teachings of the New Church made their appeal. It was enough to present them, quite for their own sake. But interest moved to Christian experience, to the service rendered by a doctrine to life, and to application and significance. A new outlook on message and work was indicated, slowly to be given expression in the re-shaping of the church's work. An effort has been made to compose a literature in the altering outlook.

In none of its organizations has the Church of the New Jerusalem promulgated a creed at the hand of a council or otherwise. Congregations do recite a "Faith." As its opening words let it be known, this is an act of worship.

We worship the One God, the Lord, the Saviour Jesus Christ, in whom is the Father, the Son, and the Holy Spirit; whose Humanity is Divine; who for our salvation did come into the world and take our nature upon Him. He endured temptation, even to the passion of the cross. He overcame the hells, and so delivered man. He glorified his Humanity, uniting it with the Divinity of which it was begotten. So He became the Redeemer of the world. Without Him no mortal could have been saved; and they are saved who believe in Him and keep the commandments of his Word. This is his commandment: that we love one another, as He hath loved us (*The Book of Worship*, p. 7).

These affirmations of Christian faith are taken from the Theological Works of Swedenborg; they come, in fact, from his culminating work, *True Christian Religion*. One or two of the affirmations recite a fact recorded in the Gospels ("He endured temptation"); others voice a common Christian conviction ("He became the Redeemer of the world"); and all reflect main teachings of the church.

Worship and prayers in the New Church are addressed to "the Lord God, the Saviour Jesus Christ, in whom is Father, Son and Holy Spirit." The one God came in Christ, manifested Himself in Him, and wrought in Him. He brought Himself near, and in that nearness is to be worshiped, according to the teaching of the New Church. Known in Christ, He is called the Lord God, the

Saviour Jesus Christ. Nor was He made known in Christ only for thirty-three years; all that the Christ became, by making His Humanity altogether God's, is forever God manifest. The New Church therefore speaks of God in the depths of His Being, or the Father; and God manifest in His Divine Humanity, or the Son; and God as He imparts Himself, or the Holy Spirit, as the one God, the Lord Jesus Christ. The teaching of the New Church thus offers a synthesis of unity and trinity in one Divine Person, who is visible to thought, tangible to prayer, and close to human life and experience.

Besides alluding to so much of the doctrine about God, the Faith gives a glimpse into another main teaching. The work of the Christ was a redemption of the world. This entailed an encounter with evil. Contact with evil was effected in the assumption of our nature with all its habitual inclinations. The Lord "endured temptation, even to the passion of the cross." He met the mass of human perversity and overcame the "hells." He put the enemies of human life and integrity under His power, and placed men in free pursuit again of their best life. Redemption was not salvation, but opened the way to it. Redemption was a reordering of man's whole moral and spiritual environment, even in the unseen world, to the expediting of the spiritual life on earth.

Salvation, in the terms of the Faith, is a manner of living, not merely a way of believing. It is more than the conviction that in Christ God effected a redemption of the world. Then must follow man's part and response. He has his life to live in the power of the redemption. With that help he has a life to attain which is motivated by love of God and charity to the neighbor. "This is his commandment: that we love one another, as He hath loved us."

The reference in the Faith to "hells," overcome by the Lord, glances at still another teaching of the church. To that teaching the world of the spirit is real, and the Christian hope of immortality can become an informed conviction and not be left a vague hope. The world of the spirit pervades our present world. The human being enters it consciously soon after the body is laid aside. Meanwhile we all are living in the midst of influences from that world. There the moral and spiritual gains of the race are garnered, and in it are all who embody those gains. These make the heavens. Also to be found in the immortal world are all the unrepented iniquities and deliberate perversions of humanity, and the men and women who embody them. These are the "hells" of which the Faith speaks. Intermediate between the heavens and the hells is a vast realm of indeterminate life into which most persons first come, there to make or complete their choices and settle their life one way or the other. In the present world we are living in spirit in this intermediate realm, learning our way, under influences out of the hells and out of the heavens.

The prominence of the thought about the spiritual world in the teaching of the New Church is owing to many things. For one thing, Swedenborg has much to disclose about that world, as he says, "from things heard and seen." During the last thirty years of his life, he solemnly averred, his consciousness was extended into the unseen world, chiefly by the avenues of the spirit's sight and hearing. He did not, of course, leave this world. He counsels earnestly against curious effort to communicate with the other world; the veiling of consciousness from it is the intended order of things. His unusual experience attended on a mission. This mission will be described in a moment; without it there would have been no sufficient ground or explanation for the experience granted him, which he always deemed an ineffable privilege.

The prominence of the thought of the spiritual world, however, is due also to various necessities of religious thinking. To speak at all adequately about Providence, for instance, means to speak of human destiny and of the goals in which history issues, and these goals and this destiny lie beyond time and space in the immortal world. The incarnation of God on earth involves a passage of His life from far above the spiritual world down through it. Truth uttered by God and finding expression in a Scripture descends through a higher grasp of the eternal Word in the immortal world —and that higher grasp is involved in our Scriptures, like a deeper sense in them. Actively thought with, therefore, and giving each chief doctrine of the New Church its shape, is an idea of the world of the spirit, of its reality, and of its active part in life here and now.

The especial teachings of the New Church deal with all the subjects and questions of the Christian faith, not only God and Christ, redemption, salvation, immortality and the world of the spirit, Providence and Incarnation, but also with the nature of man, conscience, free will, evil and sin and the distinction between them, forgiveness, charity, the processes of rebirth, the religious history of the planet, the Scriptures, revelation in general, baptism, the Holy Supper—practically any subject matter of the Christian Gospel that might be named. In the English translations into which they have been done from the Latin, Swedenborg's Theological Works amount to more than thirty stout volumes.

Filling all Swedenborg's works is the conviction that a first Christian age has been drawing to a close, and a second age is beginning. This new development is what he means by a "new church," and his mission was to herald and serve it. The truths that would inspire it are what he sought to put into words. At fifty-five years of age he turned from a concern with science and philosophy, and did so with a richly informed intellect, to this concern with Christianity. He felt divinely called to do so. He did not at once appreciate that the development he was to serve was a fulfilment of the Lord's promise to come again; that realization came as he pursued and understood his work. The Lord's return would be one in spirit and in truth. Leaving the creeds aside for the most part, Swedenborg formulated anew the teachings of the Scriptures in a body of doctrine (*New Jerusalem and its Heavenly Doctrine, The Four Leading Doctrines, True Christian Religion*). He expounded a spiritual sense in Scripture, leaving exegesis of the more obvious meanings to continue on its course (*Arcana Coelestia, Apocalypse Explained, Apocalypse Revealed*). Two works (*Divine Love and Wisdom, Divine Providence*) are of a more philosophical nature, and present a concept of the world as a spiritual-natural world, created and guided by a love and wisdom that are one and infinite. There are still other books and other bodies of thought. So little was any of this wealth of teaching his (his religious ideas from his earlier period were drastically revised), that Swedenborg did not set his name to these volumes for many years, and when he did, subscribed himself "servant of the Lord Jesus Christ."

The teachings of the New Church exalt the Word which we have in our Scriptures as "the crown of revelations" (*True Christian Religion*, No. 11), and aim to renew the power of the Christian Gospel in thought and life. Swedenborg criticized many a dogma prevalent in his day—the reliance on a mode of belief, for example, for salvation, the theory of predestination, the persuasion that non-Christians are lost if they are without a knowledge of

Christ, the notion that infants who die are disadvantaged hereafter for lack of being baptized. The doctrines which he strove to separate from Christian thought have for the most part lost their hold. And in the doctrines of a "new" church he was intent, not on formulating beliefs, but on laying hold of the truths of mankind's spiritual life. A supreme motto with him was a sentence beginning in his Latin with the words *Nunc licet*—"now it is men's privilege to enter with the understanding into the things of faith." As this path of inquiry and education was taken, the Word in the Scriptures and the Gospel in the churches would benefit by a widespreading new light. In this conviction he sent his books to universities and to leaders among the clergy. He himself founded no church and certainly strove for no personal following. He passed into the spiritual world in 1772, and not until 1787 did readers of his books organize a church, and then in considerable debate over the wisdom and rightness of the step. This debate has had a reflection in very recent years in an earnest consideration in the General Convention of "the aims of a church," to the end that the organizations of the church and all their activities may be addressed, not to separatist aims, but to the essential and common Christian object of promoting the kingdom of God on earth and establishing the spiritual life in the total contemporary culture. The General Convention has welcomed opportunities to participate in local and state church federations and in movements toward Christian unity. The teachings of the New Church picture and enforce memorably the vision and nature of Christian unity.

BIBLIOGRAPHY

For history of the Church of the New Jerusalem:
> *The Rise and Progress of the New Jerusalem*, Robert Hindmarsh (1861).
> *The New Church in the New World*, Marguerite Block (1932).
> *Transactions of the International Swedenborg Congress* (1910).
> Most encyclopedias.

On liturgy:
> *The Book of Worship* (The General Convention, 1912).

For statistics, organization, current efforts:
> *The Journal of the General Convention* (published annually).

Report, 1936, U. S. Department of Commerce, Bureau of the Census, Vol. II, Pt. 1, pp. 499–511.
The Federal Council Year Book.
For current interests and tendencies:
Reports of Committees in The Journal of Convention.
The New Church Messenger.
The New Christianity.
The Significance of Swedenborg for Contemporary Theology (pamphlet), Walter Marshall Horton (1938).
Swedenborg's Vision of a United Christianity (pamphlet), Walter Marshall Horton (1946).
For life-sketches of recent workers:
Dictionary of American Biography, Vol. XV, p. 448 (James Reed); Vol. XVI, p. 606 (Frank Sewall); Vol. XVII, p. 376 (Julian Kennedy Smyth).
The Promise of Peace (1900) in introduction, pp. 5–21, sketch of the life of John Worcester.
On Swedenborg:
Emanuel Swedenborg, J. J. Garth Wilkinson (1886).
The Life and Mission of Emanuel Swedenborg, Benjamin Worcester, 5th ed. (1901).
Swedenborg: Life and Teaching, G. Trobridge (1935).
Swedenborg: a Study of His Development into Mystic and Seer, Martin Lamm (Swedish, 1915; German, 1922; French, 1929).
Swedenborg (address at London Congress), Julian Kennedy Smyth (1910).
Swedenborg the Scientist, J. G. Dufty, F.R.M.S. (1938).
The Story of the Swedenborg Manuscripts, S. C. Eby (1926).
A Bibliography of the Works of Emanuel Swedenborg, original and translated, James J. G. Hyde (1906).
The encyclopedias.
For summaries of the teachings of the New Church:
Almost any biography of Swedenborg.
The encyclopedias, especially the *Britannica* and the *Catholic Encyclopedia.*
The Path of Life (excerpts from Swedenborg), John Curtis Ager (1913).
The Gist of Swedenborg (excerpts from Swedenborg), Julian Kennedy Smyth and William F. Wunsch (1920).
An Outline of New-Church Teaching, William F. Wunsch, (1926).

My Religion, Helen Keller (1927).

God Winning Us, Clarence Lathbury, 9th ed. (1925).

Swedenborg und die Uebersinnliche Welt (a discussion, 395 pp., in the domain of psychic research), Henry de Geymuller (1936) (translated from the French by Paul Sakman, and edited and introduced by Hans Driesch).

The Kingdom of Heaven as seen by Swedenborg, John Howard Spalding.

The Living Thoughts of Swedenborg, Eric Sutton (1944) (in "Living Thoughts Library").

LIBERAL PROTESTANTISM

The selection of Professor Conrad Moehlman to represent the cause of liberal Protestantism in this symposium was inevitable. He is without any question an outstanding name in this field in America. All his professional life he has stood up for the cause in the church, the way of the liberal not always being easy nor popular. He has stood his ground within the historically free Baptist church; but he belongs to the whole circle of prophetic leadership within Protestant Christianity.

Born at Meriden, Connecticut, in 1879, Dr. Moehlman received his higher education at the Universities of Rochester, Michigan (Ph.D., 1918), Chicago and the Rochester Theological Seminary. His professional life has been spent at the latter school almost without interruption since 1907 until his retirement in 1944, teaching in the fields of Hebrew literature, Biblical languages, New Testament interpretation, church history (holding the James B. Colgate professorship in the history of Christianity since 1928 in the newly consolidated Colgate-Rochester Divinity School), succeeding the famous Walter Rauschenbusch.

His interests have always been cosmopolitan although a specialist in his field. A prolific writer, his more than a dozen books represent consistently the prophetic note in scholarship and interpretation. Among them are: "A Syllabus of the History of Christianity"; "The Unknown Bible"; "What is Protestantism?"; "The Catholic-Protestant Mind"; "The Story of Christianity in Outline"; "The Christian-Jewish Tragedy"; and the latest vigorous publication "The Church as Educator." His membership in learned societies has afforded him the opportunity to present the fruits of his studies in the form of numerous scholarly papers. In 1933 he served as president of the American Society of Church History. His students honored him recently with a "Festschrift" published under the title "Christian Leadership in a World Society," speaking of him as one "who helped . . . theological schools in general to make the transition to the new age that was dawning thirty years ago."

Editor

LIBERAL PROTESTANTISM

CONRAD HENRY MOEHLMAN

LIVING REQUIRES the continuous adjustment of the organism to its changing environment. The manner of response to this insistence upon adaptation determines the two principal attitudes characteristic of the history of civilization, namely, authoritarianism and personalism. The different expressions of these attitudes emerge, flourish and disintegrate but the two trends persist.

I

When the response to the demand for change is slow, hesitating, conservative and even reactionary in the hope of conserving the inherited cultural values, authoritarianism develops. It is usually preferred to revolution by the people because any social group regards change with dread and worships what has been as the best that can be. The majority always wishes to follow the leader. Appeal to custom, to loyalty, to the past, to suggestion, to submission to law and order is very satisfying to the masses. Ignorance and poverty help "make the society happy and people easy under the meanest circumstances."

> Now this is the Law of the Jungle—
> as old and as true as the sky;
> And the Wolf that shall keep it shall prosper,
> but the Wolf that shall break it must die.
> As the creeper that girdles the treetrunk
> the Law runneth forward and back—
> For the strength of the Pack is the Wolf;
> and the strength of the Wolf is the Pack.

As life moves on and economic, political, social, and religious lag sets in with sorrow as the consequence, authoritarian institutions seek to restrain and suppress dissent. The method employed may be conservative or radical but the authoritarian is always a short-tether person who in the end succeeds in snubbing himself. For the reactionary of one age becomes the heretic of the next. The Sadducees of the second century B.C., then arch-fundamentalists, two centuries later had evolved into arch-heretics for upholding too long the inherited faith of no resurrection from the dead.

From ancient times there have been a few heroic souls in every society who have attempted to maintain the balance between themselves and their surroundings, who desire to keep in touch with the advancing frontier of knowledge, science, social relationships, who, religiously speaking, refuse to "play tricks with their souls." This slight minority consists of long-tether persons who reverse any snubbing process before its coils permanently bind them. For them religion is faith expressing itself in love. They respect facts lest they turn their back upon truth. They believe in the dignity and worth of the individual, in loving God for His own sake and not for the loaves and fishes. They insist upon giving religion ethical content. They may adopt a particular program of action but never commit the unpardonable sin of identifying the progressive spirit which lasts on with a particular program which soon ceases to function. Programs are transitory; the soul goes marching on. As Hobhouse has said: "Liberalism is the belief that society can safely be founded on the self-directing power of personality, that it is only on this foundation that a true community can be built."

Akhnaton, poet-philosopher king of Egypt, more than three millennia ago proposed and too hastily introduced a new type of religion. Reaction destroyed the heresy but his ideas lasted on. Protagoras's "man is the measure of all things" survived the conquest of Greece. Job's assertion, "Behold, he [God] will slay me; I shall not survive; nevertheless, will I maintain my ways before him. . . . Mine integrity hold I fast and will not let it go; my heart shall not reproach me so long as I live" * is the shibboleth of liberalism today. Jesus' "why not judge ye of yourselves what is right," "they said . . . but I say" and his emphasis upon the splendor of man because of infinite value, a value not effaceable by sin, whose duty it is to cultivate a sense of humor, to acquire perspective, to use his common sense and build life upon character appeared

* Kallen's translation.

before him and after him. From Origen, the first scientific and only independent Christian theologian to Loisy, Tyrrell and Crapsey with many like Erasmus, Emerson, Theodore Parker, Mme. de Staël, Constant, Schleiermacher and Troeltsch in between, there have been individuals who refused to surrender the splendor of man to the religious dictators.

And when the lament over dead liberalism is intoned today by omniscient reactionaries, one recalls how Irving in 1826 likewise disposed of nascent liberalism by logic, "religion is the very name of obligation and liberalism the very name of want of obligation" or how Newman in 1841 published this gem: "The more serious thinkers among us are used . . . to regard the spirit of Liberalism as the characteristic of the destined Anti-Christ." Indeed, even in theology there is a "law of continuity which, whatever we may wish, is never broken off." Thus the same John Henry Newman introduced the word "development" into Catholic thought with modernistic consequences.

In essence, religious liberalism is insistence upon the freedom of the individual against any attempt to coerce him or control him. Religion is a private and personal matter. There must be no ecclesiastical discipline for heresy or for freedom of teaching in university or theological seminary.

Applied to theology, liberalism is that kind of theological science which refuses to work with any other means and methods of research and interpretation than the scientific. It believes in process, not miracle; in separation of church and state; in rejecting all offers of state patronage.

In discussing Protestant liberalism, one is concerned with only a few of the modern expressions of the liberal trend in life and by these it was conditioned and guided. Any complete description of liberal Protestantism calls for more attention to the environmental factors which produced it than can here be given.

II

The individualism of primitive Christianity in the second century surrendered to "apostolic" creed, canon, and episcopate. Later appeal was to infallibility of church and papacy. Liberty was sentenced to life imprisonment within tradition and hierarchical organization.

Complete success in enslaving free intellect and conscience was never attained. Incipient rebellions outwardly suppressed had a habit of continuing in under-cover ways. The objective always remained of "withdrawing Christianity altogether from human expression and the operation of ordinary laws of thought."

Thereupon between 1450 and 1650 there rolled in upon Christendom the first wave of the future. Its first achievement was the destruction of the former aristocracy of learning by the invention of printing. The authority of the pope was questioned by Luther. Protestantism emerged and engaged in a century of war with Catholicism. By 1650 it was crystal clear that Catholicism and Protestantism must live together in the same Western world, their disagreements the guarantee of religious toleration and liberty. The differences within Protestantism meant the organization of innumerable types from Socinian and Anabaptist to Lutheran, Calvinist, Anglican and democratic types.

Protestantism soon capitulated to the infallibility of the scriptures, burying the free spirit of the Protestant within the solid wall of biblical literalism. The creative spirit of the earlier Protestantism was embalmed and preserved within the Westminster Confession of Faith, 1647. But the clay soil of medieval totalitarianism had been mixed with modern ideas resulting from discovery of the Americas, expanding commerce, contact with new peoples, the slave trade, the new astronomy and so on and the non-coherent mixture resisted baking into the former mold. Liberalism of a semi-modern pattern was coming to birth.

III

The second wave of the modern age lasted from mid-seventeenth to about the end of the eighteenth century, from the Christianization of interest to the adoption of the I Amendment to the Constitution of the United States. The environmental demand for individualism is considerable. The state takes over control of marriage and to some extent of education. Commerce and business start managing themselves. The people become the source of political sovereignty. In England religious toleration for most is accepted; in the United States religious liberty becomes basic from the federal point of view. Sired by the seventeenth century, born in the eighteenth, Protestant liberalism comes to group expression. It was vigorous, hopeful but also sternly realistic. In the discussion regarding the scriptures, the three substitutes proposed were the authority of the Church, of the Spirit, of Reason. But the first was a return to Roman Catholicism and the disparagement of the Reformation; the second produced vagrant individualism, discord, violent debate; the third seemed rather secular. When the shibboleth, "revelation" was monotonously acclaimed, Reason asked about its source—inner light, authority, self-evidencing scripture? And thus one returned to dangerous Reason again.

The English Act of Toleration, 1689, enabled Deism to express itself in many books. By 1700 the deists were saying that no one any longer defended *credo quia absurdum*. Deism measured religious truth against the standard of an assumed golden age, denied mysticism, overemphasized the intellect, believed in a too easy optimism, underestimated the value of struggle, made God too absentee, and furnished no substitute for the Father who has counted the hairs on one's head. Deism provoked discussion, gave an impulse to biblical investigation and the comparative study of religion, appealed to common sense, and fertilized thinking in France and Germany and the British colonies in North America.

In New England Calvinism, liberal emphases were present from the beginning although they did not manifest themselves in compact and organized forms until the close of the colonial age. Extra-church liberalism appeared in Franklin, Jefferson, Madison, Paine, Allen, Parker, while ecclesiastical liberalism found expression in Unitarianism, Universalism and the Free Will Baptist Church.

Within three decades after the landing of the Pilgrims, the love of God had been entered into Calvinism's ledger on the atonement. The early New England controversy over the form and person of baptism had greatly disturbed religious harmony in Massachusetts. The Manifesto of the Brattle Street Church of Boston made the public relation of Christian experience unnecessary, permitted the sacraments to be administered by any minister and all contributing members to help choose a minister, and sought communion with other churches. "The Lord's Prayer was to be used every Sunday in regular worship and not reserved for the regenerate only at communion." Some ministers insisted that God's revelation in nature and reason must be equated with that in the Bible. Calvinistic fatalism was being opposed. Arminianism was raising "its horrid head." In 1766 a prayer was uttered at a funeral in Boston!

The Great Awakening was a preparation for liberalism. It seriously reduced hyper-Calvinism. Church members by birth and baptism were in conflict with church members by regeneration and covenanting. The "half-way covenant" was very useful in eighteenth century New England and the middle colonies when the type of immigrant came from much lower levels. Jonathan Edwards by holding that "the sacraments are not converting ordinances: but that as seals of the covenant, they presuppose conversion, especially in the adult; and that it is a visible saintship, or in other words, a credible profession of faith and repentance, a solemn consent to the gospel covenant," was insisting upon a rather exalted requirement for the American frontier. Within a decade after the inauguration of the revival, he was writing, "multitudes of fair and high professors have backslidden, sinners are desperately hardened, experimental religion is more than ever out of credit with the far greater part." Between 1744–1748 his church was utterly dead to spiritual things and in 1750 Edwards was deprived of his pastorate and exiled not only by his church but by the association. And during the next one-half century, New England lived on the lower road of moral and religious indifference. Too much of the following exhortation hardens the sinner:

> My thoughts on awful subjects roll,
> Damnation and the dead,
> What horrors seize a guilty soul
> Upon a dying bed.

> ———————

> You can and you can't,
> You will and you won't,
> You'll be damned if you do,
> You'll be damned if you don't.

The rise of Universalism among disciples of George Whitefield demonstrated that Calvinism itself finally requires the salvation of all. Such texts as Romans 5:12 and 11:15, 25f, 32f were "in the Bible too."

Unitarianism "began as a protest against the rejection of reason.

It pledged itself to progress as its life and end, but it has gradually grown stationary and we have a Unitarian orthodoxy" said Channing. Recovery came through Channing, Emerson, Parker where they "learned to love the all-beautiful and altogether lovely God of the Universe." Any liberal movement which refuses to change its platform disintegrates in a changing world.

IV

During the third wave of the modern age, 1791 to 1899, liberalism was at bat most of the time. It was now that the word "liberal" appeared, rapidly changing its content. It first meant "worthy of a free man." For Western Catholicism it became during the nineteenth century "total or partial emancipation of man from the supernatural Moral or Divine Order" and was therefore condemned. Catholic liberalism is of two kinds, ecclesiastical and anti-ecclesiastical. The latter type must be vigorously opposed at all times; the former when it produces modernism.

The nineteenth century, "the shift in civilization," the transition from hand tool to the machine, from muscle of beast and human to electric energy and the newer chemistry and physics, from rural, agrarian civilization to urban skyscrapers, from joy in work to the impersonal gadget, from individualism to socialization of industry, from fiat creation to process view, was made to order for liberalism. But it was an optimistic liberalism undermined by political and economic realities which resulted in world wars. In Germany it was not sufficiently critical of *Volksreligion*. In the United States it failed to discern that Christianity is only one of many religions and thus let the missionary movement remain within a sectarian groove, that Jesus' view of the Kingdom of God cannot be identified with the modern developmental theory, that a religious education which only compromises with modern ideas cannot be very effective. Above all, much nineteenth century liberalism became satisfied with its achievements and occasionally blocked the way to the future. The Societies for Ethical Culture, 1876 on, probably represent the first permanent organized group movements for religious liberalism in the United States.

In 1799 Schleiermacher published his eleven addresses, *Ueber die Religion an die Gebildeten unter ihren Veraechtern.* He dared confront German culture with the values of religion. This was a very heroic adventure, yet it influenced nineteenth century theology more than any other work. Even Brunner recognized this when he wrote, "He is the only really great theologian of the past century, the root from which as a shoot the 'Christian mysticism' of modern theology grows."

In 1860 *Essays and Reviews* was published by a group of Anglicans including Frederick Temple, Baden Powell, Mark Pattison and Benjamin Jowett. Within the year three American editions were printed under the title: *Recent Inquiries in Theology*. It denoted a new era in Anglican theology. It demonstrated that Romanism was the only alternative to rationalism and that the scriptures must be historically understood. "It is not a useful lesson for the young student to apply to Scripture principles which he would hesitate to apply to other books; to make formal reconcilements of discrepancies which he would not think of reconciling in ordinary history; to divide simple words into double meanings; to adopt the fancies and conjectures of Fathers and commentators as *real* knowledge."

By 1870 theology in Germany had reached the nadir of scorn. Leipzig students objected to being represented at a political conference by a theological student! It was then that Harnack helped found the *Theologische Literaturzeitung* to give theology standing. For half a century the battle went on.

In 1900 Harnack published *Das Wesen des Christentums*—repudiated at the time by conservative evangelicals; it is today employed by them to sustain their faith! It was one of the books which enabled Germany to survive Haeckel's *Riddle of the Universe*. It was translated into at least fifteen languages. Scores of books violently questioned its findings. The evangelicals who then prayed that Harnack might be smitten with blindness, later were on their knees thanking God for a book which could be put into the hands of those reading Hitler's *Kampf* and Rosenberg's *Mythus*.

Harnack changed Church History into the history of Christianity—"whatever I have learned I learned in Church History. If I have gone beyond its limits, it pointed the path. Nothing human is alien to Church History."

Space permits only a brief, partial summary of what nineteenth century Protestant liberalism achieved. Harnack and his disciples made the intellectuals again respect Christianity. Bousset proved that religion is not only search after God but also search after the higher values of life; that religion gave the world art, sculpture, music, poetry, the alphabet, calendar, medicine. Troeltsch likewise insisted upon the recognition of the rights of religion in the development of any culture. Nineteenth century Liberalism popularized Luther. It introduced historical method in the interpretation of the gospels in particular and the Bible in general. It formulated the significant problems in theology and provided a proper perspective. It subjected itself to a searching self-criticism. It recovered the Jesus of history. It discovered the true history of the creeds and of the organization of the churches. It has shown how impossible it would be to return to Westminster, Geneva, Augsburg, Chalcedon, or Nicaea. The inerrant Bible has vanished. Biblical literalism is always selective, sterile, and external. Historical method must always remain a tool but it is a good tool. And the modern love of truth, search for truth and joy because of the discovery of truth may be dedicated to the advancement of the good life. Liberalism and science are allies, not enemies.

V

In 1899, a century after Schleiermacher delivered his famous addresses, the year of the death of Dwight L. Moody, Starbuck's *Psychology of Religion* was being read with acclaim and dread by American defenders of the faith. It was published as the fourth wave of the modern age, 1899 to 1945, began to dash upon a bewildered world. For war was in the Hinterland and psychology, sociology, history of religions, racialism were prepared to collect from a Christianity in serious cultural lag. Looking backward, it was not quite ready to do battle with the accepted scientific results of the nineteenth century.

Theological reaction came to bat after the close of the war of 1914–1918, making fun of liberalism but doing nothing against *Volksreligion*, emerging Nazism, and approaching war. It damned the Social Gospel but withdrew from a troubled world. The Barths and Gogartens over there and the echoes of German pessimism over here announced repeatedly the decease of liberalism. A theology still in its adolescence and, in spite of disruptive schisms, espousing a theology which did not survive nationalism and built upon confrontation by God beyond consciousness, sat in judgment upon the death of liberalism. But symbolism merely postpones the defeat of an interpretation approaching bankruptcy. A statement which is only symbolically true ought not to be made to literalists. If apostolic succession never happened, we can't get it because we need it. Protestantism to survive must be disturbed by facts. When fact and faith collide, it must go with fact. Bratton's characterization is unequalled: "Religious authoritarianism has indeed assembled some strange bed-fellows. In the writings of Barth, Berdyaev, Belloc, T. S. Eliot, Ralph Adams Crane, Paul Elmer More, Christopher Dawson, Maritain and Peter Oliver lie the seeds of *philosophical totalitarianism.* These are the enemies of the liberal spirit, for they all agree that man is hopeless and that the only path to a better world is through the intervention of God. They have abandoned reason and experience. The evangelical ideology of the Reformation stood for the competence of the individual. The typical Protestant philosopher as contrasted to Thomism is experiential. *Neosupernaturalism, in short, betrays the best thought of the last 400 years."*

Within Protestant liberalism after World War I, two trends became noticeable which may be called compromising and uncompromising liberalism. The former engaged in war with Fundamentalism over biblical literalism, premillenarianism, supernaturalism. Shibboleths like virgin birth, physical resurrection of Jesus, inerrancy of the Scripture, second coming were shouted at candidates who sought ordination to the Christian ministry. With the help of the middle-of-the-road group, compromising liberalism managed to prevent major schisms, but sapping continues to now.

Paying little attention to the Barthian and Fundamentalist reaction, uncompromising liberalism marched on, confident of the new age. It was soon labelled "Humanism." It redefined religion as "the spirit and quality of human living . . . the strategy of human life in the face of destiny . . . the self-conscious human life functioning in the face of its problems. . . . A humanist religion cannot be a passive thing; it must cry out the command for the cooperative creation of the good life upon the earth"—according to Sellars.

Dietrich defined humanism as: "1. Belief in the supreme worth of human life and of man; 2. The effort to understand human experience by means of human inquiry; 3. The effort to enrich human experience to the utmost capacity of man and of his environment; 4. The acceptance of responsibility for the conditions of human life and the entire reliance upon human effort for their improvement."

Its critics admit that "if humanism is to be refuted, it must be shown to be inadequate to those who live on the thought-level where it appears, that is, to those who fully accept in principle the evolution of religion and its Gods. . . ."

VI

The fifth wave of the modern age began to roll in with the defeat of the Axis powers—Germany, Italy, Japan—in 1945. It may in time be known as the Atomic Age. The San Francisco Conference and the first meeting of the U. N. have brought to pass the "one world" humanity has been pointing toward during the five centuries of transition which began with the introduction of printing. Christendom, defined as the solidarity of the civilization of Europe with Christianity, is no more. The medieval synthesis is not only dead but buried. Men consult the Doctor of Medicine today far more than the Doctor of Divinity. The painful reconstruction of our thinking during the modern age has been calling to us to fashion a new synthesis adequate to life in "one world." And a new religious synthesis based upon science and the democratic faith is in the making. A new kind of reverence is here. "Original sin and guilt" basic in the medieval religious synthesis are rejected by the modern man although he often still presents his children for baptism. For some years ahead, the rites and ceremonies of the inherited religions will be practiced the world over. But underneath, understanding of religious variation is growing and ere many decades have come and gone, religion may no longer divide but unite the nations of the world.

The task of Christian liberalism in this "one world" of today and much more of tomorrow will be what it has always been, *rightly* to interpret the signs of these times. The desperado theology of Europe cannot help disillusioned men and women the world over to their feet. It is out of one-world context. "Original sin and guilt" will some day give way to sin understood as a stage of evolution toward the good. "All our theories of salvation are ideologies of men who have reflected the limitations of their age and perspective," writes Ferm in his "Oceanic Christianity." And they will continue to be. But an interpretation based upon the present facts of life is always more satisfying than one built upon the guesses of the Fathers.

The liberal spirit cannot die—if it could, the clutch of death could not contain it. Dissent and questioning have ever been. The precise pattern fashioned by liberalism has been different in each age. New emphases are necessary today, but the mood in which creative thinking is done is not transient. A Barthian trapeze cannot swing anyone far enough away from today's problems to the crisis of confrontation—he takes himself along. Possibly in the end, liberalism will again be called upon to fight for the self-respect of a Christian theology which has lost its connection with ongoing life. The final interpretation of Protestantism will seek to recover some of its original tolerance, that is, the freedom of the Christian man. It will abandon the vain attempt to secure unity through doctrinal statement or the establishment of a universal church. Rather it will seek to offer a new view of God, a new interpretation of man, a new goal for life to the famishing folk of this day of bewilderment. Since retreat toward the comfort of traditional dogma and literalism is cut off, the towering heights of the Christian way of life must be scaled. The age-long tension in Protestantism resulting from its appeal to the Bible and its appeal to the right of the individual to experience God in his own way cannot be solved by further subdivisions in the many existing varieties of Protestantism, but only by observing that the actual "marching orders" of Christianity are, "Be ye the salt of the earth, be ye the light of the world."

BIBLIOGRAPHY

The thesis proposed and defended here will be found more completely described in the author's *The Church as Educator* (N. Y., 1947).

F. G. BRATTON, *The Legacy of the Liberal Spirit* (New York, 1943).
JOHN DEWEY, *A Common Faith* (New Haven, 1934).
ORTEGA Y GASSET, *The Revolt of the Masses* (New York, 1932).
A. E. HAYDON, *The Quest of the Ages* (New York, 1929).
CHARLES MORRIS, *Paths of Life* (Chicago, 1942).

V. L. PARRINGTON, *Main Currents in American Thought*, 3 vols. (New York, 1927 to 1930).

ROBERTS AND VAN DUSEN, editors, *Liberal Theology* (New York, 1942).

R. W. SELLARS, *Religion Coming of Age* (New York, 1928).

C. R. SKINNER, *Liberalism Faces the Future* (New York, 1937).

VERGILIUS FERM, "Oceanic Christianity" (Presidential Address delivered before the American Theological Society in New York City in 1945) appearing in the *Crozer Quarterly*, January, 1946, Vol. XXIII, No. 1.

ANGLO-CATHOLICISM

One of the younger theologians of distinction in America is Norman Pittenger. Liberally minded, he is nevertheless a strong advocate of the Anglo-Catholic position and tradition and a staunch leader of ecumenicity.

He was born in 1905. His theological training was had at Princeton, Union and General Theological Seminaries, at Columbia and Oxford (Ripon Hall) Universities. He holds the degrees of Bachelor and Master of Sacred Theology.

Active in Episcopal Church circles he is vice-president of the Church's Congress, chaplain of the Guild of Scholars, member of the presiding Bishop's Commission on the Intellectual Life of the Church and holds the position of fellow, tutor and instructor in the General Theological Seminary of the Episcopal Church, New York City. He has been the Bohlen lecturer at the Philadelphia Divinity School, Anniversary lecturer in the Episcopal Theological School in Cambridge and serves as lecturer in religion at Columbia University.

His authorship has found expression in many journals, symposia and books. He is the American editor of "Theology" and editor of the medieval section of "Christian Classics"; author of "The Approach to Christianity" (1939); "Christ and Christian Faith" (1941); "As His Follower" and "Christian Faith and Worship" (1943); "The Christian Way in a Modern World" (1944); "His Body the Church" (1945); and "A Living Faith for Living Men" (1946). Many articles of his appeared in "The Dictionary of Philosophy" and in "An Encyclopedia of Religion."

Editor

ANGLO-CATHOLICISM

W. NORMAN PITTENGER

THE ANGLO-CATHOLIC movement in the Anglican Communion—whose American branch is known as the Episcopal Church—has for its purpose the awakening of the Anglican Communion as a whole to its Catholic heritage, so that a Catholicism which is non-papal, dynamic, and free to develop its essential beliefs and forms may be shown as a reality that can command the allegiance of modern man. The term itself has a certain ambiguity, since it can mean either the movement which is directly concerned with awakening the entire Anglican Church to its traditional position, or the actual position of that Church itself, as stated in its *Book of Common Prayer* and indicated by its historic development since the days of the English Reformation. Those who are actively within Anglo-Catholicism in the former sense, however, have no doubt about its application in the latter: the genius of the Anglican Communion, wherever found, is a free and dynamic Catholicism.

By Catholicism is meant that traditional faith expressed in the days of "the undivided Church" (prior to the break between East and West in 1054 and the Reformation in the 16th century), the centrality of eucharistic worship as distinctively Christian and expressive of the true nature of the Church, and the ministry of bishops, priests and deacons, which (in the words of the *Book of Common Prayer*) has existed "from the Apostles' time . . . in Christ's Church." Coupled with this basic historic faith, worship and ministry, there is to be found in Catholicism, of all brands, a strong emphasis on the Church as a divine community, "the mystical Body of Christ, which is the blessed company of all faithful people." The Church is believed, therefore, to be in some genuine sense "a divine creation," extending the person and the work of the Incarnate Lord Jesus Christ through the centuries which have followed "the days of his flesh," and making that person and the "benefits" of his work available for succeeding generations of believers. By free and dynamic, the Anglo-Catholic means that the sheer "dead-hand" of the past does not prevent the development and growth of the given tradition, nor inhibit the freest and fullest enquiry into scientific, biblical and other matters which are relevant to the faith. The most generous attitude towards all new truth, from whatever area it may proceed, is demanded by the conviction that Catholicism is not an exclusive but an inclusive reality, to which all truth has a direct relation.

The Anglo-Catholic movement is based on the belief in the deep reality of God and his prevenient action in history, his wide self-revelation throughout the world and his particular self-disclosure by Christ, in whom "for us men and for our salvation" he entered human history as true man, while remaining true God. This basic belief has as its corollary the acceptance of the *consensus fidelium*, or commonly accepted interpretation of the faithful, as the test of the truth of developing dogma; such a *consensus* has been given in the early "general or ecumenical councils" (usually Nicaea 325, Constantinople 381, Ephesus 431, Chalcedon 451), and is summed up in the traditional creeds: the Apostles', the Nicene and the Athanasian. But the creeds are interpreted not in a static fashion, but as pointers towards truth and lines of growth. The context in which this entire position is held is, as indicated above, the belief in the Church as the divine community, whose indwelling life is Christ himself and whose guiding spirit is the Holy Spirit.

The "one, holy, Catholic and apostolic Church", belief in which is declared in the creeds, possesses certain "structural forms," the Anglo-Catholic asserts. These are a set of *dogmatic convictions* concerning God, Christ, man and redemption; a *sacramental manner of functioning* (concerning which more will be said at a later point in this essay); a *manner or quality of life* which is characteristic of traditional Christianity and which may conveniently be called "life in grace," marked by a sense of the reality of the Supernatural or God and externally expressed in charity and holiness; and finally a ministerial articulation, in which the Church as "Body of Christ" functions and through which its various activities are conducted. For the modern Anglo-Catholic, although not for his ancestors who did not possess the requisite historical and biblical knowledge, there is no difficulty in recognizing the truth that these four "structural forms" developed from germinal beginnings in the life of Christ or in the primitive days of the Christian fellowship. His conviction that the Holy Spirit has guided the Church emboldens him to believe that the several "forms" grew naturally and rightly from the seedlike beginnings; it is rather as if the infant Church, emerging from the womb of Judaism through the first few years, became self-conscious and struck out lines of growth which determined its persisting nature and established its *type*.

It is at this point that a marked difference of opinion, sometimes acrimonious in expression, has been found in Anglo-Catholicism. The older type of Anglo-Catholic has sometimes been reluctant to make the concessions allowed in the last paragraph, while the more modern-minded Anglo-Catholic, now plainly in the ascendant and majority, has not been unwilling to allow this gladly, even at times to allow much more than this in regard to the development of traditional Catholicism. During the first quarter of the present century, it was not unlikely that the latter kind of Anglo-Catholicism would be described as "liberal Catholicism"—as in the famous symposium *Essays Catholic and Critical* and the American volumes entitled *Liberal Catholicism*. But the fact that a theosophical sect had preempted this name and the growing disrepute which for some reason has come to be attached to "liberalism" in later years (one of the saddest chapters in current history, if a personal comment may be added, for the word and much for which it stood is the best the human race knows and can know), have led to the disuse of the term and a general willingness to be known as Anglo-Catholic *sans phrase*.

For the outsider, the two things that most strike his attention in Anglo-Catholicism are doubtless the centrality of the Holy Eucharist, sometimes called the Mass, with dignity and even colour, incense and other accompaniments in its celebration; and the continued insistence on the episcopate and priesthood, which has appeared over and over again in all discussions of Christian reunion in which the Anglican Church, or its American representative the Episcopal Church, has been engaged. As to the former, the Anglo-Catholic movement, following the plain intention of the English Reformers of the 16th century, has made the Eucharist the chief service of worship, believing it to be "the continual remembrance of the sacrifice of the death of Christ," as the Prayer Book Catechism puts it, and also a "holy communion" with Christ whose "Body and Blood" are truly present as "the inward part, or thing signified" in and by the eucharistic elements of bread and wine. The requirement of attendance at the Eucharist on Sundays and major festivals is laid on the faithful by Anglo-Catholicism, in view of the high doctrine of the sacrament which is entertained. For the same reason, the celebration is surrounded by such dignity and beauty as shall be worthy of the worship of Christ in this eucharistic action.

As to the episcopate and the priesthood (and the diaconate, although not so much has been said about the third order of ministry), the position of Anglo-Catholicism is based on what is regarded as the traditional Catholic "structural form" in ministerial articulation and on loyalty to the Anglican view itself, as expressed in the preface to the Ordinal in the Prayer Book. When the Reformation occurred in England, the form of ordinations was printed with these words: ". . . to the intent that these Orders"—viz., bishops, priests and deacons—"may be continued, and reverently used and esteemed in this Church, no man shall be accounted or taken to be a lawful Bishop, Priest, or Deacon, in this Church, or suffered to execute any of the said Functions, except he be called, tried, examined, and admitted thereunto, according to the Form hereafter following, or hath had Episcopal Consecration or Ordination." By "these Orders," the Ordinal means the traditional ministry which obtained *before* the English Reformation; the intention, therefore, is to continue that ministry unchanged in office and work, as the Archbishops of Canterbury and York stated in their reply to the papal condemnation of Anglican orders at the close of last century.

The view of the ministry held by modern Anglo-Catholics is what might be termed a "representative and functional theory." The Church as the Body of Christ requires for its operation certain ministerial agents: to act as chief pastors and to ordain, to celebrate the sacraments and chiefly the Eucharist, to shepherd the flock and to provide assistance in divine service and other ministrations. These operations of the total Body of Christ are delegated to specific agents, known as bishops, priests and deacons, whose ordination is by Christ in his "Church-Body" and who by that ordination are "authenticated" to be true ministers in the succession of such "functional agents." By episcopal "laying-on of hands," it is believed, continuity in office and identity in function are preserved, so that the minister acts not for some contemporaneous group nor for some small segment of believers but for the entire Church of Christ throughout the world and through the centuries. Far from such a conception of the ministry *creating* a problem, it is the Anglo-Catholic conviction that it is the *solution* of a problem. It provides the answer, divinely given through a developing community which is divinely guided, to the problem of securing continuity and identity—that is, *apostolicity*— in the Body of Christ. That is to say, it is the sacrament or "outward and visible sign" of the true nature of the Church as Christ's person and work humanly extended beyond the days of his walking in Palestine. On the other hand, the "democratization" of the episcopacy and the removal of all sacerdotal *pretension* (although not of sacerdotal *functioning*, which is required on behalf of the true *Sacerdos,* Christ in his Church) are eminently agreeable to the modern Anglo-Catholic.

It is only the fact of current controversy and misunderstanding that has led to our giving such undue attention to the nature of the ministry. In actual practice, the principal distinguishing features of Anglo-Catholicism are its eucharistic worship, its maintenance of the traditional faith with a willingness for scholarly examination and critical study, and its strong hold on the life of discipline. The last of these requires further mention, which may properly be made in connection with a survey of the whole sacramental scheme.

Anglo-Catholicism, like Eastern Orthodoxy and Roman Catholicism—the three are very close in this as in other respects—lays tremendous emphasis upon a general sacramentalism. Regarding man as an amphibian who lives in "the world of spirit and the world of sense," and seeing that the universe itself is a system in which value, purpose, ideal and meaning are declared by and operate through matter, stuff, body, the Anglo-Catholic feels that Christianity is rightly conceived as a religion of sacramental expression. While he would agree with Hugh of St. Victor and other medieval writers that in this sense there are countless sacraments, he would single out, with the Western Church generally as well as with the Orthodox, two as "sacraments of the gospel"—namely, Baptism and the Lord's Supper—and five others as sacramental rites which also have outward signs and inward grace or reality. These last are Confirmation, Penance or Absolution, Holy Order, Matrimony and Holy Unction. By Baptism, a child or adult is "grafted into Christ's Body" and made "a living member of the same"; Confirmation, historically the continuation of the whole rite of initiation, is the gift of the Holy Spirit for responsible life in the Church; Penance or Absolution is the receiving of divine forgiveness from a priest of the Church, who so acts on behalf of Christ in his Body upon evidence of sincere contrition by the penitent; Holy Order is the gift of grace for ministering in the Church; Matrimony is the Church's blessing upon a marriage between two properly approved persons; Unction is blessing with the use of oils, for those who are ill or dying. The Eucharist, already mentioned, is the chief sacrament, since it is "the memorial [the] Son hath commanded us to make" and is the means for "the strengthening and refreshing" of the believer.

The sacramental life, so available to the Christian, demands as its preparation and consequence a discipline or *ascesis*. Fasting and abstinence, as bodily training to help the soul's development; special occasions of prayer, as during Lent; self-examination and confession, as part of the life in penitence, are all included in this discipline. The Prayer Book speaks of certain times when such discipline shall be engaged in "as is more especially suited to extraordinary acts and exercises of devotion." The purpose, then, is positive; the way to achieving it is negative, in that certain denials are made so that room may be found for more fruitful devotion and holiness.

For those who wish to give themselves more directly to "extraordinary acts and exercises of devotion," the religious life is provided in the Anglican Church. By this is meant the organization of men or women into groups, called "monks" or "nuns," living in community and together entering upon a particularly rigorous discipline. In America, such orders include the Order of the Holy Cross, the Society of St. John the Evangelist (more exactly, this is a society of "mission priests," but their life is "regular"), the Franciscans and the Benedictines, for men; and the Communities of St. Mary, St. Margaret, St. Anne, the Holy Nativity and the Transfiguration, for women. In England and in other countries, there are still other groups—notably the Community of the Resurrection and the Society of the Sacred Mission in England, both of which have been important centres not only of devotion but of theological study.

One of the important developments in the Anglo-Catholic movement has been a renewed emphasis upon missionary work. At first concerned more immediately with awakening the Anglican Communion to a sense of its Catholic heritage, the movement has gone on to a strong conviction of its obligation to reach others in non-Christian lands; hence the work in Africa, India, the Philippines, Japan and China, and elsewhere. The Anglo-Catholic missionary has had a guide-book for his work since the late "twenties" of this century, when *Essays Catholic and Missionary* was published. This volume, most of the contributors to which are themselves missionaries, insists on a generous attitude towards other religions, at the same time asserting that Christianity in its Catholic form comes as "crown and criterion" of these faiths, its purpose being not to destroy but to fulfill their partial truth in the inclusive fellowship of Christ's Body the Church. As Dr. Taylor remarks in his *Faith of a Moralist,* the Anglo-Catholic can never, without blasphemy, deny the God-given "graces and mercies" found in the non-Christian religions; on the other hand, he must seek to share his faith, which he believes to be supreme, with all men.

That faith which Anglo-Catholicism maintains to be truly "Catholic" (i.e., universal and required for full Christian "appurtenance," in von Hügel's phrase) is sufficiently stated, in its main outlines, in the three creeds and the "ancient Fathers." This appeal to the age of the Fathers—roughly the first through the sixth centuries —is typical of Anglicanism from its earliest days. The Anglo-Catholic does not consider that the Bible is "the only infallible rule of faith and practice," as would a Calvinist, for example. His view is expressed in words from the Thirty-Nine Articles, that the Creeds (which for him, as for the historic Catholic communions generally, are the *regula fidei*) "ought thoroughly to be received and believed: for they may be proved [that is, in the English of our time, "tested"] by most certain warrants of Holy Scripture." The old Anglican adage, "The Church to teach, the Bible to prove [read, 'test']", states this position succinctly. In more recent times, Anglo-Catholic scholars have tended to go beyond this; they would now affirm that whereas the Protestant groups appeal to "the Bible only," and Roman Catholicism to "the Bible and tradition," the real appeal for historic Christianity is to *tradition,* classically and normatively stated in the Scriptures as being the record of the response made to the revelation of God in history through Christ; to reason, by which the tradition is studied and tested; and to experience, through which that which is historically recorded and reasonably tested may be experimentally confirmed in "the Christian consciousness." Such a study as *Dogma, Fact and Experience,* by the present Bishop of Derby (Dr. A. E. J. Rawlinson), illustrates this tendency, as does also the more recent *The Gospel of God and the Authority of the Church,* by W. L. Knox and A. R. Vidler.

Despite this attitude towards the Scriptures in relation to the tradition of the Church, the Anglican Communion is deeply grounded in Holy Writ. Not only do the Scriptures provide the basis for the daily offices of Morning and Evening Prayer, which canon law or usage requires every clergyman to say each day, but the Anglican eucharistic office is eminently scriptural as well, while the Church officially declares that although the Christian community is "a witness and a keeper of Holy Writ" it cannot "enforce anything to be believed for necessity of Salvation" save that which may be found therein. As we said above, modern Anglo-Catholicism would say that this must be interpreted as implying that which is *germinally* found in Scripture, since it is apparent that the full-grown Catholic position cannot be forced back into the perambulator of the biblical record. The net result, then, of the process has been a conviction that the Vincentian canon (dating from St. Vincent of Lerins, in the fifth century) which states that the Church may teach officially only that which *ubique, semper et ab omnibus creditum est,* must be understood as meaning "that which in the tradition has developed from evangelical or apostolic faith and practice, and has commended itself to the Christian consciousness over a long period of time and to the major portion of Christian communicants and faithful, as being consonant with the fact of Christ and its significance."

A sketch of the history of Anglo-Catholicism will now be in order. When the English Reformation occurred under King Henry the Eighth, it took a different form from the Reformation on the Continent, although it was naturally influenced by that Reformation. England had for a long time been chafing under the papacy, with its pretensions to power and its financial drain upon the nation—so much so that from the time of *Magna Carta* there had been protest after protest, finally winding up with two parliamentary acts, *Provisors* and *Praemunire,* designed to curb the power and influence of the Roman See in "the realm of England." The time was ripe for more overt action, which doubtless would have occurred in any event. But the actual occasion of the break with Rome was the matrimonial ambition of the King, with which the Roman pontiff—for political rather than religious reasons, since he had granted to others such permission for annulment and re-marriage as Henry asked—interfered. But the commonly repeated statement that Henry the Eighth "founded" the Church of England, which is the mother-church of all Anglicanism, is totally false. No reputable historian would affirm this today. Even the Roman scholar G. Constant rejects the common misunderstanding. What occurred was that the English provinces of the Catholic Church, without change in "doctrine, discipline or worship" or type of ministry, declared that the Pope had usurped powers which did not belong to him and claimed for himself privileges which belonged to Christ alone; hence, his powers and privileges "in this realm" were abrogated. It was not until much later, during the reign of Queen Elizabeth, that a succeeding Roman pontiff excommunicated England; his predecessors, without questioning the continuing Catholicity of the Anglican Church, had sought in various ways to bring the two provinces back into the papal fold.

The history of the Anglican Church for many years was a chequered one. The Continental Reformers, either forced or persuaded to come to England—in the former instance because of persecution in Europe, in the latter because of their scholarship and opposition to Roman claims—brought with them ideas which were not consonant with the normal Anglican position as expressed in the various credal writings under Henry and in the First Prayer Book of Edward the Sixth, in which the Anglican type of Catholicism was first liturgically expressed. During a period of years, Anglicanism swung left to a more Protestant position, then retracted to a more Catholic one, and finally in the Elizabethan Settlement, effected in most respects by 1559, settled down to a "reformed Catholicism." The next hundred years, apart from the tragic period under the First Charles and the Protectorate of Cromwell, were devoted to a consolidation of this point of view. The writings of the so-called "Anglo-Catholic Fathers," from Richard Hooker to Launcelot Andrewes and Thomas Ken, and including such men as Jewel, Cosin, Laud and others, set the standard for the whole Anglo-Catholic emphasis; a finely conceived and executed anthology from these men has been published under the title *Anglicanism,* edited by Paul Elmer More and F. Leslie Cross (New York and London, 1935). During the time of the Exile, when the Stuarts fled to France, the peculiar genius of Anglicanism emerged clearly under persecution; against Rome on the one hand and Continental Protestantism on the other, the Anglican *via media,* as it was called, was defended with scholarly acumen and literary skill.

From England, Anglicanism spread to the British colonies, including America, where the first Anglican service was held at Jamestown in Virginia, in the early seventeenth century—before the Pilgrims landed in Massachusetts. Since that time, the Anglican Church has won converts or gone with English colonists in almost every corner of the globe, excepting Continental Europe and the areas where the Eastern Orthodox Church is mistress. There are now something in the neighbourhood of 40,000,000 Anglicans, including more than 2,000,000 in the United States. The Communion is organized on "national" lines; that is, each country or dominion has its own indigenous organization, with presiding bishop or metropolitan, with a governing assembly (called in the United States "the general Convention"), with dioceses each with its bishop and council or convention, and with its own particular Prayer Book. The whole is bound together by a common tradition, by a common ministry and a common faith, and by the fact that the liturgies are all variants of the English *Book of Common Prayer.* The Archbishop of Canterbury, head of the Church of England, is regarded with respect as the "first bishop" of the Anglican Communion; he has no powers over other branches, however. Neither has the Lambeth Conference, held each ten years and attended by all the bishops of the Anglican Church. Lambeth meets to discuss policy and principle, but not formally to legislate; its conclusions are published in an agreed report, but their influence is one of prestige rather than power.

During the period from 1670 to the latter part of the eighteenth century, Anglicanism tended to a dull respectability with a fear of "enthusiasm" or "exaggerated" piety; the Church seemed almost, in England, to be a department of the state. With the Evangelical Revival under Charles Simeon, with his friends who were influenced by the Wesleys (themselves priests of the Anglican Church, whose almost forced defection because the English authorities disliked their "enthusiasm" is one of the great tragedies of Anglican history), new life began to appear in the Church. This revival of strong personal religion was the precursor of the Oxford Movement of the 1830's, which under John Keble, E. B. Pusey and John Henry Newman (who later went over to Rome, in disappointment because official Anglicanism did not respond quickly enough to the ideas of the group, making him doubt the essential Catholicism of his mother-Communion), began to re-emphasize the principles for which the Anglo-Catholic Fathers had stood. Beginning with the famous Assize Sermon of Keble, preached at St. Mary's Church in Oxford and demanding that the Church of God should be free of governmental interference in her spiritual life, the Oxford Movement spread rapidly. It led to a revival of Catholic piety—never dead, but for a long time slumbering—and a renewed sense of the Anglican Church's liturgical life. Through several phases, it developed until it has profoundly modified the entire Anglican Church, ceremonially and doctrinally. When we say "modified," we mean that the movement has been responsible for a rediscovery of an almost forgotten heritage of Catholic doctrine, worship and polity, although throughout its history these have nominally prevailed.

In the latter part of the last century, the Oxford Movement came to be better known as "the Anglo-Catholic Movement," its purpose being to awaken the entire Anglican Communion to its implicit Anglo-Catholicism, rather than to impose anything new upon that Communion. By the present time, its work has by no means been accomplished in full, but it has deepened and strengthened the "churchliness" of Anglicanism, led to a great enrichment of its worship and piety, brought the Eucharist back to its traditional and Prayer Book position of centrality, and strongly defended the inherent Catholic dogmatic position of the Church. One crisis occurred in this period, when Bishop (as he later became) Charles Gore and some friends in Oxford edited a volume entitled *Lux Mundi,* appearing in the eighties when new knowledge of the Bible was emerging in scholarly circles, while scientific development went on apace in other fields. Gore and his colleagues endeavoured to show that the Catholic faith as the Anglican Communion has received it could be re-stated in such a fashion that it would take account of and provide room for the new data. Old Canon Liddon of London, a power in Anglo-Catholic circles, was so disturbed by the book—especially by its admission of ignorance in the human knowledge of Jesus—that he became ill and died in despair. But the younger men were not to be stopped; following their work, others have carried on the work of re-statement and revision, along lines which we have indicated above. Although there have been repercussions of a "conservative" attitude in this respect, nothing like "fundamentalism" has ever appeared in the Anglican Communion, and the likelihood is that a dynamic and free Catholicism will continue without hindrance.

It may be asked how widely Anglo-Catholicism in the narrower sense of the term has spread through the Anglican Communion or Anglo-Catholicism in the wider sense. The answer is that it has so permeated the entire Communion that statistics are impossible. Roughly, a quarter to a half of the *clergy* are Anglo-Catholics in some meaning of the term, in its narrower sense; various other groups in the Communion have coalesced into one smaller unit often called "liberal Evangelical," but even this group in its newer phase affirms the Catholicity of Anglicanism and differs mostly in matters of emphasis and interpretation from a "liberal" Anglo-Catholicism. That such is the situation is shown by a recent article in which a neo-orthodox Protestant, Dr. Paul Lehmann of Wellesley College, discussed the genius of Anglicanism, finding its inherent Catholicism stated adequately in a symposium published by a group of professed "liberal Evangelicals." Indeed it may be said that if certain contemporary problems are surmounted, the chief one being reunion discussions with explicit Protestant denominations, the Anglican position as a whole will emerge clearly, despite some incidental exceptions and protests, as a "reformed Catholicism" such as the Caroline divines mentioned above declared was the true genius of their Church.

Perhaps nothing has brought Anglo-Catholicism, as a fact and as a religious position, so plainly into general discussion these past few years as the conversion of several distinguished literary men and scholars who had been agnostic or atheistic in their point of view. Dr. A. E. Taylor, one of Great Britain's outstanding philosophers, was one of the first of these; his great book, *The Faith of a Moralist* (the second part of which is an *apologia* for Anglo-Catholicism), is included in the bibliography. Paul Elmer More, American literary critic and humanist and author of the many volumes of *Shelburne Essays,* was another convert. T. S. Eliot, author of *The Wasteland* and a famous contemporary poet, became an Anglo-Catholic during the "twenties"; more recently, W. H. Auden, the brilliant young Anglo-American poet and critic, has been converted. Many other names might be mentioned, both in England and in America; it may be sufficient to say that the recently organized Guild of Scholars in the Episcopal Church, explicitly Anglo-Catholic in outlook, includes some of America's leading scholars in literature and arts, as well as a distinguished group of biologists, chemists, physicists and psychologists.

These men and women believe that the Anglo-Catholic has a position which is invaluable in our own day. They conceive of the great tradition in Christianity as both authoritative and supernaturally grounded, and yet free and capable of constant development. To be true to itself, they say, Christianity must hold to the central doctrine, discipline, worship and ministry which have come down through the years, but it must be free also to restate and expand that tradition as the need arises. Thus authority is dynamic, with no static law-giver, no oracular voice, but rather with a genuine *consensus fidelium,* freely given and freely received, a common agreement of saints, scholars and humble folk. This is the ideal of a truly "liberal," yet genuinely traditional, Catholicism. And this ideal is realized, so it is believed, in the Anglican Church, with its "reformed Catholicism" which has been its genius since the days of the English Reformation.

The fearless yet humble reinterpretation of the great tradition has indeed been the peculiar task of Anglicanism. The findings of modern science, biblical criticism and the several other departments of human enquiry have been pressed into service, for they are parts of God's continuing self-revelation to men along various avenues of experience. Every insight into new truth, the apprehension of beauty and submission to goodness, all of human life and activity, are capable of mediating God and enlarging the knowledge of him. The same is true of the non-Christian religions. These may be inadequate, but all are man's quest for God, a quest incited and sustained by him, and rewarded at every stage by some revelation of himself, until in Christ and his Church the two movements meet supremely and richly.

Hence Anglicanism, as the Anglo-Catholic understands it, presents a Catholicism based on the central Christian heritage, firmly rooted in history, rich in sacramental worship, maintaining the institutional and ministerial stress which has been the strength of Catholic Christianity, and nourishing the fragrant holiness and warm personal piety which keep religion alive at its heart. But on the other hand, it presents a Catholicism which is open towards all truth no matter where it may be known, which finds a place for the priceless revelation of himself given by God through science, art, philosophy, the non-Christian religions, and every other human experience. Finally, it is convinced that this Catholicism has wide social implications, since it is necessarily concerned with the nature and rights of men as sons of God, and with the fundamental principles of justice and love in human relationships. The study of these matters has been a continuing interest of Anglo-Catholicism, from the days of the Guild of St. Matthew in England to the Church League for Industrial Democracy in this country. A modern Catholicism must be vitally related to the life of every age; in our own, the emerging social order engages its attention and concern. Hence the various Anglo-Catholic conferences on sociology, with the determination to assist in building upon earth a society in which justice, goodness and truth prevail, where men can serve God with their whole lives and live abundantly, significantly, and with that degree of security which the conditions of time and space allow.

BIBLIOGRAPHY

A. R. VIDLER AND W. L. KNOX, *The Development of Modern Catholicism* (London and New York, 1933).

N. P. WILLIAMS (editor), *Northern Catholicism* (London, 1933).

A. E. TAYLOR, *The Faith of a Moralist* (London and New York, 1930).

E. G. SELWYN (editor), *Essays Catholic and Critical* (London and New York, 1926).

H. L. STEWART, *A Century of Anglo-Catholicism* (London, 1929).

A. G. HEBERT, *Liturgy and Society* (London, 1935).

C. B. MOSS, *Christian Doctrine* (London and New York, 1944).

Signposts (twelve pamphlets by various authors), editor E. L. Mascall (London, 1943–4).

W. NORMAN PITTENGER, *The Christian Way in a Modern World* (Louisville, 1944).

FRANK GAVIN (editor), *Liberal Catholicism* (Milwaukee, 1935).

W. A. VISSER 'T HOOFT, *Anglo-Catholicism and Orthodoxy (A Protestant View)* (London, 1933).

CHURCH OF JESUS CHRIST OF
LATTER-DAY SAINTS

Dr. Cowles is president emeritus of the University of Utah. He was born in Chester, Utah, in 1880, studied at Weber Academy in Ogden and then at the University of Chicago where he earned his Ph.B. and M.A. degrees (1910, 13). He did graduate work at the University of California (1920–21) and won his Ph.D. degree from that institution in 1926.

His professional life has followed that of an educator, first in the public schools of Utah and then in university work, rising through the ranks at the University of Utah to which place he came in 1915, to the headship of its department of educational administration, dean of the lower division of studies and president in 1941. An interim appointment he held as teaching fellow at the University of California, 1920–21. He is a member of numerous academic associations. Earlier in his career he was a missionary for the eastern states of his church, 1898–1900.

His books include titles dealing with educational problems of his state, his last one called "Organization and Administration of Education in Utah" (1934).

Living the greater part of his life in Utah and holding places of responsibility within his church, Dr. Cowles writes out of intimate knowledge of his subject. The present article carries the imprimatur of the First Presidency of the Church.

Editor

CHURCH OF JESUS CHRIST OF LATTER-DAY SAINTS

LE ROY EUGENE COWLES

THE CHURCH of Jesus Christ of Latter-Day Saints, commonly known as the Mormon Church, is a religious organization numbering approximately a million people. Headquarters of the Church is in Salt Lake City, Utah. The majority of the membership live in Utah, Idaho, Arizona, and California, but they are found in every state in the Union and in most foreign countries.

The Mormons believe in the heavenly Trinity and accept Jesus Christ as the Divine Savior of the world. They believe that through His atonement all mankind may be saved by obedience to the principles of the gospel. They believe that the gospel principles are revealed to man, not only in the Bible but also in the Book of Mormon. They further believe that modern revelation supplements and clarifies the ancient written word. They believe that Jesus established his church on earth during his mortal ministry, but that it was reestablished with its authority and priesthood through Joseph Smith more than a hundred years ago. The Mormons are not, however, intolerant towards people of other churches. They declare in their official articles of faith: "We claim the privilege of worshipping all-mighty God according to the dictates of our own conscience, and allow all men the same privilege. Let them worship how, where or what they may."

History

On April 6, 1830, at Fayette, Seneca County, New York, Joseph Smith and a few associates, in conformity to the laws of the State of New York, organized a new religious society. Besides Joseph Smith Jr. there were Hyrum Smith, Samuel H. Smith, Oliver Cowdery,

David Whitmore, and Peter Whitmore, Jr., in the original group. This was the beginning of the Church of Jesus Christ of Latter-day Saints.

Joseph Smith, when a boy in his early teens, had declared that he had been visited by heavenly beings in answer to his prayers for wisdom and divine guidance when he was perplexed as to what church to join. He said he had been told that if he were faithful "the fullness of the gospel" would at some future time be made known to him. He later reported other visitations and divine instructions, including the revelation which led to procuring and translating the golden plates of the Book of Mormon. This book is accepted by the Church as an authentic history of people who lived on this continent in the centuries just preceding and succeeding the dawn of the Christian era. The Book records the visit of Jesus Christ to these people after his resurrection, and the establishing of His Church among them. The book was first published in Palmyra, New York, in 1830. Since that time there have been many editions printed and it has been translated and published in many languages.

The Church increased rapidly in numbers due to active missionary work both in the States and abroad. The nucleus of the Church moved from New York to Kirtland, Ohio, where the first stake of Zion was established, the first Mormon temple was erected, and the priesthood of the Church was more thoroughly organized, including the creation of the first presidency of three, with Joseph Smith at the head, and a Quorum of twelve apostles.

As early as 1831 a colony of Mormons settled in Jackson County, Missouri, on land purchased from the federal government and consecrated by the prophet as a site for their central city. The Mormon settlers were mostly from the North and East and consequently were opposed to slavery. This and other matters got them into trouble and in 1833 they were forcibly and cruelly driven out of Jackson County into Clay, Caldwell, and Daviess counties in the same state.

The leaders in the latter part of 1837 decided to move the headquarters of the Church to Missouri. They established the city of Far West (now Kerr) as a gathering place.

The Mormon missionaries in England had, by this time, baptized about two thousand converts, most of whom came to America and joined their co-religionists in Missouri. This was but the beginning of a stream of immigrant converts from European countries.

The "old settlers" of Missouri and "new saints" did not get along well together. Friction soon developed; clashes of armed bands of both parties resulted in riots and bloodshed in which many were killed on both sides. The Governor ordered out the Missouri militia and the Mormons were forced to leave the state in mid-winter, 1838–39.

The main body of the Saints made a fairly orderly withdrawal into the state of Illinois. They soon purchased land on the east bank of the Mississippi River, about one hundred and ninety miles north of St. Louis and opposite Montrose, Iowa. On this site in the great bend of the majestic river they built the city of Nauvoo.

Within five years, the settlement grew to a city of approximately 20,000 population. Wide streets were well laid out, the buildings were of good material, many of them of brick and stone. Fine old two story dwellings are still pointed out to visitors as relics of the residential sections that once existed.

Joseph Smith requested and secured from the state a charter for the city of Nauvoo delegating to the city many unusual rights and prerogatives among which were the right to establish a University of Nauvoo and an independent military force called the Nauvoo Legion, constituting a body of troops quite separate from and independent of the state militia.

Suspicion, jealousy and trouble arose. Political opposition was intensified when Joseph Smith announced himself as a candidate for the presidency of the United States. In 1843 Smith claimed to have received the revelation proclaiming the doctrine of plural marriages, and it was contended that he, himself, married plural wives. Enemies of the church seized upon every reference to polygamy and used it against the prophet and his people. The articles that had been published and the inflammatory speeches and distorted accounts of Mormon practices aroused the entire country around Nauvoo, and brought about a series of tragedies that finally culminated in the expulsion of the Mormons from Illinois.

Governor Ford requested the prophet to appear at Carthage, Illinois, to answer to charges. He complied and with his brother Hyrum and others went to Carthage on the pledged word of Governor Ford that they would be protected. The pledge was broken. The jail in which they were imprisoned was attacked by a mob of about two hundred men, with blackened faces, who shot to death both the prophet and his brother Hyrum. This occurred on the 27th day of June, 1844. Joseph Smith had reached the age of 39 years, 6 months and 4 days.

On August 8th, at a great mass meeting of the Church members, the problem of succession was discussed and settled. The doctrine prevailed that the presidency was dissolved on the death of the president, and that the authority to govern the church rested with the quorum of the twelve apostles. Brigham Young, the president of the quorum, was recognized as leader and was later sustained as president of the church.

Those who believed in lineal succession to the presidency rejected Brigham Young and some of the doctrines he taught. These people established the Reorganized Church of Jesus Christ of Latter-day Saints. This organization at the present time has its headquarters at Independence, Missouri. The membership is said to be in excess of 100,000. The doctrines of the two organizations are quite similar, except that the Reorganized Church has never accepted polygamy and some other beliefs and practices of the larger group.

Brigham Young assumed the responsibility of leadership and began his administration at a most critical and difficult period. He was strong, energetic and capable, and he believed implicitly in the divinity of his work, but he was realistic in that he mixed good common sense with his theology.

The troubles of the Mormons, instead of quieting down after the death of the Prophet, increased. The Nauvoo Legion was disbanded and their arms confiscated. The people were left defenseless, and state authorities failed to come to the rescue. It became evident that the Mormons must leave the state or be destroyed. At great sacrifice they disposed of most of their property as best they could and prepared for the exodus.

The first party actually to leave Nauvoo consisted of the twelve apostles, the high council and about four hundred families. They crossed the Mississippi on the ice on the 11th of February, 1846, and started westward—men, women, and little children. Other companies continued to follow until by late April the great body of the Church had left Nauvoo.

It is well known that Joseph Smith had thought of a possible refuge in the West for his people and Brigham Young carried out the idea practically. At the head of a picked company including 143 men, three women and two children, he started from Council Bluffs, in April, 1847, to cross the great plains to the Rocky Mountains. The caravan consisted of wagons drawn by mules and oxen, carrying ploughs, other implements, a year's supply of food and seed grain. On July 24th, the little company entered Salt Lake Valley, and Brigham Young made the now famous declaration, "This is the place."

The first party was followed by other groups, and as the seasons came and went, the wagon trains and the handcart companies brought these "modern children of Israel" to the promised land. The faith and dogged determination of the people are proclaimed eloquently by what they endured.

Between July, 1847, and the completion of the railroad to the valley in May, 1869, thousands of settlers came overland from the East, and other thousands via Cape Horn and California. It was a tremendous task to care for all of these people and to get them placed in settlements where they could become adjusted to new ways of living in a strange environment.

Brigham Young immediately began sending exploring parties and scouts to all parts of the country between the Rocky Mountains and the Sierra Nevada Range. As rapidly as possible he established settlements in the fertile valleys and the strategic positions. Towns and cities were laid out with wide streets when there were only a few cabins to be seen. The later development proved the wisdom and foresight of the leader. The settlements grew and the population increased rapidly, but not without hardship and difficulties. The Indians were a hazard and sometimes a real menace. Crops failed because of drought, or were destroyed by hordes of crickets.

When the first pioneers came, practically all of the region west of the Rocky Mountains belonged to Mexico. It did not become U. S. territory till the close of the Mexican War. For more than two years the settlers were governed by the ecclesiastical authority of the church. There was no other government. In 1849 the people requested admission into the union of states under the name of the state of Deseret. Assuming that Congress would act favorably on their request, the people held a constitutional convention, drafted and adopted a constitution and set up the provisional government of the state of Deseret. The constitution provides that "no subordination of preference of one sect or denomination to another shall be established by law, nor shall any religious test ever be required of any officer of trust under the state." This clause reflects the strong conviction of the people that schools should be secular and not religious institutions.

The first regular session of the Deseret Legislature convened in December, 1849, and continued in session until late March, 1850. It was in this session, on February 28, 1850, that the University of Deseret was created, which later became the University of Utah.

The Congress of the United States, after some delay, declined to grant statehood to Deseret but instead organized Utah territory. Brigham Young was appointed first governor of the territory. He was followed by a succession of more or less capable men, each appointed by the President, until statehood was granted in 1896.

During the territorial days, the Church had some very serious trouble over issues, some entirely domestic and some that concerned the federal government. In the summer of 1857 the horrible massacre at the Mountain Meadows occurred in which 120 men, women, and children were killed by Indians and Mormons. The church was not responsible for this crime, as has been demonstrated by the courts, both territorial and federal.

Polygamy also caused much trouble. Though the practice was begun before the migration to Utah, it was not openly promulgated and defended until about 1853. The federal government through the Edmonds law forbade the practice and fixed penalties for disobedience. The Edmonds Tucker law a little later was more severe. It prescribed longer prison terms, heavier fines, the disfranchisement of men who practiced polygamy, and confiscated all the property of the church, including the temples and houses of worship.

The Mormons challenged the constitutionality of the law, and a test was made of the George Reynolds case. When the United States Supreme Court upheld the decision of the lower courts, the Mormons gave up the struggle and promised to obey the law. In 1890 a manifesto was presented to the general conference of the Church by President Woodruff, and the Church withdrew its sanction of further plural marriages. Much of the Church property that had been confiscated was returned, and full citizenship was restored to most of the men who had been disfranchised. An era of general good feeling between Mormons and gentiles began. Statehood was granted in 1896 and there has been but little cleavage politically between Mormons and non-Mormons since.

Church Organization and Administration

Authority in the Mormon Church is vested in the priesthood, but there is no priestly or ministerial class. Every male member of the Church twelve years of age and upward may, and usually does, hold the priesthood. There are two main divisions of the priesthood, the Aaronic or lesser and the Melchizedik or higher.

For administrative purposes the church is divided into territorial units somewhat analogous to our state, county, town, and precinct organization. The primary unit is the ward, presided over by a bishop and two counselors. The normal population of a ward is from 500 to 1,000 people, varying much with the density of population. Every ward is subdivided into districts or blocks. Two teachers are assigned to help the bishop in each block. The wards are grouped together into stakes, analogous to counties. Every stake is presided over by a president and two counselors, assisted by a group of twelve men known as the stake high council. There are at present about 1,200 wards and 155 stakes in the entire church besides 121 "branches" and 38 missions.

The First Presidency is assisted by the Council of the Twelve and by the first Council of Seventy (seven men) and a Presiding Bishopric consisting of a presiding bishop and his two counselors.

Education

The Mormons exalt intelligence and learning. They point out that according to Genesis in the beginning man was told to subdue the earth and was given dominion over the fish and fowl and every living thing on the earth. Man cannot do this in ignorance. Jesus said we should love the Lord with all our "minds." This means intelligence and understanding. Every Mormon knows the saying, "The glory of God is intelligence." Brigham Young taught that the Mormon faith "will not clash with nor contradict the facts of science in any particular."

The leaders of the church from the first advocated learning. The following are quotations from the revelations to Joseph Smith:

Teach ye diligently . . . of things which have been, things which are; things that must shortly come to pass, things which are at home; things which are abroad. The wars and the perplexities of the nations. . . . Seek ye diligently and teach one another words of wisdom, seek learning. . . . Obtain a knowledge of history, and of countries, and of kingdoms, of laws of God and man. . . . It is impossible for a man to be saved in ignorance.

The Mormon people have always supported and encouraged education. In fact, the church itself is really a great educational institution. There are five chief auxiliary organizations in every ward: The Primary organization is for boys and girls up to twelve years of age; the Sunday school has departments and gradations to accommodate people of all ages, beginning with the kindergarten department and extending to adult classes for parents. The Young Mens' Mutual Improvement Association and the corresponding organization for young women over twelve years of age furnish religious and literary instruction and also opportunity for wholesome athletic sports and social life.

The womens' Relief Society is made up of the women of the church, young and old, who devote their labors especially to relieving the poor and the sick.

These auxiliary organizations in the wards are supervised and directed by a stake board and presiding officers, who guide and unify the work in the wards. For each of the auxiliaries there is a central "general board" to supervise all the stake organizations of every auxiliary respectively in the church. The general directive authority for all organizations and quorums is vested, of course, in the First Presidency.

In the Mormon church there is something for everyone to do—not merely "busy work" but interesting and beneficial activity that aids society and develops the individual.

It has been truthfully said by a student of Mormonism, not himself a member, "The various organizations of the church furnish the means of a liberal education."

Schools were established by the Mormon church as early as June, 1832, in Kirtland, Ohio. Not only did the people want schools for the children, but also for adults. Reference is made in Joseph Smith's Journal to "The Kirtland High School" held in the temple. The Saints established a "School of the Prophets" in Independence, Missouri also, and by 1836 they had built a "large and comfortable school house" at Far West, Missouri.

In accordance with the city charter, the University of Nauvoo was established on December 16, 1840. A board of regents was appointed consisting of 23 men exclusive of the chancellor and registrar.

Elementary schools were planned for every ward of the city and were placed under the direct supervision of the chancellor and board of regents of the University of Nauvoo.

The University had a small but apparently an excellent faculty. Degrees were granted, both earned and honorary.

On the "long trek" across the plains and over the mountains attempts were made to instruct the children in improvised school houses, and after arrival in the valley, schools were of first concern to the settlers. At the meeting of the first territorial assembly in Utah, in 1851, the legislation of the provisional government of Deseret establishing a University was reenacted, and measures were passed providing for a system of common schools. The chancellor and regents of the University were authorized to appoint a territorial superintendent of schools.

The earliest type of local control of public schools in Utah was the small district under the supervision of three elected trustees, and it remained so until 1890 when the cities with a population of 5,000 or more were made independent school districts. The counties and small towns remained under the three-trustee district system until 1905 when the legislature made it optional for counties to consolidate their schools into county districts. By 1915 the plan had proved to be so beneficial and popular that county consolidation was made mandatory in the entire state, and the three-trustee-districts went the way of the oxcart and the hand sickle. The Utah Consolidated plan for administration of elementary and secondary education is among the best in the Union from the point of view of economy and efficiency.

By constitutional provision and legislative enactment the public schools are public enterprises and entirely separate in control and support from any church. But inasmuch as the Mormons have always been in the majority in Utah, it is quite likely that the present school organization was possible because of the familiarity of so many people with the successful cooperative undertakings in the church.

The University of Deseret (now the University of Utah), founded in 1850, the oldest state university west of the Missouri river, opened its doors for students in 1851, but in about a year it was closed temporarily. The school was opened again in 1867 and since that time the school has had a steady and a continuous growth. In 1892 the name was changed from University of Deseret to University of Utah.

The State University and the Utah State Agricultural College, established as a land grant college by legislative enactment of 1888 are the two public institutions of higher learning in the state.

Public secondary education was slower in getting started in Utah than was elementary or higher education. Public high schools were few and far between prior to 1900. The enrollment of public high school students in the entire state in 1907 was 2,343 and in 1926 it was 25,967, an increase of about 1,000%. It is true, however, that between 1870 and 1900 many students received secondary instruction in church schools maintained by the Mormons, the Catholics, and several Protestant churches. As late as 1910–11 there were just about as many students in the secondary schools of the Mormon church (4,289) as there were in the public high schools (4,261). This does not include some hundreds of students in other denominational secondary schools. As the public high schools increased the Mormon secondary schools and most of the other denominational schools closed. At the present time nearly all young people of high school age attend the public high schools.

The Mormon church maintains one institution of higher learning, the Brigham Young University at Provo, founded in 1875 and maintained and controlled entirely by the church. It is an excellent institution of good repute. The arts and sciences are stressed with special attention to the fine arts, besides courses in theology and church history. There have been many attempts to measure public education in Utah as compared with other states. In every such measurement, where several criteria were used, Utah stood at or near the top.

A survey of education in Utah in 1926 was made by the U. S. Office of Education, and records the following: "Utah has succeeded in enrolling in school a larger percentage of the population of secondary school age than any other state." That statement still holds. Furthermore, a recent study made by the National Education Association shows that practically the same relative condition prevails for elementary schools and colleges.*

*J. R. Mahoney, *Extent of Schooling of the Population of the U. S. 1945.*

Besides maintaining the Brigham Young University the church supports seminaries and institutes of religion in many places in Utah and adjoining states. Every seminary is located near a high school but is entirely distinct from it in control and support. Students are permitted to attend classes in church history, Bible study and theology at the seminary at hours that will not conflict with the courses in the high school. There are 204 seminaries, of which 111 are for senior high school pupils and 93 for the junior high.

Institutes of Religion are likewise conducted near the campus of a number of higher institutions including the University of Utah, Utah State Agricultural College, the University of Wyoming, the University of Idaho, the University of Arizona, and some others. At present (1946) there are 13 institutes of religion in operation. The total annual budget appropriations for both the institutes and the seminaries is about $426,250, exclusive of capital outlay. The budget is supplied entirely by the church. The students pay no fees and no support comes from taxation.

Temples

The Mormons have been rightly called "a temple building people." In 1836, six years after the date of organization of the church, a Mormon temple was dedicated in Kirtland, Ohio. When the saints moved to Missouri, a temple site was selected and dedicated in Independence, Missouri, but the Mormons were driven from the state and the temple was never erected.

In Nauvoo the church erected, furnished and dedicated a splendid temple, which was characterized as "the crowning glory of 'Nauvoo the beautiful' ". But the temple was seized by a mob, desecrated, and destroyed. The building stones were later used for other structures.

In the winter of 1853, the excavation for the Salt Lake Temple was begun. For forty years the work went on slowly but surely. For the first dozen years of construction it took four days with an ox team to bring one block of granite from the quarry twenty miles to the south. Four million dollars contributed by a pioneer community went into its construction. It was finally dedicated in April, 1893.

Meantime other temples, less pretentious, were being erected. The St. George temple, in the south-west corner of the state, was finished and dedicated in 1877. Timber was brought distances of from 70 to 90 miles. The baptismal font and its accessories weighing 18,000 pounds were cast in Salt Lake City and hauled more than 300 miles to St. George by ox teams.

The Logan Temple in northern Utah, dedicated in 1884, and the Manti Temple in central Utah, dedicated in 1888, were also erected while the Salt Lake Temple was under construction.

The Canadian Temple at Cardston, Alberta, Canada was begun in 1913 and dedicated in 1923. The Arizona Temple at Mesa, Arizona was dedicated in 1927.

The lovely Hawaiian Temple at Laie, Oahu, Hawaiian Islands is the only Mormon temple off the American mainland. It was finished and dedicated in 1919. Like the Arizona and Canadian Temples, its architectural style is markedly different from the earlier temples.

The latest temple finished is the Idaho Falls Temple which was dedicated in 1945. All of the temples are on carefully chosen sites, and are impressive structures—all of them beautiful—some are majestic.

A magnificent California temple was planned for Los Angeles, the site was determined and the land purchased but the war caused a delay and actual construction has not yet begun.

The temples are not merely chapels or meeting houses for public worship. They are more in the nature of "houses of the Lord" where the most sacred services are held and ordinances performed such as baptisms and marriages.

The Mormon people believe that the life hereafter is very real, and closely connected with the life on earth. They believe that the family ties formed here may be perpetuated in the next world; that marriages performed in the temple under the authority of the priesthood unite the contracting parties not only for this life, but for "time and eternity." Such a ceremony brings a new sanctity to the home and a new dignity to the marriage covenant. The efficacy of temple marriages is indicated by the extremely low divorce rate among those so married as compared with general divorce statistics.

The Mormons believe, too, that the living may be baptized for those who died without heeding or hearing the gospel message and that church marriages may likewise be made vicariously by the living for the dead. Children born to parents married only by secular law may be "sealed" to their parents for eternity.

There are many religious instructions given and blessings pronounced in the temples, all conditioned upon righteous living. The ordinances embody certain obligations on the part of the individual, such as promises to observe strictly the law of virtue and chastity, to be charitable, benevolent and tolerant, and to devote both talent and material means to the spread of truth and the upbuilding of the race.

Only those who are members of the church in good standing and have official recommendations from their bishops and stake presidents are admitted to the temple and then only for specific purposes. Opening the doors to all manner of visitors would bring crowds of sightseers and those trying to satisfy irreverent curiosity. The legitimate work of the temple would be disrupted. Hundreds and possibly thousands of church members are passing through the temples every day, partaking of the opportunities offered.

Missions

Mention has already been made of the extent and effectiveness of the missionary work of the church in the states and in foreign lands. Through all the troubles of mob violence, ejections, long treks, pioneering of new country and establishing settlements the missionary system was still maintained and through it, many thousands of persons were converted.

A good Mormon boy looks forward with anticipation to the time that he can go on a mission. Fathers and mothers esteem it a privilege for their sons to go. Most, if not all, of the missionaries have a deep conviction that they are rendering a service to their fellow men. Fathers and mothers share the faith; they or their parents or grandparents received the "glad tidings" from missionaries, and the only way they can pay the debt is to bring similar happiness to others. Of the thousands of boys on missions there is very rarely one who deserts his ideals of faith, service, and chastity.

In a material sense, the missionary system is a monument to the idealism of the Mormon people. Except for the years of World Wars I and II, more than 2,000 missionaries were abroad all the time. More than a million dollars was sent in cash to those missionaries every year by their relatives and friends without hope of one cent of money in return. Not only must the missionary be maintained in his field of labor, but he and the folks at home sacrifice also what he would normally produce if at home. As an evidence of faith and idealism this tremendous outlay for missionary work challenges the world. There is no coercion, no ostracism of the youth who does not go, but it is regarded as a real privilege to go. Since the close of hostilities, the church has taken steps to reestablish the missionary system in a number of foreign countries.

Temporal Phases

The income of the church is derived principally from four sources:

1. First is the tithing fund. Every church member is supposed to give to the church a voluntary, wholly free-will contribution of one tenth of his annual increase. The donor himself is the judge of the actual amount. The total expenditures of the church from the tithing fund in 1945 was $4,617,681.

2. The fast offerings. Every member is asked to fast for two meals on the first Sunday of every month and to give to the church as a wholly voluntary contribution the equivalent of those meals, which is used for the support of the poor. More than 166,000 persons made contributions to this fund in 1945, and there was expended from this fund during the year, $637,558.

3. From auxiliary organizations. Small voluntary contributions to the auxiliary organizations are made by their members to cover costs of publications, editorial and clerical help and similar purposes.

4. Income from invested surpluses of the church. The investments have been made in local Utah securities, chiefly financial institutions and commercial industries. The church has made its investments primarily to encourage local enterprises and to serve the general welfare of the people, members and non-members of the church.

The total expenditures of the church, both budget and non-budget for the year 1945 were about nine and a third million dollars.

Church Welfare

Taking care of the poor, the sick, and the needy has always been a major responsibility of the Mormon Church. But every individual should be responsible for earning a living for himself and those who are dependent upon him as long as it is possible to do so. The best kind of aid according to church theory in such cases is to assist the needy person to find employment suitable to his skill and strength.

The church decries idleness, but encourages industry, thrift and economy. A leading member recently said, "Honesty, truthfulness, sobriety, willingness to give, love for fellowmen, sympathy for woe, misery and want, service to and for others, are used to the point of command."

"We Mormons have cared for the essential needs of our own in the past, we can do it now."

Such has been the spirit and practice of the Mormons since the beginning of the church through all their hardships and migrations.

Ordinarily the bishops of wards, assisted by the ward teachers and the Relief Society, could take care of all needy cases. But when the depression came after 1930, the need for food, shelter and clothing became much greater and many accepted assistance through federal and state relief agencies.

Wards and priesthood quorums conducted various projects to increase the supply of food and clothing, to raise money, and to provide housing where necessary. "In one case the elders quorum of a stake farmed 950 acres of land and raised 15,000 bushels of wheat, which, because of its high grade, was sold at a premium for seed wheat, and the money realized was used for the welfare program of the stake."

In many agricultural areas the wards set up canning and preserving units to care for the surplus fruits and berries. All such products go into the bishop's storehouse for distribution to those who need it.

About 1933 it was becoming evident that church welfare was assuming such proportions that the wards and quorums could not handle it adequately and there was a need for an over-all organization and coordination of effort. Announcement of a church-wide program of welfare was made in a message of the First Presidency at the April conference, 1936. The basic objectives of the program were: to produce and store enough goods, commodities and clothing to care for the wants of the unemployed and needy and to assist the unemployed to find work that they might become independent and free from the curse of idleness and the evils of the dole.

The program has greatly expanded in its organization. The various stakes were grouped into nineteen regions for administration purposes. The central committee, as enlarged, includes experts in various fields, such as agriculture, industry, manufacturing, construction, cooperatives, marketing, and engineering.

The financial and statistical report of the church for the year 1945 reveals an amazing variety and extent of production of the welfare program, too lengthy to include here. The total cash expenditures for relief for the year 1945 amount to $1,181,239.

Under the heading of emergency activity, the following is reported as typical. On August 19, 1945, a rainfall of cloudburst proportions fell on the foothills to the northeast of Salt Lake City resulting in a destructive flood that ran through the Salt Lake Cemetery and southward where it did great damage to streets, grounds and houses. Four wards were involved. The Stake and Ward Welfare Committees assumed responsibility for the work of cleaning up the area. The homes of members and non-members alike were cared for. The Welfare organizations of neighboring stakes came to help. Before the work was finally completed several furnaces and water heating units were dismantled, cleaned, and rebuilt. Food, clothing, and furniture were provided where needed. Cash funds required were secured from the Ward and Stake Fast and Welfare offerings. The work group on the first evening had 100 men; one work group on one evening had 900 men; neighboring stakes sent 1,250 men, who furnished 2,500 hours of work. Three thousand more men than were needed volunteered to help. All told, 8,000 man-hours were used in the project. The Relief Society of the stake and wards provided refreshments for the workers.

The incident reported is a demonstration of what the Welfare Program can and does do in cases of dire emergency.

The latest development of the church welfare program is the effort to relieve the suffering of Mormon church members in Europe. Immediately after V. E. Day the welfare committee undertook the work of getting food, clothing, and medicine to the sick and needy in the European branches of the church. One of the twelve apostles was sent over to direct the distribution of relief and to supervise the rehabilitation of the different missions.

Fifteen carloads of food, twelve carloads of clothing, and 4,532 packages of vitamins were sent to Europe between November 15, 1945 and May 3, 1946. These were distributed in Belgium, Czechoslovakia, Denmark, Finland, France, Germany, Holland, Norway, and Sweden. In a letter to the writer, Elder Harold B. Lee, Director of Church Welfare, said, "These shipments will continue until we will probably have sent, by the first of June, another ten or twelve cars."

Because of postal regulations, parcel post packages were limited to 11 pounds each. Although the food, clothing, and vitamins already sent constitute a very small fraction of what Europe needs, it is a very real and important effort of the church to take care of her own.

BIBLIOGRAPHY

A good, brief bibliography of the Church of Jesus Christ of Latter-Day Saints is to be found in the *Encyclopedia Britannica* (1929), article, "Mormonism."

M. LYNN BENNION, Ph.D., *Mormonism and Education* (1900).

J. REUBEN CLARK, First Counselor to the President of the Mormon Church, *Church Welfare Plan* (1939).

LELAND H. CREER, Ph.D., "Utah and the Nation," *University of Washington Publications in Social Science,* Vol. 7 (1929).

Financial and Statistical Report of the Church of Jesus Christ of Latter-Day Saints, *Deseret Evening News,* April 6, 1946.

ANDREW L. NEFF, Ph.D., *History of Utah* (1940).

GEORGE SESSIONS PERRY, "Salt Lake City," *Saturday Evening Post,* March 9, 1946.

THE BAHAI CAUSE

The name of Mirza Ahmad Sohrab has been favorably known among book-lovers ever since the publication of his large and beautiful volume called "The Bible of Mankind." To a more circumscribed circle he is well known for his many volumes and pamphlets dealing with the Bahai Cause.

Born in Esphahan, Persia, in 1891, he was educated in a missionary school in Julfa and then graduated from the Imperial University of Teheran. His uncle was the leader of the Bahai movement in his home city and took young Sohrab with him after his house was pillaged at the hands of religious persecutors. The two wandered as dervishes, visiting many cities and finally arriving in Bombay, India, where the Zoroastrian Bahai colony welcomed them as religious refugees. Then followed travels in Egypt, Acca and on to Palestine where he stood before the presence of Abdul Baha and learned first-hand the teachings of the cause. Abdul Baha sent him to Washington, D. C. to join a famous Bahai teacher, Mirza Abul Fazl. Through a set of curious circumstances, Sohrab became secretary of the Persian Minister to the U.S.A. and later set up the "Persian-American Educational Society" and the "Orient-Occident Unity."

In 1912 when Abdul Baha visited the United States, Sohrab travelled with him for nine months as his interpreter and secretary, continuing this service in England, Scotland, France, Germany and Austria-Hungary and then back to Egypt, Acca and Palestine. During the World War he lived as companion in the house of the prophet, keeping a diary of Baha's words and teachings. In this country Sohrab continued to lecture for many years on the Bahai Cause. Since 1929 he has been a director of the newly founded group called "The New History Society" and now serves as the editor of "The Caravan," an international correspondence club of young people with some 100,000 members. In 1943–44 Sohrab devoted his full time to the preparation of the Bahai Centennial. He was co-author of the production called "The Gate" which dramatized the lives of the founders of the Bahai faith and was produced at the Metropolitan Opera House in May of 1944.

Editor

THE BAHAI CAUSE

MIRZA AHMAD SOHRAB

IN 1844, A MOVEMENT for religious and social reform was launched in Iran. In spite of its modest beginnings among a handful of students, this movement within a short while gained so much momentum that both government and church felt their institutions threatened and proceeded to take drastic counter-action. The leader, calling himself The Bab, meaning the Gate, was thrown into prison and later martyred, while his followers, known as Babis, were eliminated by mass measures, supplemented by unimaginable cruelties. The rebellion was on the way out, so the authorities thought.

Now The Bab, who was not only a reformer but also a Prophet, had foretold the appearance of a yet greater one than he to carry on the work after his departure from the scene of contest; consequently, the remaining disciples treasured the hope that all was not lost. In this group of humble persons was Mirza Hussain Ali, distinguished by the fact that he was the oldest son of Mirza Abbas of Nur, wealthy minister of the State. On joining the Cause, this young noble had recovered his family name, a custom prevalent among the Babis and had assumed the name, Baha-O-Llah, signifying the Glory of God. Thus Baha-O-Llah stepped out of the framework of court circles to espouse a people's reform movement of which he was presently recognized as one of its most fearless and powerful exponents.

In 1852, an event occurred which was fraught with terrible consequences for the Babis. One of The Bab's followers, a simple boy who had been mentally unbalanced at the spectacle of his Master's martyrdom, waylaid the Shah as he issued from the Capitol on an afternoon's promenade, and fired a pistol at him. The weapon was ineffectually charged with small shot, and the demonstration resulted merely in an attack of royal nerves, but the assailant was put to death on the spot and a reign of terror loosed in the city, the hideousness of which has few parallels in history. Among the Babis, thrown into jail as suspect in the plot, was Baha-O-Llah, and it was in the lowest depths of a series of underground dungeons in Teheran that this disciple received the revelation that he was disciple no longer but that indeed he was the leader whose coming had been foretold by The Bab.

Owing to his family connections, Baha-O-Llah was not summarily executed as were his fellow-believers. Instead, he was given benefit of a trial, at which he was cleared, largely through the intercession of the Russian Ambassador. He was, however, exiled to Bagdad, as member of a sect unwelcome in his native land, and there in company with his family and close adherents, he took up his life under the jurisdiction of the Turkish Government.

During this period, which lasted approximately ten years, Baha-O-Llah made of his house in Bagdad a center to which scholars from near and far were attracted, and many Babis found their way to him, forming a community in exile. Here he wrote three books, classics in Bahai or in any literature, namely: *Hidden Words, Seven Valleys* and *The Book of Iqan.*

This sojourn, under comparatively friendly conditions, was not to last indefinitely, for here also the revolutionary teachings of the New Cause were cutting channels in minds ready for a broadening conception of religion and social science; consequently the Turkish Government in turn became uneasy and dissatisfied. In 1863, Baha-O-Llah and his associates were ordered to move on.

Preceding his departure from Bagdad, Baha-O-Llah tarried twelve days (April 21st–May 3d, 1863) in the Garden of Rizwan, a property adjoining the city, while the poor uprooted families straggled in with their small possessions, choosing of their own free will to continue with him whatever the cost. Then when all had assembled, he stood before his distracted followers who were wailing at this second banishment, and made an unexpected announcement, one which actually broke upon the scene like a bombshell. The announcement was as follows: The One whose coming had been foretold by their Master, The Bab, was no stranger to them. He had been living with them all the while. He, Baha, was their leader and the leader of the Cause. Let those who would, follow him.

From that night on, the Babis existed no longer. Those who

recognized Baha-O-Llah as the fulfillment of prophecy turned to him, calling themselves after his name: Bahais. A very few who were unconvinced made their way back to Bagdad.

The twelve days spent in the garden near Bagdad are celebrated every year, this period being known as the "Feast of Rizwan." It is one of the outstanding Bahai anniversaries, for it commemorates a new phase in the Cause. Under the leadership of Baha-O-Llah, the movement shifted outward into an all-embracing circle. The reformation within Islam was to be a World Reformation.

The caravan of displaced Bahais made for Constantinople. A stop of a few months, then on to Adrianople. Here they took up life again for four years, and it was during that time that Baha-O-Llah addressed the kings and rulers of the earth in a series of Tablets which were sent to their destinations from the next place of exile. In these epistles is developed a system of international law to be applied to the politics and ethics of the modern world. They also contain prophecies on the status of the nations which were justified later, and repeated appeals for bettering the condition of the poor and downtrodden. If appearing in these latter years, these epistles would stand out as remarkable, but in view of the fact that they were written in the nineteenth century, they make extraordinary and impressive reading.

Again on the move, this time by sea, the weary travellers arrive at the fortress city of Acca, Turkish dominion on the shore of Palestine. It is the final exile. Baha-O-Llah and his family were incarcerated in the military barracks, a confinement which with time became less and less restricted. During twenty-four years, Baha-O-Llah lived in Acca, while the massive walls which had withstood the onslaughts of Napoleon showed themselves impotent to prevent the light of world consciousness from filtering through to a harassed humanity. The teachings of Baha-O-Llah, transmitted in secret past the city limits, were carried back to Iran, the land of their origin; back to Turkey proper, and on to Russia, China, India and Arabia. The concept of federating the nations of all the earth was beginning to germinate in the minds of the people of the East. "Let not a man glory in this, that he loves his country," Baha-O-Llah addressed Professor Edward G. Browne of Cambridge University, England, in the single recorded interview with an Occidental, concluding "let him rather glory in this, that he loves his kind."

Alongside of his plan for world unification, Baha-O-Llah made a spiritual blue-print of religion, showing that the different Faiths were illumined pathways toward the same goal. The Founders of these Faiths were one in purpose and taught identical lessons. Why then, asked the great Teacher, could not their followers serve God and men in complete understanding, sympathy and cooperation? Only superstitious imaginations and man-made laws prevented them from arriving at this state of awareness. These stumbling blocks should be relegated to the past where they belonged and cease to figure in an awakened society.

Baha-O-Llah wrote in Persian and Arabic, of which languages he was a past-master. His works are practical and poetic, inspired and human. He always thought of the world as a whole, without parts, yet the component objects of that world were very real to him. He loved children and music; he delighted in a blade of grass.

Abbas Effendi started life as the privileged son of a rich landowner. When still a child he saw his house stripped of furnishings and treasures, heard the threatening murmur of the mob, and saw his father laden with chains, the target for abuse.

Together with his mother and her younger children, he accompanied Baha-O-Llah into exile and, as he grew up, he more and more became the intimate companion of his father. At the age of seventy five Baha-O-Llah passed into the life beyond on the 28th of May, 1892, leaving his son, Abbas, leader of the Cause and interpreter of the teachings.

Abbas Effendi became known to the world as Abdul Baha, meaning Servant of Baha, a name which he chose to designate the state of servitude that was his throughout his life. He served his great father, the Bahais and the communities in Acca and Haifa during the years of his captivity, which lasted over half a century, and when, with the revolt of the Young Turks, he was set free, he issued forth to serve the world at large.

Abdul Baha undertook journeys which carried him to Egypt, France, Switzerland, Austria-Hungary, Germany, Canada and the United States, in the course of which he delivered hundreds of lectures before churches, synagogues, universities, colleges and civic organizations. As interpreter of the Bahai Cause, he summed up its teachings in a set of principles, as follows:

1. The Oneness of the world of humanity.
2. Independent investigation of Truth.
3. The foundation of all religions is one.
4. Religion must be the cause of unity.
5. Religion must be in accord with science and reason.
6. Equality between men and women.
7. Prejudices of all kinds must be forgotten.
8. Universal peace.
9. Universal education.
10. Solution of the economic problem.
11. An International Auxiliary language.
12. United States of the World.

At the termination of his arduous journeys in Europe and America, Abdul Baha returned to Palestine where he dictated *The Divine Plan,* a work in which he summoned the Bahais of all lands to go out into the world and spread the teachings of Baha-O-Llah for the unification of the races, nations and religions.

In 1921, Abdul Baha at the age of seventy-seven, terminated a life of unexampled devotion to humanity, leaving behind a will in which he appointed his grandson Shoghi Effendi as Guardian of the Bahai Cause. Under the leadership of Shoghi Effendi, the various Bahai Assemblies on this continent have been organized by the "National Spiritual Assembly," and headquarters established in Chicago, Illinois, where a Bahai Temple has been erected. According to the *World Almanac,* 1946, page 308, the Bahais in the United States number 4,489.

The Bahai Cause has no rituals. It has no priesthood. A respected person in the community who knows and understands the teachings is fitted to conduct the meetings, which consist of talks, readings from the writings of Baha-O-Llah and Abdul Baha, prayers and occasionally questions and answers. Fellowship of spirit and mutual service is the badge of association and worship. Local groups, wherever organized, are under the direction of the National Spiritual Assembly of the Bahais of the United States and Canada.

As an outgrowth of the Bahai Cause, a second movement is functioning throughout the world, with the intent of bringing the universal teachings of Baha-O-Llah and Abdul Baha to the consciousness of the youth of all nations. In 1929, The New History Society was founded in New York by Mr. and Mrs. Lewis Stuyvesant

Chanler and Mirza Ahmad Sohrab (a secretary to Abdul Baha from 1910 to 1919). This society engaged itself in public lectures and in the publishing of Bahai books, and from it, as its youth section, emerged The Caravan of East and West.

The Caravan of East and West is an educational movement, the chief activity of which is international correspondence. It numbers 1,300 Chapters in 37 countries, with an aggregate membership of 100,000 children, young people and adults. Its publications, *The Caravan* and *Pen Friends Guide,* respectively appearing quarterly and monthly, keep the large circle of its readers informed as to the growth and influence of the movement.

The New History Society and the Caravan is a movement in itself for the spreading of the Bahai ideals and principles, independent of and unaffiliated with the Bahai organization.

BIBLIOGRAPHY

Tablets of Baha-O-Llah, translated by Ali Kuli Khan, Bahai Publishing Society (Chicago, 1917).

The Mysterious Forces of Civilization (written in Persian by an eminent Bahai philosopher, translated by Johanna Dawud), (Chicago, Bahai Publishing Society, 1918).

Living Pictures (in the Great Drama of the 19th Century) by Mirza Ahmad Sohrab and Julie Chanler, The New History Foundation (New York, 1933).

The Human Charter, Principles of Baha-O-Llah and Abdul Baha for the founding of a World Society (The New History Foundation, 1945).

The Bible of Mankind, edited by Mirza Ahmad Sohrab (Universal Publishing Company, New York, 1939).

REFORM JUDAISM

One of the leaders in America of Reform Judaism is Dr. Louis I. Newman, rabbi of the Temple Rodeph Sholom in New York City. His many papers and books have been the voice of this movement not only in this country but abroad. A leading Zionist, he has been acting chairman of the Palestine Mandate Defense League, honorary chairman of the American Friends of a Jewish Palestine and member of the administrative committee of the Zionist Organization of America. He has served as an official observer of the Central Conference of American Rabbis at the United Nations conferences. He is trustee and member of many educational and philanthropic organizations, and has held the chairmanship of the Intercollegiate Menorah Association.

He was born in Providence, R. I., in 1893. He attended Brown University (B.A., 1913), University of California (M.A., 1917) and Columbia University (Ph.D., 1924). In 1942 Brown University conferred upon him the honorary degree of Doctor of Divinity.

Serving first with Rabbi Stephen S. Wise in the Free Synagogue of New York, Dr. Newman became rabbi in the Bronx Free Synagogue, then associate at the Temple Israel in New York City, special lecturer at Columbia, a member of the faculty of the Jewish Institute of Religion and rabbi at the Temple Emanu-El in San Francisco. For many years he engaged in journalistic work: a feature writer for the "Call-Bulletin," San Francisco, and columnist for the American Jewish Press.

Besides the works listed in the bibliography to his essay, he has published: "Studies in Biblical Parallelism" (1918); "Songs of Jewish Rebirth" (1921); "A Jewish University in America?" (1923); "Jewish Influence on Christian Reform Movements" (1925); "The Hasidic Anthology" (1934); "The Talmudic Anthology" (1945); five volumes of "Collected Sermons and Addresses" (1941 on) and many other volumes.

Editor

REFORM JUDAISM

LOUIS I. NEWMAN

REFORM JUDAISM is the name given to the liberal or progressive manifestation of Judaism. It has its main headquarters in the United States, but there is a modest Reform movement in England and France. Its "Guiding Principles" were enunciated, not in the form of a credo, but of a general statement of ideals, in the so-called Columbus, Ohio declaration of 1937, issued by the Central Conference of American Rabbis, its representative Rabbinical body. The liturgy and ritual of Reform Judaism are to be found in the *Union Prayer Book,* the *Union Hymnal,* the *Rabbi's Manual* and other publications. Rabbi Solomon B. Freehof, a former president of the Central Conference of American Rabbis, has written on *Reform Jewish Practice and Its Rabbinic Background* (1944), and the author of this essay has in preparation a volume entitled: *The Jewish People, Faith and Life* which will be a Guidebook for Newcomers into Judaism and serve as a handbook for American Jews of liberal outlook and observance.

The Union of American Hebrew Congregations, founded in 1873 by the late Rabbi Isaac M. Wise, and comprising—in 1945—320 congregations is the central organization of American Reform synagogues, with its headquarters in Cincinnati, Ohio. Its publications include *Liberal Judaism, The Jewish Teacher, The Synagogue, Youth Leader, The Jewish Layman Topics and Trends.* Its Commissions include those on Jewish Education; Synagogue Activities; Information about Judaism; Institutes on Judaism. The Hebrew Union College at Cincinnati, founded in 1875, has graduated nearly 600 Rabbis, and the Jewish Institute of Religion, founded by Rabbi Stephen S. Wise at New York in 1922, has graduated nearly 200. Associated with the Union of American Hebrew Congregations are the National Federation of Temple Brotherhoods, the National Federation of Temple Sisterhoods, and the National Federation of Temple Youth. The Central Conference of American Rabbis, which was founded in 1889, had in 1945 a membership of 475.

Reform Judaism is a direct derivative from traditional Judaism and stands in friendly relationship to Orthodox and Conservative Judaism, as well as co-called Reconstructionist Judaism, of which Rabbi Mordecai M. Kaplan is the founder and chief spokesman. Its approach, however, to matters of ritual, belief and organization is eclectic and voluntary. While all Judaism, including Reform, stems from Biblical, Talmudical and Medieval Judaism, as codified in the *Shulhan Arukh (The Prepared Table)* of the 16th century and thereafter, nevertheless Reform Judaism has particular points of emphasis which are characteristic of it. For example, the wearing of hats or other head-covering at divine worship is optional with the individual, though most Reform Jews do not cover their heads at prayer. Reform Judaism enjoins the observance of only one day of the holidays of *Sukkoth* (First and Seventh Day), of Passover (First and Seventh Day) and of Pentecost or *Shevuoth* (First Day). Reform Rabbis do not ask that a person divorced under the laws of the state also secure a Rabbinical divorce or *Get*. The ritual of Reform Judaism, while thoroughly traditional, is nevertheless abbreviated in length; more prayers in the English or other vernaculars are to be found in the Reform Prayer Book than in the Conservative or Orthodox. Reform Jews hallow the Seventh Day Sabbath, but do not observe the minutiae of the regulations concerning Sabbath rest and worship.

Among Reform Jews, each individual is free to formulate his own viewpoint with respect to Zionism, but the Central Conference of American Rabbis has enunciated the principle that Reform Judaism and Zionism are not incompatible. Each individual is also free to observe the Dietary Laws throughout the year and at Passover to the degree that he or she elects. The Rabbis, however, do not preach from their pulpits or teach in their classes that an observance of the Dietary Laws, in whole or in part, is a desideratum of Jewish life. Many Reform Jews observe the food laws as a symbol of fealty to Jewish tradition, and not for hygienic or health reasons.

The theology of Reform Judaism has been ably expressed by Rabbi Kaufman Kohler and, more recently, in the "Guiding Principles" enunciated at Columbus in 1937. God, Prayer, Immortality, Free Will, the Mission of Israel, the Messianic Age, the Chosen People, the Problem of Evil, the "Merit of the Fathers" and other religious themes continue to form the substance of Reform Judaism, built upon the concept of "Torah" or Jewish religious culture or religious "civilization." Reform Judaism interprets the Messianic ideal, not in terms of a person or a group of persons; it speaks rather of a Messianic Age with Israel as the "Priest People" and Humanity as its own Messiah. Reform Judaism does not believe in personal resurrection, but in personal and collective immortality, having restored to its liturgy the magnificent prayer: "God, Full of Compassion" with its phrase: "May the soul be bound up in the cluster of eternal life."

For Reform Jews, Liberal Judaism is a true religion, perhaps the true religion, but we do not assert that there is only one true religion for all humanity. We believe that "the righteous of all nations have a share in the World-to-Come", as the Talmudic Rabbis declared. We believe with Lessing in *Nathan, the Wise,* that any religion which leads its adherents to the good life is a true religion, even as each ring owned by the sons in the parable was the correct ring. We cooperate actively in inter-faith activities; at the same time we preserve the individuality and integrity of our family faith.

Reform Judaism is not a proselyting religion, but we are ready to welcome newcomers into our midst through marriage or otherwise, after a period of training with respect to the Jewish people, faith and life. We do not insist for either the man or woman newcomer a strict fulfilment of ritual laws, but sincerity of purpose and basic information regarding Jews and Judaism are asked. Through our Temples and Temple Centers we encourage social comradeship among Jewish young people, but the door is open to those who wish to enter into our fellowship. If a Rabbi lends the benediction of the Liberal Jewish faith, it is understood that any children born to the couple are reared within the fold of Israel. We recognize as valid any marriage performed by a civil magistrate, but we prefer that the religious ceremony be performed initially or in addition. The spirit of Reform Judaism is entirely voluntary, and there is no element of compulsion within itself whatsoever.

Reform Judaism began in Germany in the early years of the 19th century and gained its greatest vogue in the United States. While the number of members in Reform synagogues is far less than those identified with Conservative or Orthodox Judaism, the Reform Temples and Temple Houses are great meccas of activity and community service. The Confirmation rite for boys and girls on the day of Pentecost *(Shevuot)* has been highly developed in Reform Judaism, and cantatas like "The Law God Gave on Sinai" are now popular. Within recent years, through the influence of Rabbi Jacob D. Schwarz of the Union of American Hebrew Congregations there has been an increasingly strong emphasis upon pageantry, symbolism and ceremonialism in Reform Judaism, not for esoteric purposes, but in order to add color, zest and poetry to our cult.

The author of this essay in *Biting on Granite* (1946) has written of "A New Reform Judaism and the New Union Prayer Book." In this exposition he has sought to describe so-called "Renascence Reform Judaism" and its indebtedness to the new folk-movements in Jewry and to Zionism in particular. The Hebrew revival in Palestine within the past sixty years has tended to deepen and enrich the content of Judaism the world over, including the United States. Reform Jews, who are frequently to be found among the affluent and the middle-class, are concerned not merely with philanthropic aid to the distressed and displaced survivors of Hitlerism and Fascism, but also with the championship of the cause of minority rights where the situation favors this program, and of Palestine as the Jewish Homeland under the Mandate. Within the synagogue an endeavor is being made to increase participation by worshipers in the ritual and in congregational singing, to the end that the Order of Worship may be livelier and less aloof. The Hasidic movement, chiefly through the publication of its ethical and homiletical masterpieces, has come to exert an influence upon the preaching of many Reform Rabbis.

Reform Judaism espouses no particular or concrete economic system, but through the pronouncements of the Social Justice Commission of the Central Conference, it seeks to formulate principles which may guide the individual to the advocacy of progressive programs of social, economic and international action. Though many of the members of Reform Temples belong to the "Sadducean" group (to borrow a phrase of the late Justice Louis D. Brandeis), nevertheless they appreciate the necessity of preaching and disseminating the principles of liberalism, regardless of party affiliations, in accordance with the message of the Hebrew Prophets. It is upon Prophetic teachings that Reform Judaism lays its chief stress. At the same time, it has place for "inner religion" and one of its most eminent Rabbis has written a now-celebrated book entitled: *Peace of Mind.* Moreover, the late Rabbi Morris Lichtenstein, author of a book with the same title several years ago, and one of the founders of so-called Jewish Science, was a Reform Rabbi.

Reform Judaism is hospitable to the new psychology, to the findings of science in all its domains, and to the content of constructive sociological movements. Its attitude towards Revelation is expressed in the words from the *Union Prayer Book:*

> O Lord, open our eyes that we may see and welcome all truth, whether shining from the annals of ancient revelations, or reaching us through the seers of our own time; for Thou hidest not Thy light from any generation of Thy children that yearn for Thee and seek Thy guidance.

It is not surprising, therefore, that many Reform Rabbis were in the forefront of the battle to defend science when the Fundamentalists in the name of a literal interpretation of the Bible sought to ban it from publicly-supported schools and colleges.

Reform Judaism has been interested in examining the merits of Humanism, but the latter movement has found few spokesmen in the Reform Temples. Liberal Judaism is rationalistic, but it remains a mystical movement, determined to conserve the best elements of classic Judaism. It functions in the mood of the words of Samuel Taylor Coleridge that "Sublimity is Hebrew by birth." We have great appreciation for such movements as the Community Church, Ethical Culture (which sprang largely out of Jewish leadership) and progressive Christianity, particularly Unitarianism, but no one of these reflects aright the intention, the message and the practice of Reform Judaism. In the words of the late Jacob Voorsanger, for example: "Unitarianism denies the Trinity of God; Judaism affirms His Unity." Jesus of Nazareth remains for Reform Jews an extraordinary personality, akin to the Prophets and the Rabbis, but we do not accept him as the *Christos,* or the Messiah; we regard him, as does Joseph Klausner in his great book, as a "great teacher of morality and an artist in parable."

We believe that Reform Judaism is a highly meritorious expression of modern Judaism in particular and modern religion in general. It is reasonable, sensible, aesthetically appealing, lofty in spirit and at the same time intimate and personal. It has great devotion to Jewish scholarship and tradition, selecting out of the past freely and without inhibition that which seems to apply effectively to the needs of the present. Reform Judaism has fashioned a religion which does not lie too heavily or oppressively upon its adherents; it encourages a sustained rather than a sporadic piety; it seeks to integrate the modern Jew into his environment without minimizing his attachment to the Jewish community and the Jewish people; it aspires to inculcate in Jewish children and young people a staunch fidelity to the best in our legacy, at the same time that we wish to include within our consciousness, our memory, our feelings and our way of life the best which the general commonwealth has to offer with respect to the humanities and amenities of living.

Reform Jews teach that a complete Jew is a person who is a member of the Jewish people by birth or adoption, who believes in the fundamental doctrines of the Jewish faith, and who observes the practices and upholds the movements of Jewish life. We do not wish to wean away a single Orthodox or Conservative Jew from his household fealties; nor do we go forth into the market-place to draw to us the non-Jew. We do, however, seek to overcome skepticism, agnosticism and unbelief; we wish to convince the unaffiliated and the irreligious that Judaism, in our opinion, is a majestic faith. It has the power to create solidarity; it lifts the eyes of its adherents to the God who is the Father of all mankind. It turns us inward to commune with our indwelling spirit, but at the same time, it sends us forth as members of a "kingdom of priests and a holy nation" to endeavor to bless the world.

BIBLIOGRAPHY

Articles in the *Universal Jewish Encyclopaedia* and the *Jewish Encyclopaedia* on Reform Judaism.

LOUIS I. NEWMAN, *The Jewish People, Faith and Life* (1941, 1947); *Biting on Granite* (1946).

DAVID PHILIPSON, *The Reform Movement in Judaism* (1907).

Yearbooks of the Central Conference of American Rabbis, Vols. 1, 15 20, 24, 26, 28, 29, 33, 35, 37, etc.

Tracts issued by the Central Conference of American Rabbis.

KAUFMAN KOHLER, *Jewish Theology* (1910 and 1917).

SOLOMON B. FREEHOF, *Reform Jewish Practice and Its Rabbinic Background* (Cincinnati, 1944).

ELMA AND L. J. LEVINGER, *Folk and Faith; Israel and Its Religion* (1942).

H. G. ENELOW, *A Jewish View of Jesus* (1920).

CONSERVATIVE JUDAISM

Dr. Simon Greenberg has recently transferred his activities from Philadelphia to New York where he is now Provost at the Jewish Theological Seminary. For twenty-one years, until 1946, he served as rabbi at Har Zion Temple in Philadelphia, during which period he also lectured at the Jewish Theological Seminary. In many capacities he has been associated as a leader of the organizations of his faith. He has been vice-president (1935–1937) and president (1937–1939) of the Rabbinical Assembly of America; he has been a member of the national executive committee of the Zionist Organization of America. He has served as director of the Philadelphia Psychiatric Hospital and has been a member of the chaplains' council of the University of Pennsylvania, not to mention many associations with civic and philanthropic organizations.

He was born in Horoshen, Russia, in 1901 and came to America as a mere boy. He attended the University of Minnesota from 1920 to '21 and the College of the City of New York where, in 1922, he was given his B.A. degree. He graduated from the Teachers' Institute of the Jewish Theological Seminary and received his rabbinical degree from that institution in 1925. During the preceding year he studied at the Hebrew University and the American Academy of Oriental Research in Jerusalem. In 1932 Dropsie College conferred upon him his Ph.D. degree.

He has had published numerous articles and sermons in magazines. His books include: "Living as a Jew Today" (1939); "Harishon Series of Texts for the Study of Hebrew" (in five volumes); "Ideas and Ideals in the Jewish Prayer Book" (1940); and "The First Year in the Hebrew School—a Teacher's Guide" (1946).

Editor

CONSERVATIVE JUDAISM

SIMON GREENBERG

CONSERVATIVE JUDAISM designates that current in modern Jewish religious life and thought which occupies the extensive area between Reform and Orthodox or Neo-Orthodox Judaism. It is often spoken of as the "middle of the road" traditional Judaism, though there is no known center between Orthodoxy and Reform. Frequently and more correctly, it is referred to as the school of Historical Judaism, because in all of its activities and thought it ascribes pre-eminent significance to the sense of historic continuity. Hence, it has always laid great emphasis upon thorough scholarly investigation of the historic development of every aspect of Jewish life and thought. It originated in Germany in the middle of the nineteenth century and centered around the Jewish Theological Seminary of Breslau, founded in 1854 and directed for the first two decades of its existence by Zacharias Frankel (1801–1875). Protest against the excesses of the Reform Jewish school was the immediate cause which brought it into being. But the founders of historical Judaism were not interested merely in preserving Judaism as they had received it from their immediate fathers. They knew that no living organism can remain static. Change, leading to growth or decay, was inevitable. They believed that no living organism can develop normally if it breaks sharply, completely and suddenly with its own past. Hence, they sought to guide Jewish life in a manner that would effect the necessary changes without destroying or impairing the essential continuity of Judaism in all of its phases. They looked upon a knowledge of history as indispensable for the achievement of this continuity within change or change within continuity. The main contribution, therefore, which the movement made in the first half century or more of its existence consisted in works of great scholarship delineating the history of Jewish communities, customs, religious ideas and personalities. It consciously avoided the formulation of a new theology, metaphysic or even a general philosophy of Jewish life. Zunz, the universally acknowledged father of modern Jewish scholarship, and Heinrich Graetz, the first great modern Jewish historian, as well as a host of other eminent scholars contributed to the development of this trend in Judaism.

In the United States the movement centered around the group which created The Jewish Theological Seminary of America (1887). Sabato Morais (1823–1897), the founder of the Seminary, Alexander Kohut (1842–1902), Benjamin Szold (1829–1902), and Marcus Jastrow (1829–1903), the greatest Jewish scholars in America in their day and such lay leaders as Solomon Solis-Cohen (1857–   ) and Mayer Sulzberger (1843–1923) sought individually and as a group to stem the ever widening and deepening chasm which was being created by Reform Judaism between the Jewish past and the Jewish present. For fifteen years the Seminary was a weak and ineffective institution. In 1902 the Seminary was reorganized. Doctor Solomon Schechter (1847–1915) at that time reader in Rabbinics at Cambridge, accepted the call to become the president. He brought to the new institution a group of brilliant young scholars who have since then richly fulfilled the promise of their youth, such as Louis Ginzberg (1873–   ), Alexander Marx (1878–   ), Israel Friedlaender (1876–1920), and Israel Davidson (1870–1939).

At the present time, Conservative Judaism in America has three main organs through which it functions. I.) The United Synagogue of America, composed of some four hundred congregations under the spiritual leadership of graduates of The Jewish Theological Seminary and other members of The Rabbinical Assembly of America. II.) The Rabbinical Assembly of America, composed of some three hundred fifty Seminary graduates and a number of similarly-minded individuals trained elsewhere for the Rabbinate. III.) The Jewish Theological Seminary of America whose program of activities has been progressively expanded in conformity to the changing needs of Jewish life in modern times.

The basic attitudes characterizing the vast majority of the members of Conservative Jewry may be formulated as follows:

1. Change in thought and in action is inevitable. It is not, however, necessarily an indication either of progress or decay. It all depends upon the character of the change.

2. Truth scientifically established beyond a reasonable doubt

cannot be denied by a mere appeal to authoritarian dicta. Such truths must be assimilated into the formulations of Judaism.

3. An effort is made to preserve all Jewish religious practices which have been hallowed by Biblical injunction, Rabbinic teachings and centuries or generations of usage. The creation of new forms and practices embodying the ancient teachings is encouraged. Since there is no authoritarian hierarchal organization within Judaism generally nor within the Conservative movement in particular, a considerable variety of practice prevails even within the ranks of the Conservative movement.

4. Judaism, being more than a system of abstract universal ethical data but an all-embracing comprehensive way of life, should seek to express itself in all forms of literature and art and communal organization, as well as in Festivals, Sabbaths, Holy Days, daily ritual and the synagogue.

5. The re-establishment in Palestine of a large, flourishing autonomous, Hebraically and religiously dominated Jewish community is an integral part of Judaism's hopes and teachings. Hence, Conservative Jews have almost unanimously been identified with every phase of the modern Zionist movement.

6. A knowledge of the Hebrew language, of Jewish history and literature being indispensable to rich Jewish living and meaningful Jewish continuity, the Conservative movement has always emphasized the need for intensive Jewish education. The movement's achievements thus far in the field of intensive Jewish education have not been too impressive. An intense dissatisfaction with the results and a restless search for more effective educational procedures characterize today's Conservative Jewish ranks in America.

7. In regard to national and international problems, Conservative Judaism, basing itself upon the central Jewish teaching regarding the sanctity of all of life and of human life in particular, has through the Rabbinical Assembly of America and the United Synagogue of America repeatedly made public pronouncements supporting all action which would help implement the ideals of human brotherhood, equality, freedom and peace.

8. Judaism has always been a universal religion. Its hopes for the future envisage a mankind living in brotherhood and peace without, at the same time, necessarily being uniform in language, religious beliefs and social practices. However, one need not be born a

Jew in order to be accepted within the ranks of Judaism. He may through voluntary action accept the teachings and the discipline of Judaism and identify himself with Jewish life, thus becoming eligible for membership within the Jewish fold. Nor are the practices of Judaism limited to any given geographic area. Conservative Judaism naturally partakes of this universalism. It thus also believes that co-operation among the religious groups of America and an unrelenting effort for the better understanding among them are indispensable to the welfare of religion generally, the religious groups themselves, and the spiritual growth of America as a whole.

BIBLIOGRAPHY

Beliefs and Practices of Judaism by Louis Finkelstein (1941).

Conservative Judaism—An American Philosophy by Robert Gordis (1945).

Students, Scholars and Saints by Louis Ginzberg (1928), pp. 195–203.

Living As a Jew Today by Simon Greenberg (1940).

Judaism As a Civilization by M. M. Kaplan (1934).

Proceedings of The Rabbinical Assembly of America (Vol. I; Vol. VII).

Seminary Addresses and Other Papers by Solomon Schechter (1915).

The Jewish Theological Seminary—Semi-Centennial Volume (1939).

United Synagogue Recorder (1913; 1927).

ETHICAL CULTURE

Ethical Culturists will agree that Henry Neumann is an authentic voice of their group. Since 1911 he has been a leader of the Brooklyn Ethical Culture Society and has contributed important volumes to the large and expanding literature of this faith, including "Education for Moral Growth," "Modern Youth and Marriage" and "Lives in the Making." Born in New York in 1882 Dr. Neumann received his formal education on the eastern seaboard, graduating from the College of the City of New York in 1900; he pursued graduate studies at Cornell, Columbia and New York Universities, the latter conferring upon him the Ph.D. degree in 1906.

Essentially an educator, he has taught at many American universities: his alma mater, Wisconsin, Ohio State, California, Utah, Arizona, as well as at the University of Hawaii, lecturing in the field of his specialty which is moral education. He has been secretary of the American Committee at the 2nd International Moral Education Congress at the Hague (1912), a member of the N.E.A. Committee on the Reorganization of Secondary Education, vice president of the Lincoln Settlement for Negroes, a former head-worker at the Madison House Settlement in New York and chairman of the Brooklyn Ethical Culture School Board. His many activities in the social and religious fields have included also leadership among numerous academic fraternities.

Editor

ETHICAL CULTURE

HENRY NEUMANN

THE ETHICAL CULTURE SOCIETY held its first formal meeting in Standard Hall, New York City, May 15, 1876. The founder was Dr. Felix Adler (1851–1933), son of a rabbi and for two years a lecturer in Oriental Literature in Cornell University.

His chief reasons for leaving his ancestral fellowship were not such rationalist objections to dogma as were being spoken by other men too like Robert Ingersoll and Thomas Huxley. He was still devoutly religious, as indeed he remained all his life. He felt intensely that a freshening influence was needed to replace the earlier belief; and it had to be the profoundly moving, affirmative conviction which we call consecration. It was his faith that there might arise in the world a new birth of religion and that the way to this was to increase moral excellence.

In his opening address, the young founder dwelt on the urgent moral needs of the days. This was the period following the Civil War, the age of Tweed and of the scandals in President Grant's Cabinet, when, though people went to church in much greater numbers than they do now, political corruption was never more shameless. It was a day of bitter strife between masters and employees. Said Dr. Adler: . . . "Statesmen and philanthropists are busy suggesting cures for these great evils. Whatever measures may be devised, all depend in the last instance upon the fidelity of those to whom their execution must be intrusted. They will all fail unless the root of the evil be attacked, unless the conscience of man be aroused, the confusion of right and wrong checked, and the loftier purposes of our being again brought powerfully home to the hearts of the people."

Organized expression of this motive followed soon. Members shared with a group of printers in starting a co-operative as one way to improve industrial relations; and when this failed, they decided to begin with an ethical education for children. Thereupon in 1878 the Society founded The Workingman's School, the first free kindergarten east of the Mississippi. Out of this came the present group of Ethical Culture Schools (Midtown at 33 Central Park West, The Little School, and Fieldston, in Riverdale, New York City) known to educators the world over for progressive methods in the building of character. The Ethical Culture School of Brooklyn (maintained separately by the Society in that borough) was organized in 1922 by Julie W. Neumann, a graduate of the original school. Scholarships provide for pupils unable to pay. Two social settlements, Hudson Guild and Madison House, were created in New York. When Societies were organized elsewhere, Henry Booth House was set up in Chicago, Self-Culture Hall in St. Louis, Southwark Neighborhood House in Philadelphia. More recently, the Society in New Rochelle, N. Y., established a clinic for problem children. Felix Adler was one of the founders of the National Child Labor Committee and for many years its Chairman. The Child Study Association of America was originally a group of mothers in the Ethical Culture Society. The International Union of Ethical Societies was responsible for the International Moral Education Congresses begun in London in 1908 and held at four year intervals in other cities until 1936. The first Universal Races Congress, London, 1911, (under the same auspices) was occasioned by the growing tensions between peoples of differing color. The improving of race relations is a major concern in all Ethical Societies to-day.

The American Ethical Union (headquarters, 2 West 64th Street, New York City 23) is a federation of the societies of Brooklyn, Chicago, New York, Philadelphia, St. Louis, Westchester, and whatever new groups are voted into admission. It originated and for twenty-five years issued *The International Journal of Ethics,* now published at Chicago University as *Ethics.* It is responsible for *The Standard,* printed every month from October through May, for some of the books by Leaders, and for pamphlets on various ethical problems. In England there are now, besides smaller groups in London and elsewhere, the South Place Ethical Society (1887) and the West London Ethical Society (1892), known now as the Ethical Church, founded by Dr. Stanton Coit and later including Lord Harry Snell of the British Labor Party. (Among members of the West London Ethical Society were Henry Sidgwick and Leslie Stephen.) A vigorous society in Vienna, which besides offering the usual functions of such a group, specialized in aid to the mentally distressed, was broken up by the Nazis in 1938; and its Leaders, Wilhelm Boerner and Walter Eckstein, were imprisoned. The total membership in the societies is five thousand, although many more thousands are reached every year by the weekly addresses, radio talks, *The Standard,* the pamphlets, books, classes, forums, institutes.

Leaders of the societies, like members, have come from many religious ancestries. Wilhelm Boerner of Vienna and Cecil Delisle Burns of London were of Catholic origin. Nathaniel Schmidt of Cornell University came of a Lutheran family. Out of a total of twenty-seven Leaders from 1876 to 1946, seven were from Jewish homes, two from Catholic, eighteen from Protestant.

The societies conduct weekly meetings, chiefly on Sunday mornings, and except in Chicago, in buildings which they own. At these meetings, Leaders and guest-speakers discourse on problems of the inner life, or on questions of current social importance, or on both. Forums, classes, institutes, meetings of Men's Clubs, Women's Clubs, Young People's Associations afford occasion for discussions of these matters and of practical ways to deal with them. Sunday classes for boys and girls are of special help with children of inter-marriage because the ethical interest unifies where creed (or ancestral affiliation such as the Hebrew) may separate. Leaders are empowered to conduct marriage services; they officiate at funerals and naming-ceremonies; and they offer personal counsel to members and non-members.

The Ethical Culture Society is to us a religious society in the sense of giving us a cause entitled to chief claim upon our energies, our most inclusive fellowship, our most satisfying way of reading life's meaning, our best long-run incentive, our deepest assurance and hope. As in some traditional ethical religions, we hold that human behavior is good according as it is animated by faith in a supreme excellence, that at all times the test of such faith is conduct, and that the truest way to cooperate with the noblest life in the universe is to ennoble the life of man.

We acknowledge our indebtedness to the religious teachings of our forefathers; and we appreciate the labors which have turned the main current of religion more and more away from belief in magic to increased concern with ethical progress. We respect the convictions which send our friends to the churches and temples for their leading inspiration in this forward-reaching endeavor. We still think, however, that the founders did well to establish this independent fellowship. Our bond of union is broader than the racial tie of the temples. While Jew and Gentile cooperate in most secular enterprises, there is need for a fellowship which unites them in the one over-arching devotion which is religion. The churches, howsoever liberal, are Christian; and for all our reverence for the teachings and the life of Jesus, we think that the supreme ideal for human life is too richly varied to be incarnated in any one person, no matter how sublime.

Nor can we commit ourselves to the belief that the best ethical behaviors require trust in a Creator. We think that the best in the God-belief itself points to a very different truth. The very progress from a god of magic to a God who expects mankind to do justice and mercy indicates how ethical thinking and ethical practice decide what kind of God-belief, if any, people will reach. Likewise, the best in the belief in immortality is the hunger for continued fellow-ship and the desire that human goodness shall grow to perfect flower. At their best these beliefs are ethically motivated. Their finest out-come is ethical practice.

On these traditional beliefs, we leave our members free to decide for themselves. Experience has taught us that most of those who come to us do so because they want a fellowship where the conviction is stressed that first-rate living can and should be sought because of its own inherent appeal that human spirits, human hands, must do the necessary labors and that the most deeply satisfying meaning of life is to be found in the process of such striving and in the reflections which it enlightens. Because this is an experiment in a new way of living, Ethical Societies are needed to organize, direct, and inspire such efforts.

Our leading purpose, we think, must be reaffirmed and em-phasized today in view of the fact that many important recent move-ments also get on without theological sanctions. Ardent social re-formers are at work in countless good causes; industrial and other workers are organizing unions and labor-parties. Russia and Ger-many divorced the State from religious affiliation and captured people, especially the young, for a loyalty which was markedly secu-lar. Fascism and Communism bear many resemblances to traditional religion. They unite around a supreme allegiance. They declare their gospel to be the one hope of all mankind. They have their ceremonies, their hymns and other ritual. They enjoin an austere morality of its own kind. They persecute non-conformists and justify such suppressions as indispensable to their basic unity. Mixed as their motivation has been, it is essential to remember that both Fascism and Communism arose in response to widespread and acute distress out of which no other way of escape seemed to the leaders likely to be successful. In both of them, features can be found which discriminating observers can respect.

The fact that these movements are secular inclines some people now to turn to church and temple. But the traditional religions, even when they no longer persecute, have doctrines and practices which shut too many persons out. The Ethical Culture Society stands for world-embracing ideals which refuse to set up a nation, a race, or a church as the one hope of humanity. Far from suppressing non-conformists, it insists that the very differences among people are to be worked over into harmonies which are all the grander for the interplay of diverse excellence. An important reason for moving out of the historic religions was the conviction that to no one group of any kind can truth ever be finally revealed, that the quest of truth must never end, and that all men and women are needed to bring whatever is good in their own way of life into creative relation with the different good in other lives. Above all else, the Ethical Society insists upon the worth and dignity of every human soul even when to the outward eye little or no reason can be seen for according such honor.

As against the steam-roller methods of bringing people into unity, Ethical Culture is working to create a world where the best of those freedoms already attained by the democracies will be still better. It regards as the chief fact about people that distinctive quality called by such names as personality, worth, basic human dignity. This is impossible to define with complete precision, because it is itself presupposed in making ethical judgments. That is, we protest against injustice not only because such conduct brings pain. Animals, too, suffer from inhumanity; they resent it and take revenge when it is inflicted. Human beings are to be respected in a profounder sense. Something fine exists in them, even though only in germ, which is not to be outraged by oppression or other wrong. Instead, it is to receive all encouragement from individuals and communities.

No isolated or entirely private affair, this essential worthwhileness in people best manifests itself to the degree that it promotes rather than hinders the best self-expression in others. It is this fact which gives us the leading maxim of Ethical Culture Societies: "So act as to encourage the first-rateness in other people, and thereby in yourself."

Today we see with renewed clearness how important this principle is. Yet even if it were still more widely applied to the dealings of person with person, this would not be enough. It needs to rule the relations of whole groups. Individual white men get on fairly well with individual Negroes. Whites as a group, however, still fail lamentably in their relations with Negroes as a race. So do workers and their employers; and so likewise do other groups. The two types of relationship, the one within the group, the other in the dealings toward whole groups, work together for better or worse. The nations which have most seriously offended against international ethics are those which at the same time have most mistreated individuals and groups within their borders. In related fashion, Negroes in America suffer their worst hardships in states where organizations to suppress such whites as Jews, Catholics, or labor unions, are most common. Negroes will get justice from whites when white men are more just to one another. So Jews will receive better treatment from Gentiles when Gentiles treat one another more justly. Back and forth and on constantly broader lines the heart of our Ethical Society's teaching cries aloud for application: "Both in individual and in group relations, evoke the best in yourself by seeking to promote the best in others."

From its very beginning, Ethical Culture has held that individual and social ethics are inseparable. Today's disorders give new point to this teaching. The growing tensions in the world reveal that far below the surface, deep-seated group-interests are clashing. These interests, though intertwined with personal or national animosities of various kinds, are so connected with problems of livelihood and property that basic changes in our economic society are needed sorely. Our members differ over the immediate steps to effectuate such changes. We agree that an ethical program which concerns itself exclusively with individual consciences may be thwarted by the operation of these larger economic influences, and that far from postponing the re-direction of such influences until individual souls have been improved, the very interests of such personal advance oblige us to work today for a more ethical economic order. Economic power is much too important to be permitted irresponsible exercise, such as has already come from practices which put first the seeking of individual gain.

Arbitrary conduct has come from labor unions too. But because far more power is wielded by the big employers, and because in a strike people are much quicker to see their own discomfort or hardship than the hidden pressures exerted by the wealthier camp, much of the ethical teaching of the day still has to call attention to the differences in advantage. Serious obligations rest upon the public and upon both parties to the conflicts, all three. Failure to recognize this fact was a major reason for the rise of the two powerful secular movements already mentioned. Ethical democracy must meet their challenge in its own way and before the harm done by neglecting it destroys whatever else may be gained.

Here the leading motive, as we see it, is the conviction that human worth requires the fullest honor from every influence, direct or indirect, which in any way affects it. Men and women who wish to be self-supporting workers must not suffer that corroding of their self-respect which ensues from idleness or taking charity, or being shut out from decisions affecting their lives. Young people, eager to be of use in the world, to marry and set up homes of their own, must not be at the mercy of forces which deprive them of this chance to grow up. Parents owe it to their children to rear them in homes fit for human habitation. They will be better parents when their minds are not haunted by needless worry, by economic strife, by working conditions which stunt their intelligence and arrest their own development as persons. As citizens all people need to do their part in promoting a true democracy. They cannot do this when their work-lives are subject to such arbitrary, irresponsible forces as rule much of our economic life today. Freedom to vote is often mocked by this other unfreedom.

Should Ethical Societies as a whole, therefore, commit themselves to, for instance, Socialism? Upon any such proposal, intelligent, public-spirited members differ, as Socialists themselves disagree over the special next directions to which their doctrine must lead. For the same reason that an Ethical Society cannot bind itself to the ancestral commitment of Judaism or to the sectarian ties of the churches, it cannot commit all its members to any one specific social ethic. It leaves its leaders free to speak whatever convictions they hold. It offers such freedom likewise to its members and to groups within its organization. Still more, it encourages all to give themselves to continued study of such problems and to apply in practice whatever outcomes thereby suggest themselves. As a body the Society itself is pledged only to the heartiest promotion of such a quest. The words over the platform in the Meeting House in New York read: "The place where men meet to seek the highest is holy ground." No one group is privileged to say that it has already found the one conception of highest life which all of us must accept. Instead the truth is to be sought ever afresh—and sought cooperatively. Here a prime essential is that each group respect the freedom and the responsibility of other groups to seek out and to practice what each finds best. Not the findings of any one body, but the spirit of reciprocal encouragement in the quest, is what unites us.

We are aware that these principles and practices have never found full expression anywhere on our globe, that vast numbers have never heard of them and might not even understand, that other multitudes today take a positive delight in rejecting them, and that even in the relatively small portion of the earth where acceptance has come, recent events show how mistaken it is to assume this gain as beyond all question permanent. No guarantee exists that ethical progress will continue.

This is but one of the many obstacles with which an ethical way of living must reckon. Such obstacles are met with in our private lives too, where sickness, bereavement, defeats of many kinds, enter. What keeps us going—those of us who look to no Divine Providence or a life beyond the grave? We answer that we have been privileged to glimpse what human life might become if men's better leadings attained their due ascendancy. We see in vision life not only cleansed of the shame in living at the expense of other life, but finding itself in the very process of liberating other life. The vision brings its own imperative—to act at all times under its prompting. Out of our failures we are to learn to do better. Where such further chance is denied us, we find our strength in the thought that whatever is good and worthwhile in the deeds which have come from us has its own living quality which may engender fresh life in at least one other spirit. Whether it does or not, it is good to try to be part of the power which ennobles human living. The beauty and the holiness of such life are their own justification; and our deepest satisfaction is in seeking, even to the last, to be worthy of sharing in it.

BIBLIOGRAPHY

Fiftieth Anniversary of the Ethical Movement (New York, 1926).

FELIX ADLER, *Moral Instruction of Children* (New York, 1895).

————, *The Reconstruction of the Spiritual Ideal* (Hibbert Lectures) (New York, 1924).

————, *An Ethical Philosophy of Life* (New York, 1925, Revised 1946).

H. J. BLACKHAM, *The Ethical Movement during Seventy Years,* Pamphlet, Union of Ethical Societies (London, 1946).

HORACE J. BRIDGES, *The Religion of Experience* (New York, 1916).

————, *Taking the Name of Science in Vain* (New York, 1928).

————, *The Emerging Faith,* American Ethical Union (1937).

————, *Some Applications of Ethical Religion Today,* American Ethical Union (1944).

————, *Humanity on Trial* (New York, 1941).

HORACE J. BRIDGES (Editor), *Aspects of Ethical Religion,* American Ethical Union (1926).

————, *The Ethical Movement,* Union Ethical Societies (London, 1911).

C. DELISLE BURNS, *Old Creeds and the New Faith* (London, 1911).

PERCIVAL CHUBB, *On the Religious Frontier* (New York, 1931).

STANTON COIT, *National Idealism and a State Church* (London, 1907).

————, *The Soul of America* (New York, 1914).

W. EDWIN COLLIER, *Phases of Ethical Faith,* American Ethical Union (New York, 1945).

Ethical Religion—(A Symposium), American Ethical Union (New York, 1940).

HORACE L. FRIESS (Co-author with Herbert W. Schneider), *Religion in Various Cultures* (New York, 1932).

————, *Our Part in this World: Interpretations by Felix Adler* (1947).

A. EUSTACE HAYDON, *The Quest of the Ages* (1929).

————, *Biography of the Gods* (1941).

ALFRED W. MARTIN, *Great Religious Teachers of the East* (New York, 1911).

DAVID S. MUZZEY, *Ethical Religion,* American Ethical Union (New York, 1943).

———, *Ethical Imperatives,* American Ethical Union (New York, 1946).

JEROME NATHANSON (Editor), *Publications of Conference on Scientific Spirit and Democratic Faith* (New York, 1944, 1945, 1946).

HENRY NEUMANN, *Education for Moral Growth* (New York, 1924).

———, *Modern Youth and Marriage* (New York, 1929).

———, *Lives in the Making* (New York, 1932).

WILLIAM M. SALTER, *Ethical Religion* (Boston, 1899).

NATHANIEL SCHMIDT, *The Coming Religion* (New York, 1930).

WALTER SHELDON, *An Ethical Movement* (New York, 1896).

———, *An Ethical Sunday School* (New York, 1900).

HENRY SIDGWICK, *Practical Ethics* (London, 1898).

V. T. THAYER, *American Education Under Fire* (New York, 1944).

The Standard, the monthly publication of the American Ethical Union (October through May) is issued at 2 West 64th Street, New York City 23.

THE SALVATION ARMY

Commissioner Donald McMillan, National Secretary of The Salvation Army with headquarters in New York City, was born June 8, 1887.

Although born of Scotch parents in England, he entered the Army Training College from Chicago, and received his first appointment as Lieutenant in New York City in July, 1906. In a wide Salvation Army experience he has held Corps, Divisional, Provincial, Financial, Men's Social Service, and Training College appointments.

The Commissioner is a son of the regiment—his parents were Army Officers in the early pioneering stage of the movement, serving in Scotland, England, Canada and the United States.

During his forty years of officership, he has been General Secretary in three Divisions of South Atlantic, Chesapeake, and South Eastern Pennsylvania; also, Divisional Commander for Florida and Georgia and Western New York. In September, 1936, he was appointed Provincial Commander for New England, and in 1939 assumed the Chief Secretaryship of the Eastern Territory and second in command of all the work in the eleven eastern states.

Just prior to Pearl Harbor, the Commissioner was appointed as Territorial Commander of the Western Territory with Headquarters in San Francisco and responsible for all activities in the eleven western states and Hawaii.

As a member of the Board of Directors and the Executive Committee of the United Service Organizations, Commissioner McMillan from its inception has played a prominent and important part in the Salvation Army's war service activities. He is also international representative for the Salvation Army at all United Nations meetings.

Among his associates he is known as a man who possesses keen mental and executive endowments, a good physique that stands stress and strain, and sterling spiritual gifts and capacities. These qualities have eminently fitted him for the position he now holds, calling for both administrative judgment and inspired spiritual leadership.

Editor

THE SALVATION ARMY

DONALD McMILLAN

THE SALVATION ARMY is a religious body operating in 98 territories of the world, preaching the gospel of Christ in 102 languages, and ministering to emergency needs of humans. Trained officers numbering 27,000 guide its over 5,000,000 followers. The ultimate purpose of all Salvation Army activities is to lead men and women into a proper understanding of their relationship to God, with particular regard for the erring, the bewildered and the unfortunate. It endeavors to accomplish this through the teaching and practice of the religion of Christ. It is essentially an evangelical organization practicing its precepts through a vast system of social services.

Its spiritual purpose is paramount. Founded originally for the religious enlightenment of the masses, its primary and persistent aim still is to proclaim and exemplify, through song, word and deed, the regenerating revitalizing message of the Scriptures. The Social Service Work is supplementary. As far-reaching as is its welfare program, including hospitals, nurseries, homes, and a host of other activities and institutions, it should be recognized as a manifestation, an expression, or a practical application of the dominating spiritual motive.

Knowledge of this relationship between its two functions is essential to a proper and complete understanding of the organization. It does not mean that material assistance is withheld from those who hesitate or decline to accept spiritual advice or guidance. Care is freely given whenever and wherever the need is apparent. It does mean that The Salvation Army aims at the permanent regeneration of the "whole man", not merely at the alleviation of his immediate and temporary physical necessities. Through spiritual exhortation, and an earnest appeal to his better nature, it aims not only to put him back on his feet, but to keep him there.

The Salvation Army teaches God is Love. It believes that Charity, to be permanently reconstructive, must be understood as the beneficence of God. Therefore, it wants its welfare service recognized, not merely as the doling of alms, in response to a sentimental impulse, but as Love in Motion, Christianity in Action.

This principle is observable in every activity and branch of endeavor. It must be kept constantly in mind, if the aim of any phase of The Salvation Army is to be accurately appraised and appreciated.

The most impressive fact about the history of The Salvation Army is the short span of time it embraces. The organization has developed rapidly into a moral force of world-wide influence, yet it was only eighty-one years ago that its humble foundations were laid in the East End of London, and only sixty-six years ago that its flag was first planted in America.

The founder, General William Booth, a Methodist minister, defied church tradition of the 1864 era by holding meetings for the poor in London's slums. When converts were refused membership in churches, Booth united them to form The Christian Mission. In 1878 the organization became The Salvation Army, uniforms for men and women were inaugurated, and a semi-military system of leadership adopted.

Unity of thought, method and purpose is an outstanding characteristic of The Salvation Army throughout the world. In a movement which has penetrated so many strange and dissimilar fields, this is a fact of exceptional interest. It is explainable partly by the simplicity of its mission and its direct method of approach; but largely is it due to the element of military discipline as the controlling force in an ingeniously devised plan of organization and administration.

In conformity with this general plan, The Army has divided the United States into four territories, with headquarters in New York, Chicago, Atlanta, and San Francisco. These Territorial Centers, each under the authority of a Territorial Commander, are coordinated through the National Secretary at National Headquarters, New York, which office is responsible to International Headquarters in London, England.

The distinguishing feature in the religious life of The Salvation Army is its insistence upon active participation rather than passive adherence on the part of its followers. There is no such thing as in-

active or nominal membership. Christianity is considered synonymous with service. A person may attend meetings on Sundays, but if
he is not willing to demonstrate his faith in the form of tangible
helpfulness to others, or to the organization as a whole, he is not regarded as a good soldier. In short, The Salvation Army regards itself
as engaged in a continual fight against evil, and all its operations are
incidental to that end.

The primary object of the average Salvation Army meeting is to
win men to Christ and enlist recruits for its crusade against sin. The
unregenerate are urged to seek pardon and deliverance from sin,
and return to active membership in their own churches or enroll as
fighting soldiers in The Salvation Army Corps.

Salvationists enjoy their religion; they do not subscribe to it
merely in duty or obligation. They are keenly conscious of the
presence of God as a kindly and beneficent Deity, as the unfailing
source of happiness and satisfaction. Therefore they find real joy in
serving as well as praising Him.

This cheerful quality is exemplified in the character of the music
which takes so important a part in all the services. Every Corps is expected to create a brass band out of its membership, and if any member can play a guitar, a mandolin or even a harmonica, he is invited
to make use of it. The hymns and marches are for the most part
rhythmical and lilting, and frequently the popular tunes of the day
are given religious words and used on the street-corners. To some
observers these methods may seem offensively spectacular but they
are fully justified, not only as a means of attracting attention, but in
dispelling the notion from many minds that there is not happiness or
light-heartedness in the religious life.

Every soldier is given something to do, and he remains in good
standing only so long as he does it. He is expected whenever possible
to participate in open-air meetings on the street-corners; he may
make a special study of the Bible and teach it at the young people's
meeting; he may learn to play an instrument and join the band, or
he may be asked to assist the Corps officer in visitations among the
poor and the sick or in general welfare work. If particularly depend-
able, he may be appointed a "local officer", such as sergeant, or
sergeant-major, which are comparable to the non-commissioned
ranks in any other military organization. There are scores of duties
to be performed, and something to which every member can readily

turn his hand, no matter what his individual aptitudes or inclinations may be.

This explains why conversion in The Salvation Army is usually more lasting than the mere profession of faith demanded in so many evangelical campaigns of a sporadic nature. The faith of the convert is made permanent by his being kept busy.

Such an exacting standard of Christian service in The Salvation Army reacts in a measure against its own numerical strength. The membership of almost any Corps could easily be doubled if passive adherence were accepted and if demands upon the time and attention of the individual were not so heavy.

Many people who find salvation in a Corps meeting shrink from the obligation of soldiership and therefore do not enroll. They may be sincerely converted, and live virtuous lives thereafter, but they join a church rather than don the uniform and accept the responsibilities of Salvation Army warfare. In this way the organization performs a continuous and incalculable service to the churches of all denominations.

In this connection it should be noted that the open-air meetings exercise an even wider influence upon the religious and social life of the community. Thousands of men and women, once confused, bewildered or desperate, have testified how a chance word or strain of music from the "open-air ring" on the street corner has at one time or another turned them away from a vicious or dangerous line of thought, and has resulted in their return to active membership in a church they had once attended. No record can be kept of this influence. Such people may stand on the edge of the crowd for a short time without visible interest in the proceedings and then pass on. But the seed has been sown and the result becomes apparent later on in the roster of a denominational congregation.

The deepest motivation of all Salvation Army service is found in its religious faith. Its doctrinal roots are firmly embedded in the historical traditions of evangelical Christianity. The elements of its fundamental beliefs are closely and positively set forth in its "Foundation Deed" of 1878 by eleven cardinal affirmations. These statements document the organization's recognition of the Bible as the only rule of Christian faith and practice; one God who is the Creator and Father of all mankind; The Trinity of Father, Son and Holy Spirit; Jesus Christ, Son of God and Son of Man; Sin, the great destroyer of man's soul and society; Salvation, God's remedy for sin and man's ultimate and eternal hope made available through Christ; Sanctification, the individual's present and maturing experience of a life set apart for the holy purposes of the Kingdom of God; and an Eternal Destiny that may triumph over sin and death.

The very word "Salvation" that describes the Army's hope for broken and bewildered humanity is the term most descriptive of the Army's idea of God's love for all mankind. For, it is His will not one should be lost but that all may come to know the blessing of His Salvation. Into earth's darkness the Salvationist brings the saving light of the Gospel, seeking to place the hands of straying, stumbling souls into the strong saving hands of God.

Although the Army meets a distinct need in the religious life of the community, which is practically untouched by any other organization, it cooperates in every helpful way with the churches of all denominations and is always ready to participate in any concerted movement for the advancement of the general cause of religion.

The spiritual work centers in the local Corps, which is the Army designation for the individual congregation or church organization. The work is organized in the military manner, and military terminology is used throughout. The Corps building or hall is generally known as the "citadel"; the pastor is an "officer," and the members are "soldiers"; the sphere of activity is the "field" and the member becomes formally attached by signing the "articles of war" and being publicly enrolled, which indicate that from then on he is to engage in actual warfare against sin, poverty and distress. The reason for the military forms of organization is that it is the one certain way of getting things done quickly and efficiently. It keeps up the mood of emergency, the spirit of urgent activity, and makes it less easy for the work to fall into a lifeless and unprogressive routine.

Each Corps is required to hold a standard number of meetings each week, most of which are preceded by open-air meetings. The open-air meeting is the most practical method of carrying out the original and fundamental purpose of the organization: to take the Gospel to those who need it where they are. The open-air meeting is followed by a march to the citadel in which the street-corner congregation is invited to join. Upon arrival the service is continued. Many types of meetings are held, sometimes in hired auditoriums or theaters, but the basis of the continuous evangelical campaign is to be found in the Corps services on the streets and in the halls, held during the week as well as on Sunday morning and evening.

During these meetings the soldiers are expected to wear uniforms and assist in dealing with converts and recruits, but the commissioned officer at the head of the Corps is that member of the group who is under total Army authority and receives a weekly salary.

Each Corps has a program of youth activities providing religious education, recreation, and informal education for both members and non-members of the organization. A Sunday School functions in each Corps, also a Vacation Bible School. Other groups include the Young People's Legion, offering Graded Class Work for the various age levels from six to twenty-five; Cubs, Boy Scouts (for boys), Sunbeams, Guards (corresponding groups for girls). In addition to the foregoing, many Corps conduct special interest groups, playground activities, summer camping programs, athletic leagues, music bands, recreation and neighborhood centers.

While each Corps conducts a youth program as a part of a total program there also exist separate institutions with full-time professional leadership devoted entirely to youth. Such are the Boys Clubs operated by The Salvation Army, some of which have boy memberships exceeding one thousand. Some of these institutions provide co-ed activities and are then known as "youth centers".

The Home League is a vital part of the Corps life in all lands where the Army is at work. It is the women's organization calling for advancement of ideal home life through Christian fellowship, with a program to fill spiritual, educational and recreational needs. The branches of the Home League throughout the country assumed a lion's share of the Army's World War II activities, rising superbly to a wide variety of calls for help. The post-war work of these women's groups embraces among other important fields the readjustment of war-working wives to domestic living and the making of home life more attractive for returned veterans. The long range aim of the Home League continues to be "a better world through better homes".

The charitable and humanitarian social service work has developed in many different directions in response to human needs as they have been discovered, and has not been restricted or limited by any preconceived or arbitrary plan. This explains its extraordinary variety and scope.

Social service had no part in the plan as at first conceived by the founder. The original purpose was exclusively evangelical. The Salvationists were to take the Gospel to those who would not seek it in the churches. They were to invade the highways and byways and preach salvation, through Christian grace, to the spiritually blind and poor in heart. That was to be their one and only mission.

But it was not easy to talk spiritual salvation to people who were dazed and bewildered by acute physical need. That such people responded to the preaching with manifest eagerness made the task all the more perplexing. Their ears were attuned to the "voice crying in the wilderness"; but—what were they to do about it? The man without a job, enervated through privation or dissipation; the girl facing motherhood out of wedlock, dismayed and alone; aged men and women without homes in which to spend their declining years; the youth, realizing the futility of indulgence, but puzzled as to which way to turn; the criminal brooding in his cell; the widow, with her children, valiantly waging a losing battle against poverty and disease; the wayward, the degenerate, the irresponsible, the weak of will— all of these saw the light of hope in the message that was brought to them, but it seemed far off, intangible beyond their reach. It was clear that in addition to the Gospel they needed material assistance and patient guidance from people who could understand their troubles.

It was in response to such need that the Army entered the realm of social service. Today, every Corps, or religious unit, is at the same time a center of humanitarian activity; and the evangelical work is supplemented by two great branches of the organization known as the Men's Social Service Department and the Women's Social Service Department. The functions of these departments have grown to such proportions as to convey the erroneous impression to many minds that the Army is primarily a social service agency. But, as already emphasized, these functions must be understood in their entirety as a humane demonstration of the religion of Christ. Religious exhortation, however, is not forced upon the beneficiaries, and no person is expected to change his religion if he already has one. His religion is expected to change him.

Men's Social Services include Centers, Workingmen's Hotels and Employment Bureaus. The centers are institutions in which hard work and simple religious truth are combined as a cure for human waywardness. Unfortunate men spend varying periods in them for the purpose of working themselves back to respectability. Workingmen's Hotels are homelike hostelries in which temporarily embarrassed or low-wage earning men are provided with comfortable lodgings in a wholesome atmosphere either at nominal prices or without charge. Employment Bureaus are systematically organized and operate in close cooperation with governmental, business and industrial establishments. No charge is made for service.

Women's Social Services include Maternity Homes and Hospitals, Settlement Houses and Nurseries, Children's Homes and Hospitals, Working Women's Hotels, Employment Bureaus, and Young Women's Residences. Maternity Homes and Hospitals are maintained to provide care for unmarried mothers. Girls are given the best of medical and surgical treatment and provided with a homelike haven before and after the birth of their children. Understanding and untiring effort are directed towards helping each mother work out her own best plan.

Settlement Houses and Nurseries are maintained in the larger cities where, in addition to the nursery work, there is a professional staff of visitors and instructors who advise and help the families in the homes from which the children come. Children's Homes and Hospitals are maintained for orphans or children whose parents are temporarily unable to care for them. Working Women's Hotels are for middle-aged working women who have no homes of their own. Young Women's Residences provide a wholesome environment for self-supporting girls. The extremely reasonable rates include a pleasant room, two meals per day, facilities for laundry work, a reading room, a library, private lounges for the entertainment of guests, and sometimes gymnasium and swimming pool.

Another important welfare service is family service. In local units family service consists simply of relieving acute material needs and making sure that other needs are met through the proper local agencies.

In larger areas, however, the work has intensified far beyond momentary aid; it is carried to its deepest possible helpfulness, reaching into individual analysis of the cause, and the sociological and spiritual treatment which help fit the man or woman back into constructive, well-adjusted community living.

For more than fifty years, The Salvation Army has been recognized as a semi-official adjunct of the penal system of the country and is believed by many criminologists to have the only lasting solution to one of society's perplexing problems—the restoration of prisoners to constructive civilian life. Untiring effort is devoted to understanding each individual, regardless of race, creed or previous record. Religious meetings and song services are held in practically every state and federal prison and house of correction in the United States. Inspirational literature is provided regularly.

Under the guidance of Salvation Army welfare officers, Brighter-Day Leagues flourish behind the gray walls. The worst offenders—the "life termers"—are invited to join the Army's Lifers Club. Usually a member is found to be without a friend in the world, disowned and ignored by his family. The first step towards arousing his interest in a better life is to put him back in touch with his relatives. One of the outstanding follow-through efforts is the establishment of sympathetic employer relationships based on full knowledge of the man's prison record in advance of his employment.

Quite distinct from the Prison Department for Men, virtually every penal institution in which there are women is regularly visited, and, in larger cities, the police courts are attended by specially qualified women officers in the interest of young girls. These officers are also called upon by the courts to act in parole cases.

The Salvation Army also maintains camp sites on the outskirts of practically all large cities where thousands of needy mothers and children are taken for summer vacations. Other on-going activities include aid during emergencies, Christmas cheer in various forms, maintenance of medical and dental clinics and the work of the Missing Persons Bureau.

In the light of today's national issues The Salvation Army has set a goal for expanded programs in all fields. Particular emphasis has been placed on the recapture of a normal mental outlook; care and recovery of the sick and maimed; food and clothing for the needy; a broad program of employment; the return of family life to a normal peace-time basis; building up of health and character for the children of the nation.

INTERNATIONAL STATISTICS

Trained Officers	27,995
Followers	5,000,000
Corps and Outposts	17,996
Social Operations	1,864
Number accommodated	158,528

BIBLIOGRAPHY

General Booth (1912), by Commissioner G. S. Railton, his right-hand man for many years.

The Life of William Booth (1920), by Harold Begbie. A two-volume study of General Booth and the beginning of The Salvation Army.

God's Soldier (1935), by St. John Ervine. A study of William Booth and the Army with an attempt to trace the Army's structural development from a local mission to a modern world-wide organization.

God in the Shadows (1932), by Hugh Redwood. Modern true stories from the slums of England that read like fiction.

Darkest England and the Way Out (1890), by General Wm. Booth. A pioneer study of the cause and cure of social conditions during the latter part of the nineteenth century. A cornerstone not only of the Army's philosophy and program of Social Service but public and private Social Work in general.

Evangeline Booth (1935), by P. Whitwell Wilson. The fascinating story of American Salvationism and its foremost leader.

The Angel Adjutant (1936), by Mrs. General G. Carpenter. The beautiful story of Kate Lee as the simple but powerful instrument of divine transformation of human personality.

Twice Born Men (1909), by Harold Begbie. About the unique ministry of a typical Salvation Army Corps Center.

Out of the Depths (1936), by Clarence Hall. The dramatic story of a New York newspaper editor and his salvation from the death grip of alcoholism.

Life of Commissioner George Scott Railton (1920), by E. Douglas and M. Duff. Commissioner Railton was the pioneer leader in American Salvationism.

Portrait of a Prophet (1930), by Clarence Hall. The Life of Commissioner Samuel L. Brengle, preacher, writer and example of the Army's ideal and experience of "Holiness."

Echoes and Memories (1928), by General Bramwell Booth. First-hand description of important events and people as they affected the course of the Army's life and thought.

Handbook of Doctrine (rev. ed., 1935). A systematic and authoritative statement of Salvation Army religious thought and interpretation.

My 58 Years (1943), by Commissioner Edward J. Parker. An informal autobiography of an American leader who reviews with insight and humor the Army's unique methods and accomplishments.

Year Book. An annual publication issued at International Headquarters giving a brief outline of the work throughout the world.

God in the Slums (1931), by Hugh Redwood. A modern story describing various characters in the London slums redeemed through Salvation Army interest.

An Outline of Salvation Army History (rev. 1936). A brief digest giving the origin and development of the organization and emphasizing certain special areas of activity.

CHRISTIAN SCIENCE

Dr. Todd is well qualified to present the faith of Christian Science and its relation to the world of today. Since 1944 he has been manager of the Washington, D. C. office of the Committee on Publication of the First Church of Christ, Scientist, Boston, Mass., and he is at home in the field of social problems, having held important academic professorships in the field of sociology, is an expert counselor for social organizations and an author of widely recognized publications in that field.

Born in 1878 in Petaluma, California, he was first educated in the public schools of that state and graduated from the University of California with a B.L. degree in 1904. He studied at the Universities of Aix-Marseilles, Paris and Munich and won his Ph.D. degree at Yale in 1911. He was director of boys' work Coll. Settlement, West Berkeley, at South Park Settlement, San Francisco, chief probation officer of that city, before he began his professorial work. At the University of Illinois he was an instructor in sociology and then associate, 1911–1914; the following year professor and head of the department at the University of Pittsburgh; director of training courses and professor at the University of Minnesota for six years and then director of industrial relations for the B. Kuppenheimer Company of Chicago from 1919 to 1925. From 1919 until his retirement in 1943 as emeritus professor he taught at Northwestern University, serving also as chairman of the department of sociology. His membership in academic fraternities and social councils has been wide. Among his some dozen books, mention can be made of only a few: "The Primitive Family as an Educational Agency" (1913); "Theories of Social Progress" (1918); "The Scientific Spirit and Social Work" (1919); "Industry and Society" (1933); and editor of "Recreation Survey of Chicago", a work in five volumes (1937–1940).

Editor

CHRISTIAN SCIENCE

ARTHUR JAMES TODD

CHRISTIAN SCIENCE is the system of religious thought and the denomination founded by Mary Baker Eddy in 1879 as the outcome of her discovery of this religious truth at Swampscott, Massachusetts, in 1866, and her publication of the first edition of its basic textbook, *Science and Health with Key to the Scriptures,* in 1875. From childhood Mrs. Eddy had been deeply religious and a profound student of the Bible, and had long been inclined to attribute all causation to God, and to regard Him as infinitely good, and the Soul and source of all reality. But in 1866 a lifetime of ill-health was climaxed by what was regarded as a fatal injury from which she recovered almost instantaneously after reading an account of healing in Matthew's Gospel. That seeming miracle set her mind to work. It appeared to her as a divine revelation, the prophecy of a revolution in human thinking, and an inspired call to action. She describes (in her brief autobiography *Retrospection and Introspection*) how she withdrew from society for about three years "to ponder [her] mission, to search the Scriptures, to find the Science of Mind that should take the things of God and show them to the creature, and reveal the great curative Principle,—Deity." In this process of seeking for a solution of the problem of Mind-healing she readily grasped (as recorded in her textbook) "the Principle of all harmonious Mind-action to be God, and that cures were produced in primitive Christian healing by holy, uplifting faith." But that was not enough. She insisted on knowing the process, the method, the rationale, the Science of such healing, and finally reached absolute conclusions. But again mere theory, however well-founded and consistent, did not satisfy her. Hence for several years she put her discovery and conclusions to practical test by healing many sorts of disease and human disorders, both organic and functional, and by teaching students to heal. This experience led her to write and publish her basic book. It

357

had been her earnest expectation that her discovery would be welcomed as a fresh spiritual dynamic by all religious denominations of those who professed belief in the Bible and in the word and works of Jesus the Christ. But it soon became evident that her discovery was ahead of the general frontage of contemporary Christianity; therefore it appeared necessary to found a separate church to preserve the purity of the teachings and practice of Christian Science and to more effectively present it to the world. Accordingly in 1879 she and her small band of followers organized the Church of Christ, Scientist, in Boston for the avowed purpose, as expressed by her, "to commemorate the word and works of our Master, which should reinstate primitive Christianity and its lost element of healing." Ten years later this Church was dissolved, and in 1892 the present Church, The First Church of Christ, Scientist, in Boston, Massachusetts, known as The Mother Church, was organized. At present there are approximately 3,000 authorized branches of this Church established throughout the world. It is contrary to the basic governing Manual of The Mother Church, written by Mrs. Eddy, to give out statistics of membership, but authoritative newspaper accounts of the dedication of the Extension of the Original Mother Church in 1906 expressed astonishment at a movement which in thirty years had grown from a "mere handful of members" to a body of adherents numbering probably a million. Mrs. Eddy in a Message to her Church in 1901 answering a critic of her work, challenged him to match a record which "could start thirty years ago without a Christian Scientist on earth, and in this interval number one million." It may be asserted with confidence that the number of adherents has rapidly increased in the forty-five years since that challenge was issued.

Such in brief is the outline of the first eighty years of Christian Science history. Against this background certain significant details may now be presented. First, how does the Discoverer and Founder of Christian Science define it?

In her little volume *Rudimental Divine Science,* she defines Christian Science as "the law of God, the law of good, interpreting and demonstrating the divine Principle and rule of universal harmony." Any work of scholarship is primarily an extended definition of its primary concept or theme; hence it is not surprising to find on nearly every page of Mrs. Eddy's writings some new turn of thought, some phrase or term which adds a new flash of meaning to the expression Christian Science. Perhaps the most compact summary of her revelation opens the chapter on Science, Theology, and Medicine in her textbook: "In the year 1866, I discovered the Christ Science or divine laws of Life, Truth, and Love, and named my discovery Christian Science." But elsewhere occur such revealing synonyms as Science of Mind, Mental Science, Science of Mind-healing, Science of mental healing, Divine Science, Science of Christianity, Science of God, Science of good, Science of Life, Science of being, Science of man and the universe, etc. The purpose of Christian Science is to correct wrong human thinking and to replace it with Godlike understanding. Indeed on the very first page of the Preface to *Science and Health* Mrs. Eddy sounds the trumpet call: "The time for thinkers has come." In so far as clarifying terms or phrases will wing their way to the target of human consciousness she utilizes them to the utmost.

Through Christian Science the redoubtable term "metaphysics" takes on new significance. In the correction of false human thinking Christian metaphysics is the essential tool. Mrs. Eddy posits mental causation as primary by saying, "Christian Science explains all cause and effect as mental, not physical," and at once relates causation to divinity by declaring that "God is the Principle of divine metaphysics."

At this point it should be stressed that Christian Science is not, as many have supposed, just a recrudescence of deistic philosophy, nor primarily a method of healing. It is a philosophy of God, man, the inter-relationship of God to man, and man to man, and of the universe of which God is the sole creator and man His indispensable expression. It is a system of healing, but as its Discoverer clearly pointed out, "the mission of Christian Science now, as in the time of its earlier demonstration, is not primarily one of physical healing. Now, as then, signs and wonders are wrought in the metaphysical healing of physical disease; but these signs are only to demonstrate its divine origin,—to attest the reality of the higher mission of the Christ-power to take away the sins of the world."

Hence Christian Science is a religion based upon a specific content of spiritual truth. It has a literature, an organization, a basic Manual and a varied pattern of activities. But have Christian Scientists any religious "creed"? Mrs. Eddy squarely anticipated this question and answered it in her text book: "They have not, if by that term is meant doctrinal beliefs. The following is a brief exposition of the important points, or religious tenets, of Christian Science:—

1. As adherents of Truth, we take the inspired Word of the Bible as our sufficient guide to eternal Life.

2. We acknowledge and adore one supreme and infinite God. We acknowledge His Son, one Christ; the Holy Ghost or divine Comforter; and man in God's image and likeness.

3. We acknowledge God's forgiveness of sin in the destruction of sin and the spiritual understanding that casts out evil as unreal. But the belief in sin is punished so long as the belief lasts.

4. We acknowledge Jesus' atonement as the evidence of divine, efficacious Love, unfolding man's unity with God through Christ Jesus the Way-shower; and we acknowledge that man is saved through Christ, through Truth, Life, and Love as demonstrated by the Galilean Prophet in healing the sick and overcoming sin and death.

5. We acknowledge that the crucifixion of Jesus and his resurrection served to uplift faith to understand eternal Life, even the allness of Soul, Spirit, and the nothingness of matter.

6. And we solemnly promise to watch, and pray for that Mind to be in us which was also in Christ Jesus; to do unto others as we would have them do unto us; and to be merciful, just and pure."

Christian Science is in the line of Christian tradition, indeed of Protestant tradition, but is not to be considered as merely another Protestant sect or denomination. Current practice in radio circles and elsewhere is to set up four major religious classifications in the United States, namely, Protestant, Catholic, Jewish, and Christian Scientist. The Discoverer and Founder of Christian Science was brought up in the atmosphere of New England Protestantism, and was for nearly forty years a member of the Congregational church, taught in Sunday School, and participated actively in current theological discussions. Only when it became necessary to establish her own church did she sever the link to the church which had nourished her. But her own church in no wise disavowed historic Christianity. Mrs. Eddy never claimed to have invented any new doctrine, invoked any new powers, nor introduced any new healing methods. She did claim that Christian Science is the Comforter promised by the Master in John's Gospel. She did claim that her discovery is the answer to prophecy as recorded in both the Old and the New Testament. She did claim that her method of healing was that of Jesus and his students, disciples, apostles. Thus she traces Christian Science practice directly to Christ Jesus.

Christian Science is not new: it is as ancient as God-like thinking and spiritual perception. Why then did it need to be "discovered"? Mrs. Eddy replies: "Our Master healed the sick, practised Christian healing, and taught the generalities of its divine Principle to his students; but he left no definite rule for demonstrating this Principle of healing and preventing disease. This rule remained to be discovered in Christian Science."

Hence the ideal set forth by Mrs. Eddy is to make every Christian Scientist his own practitioner. Is not that the significance of her prophecy: "When the Science of being is universally understood, every man will be his own physician, and Truth will be the universal panacea"?

Let it be reiterated that Christian Science does not actually claim nor enjoy a monopoly on spiritual healing. Some two score religious denominations listed by the United States Census indicate that "divine healing" occupies some place more or less significant in their systems of belief. It remained, however, for Christian Science to bring out into the foreground what the other sectors of Christendom had allowed to lapse, become obsolescent, or be relegated to back stage as peculiar to some remote "apostolic age."

Enough has been said now to warrant turning to answer certain inevitable questions. For example, how can Christian Science reject the idea and the fact of evil, since it is so obvious, so universal, so persistent, so powerful? First, let it be clear that to deny the reality or power of evil is not to ignore it. Hundreds of references to evil in Mrs. Eddy's writings prove keen awareness of the problem. In both the teaching and practice of Christian Science students are warned to detect, recognize, uncover, handle and destroy the claim of any particular form of error or evil to existence, reality, or power to injure. This rejection of evil is fundamental to Science: to admit it would nullify spiritual healing from the outset.

It is obvious that, as Mrs. Eddy declares, the "foundation of evil is laid on a belief in something besides God." That something is matter. Reject that belief, and error disappears with its suppositional origin, history, and effects. After such heroic surgery the world is welcome to whatever seems to remain of evil's claim to be. Thus Christian Science offers not merely an authoritative religion and a demonstrable system of healing, but also a sound and coherent philosophy of life. Indeed on this account many have accepted it who had no immediate need of its healing ministry.

But what of the demand of Christian Science to be rated as not only *a* Science but *the* Science? Certainly Christian Science claims not only to have searched for truth, but to have found Truth, to have reduced this basic knowledge of Truth to a system which is eminently communicable; to have brought to light general or fundamental laws, and to have made this organized system of knowledge available in work, life and the search for truth.

It declares that this Truth includes all known or knowable fact, phenomenon, or action. What other knowledge remains to be apprehended or organized? What becomes of physical science, socalled? How does Christian Science regard the apparent sweeping domination of contemporary thought by the physical sciences? To the extent that they base themselves upon a concept of elementary material substance or force, it rejects them as a valid statement of ultimate truth. In short, Science rejects matter as without existence, reality, actuality, substance, or power. As put in the Scientific Statement of Being, quoted from *Science and Health,* which climaxes every Christian Science Sunday church service, "There is no life, truth, intelligence, nor substance in matter. All is infinite Mind and its infinite manifestation, for God is All-in-all."

In this rejection of matter as a reality and the basis for true knowledge, Mrs. Eddy anticipated by half a century such philosophers as Whitehead, who complain that for three hundred years human science has limited itself by its assumption of basic materiality. She puts the whole trouble in a nutshell: "Matter is an error of statement. This error in the premise leads to errors in the conclusion in every statement into which it enters."

When Mrs. Eddy wrote, "We tread on forces . . . Divine Science, rising above physical theories, excludes matter, resolves things into thoughts, and replaces the objects of material sense with spiritual ideas . . . Material so-called gases and forces are counterfeits of the spiritual forces of divine Mind," such bold challenges shocked and even amused the academic world and scientific orthodoxy. But the past quarter century witnesses a steady albeit cautious approach of many of the world's leading physical scientists to a not dissimilar ideology.

For example, Sir James Jeans speaks of annihilating matter, and frankly confesses that "the universe begins to look more like a great thought than like a great machine." Professor Eddington also speaks of matter as "an imaginary something," and concludes that "the physical world is entirely abstract and without 'actuality' apart from its linkage to consciousness." Dampier in the 3rd edition of his *History of Science* devotes a whole section to the "Evanescence of Matter," and likewise speaks of annihilating matter.

Christian Science does not, however, derive its validity from such corroborative testimony of physical scientists. It maintains hold on its status as Science by its utilization of accepted scientific methods and procedures, notably revelation (spiritual enlightenment); reason (gathering of factual data and utilization of inductive logic); demonstration (practical proofs).

Christian Science is an eminently practical way of life. Its Founder and Leader had an enormous fund of common sense and a lively wit along with the deepest grasp of spiritual truth since the days of Christ Jesus the Way-shower. Hence her constant urging to beware of running ahead of one's power to demonstrate one's spiritual attainments, and her insistent injunction not to ignore evil or erroneous material beliefs. For contrary to common apprehension, as we have already pointed out, Christian Science does not ignore what it regards as unreal. This religion teaches its adherents to forsake and overcome every form of error or evil on the basis of its unreality; that is, by demonstrating the true idea and fact of reality. This it teaches them to do by means of spiritual law and spiritual power. Thus the practice of Christian Science is not merely mental; it must be also spiritual. Indeed, it is truly mental only as it is absolutely spiritual.

Christian Scientists on this present plane of existence do not claim to have realized or manifested fully the spiritual perfection which the Bible teaches from the first chapter of Genesis, through the teachings of Jesus and the apostolic doctrine, to the final scene of St. John's apocalyptic revelation. Their more modest claim derives from their Leader's teaching that perfection must be won, and that "earth's preparatory school" becomes an instrument to this end. Human experience is the arena for the regeneration of the fleshly mind through Truth and for the substitution of better for poorer beliefs until absolute Truth is reached.

We have now set forth the justification of the term Christian Science as both Christian and scientific. Moreover it ascribes to itself nothing short of being the only true and valid science, Mind-science, the revelation of the infinite divinity in all His "nature, essence, and wholeness"; and it posits the unity, indeed the identity of Science and Christianity. Hence it cannot be classified as merely a Christian sect or another denomination, for it permeates and must eventually transform every other statement of the Christian message to mankind.

Such declarations will continue to provoke in the serious inquirer's mind a flock of questions, just as they did when the Discoverer of Christian Science first issued her challenge. Topping the list would probably stand this one: Do Christian Scientists believe in God? In her Message to The Mother Church for 1901, Mrs. Eddy gave a full and direct answer: "We hear it said the Christian Scientists have no God because their God is not a person. . . . The loyal Christian Scientists absolutely adopt Webster's definition of God, 'A Supreme Being,' and the Standard dictionary's definition of God, 'The one Supreme Being, self-existent and eternal.' "

Is Christian Science, then, a rather thin modern broth of Deism? When Mrs. Eddy was asked directly, Do you believe in God?, she replied: "I believe more in Him than do most Christians, for I have no faith in any other thing or being. . . . To me God is All. He is best understood as Supreme Being, as infinite and conscious Life, as the affectionate Father and Mother of all He creates."

The concordances to Mrs. Eddy's writings reveal how the allness of God permeates Christian Science, and how it derives not from Platonic, Hegelian, or any other philosophy, but directly from the Scriptures. And yet it does not indulge in mere Bible-worship. As noted in the Tenets already quoted, it accepts the "inspired Word of the Bible." Thus the Bible is a source, a guide, but not a fetish. God alone is to be adored, worshiped, and obeyed. Hundreds of references might be cited from the approximately 2,500 which appear in *Science and Health* and the 4,000 in Mrs. Eddy's other writings.

Only the ill-informed person or the most bigoted critic could claim that Christian Science is "godless."

Next in order, Do Christian Scientists believe in man, and what do they believe about man? Mrs. Eddy considered the term Christian Science as related especially to this truth as "applied to humanity." Hence the need for a clear concept of man. This she supplies in a three-page definition in *Science and Health*, making clear the distinction between mortal, corporeal, physical human kind, and spiritual, real, immortal man, the son of God. It is just at this point that Science parts company with traditional theology and accepts the spiritual record of man's creation in God's image and likeness described in the first chapter of Genesis and in the first five verses of the second chapter. In other words, Science rejects in toto the dust-man theory and all it implies as primitive allegory and folk-belief. Mrs. Eddy epitomizes the issue in two brief sentences: "Human philosophy [and she might have included traditional theology] has made God manlike. Christian Science makes man Godlike."

Human consciousness becomes the arena in which Science, the revelation of divinity, battles with, displaces, and finally extirpates the mesmeric belief of man as material, as separated from his Father-Mother, creator and sustainer, God. That battle is the practice of Christian Science.

It is impossible in Science to mix material medicine and spiritual healing. You cannot work from two opposite standpoints and succeed. Hence a patient may not at the same time invoke both material remedies and scientific prayer. This does not mean discourtesy nor antagonism toward medical doctors or surgeons. Indeed Mrs. Eddy frequently paid high tribute to the better representatives of the medical profession.

But how can a Christian Scientist speak of healing unless he believes in a human material body which seems to demand healing? Of course man has a body. But that body is not material or physical. Human body and human mind are merely two aspects, outer and inner, of the same appearance. Human belief constructs this human body, controls it, afflicts it, and finally destroys it. Never was that body material; it was always a mortally mental concept,—although appearing to the human senses as an aggregation of organic cells. Hence the possibility of utilizing spiritual power, right thinking, spiritual prayer, to heal what appears to the corporeal senses as a sick, diseased, broken body, but which must be conceived as a sick, disordered, lawless, and fearful human mind.

Christian Science teaches further that in the so-called "experience of death," there is no interruption of life, continuity, or activity, no cessation of being, no dissipation of being into some pool of Nirvana, no absorption of individual identity into Deity; therefore body continues. Mrs. Eddy unequivocally declares: "Mortals waken from the dream of death with bodies unseen by those who think that they bury the body."

Now let us turn to certain other theological concepts and indicate the teaching of Christian Science regarding them. First, do Scientists accept immortality? Indeed they must, for they utterly reject the idea of mortality as part of the whole texture of belief in matter. Life, continuous life, is the reality, death the illusion. Man is immortal, cannot help being so, since God is Life itself and man lives in God. He is immortal and harmonious now and does not have to achieve immortality by dying. This very inextinguishable continuity of being, infinite, uninterrupted, and eternal connotes pre-existence as well as "future life." Life is not chopped into little segments by some mythical Lachesis and Atropos, is not limited by any so-called "natural lease on life," nor contingent on a mortal physical body. But this teaching does not in any way involve the complicated oriental beliefs in transmigration or reincarnation.

So large a role does this idea of immortality play in Christian Science that at least four Lesson-Sermons out of the twenty-six in the semi-annual cycle constituting the basis of church services are devoted to aspects of this subject. And this immortality is not conceived as a gray static condition in limbo, but as a continuous growth which all must experience until conscious perfection is attained.

Since all sin or sickness derives from a belief of separation from God, salvation is conscious at-one-ment with Him. And this at-one-ment is achieved by divine aid and encouragement to human effort, not by a substitutionary sacrifice or vicarious atonement by Jesus on the Cross. Jesus' life, not the belief in his death, is the important fact in Science.

One of the commonest questions addressed to Christian Science betrays a hang-over from primitive oriental beliefs about cosmology and the future life, namely: Do you believe in heaven and hell? The answer is unreservedly, yes,—but without any reference to a geographical location or to material conditions. After declaring that all is Mind and that metaphysics reduces things to thoughts, heaven and hell must be conceived as mental states. Indeed Mrs. Eddy tells us plainly that "heaven is not a locality, but a divine state of Mind in which all the manifestations of Mind are harmonious and immortal." As for hell, she says, "The sinner makes his own hell by doing evil, and the saint his own heaven by doing right."

Sin which is violation of divine law, brings inevitable penalty. Mrs. Eddy assures us that the heavenly Father who is Love and Truth, is not at war with His own image and likeness, man. Therefore the atonement of the Christ achieves the reconciliation of man to God, not vice versa. In this process of self-discovery and attainment of unity with God, the sin of belief in separation from God, of idolatrous acceptance of other gods, notably matter, must in some way be purged out of human thinking. Hence there must be active cooperation on the individual's part; he cannot merely manifest sorrow for wrongdoing, but must become convinced that sin confers no real satisfaction, must reform, and make restitution. Following St. Paul's injunction Christian Science requires that "the old man with his deeds must be put off," if man would avoid penalty, achieve spiritual maturity, and win heaven.

In this process of attaining daily *rapport* with divinity and ultimate unity or salvation, prayer is a method recognized by most of the great religions. Curiously enough, however, some uninformed critics have charged that Christian Science dispenses with prayer. Indeed, besides being called an infidel, an atheist, a spiritualist, a medium, a drug-addict, the Discoverer of Christian Science was referred to by a clergyman as "the pantheistic and prayerless Mrs. Eddy of Boston!" She promptly but lovingly gave him her answer which may be found in her volume of *Miscellaneous Writings:* "Three times a day, I retire to seek the divine blessing on the sick and sorrowing, with my face toward the Jerusalem of Love and Truth, in silent prayer to the Father which 'seeth in secret,' and with childlike confidence that He will reward 'openly.' In the midst of depressing care and labor I turn constantly to divine Love for guidance, and find rest." It was no mere accident which led the author to place the chapter on prayer at the very beginning of *Science and Health.* Nor did mere casual concern dictate in that same chapter the characterization of the Lord's Prayer as the "prayer which covers all human needs," and follow it with the inspired recognition that "only as we rise above all material sensuousness and sin, can we reach the heaven-born aspiration and spiritual consciousness, which is indicated in the Lord's Prayer and which instantaneously heals the sick."

No prayerless religion would provide that every church service must include a period for silent prayer and the audible repetition of the Lord's Prayer. Note further that Mrs. Eddy directs in the Church Manual that members of her Church should "daily watch and pray to be delivered from all evil, from prophesying, judging, condemning, counseling, influencing or being influenced erroneously." Moreover, in that same Manual she enjoins that it shall be the duty of every member of this Church to pray each day the prayer which now has attained wide acceptance: " 'Thy kingdom come;' let the reign of divine Truth, Life, and Love be established in me, and rule out of me all sin; and may Thy Word enrich the affections of all mankind, and govern them!' "

How does Christian Science view the traditional sacraments of the Christian church? It does not engage in controversy nor take sides with either those who accept the whole seven or only the two commonly adopted by Protestantism. But from the beginning Mrs. Eddy's followers retained the sacramental concept but without material expression. Thus baptism, for example, becomes not a single rite or ceremony but a continuing spiritual purifying process. Mrs. Eddy devotes to marriage a whole vigorous chapter in her textbook, which sets forth the highest ideals of chastity, purity, and stability in the marriage bond.

Communion, the Eucharist, plays an important role in Christian Science thinking and church services. Twice a year, Sacrament appears in the cycle of Lesson-Sermons. A modification of the regular order of services permits featuring a period of special communion through reading the Church Tenets and silent prayer.

Here and there we have made passing reference to such terms as spiritualism, pantheism, hypnotism, mesmerism, faith cure. Has Christian Science any kinship with them? Mrs. Eddy answered categorically in her textbook: "No analogy exists between the vague hypotheses of agnosticism, pantheism, theosophy, spiritualism, or millenarianism and the demonstrable truths of Christian Science." Chapter IV of *Science and Health* bears the title "Christian Science versus Spiritualism," and in it while displaying great courtesy and charity towards spiritualists, she leaves no doubt as to her own position. As to pantheism, Mrs. Eddy in two score passages refutes it as utterly inconsistent with Science. The reason is surely obvious, for pantheism accepts the reality of matter which Science utterly rejects.

As to hypnotism, mesmerism, or the older term animal magnetism, she devotes a brief but unequivocal chapter, "Animal Magnetism Unmasked," in her textbook. Neither in theory nor in practise can the slightest relationship be established between Christian Science and hypnotism, since Science depends upon and utilizes the divine Mind, whereas hypnotism or suggestion uses the human mind for its manipulative purposes.

How about faith cure? Since an individual seeking to be healed must start somewhere and with some inclination towards belief in the healing agency, that point of departure may be called faith. But this is faith in God, not in the healer. And many people have been healed who started with little or no faith at all. Note that faith is the first step, but even that faith in God is insufficient. Blind faith in God is limited and soon exhausted because it savors of emotionalism.

From the foregoing it must be clear that Christian Science is a universal gospel, designed to meet every human need and for the benefit of all mankind. It has already in less than eighty years spread to every part of the globe. It has permeated religious and philosophic thinking, medicine and literature, wherever such exist. Its terminology has been widely even if unconsciously accepted. State laws and courts of justice almost everywhere accept Christian Science as a recognized method of healing. In her book *Pulpit and Press,* Mrs. Eddy set down this prophecy: "If the lives of Christian Scientists attest their fidelity to Truth, I predict that in the twentieth century every Christian church in our land, and a few in far-off lands, will approximate the understanding of Christian Science sufficiently to heal the sick in his name."

The Christian Science denomination cooperates in many ways with other denominations including foreign war relief, disaster relief, and in weekday religious education (where that plan is in vogue). It is represented on the General Commission for Army and Navy Chaplains. Its members as individuals participate energetically in national and local movements for civic and moral welfare.

This admittedly cursory and inadequate doctrinal summary must suffice, although naturally a full understanding could be secured only by studying the basic source book, *Science and Health*. We must now turn to the organization or institutional aspects of Christian Science. In 1875 a few of Mrs. Eddy's students arranged with her for weekly Sabbath meetings to be conducted by her in Lynn, as their teacher or instructor, and the following year organized the Christian Scientist Association. This germinal organization continued until its dissolution in 1889, after which time it functioned merely as an alumni group of the Massachusetts Metaphysical College founded by Mrs. Eddy in 1881. Meanwhile in 1879, after a few months of preliminary discussion and counselling together, she and twenty-six of her followers organized the Church of Christ, Scientist. For a while the church did little beside hold Sunday services. Other agencies such as the pioneer Christian Scientist Association, carried on most of the distinctive activities later concentrated in the Church. The need for simplification, co-ordination, and for a focal point of administration and responsibility became increasingly clear during the ten years after the first church was formally launched. Mrs. Eddy's students had established centers of healing and teaching (sometimes called "Institutes") all over the United States; churches had been organized in several localities and even in Europe. Yet the major problem which confronted Mrs. Eddy was the need for an adequate agency to be the central administrative and executive body of the Christian Science movement. Characteristically enough, Mrs. Eddy then recommended that the Boston church organization be dissolved. This was done in December 1889. For three years the Church carried on its work in an informal way, its affairs being managed by a Board of Directors. During this time of somewhat informal conduct of church affairs the Directors were encouraged to greater assumption of responsibility. But by 1892 Mrs. Eddy had matured the plan which still remains the organizational pattern of this denomination. This plan culminated in the organization of the present Church, The First Church of Christ, Scientist, in Boston, Massachusetts. Since 1892, the denomination has consisted of The Mother Church in Boston, Massachusetts, and branch churches or branch societies wherever adherents number enough to warrant founding local organizations.

Branch churches or societies are entirely self-governing, have their own corporate existence, their own by-laws; set up their own membership qualifications; elect their own officers and Readers.

They must, however, conform to certain requirements laid down in the Church Manual. The Manual requires that branches must be "distinctly democratic" in government. The form and order of exercises for Sunday, Wednesday, Thanksgiving, and Communion services, and for the Sunday Schools are prescribed in the Manual as uniform for all churches. Each branch church maintains or cooperates in maintaining a Reading Room, and calls upon the Board of Lectureship annually for one or more lectures: a branch society, being only an incipient church, may but need not do either.

The officers of The Mother Church consist of The Christian Science Board of Directors, a President, the First and Second Readers, a Clerk, and a Treasurer. The governing body of the denomination is the Board of Directors. While each branch church has its own self-government, its roster of officers patterns that of The Mother Church. The Directors of The Mother Church are self-perpetuating, elect the President, Clerk, Treasurer, Readers, Superintendent of Sunday School, editors of publications, Board of Lectureship, Committee on Publication, and other executives. In branch churches members elect Readers, also Directors, who may or may not name the other church administrative officers.

The income of The Mother Church derives from a per capita tax provided in the Church Manual, from bequests, donations by branch churches, contributions from the field for war relief, disaster relief, or other special needs, payment by guests of the benevolent institutions, and profits from church publications.

From what has been said, quite evidently Christian Science is a "laymen's movement," in the sense that it permits no professional clergy or priesthood. Each member is his own priest. Each is eligible for election to any and all church offices. Rotation in office assures democracy and participation by members in all church activities. No titles are permitted except those conferred under laws of state or nation.

What then are the specific "activities" of the Christian Science movement? First, as might be expected, church services,—public worship. In the beginning these services included preaching of the traditional type. Mrs. Eddy herself preached sermons for several years by invitation in churches of other denominations and in the meeting halls where Christian Science services were held. As she gradually withdrew from this phase of directing her movement, other preachers took over, some of them regularly ordained ministers formerly serving other denominations. The momentous year 1895 records two significant steps in preserving and consolidating the outward aspects of Christian Science, namely, dedication of the Original Mother Church Edifice, and ordination of the Bible and *Science and Health* as the only preachers henceforth for both Mother Church and all branches.

Accordingly, reading from the King James version of the Bible and from *Science and Health* became the new order in January, 1895, for The Mother Church; and in April of the same year the branch churches followed suit. The order of services thus instituted became fixed by appropriate rules in the Church Manual.

The Wednesday testimonial meetings offer opportunity not only to hear selections from the Bible and *Science and Health,* but also testimonies of healing through application of Christian Science.

Each church may, and most do, conduct a Sunday School to which pupils up to the age of twenty may be admitted. Adult classes are no longer permitted, since the church service offers the same Lesson-Sermon for daily study, which is the basis of teaching for all but the younger Sunday School pupils.

Each branch church is required to establish and maintain a Reading Room, either on its own premises or in other quarters. Here the public may read, consult, borrow, or purchase the Bible, the writings of Mary Baker Eddy and other authorized literature published or sold by The Christian Science Publishing Society.

Since on the very first page of the Preface to *Science and Health* its author has challenged, "The time for thinkers has come," Christian Science is fundamentally committed to education. Not mere intellectual, nor cultural, nor vocational education, but education in its broadest, most regenerative sense. Mary Baker Eddy was not only well educated herself, but prized and fostered education. The nobility of her English and the originality of her style indicate an outstanding cultivated mind. But she warned against the limited knowledge gained through material senses alone, and foresaw precisely how such knowledge could be turned against its possessors and bring on disaster.

The wide circulation of the periodicals issued by The Christian Science Publishing Society offers a great variety of educational content. Of these periodicals public opinion would probably rate *The*

Christian Science Monitor as the most unique educational contribution of its founder, Mrs. Eddy. For almost forty years this international daily newspaper has been setting a standard of decent journalism, authentic news, and truth in advertising; hence its wide use by classes in public schools, colleges and universities.

The Christian Science church as such maintains no denominational school or college, but several private schools and one college are operated by Christian Scientists. Christian Science Organizations may now be found in over seventy colleges and universities in the United States, Canada, and England.

We have repeatedly emphasized that Christian Science is a religion, and not just a new-fangled form of medicine or faith healing. Yet healing is the irrefutable witness that Science does embody the word and works of Christ Jesus the Way-shower and is thus able to "reinstate primitive Christianity and its lost element of healing." Hence every genuine Christian Scientist is expected to be a healer. But it was entirely natural that certain among them should feel the special qualifications for and an urge to devote their time and energies to healing on a full-time basis. *The Christian Science Journal* at present lists over 10,000 such practitioners serving throughout the world. In most localities Christian Science practice is recognized by statute or court decision as a legal method of healing, and practitioners are permitted to charge for their services. Mrs. Eddy approved such charges.

Because of persistent misapprehension the question, What is Mrs. Eddy's relation to the Christian Science movement? must be squarely faced and answered. She is known as the Discoverer, Founder and Leader of Christian Science. She wrote its basic textbook, *Science and Health,* the *Church Manual,* and a half score of other volumes large and small. She established the first Church of Christ, Scientist, and was its first pastor. After the dissolution of this Church she organized the present church, The First Church of Christ, Scientist, in Boston, of which she became Pastor Emeritus. She also provided for the establishment of its branches. She founded the Massachusetts Metaphysical College and taught classes in it for nearly ten years. She set the pattern for metaphysical healings as witnessed by many so-called miraculous cures, including cancer, insanity, deformity, tuberculosis, enteritis, "brain fever," deafness, dumbness, stomach ulcers, ankylosed joints; and was able to restore both children and adults who manifested the common evidences and appearance of death. Pressure of other leadership activities led her to publicly decline further patients after 1885, but her healing work continued on occasion directly, and also on ever increasing scale, indirectly through inspiration and continued teaching of her students. She set up all the various boards and activities of her church, including lecturers, Reading Rooms, benevolences, publications. She launched *The Christian Science Journal* (of which she served as first editor and publisher) and every successive periodical including *The Christian Science Monitor,* which was the crowning achievement of her eighty-eighth year.

Small wonder then that Christian Scientists revere and love Mrs. Eddy, consider her as divinely inspired and guided, and pay grateful tribute to her at Wednesday testimonial meetings and in the denominational periodicals. But do they identify her *as* Christian Science? Do they worship her? Do they conider her as another Christ? The answer is an emphatic NO! The growth of Christian Science since Mrs. Eddy's passing on in 1910, however shocking to the soothsayers who predicted its immediate collapse after removal of her personality, witnesses to her genius as an organizer and to the inherent truth of her message. Mrs. Eddy never exalted her own personality, nor exacted personal homage, following, or adulation. To the contrary she constantly urged that her students follow her, their Leader, "only so far as she follows Christ." She begged them not to lean too much on her, but trust God to direct their steps. Again and again she warned her followers to beware of personalizing Christian Science or of worshiping her own personality. It was partly to avoid just this tendency of human nature to lionize and exploit personality that she withdrew from Boston and removed to Concord, New Hampshire, seventy miles away: and this at the very time her college was enjoying its highest prosperity and her fame widespread.

She never manifested false modesty as to the value and God-inspired quality of *Science and Health,* but likewise never plumed her own vanity as its author. She never considered her textbook as a substitute for the Bible, but as a scientific explanation and key to it. Hence the "only preachers" at a Christian Science church service, as she directed, are the Bible *and* the textbook.

In view of these facts one can easily comprehend Mrs. Eddy's reaction to the question of whether she was Christ. In a letter to the *New York Herald* just after the original Mother Church Edifice was dedicated, she wrote: "A despatch is given me, calling for an interview to answer for myself, 'Am I the second Christ?' Even the question shocks me. What I am is for God to declare in His infinite mercy. As it is, I claim nothing more than what I am, the Discoverer and Founder of Christian Science, and the blessing it has been to mankind which eternity enfolds. . . . There was, is, and never can be but one God, one Christ, one Jesus of Nazareth. . . ."

So Mary Baker Eddy stands as the messenger to this age of the same truth glimpsed by the prophets, taught and exemplified in its acme by Christ Jesus, practised for three centuries by the early Christian Church, overlaid by materialism and ecclesiasticism and dormant for over a millennium, again discovered, organized, and put into such form as to be available for all mankind henceforward and forever. The Christian Science Board of Directors in a public statement concerning "Mrs. Eddy's Place" which appeared in the *Christian Science Sentinel* for June 5, 1943, states in part: "she (Mrs. Eddy) represents in this age the spiritual idea of God typified by the woman in the Apocalypse." Concerning this "spiritual idea" Mrs. Eddy writes in *Science and Health*: "The impersonation of the spiritual idea had a brief history in the earthly life of our Master; but 'of his kingdom there shall be no end,' for Christ, God's idea, will eventually rule all nations and peoples—imperatively, absolutely, finally—with divine Science."

What now may be said as to the fruitage of Mrs. Eddy's leadership, the organization she founded, the church activities, the practitioners' services, and the publications? The important consideration is not the number of church members, nor church edifices, nor money value of properties, but does Christian Science maintain the healing mission its Discoverer and Leader conceived? It does. The demand for its textbook increases steadily. Many hundreds of editions of it have been issued. Dr. Lyman Powell writing in 1930 declared that *Science and Health* had become, next to the Bible, the "best seller" among serious books. But its sales have leaped to new heights since that date. It has been translated into German and French, and other translations are under consideration. This textbook contains a hundred pages of "Fruitage,"—testimonials of persons healed of desperate organic as well as functional ailments, through study of the book.

The last chapter of Mrs. Eddy's *Miscellaneous Writings* consists of seventy pages of similar testimonials. Every issue of *The Christian Science Journal* (monthly now in its 64th volume) contains several pages of authenticated testimonials of healing. An almost equal number appear in the weekly *Christian Science Sentinel*. The various *Heralds* (monthly in German, French, Dutch, Scandinavian, and Spanish languages) likewise include such testimonies. One may hear oral testimonies at any Wednesday church meeting or at Thanksgiving services. Practitioners offer healing help in every state in the Union, in Alaska, Hawaii, the Philippines, Puerto Rico, Canada, Egypt, South Africa, India, Java, Australia, New Zealand, most European countries, Argentina, Brazil, and before the recent World War, in China and Japan. Christian Science nurses are available, though in much fewer numbers, in nearly two-thirds of the United States and in Australia, Great Britain and Ireland, Netherlands, Switzerland, and British Columbia. The current issues of the *Journal* and *Sentinel* record healings of such physical and mental troubles as sprained ankle, ivy poisoning, pernicious anemia, tuberculosis, blood poisoning, nervous breakdown, broken bones (including hips and pelvis), measles, whooping cough, influenza, chicken pox, ringworm, goiter, appendicitis, chronic indigestion, grief, smoking, drinking. An analytical listing of disorders healed as published in these two periodicals for the five years 1940-45 brings together not less than 250 physical ailments both organic and functional, such as acne, Addison's disease, adenoids, angina pectoris, apoplexy, arthritis, astigmatism, blindness, Bright's disease, cancer, chorea, colitis, deafness, dementia praecox, diabetes, dysentery, encephalitis, epilepsy, gangrene, hay fever, hernia, jaundice, locomotor ataxia, malaria, neuritis, osteomelitis, paralysis, pneumonia, pyorrhea, shingles, sciatica, smallpox, St. Vitus' dance and stuttering. Note that this list includes the most inveterate and dreaded organic diseases as well as functional disorders.

Hence it is no exaggeration to assert that countless thousands in this world today are "living witnesses" and monuments to the power of Christian Science to meet every human need, to heal every type of sickness and disease, and to rescue untold numbers from a premature grave to which earnest but baffled doctors and their own fears had consigned them.

The whole field of medicine and surgery has felt the impact of

Christian Science. The "mental factor in disease" receives more and more attention from medical schools and practitioners. Mental traumatism now occupies a fixed place in medical and surgical parlance. In polite circles discussion of one's diseases and ailments tends to become "bad form." Even language reflects Science terminology: for example, the now common usage of "passed on" for died.

Not unnaturally the dramatic emergence and spread of Christian Science as a major religious phenomenon of the last eighty years finds expression in a multifarious literature. Books, pamphlets, and periodical articles abound,—some ignorantly hostile, some malicious, some well intentioned but inaccurate. Hence it has become necessary to set up in library cataloguing two categories, "authorized" (i. e. Mrs. Eddy's own writings or publications of The Christian Science Publishing Society) and "unauthorized" (miscellaneous publications of varied derivation and content).

BIBLIOGRAPHY

Mary Baker Eddy's works include, in latest edition all published in Boston by the Trustees under her will: *Science and Health with Key to the Scriptures* (1946); *Miscellaneous Writings* (1944); *Retrospection and Introspection* (1946); *Unity of Good* (1946); *Pulpit and Press* (1945); *Rudimental Divine Science* (1946); *No and Yes* (1946); *Christian Science versus Pantheism* (1946); *Messages to The Mother Church* (for 1900, 1901, 1902) (1946); *Christian Healing* (1946); *People's Idea of God* (1944); *The First Church of Christ, Scientist, and Miscellany* (1946); *Poems* (1945); *Christ and Christmas* (1946); *Church Manual* (1946). The official church periodicals initiated by Mrs. Eddy comprise: *The Christian Science Journal* (1883); the *Christian Science Sentinel* (1898); *Christian Science Quarterly* (1898); the *Herald of Christian Science* (German, 1903; French, 1918; Scandinavian, 1930; Dutch, 1931; Spanish, 1946; Braille in English, 1931). The Christian Science Publishing Society also issues many authorized publications outlined as follows with the last edition thereof indicated; the *Christian Science Hymnal* (first edition, 1898; revised, 1910; revised and enlarged, 1932) (1946); *The Life of Mary Baker Eddy*, by Sibyl Wilbur (1945); *Mary Baker Eddy: A Life Size Portrait*, by Lyman P. Powell (1946); *Christian Science and Its Discoverer*, by E. Mary Ramsay (1943); *A Child's Life of Mary Baker Eddy*, by Ella H. Hay (1944); *Historical Sketches from the Life of Mary Baker Eddy and the History of Chris-

tian Science, by Clifford P. Smith (1943); *We Knew Mary Baker Eddy,* by Lathrop, Knapp, Thompson, et al. (1946); *Twelve Years with Mary Baker Eddy,* by Irving C. Tomlinson (1946); *The Mother Church,* by Joseph Armstrong (1946); *The Mother Church Extension,* by Margaret Williamson (1939); *Mary Baker Eddy: Her Mission and Triumph,* by Julia Michael Johnston (1946). The Publishers of Mrs. Eddy's writings issued *Concordances* to *Science and Health* and to other Prose Writings by Mrs. Eddy in two separate volumes and in a single inclusive volume (1933, 1934).

JEHOVAH'S WITNESSES

Nathan Homer Knorr was born in Bethlehem, Pennsylvania, in 1905, of American-born parents. He attended school in Allentown, Pennsylvania, and graduated from high school in June 1923.

Mr. Knorr first came into contact with Jehovah's Witnesses at the age of 16, when members of his family obtained some of the "Watchtower" publications. With his family he studied such publications and became convinced of their Biblical truthfulness. Shortly thereafter he commenced to associate with Jehovah's Witnesses of Allentown in their regular meetings for Bible study. Upon beginning his association with Jehovah's witnesses he resigned membership in the Reformed Church which he had attended for several years. He became a full-time preacher at the age of 18.

In 1923 he was invited to become a member of the staff of workers at the headquarters of the Watch Tower Bible and Tract Society at Brooklyn, New York. His first duties with the Society in Brooklyn were connected with the shipping of Bibles and other publications. Week-ends were generally devoted to preaching activities; evenings to Bible study and classes arranged for by the Society. In the course of time he was assigned as coordinator of all printing activities in the Society's plant. He became general manager of the publishing office and plant in 1932.

In 1934 Mr. Knorr was elected as one of the directors of the Peoples Pulpit Association (now Watchtower Bible and Tract Society, Inc., of New York), and a year later he was chosen to be vice president. In 1940 he was made a director and vice president of the Watch Tower Bible and Tract Society, a Pennsylvania Corporation. Election to the presidency of both Societies and the International Bible Students Association, of England, came in January 1942, following the death of J. F. Rutherford.

Mr. Knorr's duties as president of the Societies are varied and multitudinous. They include the direction of policies; supervision of all editorial work; direction of the Society's fifty-seven branch offices; supervision of the Society's missionary representatives in countries where no offices are yet established; direction of the Watchtower Bible School of Gilead at South Lansing, New York; general supervision of the Society's farms operated to provide food for those working at the headquarters and the School; and oversight of activities of Radio Station WBBR, Brooklyn.

Editor

JEHOVAH'S WITNESSES OF MODERN TIMES

N. H. KNORR

JEHOVAH GOD is the Founder and Organizer of his witnesses on earth. The first witness was Abel. Such valiant witnesses as Enoch, Noah, Abraham, Moses, Jeremiah—indeed a long line of faithful witnesses—ran all the way down from Abel the first martyr ("martyr" means "witness") to John the Baptist. Christ Jesus was himself the "faithful and true witness, the beginning of the creation of God" and takes the preeminence among all the witnesses. (Revelation 3:14) This Chief Witness designated others to continue Kingdom testimony, saying, "Ye shall be witnesses unto me . . . unto the uttermost part of the earth." (Acts 1:8) The apostles and other early Christians faithfully fulfilled their commission as witnesses of the Most High, and on down through the centuries until the present time Jehovah God has had his witnesses on earth testifying to his name and supremacy. Jehovah's witnesses of modern times are merely the last of a long line of God's earthly servants.

In recent years, since 1931, they have become widely known under the name of Jehovah's witnesses. This is a name Jehovah God himself has indicated as the appropriate designation of his earthly ministers, as is evidenced by Isaiah 43:10,12, American Standard Version Bible: "Ye are my witnesses, saith Jehovah, and my servant whom I have chosen; that ye may know and believe me, and understand that I am he: before me there was no God formed, neither shall there be after me. I have declared, and I have saved, and I have showed; and there was no strange god among you: therefore ye are my witnesses, saith Jehovah, and I am God." Jehovah's witnesses of modern times have not arbitrarily assumed this God-given name, but the facts concerning their activity prove it applicable to them, that they are living up to it.

We break in on the history of Jehovah's witnesses during the seventies of the nineteenth century. It was during this decade that a young man by the name of Charles Taze Russell started a small Bible class in Allegheny, Pa. Previously Russell had explored the various religious organizations in search of truth, but in none of the denominations of Christendom did he find a religious creed that seemed to fully teach Bible truths. Hence C. T. Russell and his associates began a thorough study of the Bible, particularly concerning Christ's second coming and millennial reign. In 1874 the group published a pamphlet entitled *The Object and Manner of the Lord's Return,* and 50,000 copies were distributed to disprove the religious theory of the earth's being destroyed by fire at Christ's coming and also to proclaim that Christ's presence was to be invisible rather than a physical return. Thus started a work of gospel preaching by printed page that was to become unrivaled in history.

Actually the year 1879 opens the history of the modern organized witnesses of Jehovah, for it is in this year that the witness work took on an organized form. In July of that year the first issue of the *Watchtower* magazine appeared, 6,000 copies being distributed. From then till this year *The Watchtower* has not missed an issue, and its distribution in many languages now exceeds 600,000 semi-monthly. As early as June, 1880, *The Watchtower* published the Bible chronology proving that A.D. 1914 marked the end of the Gentile Times, and in that year the physical signs Jesus foretold as accompanying the establishment of his kingdom in heaven did begin appearing on earth. (See Matthew 24:3–51; Mark 13:3–37; Luke 21:7–36.) Down through the years the *Watchtower* magazine has uncompromisingly declared Jehovah's message and judgments and the good news of his established kingdom. It is the official journal of the Watchtower Society that sets forth the Scriptural beliefs of Jehovah's witnesses.

Early in the history of Jehovah's witnesses tract distribution played an important role in gospel preaching. By 1881 basic beliefs had gouged out a wide breach between the witnesses and the orthodox denominations of Christendom, and these differences in belief were widely publicized by tracts that eventually numbered into the millions and circulated in 13 different languages. In that year the 161-page booklet *Food for Thinking Christians,* setting forth the fundamental beliefs of the witnesses, were distributed in the United States and also abroad. The year 1881 saw Jehovah's witnesses organized into a society to undertake the preaching work, Zion's Watch Tower Tract Society (an unincorporated organization) being established, with headquarters in Allegheny, Pa.

As the Society expanded, it became necessary to incorporate it and build a more definite organization. In 1884 a charter was granted recognizing the Society as a religious, non-profit corporation. C. T. Russell was elected president and six of his close associates filled out full membership of a board of directors. The charter name, Zion's Watch Tower Tract Society, continued till 1896, when by amendment it was changed to Watch Tower Bible & Tract Society. This corporation is the legal instrument and servant of the unincorporated body or society of Jehovah's witnesses making up the congregations scattered throughout the earth.

Two years after incorporation the Society made another stride in printing, adding bound volumes to its tracts and booklets, in 1886. In that year the 350-page clothbound book *The Divine Plan of the Ages* was published, to be followed in course of time by six other volumes which made up the series known as *Studies in the Scriptures.* They were circulated by the millions and in several languages. Increased publishing activities demanded greater facilities, and a milestone in expansion was reached in 1909, when the Society's headquarters was moved to Brooklyn, N. Y. In that year a New York corporation was formed, called the People's Pulpit Association; but this was later changed, in 1939, to Watchtower Bible and Tract Society, Inc. Expansion of the work on a world-wide scale led to the creation of the International Bible Students Association, in the British Isles, in 1914.

Down through the years preceding World War I the publishing of fundamental Bible truths attracted thousands of sincere persons, who in turn engaged in the work of distribution. By the close of World War I, at which time the work was disrupted by false charges of sedition, there had been distributed 318,730,050 tracts and booklets and 8,993,166 bound books. During this forty-year period the original handful of witnesses had grown to 22,304 active house-to-house publishers. But their publicizing of the Kingdom was not limited to publication of tracts, booklets and books. Much preaching was done from the public platform. Mention of the breach between beliefs of Jehovah's witnesses and the clergy of Christendom has been made, and as the work increased religious opposition kept pace with it. The early years of the twentieth century were marked by widely advertised debates between C. T. Russell and J. F. Rutherford on the one hand and outstanding Protestant ministers on the other.

Beginning with the year 1910, the Society undertook considerable newspaper work. What was known as the Syndicate was established. The Society's president wrote sermons each week for the Syndicate, whose business it was to telegraph them to newspapers that subscribed for the service. During the first year 1,000 newspapers in the United States and Canada carried these discourses, and in 1913 a peak in this activity was reached, at which time the sermons were in 1,500 newspapers and appeared in four languages. The Syndicate service covered about five years.

The factor which brought the witness of Jehovah's servants prior to World War I to an emphatic conclusion was the Photo-Drama of Creation. It was a showing of motion pictures and stills, accompanied by recorded lectures and musical selections. There were four successive exhibitions or parts with twenty-four lectures of about five minutes each, and requiring two hours per part. The undertaking was unprecedented, for motion pictures and sound recordings were only in their infancy. Work on the Photo-Drama began in 1912 and was completed in 1914, when it was first shown in New York to an awe-struck gathering. Before that fateful year was over the Drama had spread to every city of any size in the United States and throughout Europe and into Australia and New Zealand.

Since 1880 Jehovah's witnesses had publicized the year 1914 as the end of the "times of the Gentiles", according to Bible prophecy. That year 'nation rose against nation' in history's first engulfing world war. It was the first of the series of physical evidences Jesus foretold in his outstanding prophecy in the twenty-fourth chapter of Matthew concerning his second coming and the end of the world. The witnesses as a whole understood that this second coming and end did not mean a fiery end of the literal earth, but meant the end of Satan's uninterrupted rule over "this present evil world" and the time for Christ's enthronement in heaven as King.

Christ Jesus further foretold that much persecution and Judas-like betrayals would afflict his followers after the start of World War I. In October, 1916, C. T. Russell died and was succeeded in the Society's presidency by J. F. Rutherford, in January, 1917. Soon thereafter a volume entitled *The Finished Mystery* was released, and it became a focal point of internal dissension. At the annual corporation meeting in 1918 J. F. Rutherford and other faithful directors of the Society were overwhelmingly supported. The beaten and disgruntled opposition force withdrew and set up an independent organization, but soon had a falling out among themselves and split off into many little groups of no consequence. Foretold persecution came to a climax after religious leaders, aided and abetted by some of the one-time brethren whose love had grown cold, grossly misrepresented Jehovah's witnesses and denounced them as seditionists. (See Luke 23:2; Acts 17:6, 7; 24:1–5.) War hysteria made easy the engineering of the arrest, conviction and imprisonment without bail of the Society's officers, to serve sentences of eighty years. After nine months defendants were admitted to bail, the case heard on appeal, judgment reversed, defendants discharged and dismissed and hence automatically restored to citizenship and never convicts within the meaning of the law. Similar false arrests and betrayals plagued the witnesses the world over, their trials even being added to by mobbings and beatings and raids and tar-and-feather outrages.

But soon thereafter the picture brightens with the fulfillment of another of Jesus' foretold signs of his second coming—the preaching of the good news of his enthronement in all the world for a witness unto all nations, as a warning before the final end of Armageddon. (Matthew 24:14) In 1919 at Cedar Point, Ohio, 8,000 witnesses girded themselves for the publishing work. Another convention at the same place three years later saw 20,000 witnesses acclaim the slogan "Advertise, advertise, advertise the King and the Kingdom". In the years that followed Jehovah's witnesses have done just that. Since the end of World War I their ranks have increased from some 22,000 to upward of 150,000, and in that period they have distributed Bibles, bound books and booklets totaling more than 485,-000,000, in 88 languages. This figure excludes hundreds of millions of *Kingdom News* leaflets and magazines. In 1919 a companion magazine to *The Watchtower* was introduced, *The Golden Age*, which in 1937 was replaced by *Consolation*. *Consolation* was in turn supplanted by the new magazine *Awake!*, released in 1946 at an international convention of Jehovah's witnesses held in Cleveland, Ohio, and reaching a peak attendance of 80,000. During the

1920's and 1930's the Society made extensive use of the radio for weekly broadcasts and chain hookups to publicize Christ's kingdom. But the bulk of the work was and is done by the publisher in the field, and when it is remembered that it is done under severest persecution, literally thousands upon thousands of witnesses being mobbed and mutilated, imprisoned and killed, during the past dozen years, then the magnitude of work accomplished is not short of miraculous.

By what organizational setup is the work done? First, let it be clear that no man is the leader of Jehovah's witnesses. Jehovah God has appointed Christ Jesus as their Leader and Commander, and through a visible organization the King-Leader directs affairs, just as God long ago directed Israel through a visible organization. The facts, not presumption, show that the Watchtower Society has been used as the modern channel for direction. Present headquarters are at 124 Columbia Heights, Brooklyn 2, N. Y., with chief printing plant near by, at Adams and Sands Streets. The work is directed from the headquarters, most of that in foreign lands being handled through Branch offices. The first Branch was established in 1900, in London. Fifteen new Branches organized in 1946 brought the total to fifty-six.

The witnesses earth-wide are grouped in thousands of local congregations called companies, and regularly meet at Kingdom Halls for study and instruction for service. Each company has organizational servants to oversee the various features of field activity. The companies hold large assignments of territory, which large assignments are broken up into small areas for individual publishers. Each one of Jehovah's active witnesses is a minister, ordained and commissioned by God, not by man, to preach (Isaiah 61:1, 2; John 15:16; Mark 13:10). In his individual territory the witness preaches, calling from house to house, making return visits or backcalls on those showing interest, standing on the streets with the message—all this in addition to preaching from the public platform. In so doing the witness is following in the way blazed by Christ and early Christians. (Matthew 10:7, 11–14; Luke 8:1; 13:26; Acts 5:42; 15:36; 20:20; Proverbs 1:20, 21; 8:1–3.)

Jehovah's witnesses are trained for the ministerial work. Not that they attend seminaries—neither did Jesus or the apostles. But intensive private and group study in the Bible and Bible helps equips

them. Such training has been stressed particularly since J. F. Rutherford has been succeeded in the Society's presidency by N. H. Knorr,
early in 1942, due to Rutherford's death. Since then the Watchtower
Bible School of Gilead has been established in South Lansing, N. Y.,
and yearly two hundred ministers receive special training there for
foreign missionary service. Full-time witnesses are brought from
all parts of the earth for the courses, and some 350 have already, by
the summer of 1946, been sent to foreign lands. Additionally, each
company of witnesses conducts special ministerial training schools in
their local Kingdom Halls, using as basic textbooks the Bible, and
two 384-page helps, *Theocratic Aid to Kingdom Publishers* and
"Equipped for Every Good Work."

The unquenchable zeal of these trained ministers has oft been
commented upon. It is due to their covenant obligations to God.
They have consecrated to do God's will, have studied what that will
is as set forth in the Bible, and then do it unwaveringly. They are
moved by love for God. They are not serving for money. The work
is not commercial; and the United States Supreme Cout has so
ruled repeatedly in the many court victories won by Jehovah's witnesses in the interests of freedom of speech and worship. Literature
is left on a nominal contribution, 35 cents being suggested for the
384-page bound books. Much literature is left free. The witnesses,
for the most part, are engaged in secular employment for a livelihood; but spend all their available spare time—evenings, Saturdays,
Sundays—in the field service. It is even the voluntary contributions
of these same witnesses that support the work, plus the nominal contributions for literature. Some 6,700 full-time field workers (pioneers) are aided financially by the Society. Those working at Branch
offices and Brooklyn headquarters get their room and board and $10
a month for clothing and incidental expenses. The 265 serving at
headquarters, whether president or factory worker, receive the same
allowance. The witnesses do not believe one should have to be paid
to serve God, but believe service should be motivated by love for
him.—1 Timothy 6:8.

But what are some of the other beliefs, the main tenets, of
Jehovah's witnesses? First, they believe that the Bible is God's inspired Word, written by faithful men over a period of sixteen centuries and handed down through manuscript copies and printed
pages for the admonition and learning of those now living in the

"last days". (Romans 15:4; 1 Corinthians 10:11) The Bible's Author, Jehovah God, is Creator of heaven and earth, the fountain of life and the one to whom salvation belongs. Rebellion in Eden called into question Jehovah's position as supreme Sovereign and challenged his power to put men on earth who would maintain integrity toward God under test. (Job 1:6–12; 2:1–5) It raised an issue requiring time to settle, and made necessary the vindication of God's name. The Scriptures abound with evidence that the primary issue before creation is the vindication of Jehovah's name and Word. The masses of Christendom do not even appreciate the fact that "Jehovah" is God's name (euphonious and Anglicized form), and that the Hebrew equivalent appears 6,823 times in the original Hebrew Scriptures. In due time God will establish his new world of righteousness and completely vindicate his name. (Isaiah 65:17; 2 Peter 3:13) Chiefly used to do this is Christ Jesus.

Christ Jesus, also called Logos, was the first creation of God, and was thereafter used as a Master Workman in successive creative works. (Proverbs 8:22–36; Colossians 1:15, 16) Millenniums later Christ was made flesh and dwelt on earth, witnessed to the truth, preached the Kingdom, died on the tree as a ransom for obedient mankind, and was resurrected on the third day and later ascended unto God in heaven as appointed King of the New World. Jehovah's witnesses do not believe in universal salvation through Christ's ransom, but salvation "unto all them that obey him". (Hebrews 5:9) Neither do they elevate Christ to equality with Jehovah God by belief in a religious "trinity". Jesus never taught such a thing, but said: "My Father is greater than I." (John 14:28) Bible scholars now recognize that the trinitarians' pet text, 1 John 5:7, was never in the original manuscripts but was maneuvered into the Bible many centuries later. Jehovah God and Christ Jesus are one in the same sense that faithful Christians on earth are one with Them, namely, in purpose and effect.—John 10:30; 17:20–23.

The church mentioned in Scriptures refers not to any literal building, but to the body-members of Christ Jesus, who are spoken of as living stones built up as a holy temple unto the Lord on the chief Foundation Stone, Christ Jesus. (Acts 7:48–50; Ephesians 1:17, 22, 23; 2:19–21; 1 Peter 2:5, 9) This consecrated class have been anointed with God's spirit to become a part of the "kingdom of heaven" joint-heirs who live and reign with Christ a thousand years. The Scriptures limit the number of this spiritual, heavenly church-body to 144,000.—Revelation 14:1, 3; 20:4, 6.

The focal point of the beliefs of Jehovah's witnesses is the Kingdom for which Christ taught his followers to pray. That kingdom is invisible, heavenly, and comprised of the 144,000 body-members and their Head and King, Christ Jesus. "Flesh and blood cannot inherit the kingdom of God." (1 Corinthians 15:50) Thus the Kingdom is not an earthly one, is not to be and never will be found in any political government or combine of governments on this earth. "My kingdom is not of this world," said Jesus. (John 18:36) However, the righteous rule of that heavenly kingdom will descend earthward and effect the answer to the Lord's prayer, "Thy will be done in earth, as it is in heaven."

Most striking is the belief of Jehovah's witnesses that the Kingdom is established, is at hand and is operating. This sounds strange to many, in view of continued woes and distress. However, the Scriptures foretell a transition period from old world rule to Kingdom rule, a time in which Christ would 'rule in the midst of his enemies' while Satan the Devil increased earth's woes. (Psalm 110:2; 1 Corinthians 15:25, 26; Revelation 12:1–12, 17) Christ Jesus foretold the physical signs visible during this transition period, namely: world war, famines, pestilence, earthquakes, special persecution upon his followers, world-wide preaching by his witnesses that the Kingdom is established, the appearance of a league of nations that would stand in the holy place of Christ's kingdom by being proclaimed the 'political expression of God's kingdom on earth', and which world combine would sink into oblivion for a time, only to be later revived and once more heralded by worldlings as the bringer of world peace. (Matthew 24:3–39; Revelation 17:7–13) This chain of physical evidence has been forged in world events, link by link, since 1914. And Jehovah's witnesses had published 34 years previous to 1914 (1880) that that year would mark the establishment of the heavenly kingdom of Christ. Jesus also said that the transition period would be fully accomplished during the span of the generation then living, and that the climactic end would come with the battle of Armageddon, the battle of God Almighty.— Matthew 24:21, 34; Revelation 16:13–16.

Armageddon is not a clash between earthly armies or ideologies, but is to be a battle fought by the invisible hosts of heaven. It will end in victory for Jehovah God and his King Christ Jesus, in the destruction of Satan the Devil and his demons, in the cleansing of this earth of all wickedness and evil-doers, and in the complete vindication of Jehovah's name. (Zechariah 14:3, 12; Revelation 19:11–21; 20:1–3) Jehovah God is now warning men and nations of this coming battle, through his witnesses on earth, that men of good-will toward God may heed and be preserved alive within the safety of God's organization.

Jehovah's witnesses do not believe that this battle of Armageddon will destroy the literal earth, by fire or otherwise. "The earth abideth for ever." (Ecclesiastes 1:4) Jehovah God has promised it to the meek as their inheritance, a place to dwell in eternal peace, free from war and oppression, sickness and death. Jehovah's purpose in creating the earth was to extend Edenic conditions earthwide and have it inhabited by a righteous race of men and women. (Genesis 1:28; Psalm 37:11, 29; Isaiah 2:2–4; 11:6–9; 25:6–8; 65:25; Jeremiah 33:6; Revelation 21:1–4) His purposes and promises will not fail.—Isaiah 14:27; 46:11; 55:11.

Armageddon survivors will multiply and populate the earth. Unnumbered multitudes will be raised to life by a resurrection from the dead during the time of Christ's 1000-year reign. (John 5:28, 29, *American Standard Version*) Since Jehovah's witnesses believe in the resurrection, it means they do not believe man possesses an immortal soul that never dies. (Ezekiel 18:4) The dead are completely out of existence, awaiting the resurrection. (Psalm 146:4; Ecclesiastes 3:19, 20; 9:5, 10) Moreover, Jehovah's witnesses do not believe in purgatory or eternal torment in hell-fire. They believe that the punishment for the wicked is what God said it would be in Eden, namely, death. Everlasting death, without hope of resurrection, is the punishment of the willfully wicked. (Genesis 2:17; Psalm 145:20; Romans 6:23) The Bible "hell" is merely the grave.

The foregoing is a very brief summary of some of the principal beliefs of the witnesses. Complete coverage of the message they proclaim is found in their latest book, *"Let God be True,"* and also in the books *"The Kingdom Is at Hand"* and *"The Truth Shall Make You Free."* Additionally, the foregoing shows the wide breach existing between the beliefs of Jehovah's witnesses and organized religion in general. But does this mean intolerance should exist? No; all should have full freedom to proclaim their beliefs. Beliefs made public are property for public discussion. The cause of truth is forwarded by open discussion, not by gag tactics. Jehovah's witnesses have won many cases in state courts, federal courts, and the United States Supreme Court in establishing their right to speak their beliefs. In so doing, court decisions safeguarding freedom of speech and worship and assembly have come forth that work in the interests of all. Jehovah's witnesses are glad for all to make use of these freedom-assuring victories, because they favor freedom for all, not just themselves. To disagree is not intolerant; to gag those who do disagree with you is intolerant.

During World War II Jehovah's witnesses came in for severe persecution, because they would not silence their testimony to the Kingdom. Some 6,000 suffered under Hitler in Germany, in concentration camps. Many were murdered. Even in democratic lands the work was banned. In the United States violent mobbings broke out against the witnesses. The excuse was that they were unpatriotic. Jehovah's witnesses do not salute the flag of any nation on earth, believing such to be, for them, a violation of Exodus 20:4, 5. The Supreme Court upheld their sincerity and right to refrain from the salute. But Jehovah's witnesses are law-abiding. Other persecutors assaulted them because they continued preaching as ministers and soldiers of Christ, instead of joining the armies of nations. The draft law provided for exemption of ministers, and Jehovah's witnesses rightfully claimed legal exemption. Many boards recognized them as ministers; others through religious prejudice and intolerance did not. In court thousands of such ministers were not granted the right to defend themselves against the indictments against them. Off they went to penitentiary. Now the Supreme Court has admitted their rights were denied. In all instances, sober consideration shows the persecutors, not the persecuted, to be the lawless ones. But by God's grace the witnesses survived the global war and its hysteria, and are now pushing the work in all corners of the earth.

The war and the winning of the peace thereafter created many complex problems for the nations to solve. The only solution is Christ's kingdom, and this Jehovah's witnesses declare, and will continue to declare in a sincere desire to show the way to lasting peace. This remedy seems foolish to world leaders, and the apostle Paul said it would appear as "foolishness of preaching". But man's wisdom is foolish in God's sight. (1 Corinthians 1:18–21; 3:19; Isaiah

8:9–13) Jehovah's witnesses will continue to obey God rather than men, and the work will be accomplished despite all opposition, "not by might, nor by power, but by my spirit, saith Jehovah of hosts."— Acts 5:29, 38, 39; Zechariah 4:6, *American Standard Version.*

BIBLIOGRAPHY

From and after 1927 the Watchtower Society has regularly published a "Yearbook of Jehovah's Witnesses."

The following are the latest books prepared by the Society's editorial staff and published by its printing house at Brooklyn, N. Y.:

The New World (1942). Clothbound; 384 pages; 3,270,000 copies printed as of September, 1946.

"The Truth Shall Make You Free" (1943). Clothbound; 384 pages; 3,550,000 copies printed as of September, 1946.

"The Kingdom Is At Hand" (1944). Clothbound; 384 pages; 3,786,000 copies printed as of September, 1946.

Theocratic Aid to Kingdom Publishers (1945). Clothbound; 384 pages; 175,000, first edition.

"Let God Be True" (1946). Clothbound; 320 pages; 1,000,000, first edition.

"Equipped for Every Good Work" (1946). Clothbound; 384 pages; 250,000, first edition.

"Be Glad, Ye Nations" (1946). Paper cover; 64 pages; 7,425,000 copies printed as of September, 1946.

"The Prince of Peace" (1946). Paper cover; 64 pages; 5,000,000, first edition.

THE RAMAKRISHNA MOVEMENT

Swami Satprakashananda is the Founder and Spiritual Head of the Vedanta Center of St. Louis, Missouri. He was born in 1888 at Dacca, Bengal, India. As a youth in 1901 he saw Swami Vivekananda and learned about Sri Ramakrishna and his message. Four years later he became closely associated with the Ramakrishna Movement and was greatly instrumental in the building up of the Ramakrishna Mission Center in Dacca.

He met his teacher, Swami Brahmananda, for the first time in 1908 and had the privilege of sitting at the feet of most of the other direct disciples of Sri Ramakrishna.

He graduated from the University of Calcutta before joining the Order, which he served at several places in different capacities. For nearly three years he was associate editor of "Prabuddha Bharata," the chief monthly organ of the Order, published by the Advaita Ashrama, Mayavati, Himalayas.

He was in charge of the Ramakrishna Mission Center in New Delhi, the capital of British India, for six years before leaving the country for America. It was in his time that the permanent home of the Mission was constructed in New Delhi and the Free Tuberculosis Clinic started. Throughout his stay in Delhi the Swami held regular discourses on Hindu Scriptures under the auspices of different religious organizations.

In March, 1937, he came to the United States and lectured for some weeks on the religion and philosophy of Vedanta in Washington, D. C. He conducted the Vedanta Center in Providence, R. I. for about a year. Then after visiting the different Vedanta Centers throughout the States he started the Vedanta work in St. Louis in October, 1938.

He has contributed many articles to the periodicals published by the Order and is the author of "Ethics and Religion" (1942).

Editor

THE RAMAKRISHNA MOVEMENT

SWAMI SATPRAKASHANANDA

THE RAMAKRISHNA Movement is the revival, in the modern age, of the universal religious spirit of Vedanta. It has found expression in twin institutions: The Ramakrishna Math and the Ramakrishna Mission. The Ramakrishna Math is a monastic order, the principal purpose of which is to develop its members and lay devotees spiritually by means of religious practices such as worship, prayer, meditation, study and so forth, and to train monks to be fit teachers of religion. The Ramakrishna Mission is a philanthropic body composed of both monastic and lay members and devoted to public service in all forms: religious, cultural, educational and social. Both the Math and the Mission have affiliated Centers throughout India and abroad. Though distinct—their funds are kept separate—the two organizations are inter-connected: both have their headquarters at Belur Math situated to the northwest of Calcutta, across the Ganges. The Board of Trustees of the Math is the Governing Body of the Mission, and the resident workers of the Mission Centers are mostly the monks of the Order.

I

Vedanta is the culmination of the religion and philosophy of the Vedas, the original scriptures of the Hindus and the world's oldest records of religious experience. Truly speaking, Vedanta cannot be called a religion. It is, rather, the common basis of all religions, inasmuch as it enunciates the fundamental spiritual truths underlying all religious doctrines, practices and experiences. Because Vedanta is the very basis of Hinduism, it is identified with it. But Hinduism, including many religious cults and philosophical systems, is founded not on the authority of any person, but on eternal spiritual principles; it affirms these very clearly and finds their application in life.

395

The principal tenets of Vedanta may be stated as follows:

1. The fundamental Reality is Pure Being-Consciousness-Bliss. That alone exists.

2. The phenomenal existence is an appearance; it disappears when knowledge of the Realty is gained.

3. Transcendentally one without a second—formless, feature-less, attributeless—the Supreme Being-Consciousness-Bliss, immanent in the phenomenal existence as its one all-pervasive Self, is the creator, preserver and absorber of the universe, the God of love, goodness and grace worshiped by the devotees, and the indwelling Spirit in all beings.

4. Man is essentially That.

5. To realize the innate divinity is the supreme end of life.

6. Methods of God-realization vary according to the aspirants' tendencies, capacities and conditions.

7. Different religions are so many ways leading ultimately to Godhead.

The essence of spiritual knowledge has been expressed by Vedanta in the terse formula, "That Thou Art." Resolved into the two factors, "Thou art He" and "Thou art His," it comprehends all the impersonal and personal approaches to Godhead and em-braces the entire religious life of mankind.

The real self of man is ever pure, self-illumined, free, divine. The Ramakrishna Movement holds this truth as central, whether ex-plicit or implicit, to all religions, and as the sole key to man's edifica-tion and advancement. Its practical application in modern times by the Movement is in some respects an innovation on the traditional method of Vedanta: the general tendency of the classical Vedanta has been to impart this knowledge to earnest seekers of truth and apply it to spiritual culture exclusively, while the Movement aims to teach it to men and women in various spheres of life, thereby awakening their faith in themselves and others, so that they can achieve physical, mental and moral growth individually and col-lectively, with a spiritual outlook on life, and proceed toward the Supreme Ideal from their present level of development, whatever that may be. Traditionally, Vedanta stresses the need of secluded life for spiritual aspirants and exhorts them to work out their own Liberation by Self-knowledge, while this Movement enjoins on them a twofold duty: striving after Liberation by solitary practice, and doing good to the world as a part of spiritual discipline for Self-realization.

Further, the three schools of Vedanta, dualistic, qualified monistic and monistic have in the past usually been held to be contradictory, but the Ramakrishna Movement views them as complementary, as stages of realization.

A distinct contribution of the Ramakrishna Movement to the modern world is its message that all help given to men by individuals or by society should be based on the recognition of man's innate divinity. The only way to mutual regard, love and unity among mankind, on which rest peace and progress in life, is to find an all-embracing ground of human relationship that transcends distinctions of race, nationality, color, creed, rank, merit and so forth. That this precept can be actually carried into practice has been exemplified by the Ramakrishna Movement's institutions, framed for the purpose of service of God in man. The Movement calls on its followers to see God in the needy, the distressed and the diseased and to serve them as if one were serving God. Work done in this spirit is veritable worship.

II

The Ramakrishna Movement had its origin in and draws its inspiration from the life of the great Hindu saint and seer, Sri Ramakrishna, whose name it bears. Born of devout brahmin parents in an idyllic village of Bengal in the year 1836, he had ecstatic experiences in boyhood, which intensified his inherent love of God. At the age of seventeen he went to Calcutta to live with his brother, who conducted a Sanskrit academy, and there too he occupied himself mostly with religious pursuits. Though possessed of extraordinary memory, keen intellect and artistic aptitudes, he refused to acquire secular knowledge; his brother tried in vain to give him a Sanskrit education —his heart yearned for spiritual enlightenment that would remove all darkness forever.

Three years later he was appointed priest for the worship of Kali, the Divine Mother of the universe, in a newly founded temple situated on the Ganges at Dakshineswar four miles north of Calcutta. As soon as he began worshiping the Divine Mother in the image installed in the temple, an all-consuming desire actually to see Her grew within him: he was unable to think even of food or rest; sleep forsook him, and no longer could he perform the prescribed rituals of worshiping the Deity. In the intense hunger of his soul, he practiced hard disciplines, prayed to the Divine Mother day and night, intently meditated on Her, poured out his devotion at Her feet in song, and cried bitterly like a child for vision of Her—till at last one day he entered into a state of beatitude in which She revealed Herself to him. Yet he could not rest satisfied; his heart craved continuous vision of Her. He prayed more and more and before long was able to see Her not only in trance but in the normal state of consciousness, with open eyes.

He was in constant divine ecstasy, yet even so he hankered for the realization of God in different aspects and forms. With superhuman energy, ardour and devotion he therefore practiced, one after another, various spiritual disciplines prevalent in Hinduism—from the intricate ritualism of the Tantras to the abstruse meditation of Yoga, from the ecstatic devotional practices of Vaishnavism to the transcendental Self-absorption of nondualistic Vedanta—and he realized the Divine Being through every one of them. Afterward he turned to Muhammadanism, with the same result; and later in life, Christianity. In regard to the latter, he had a vision of Jesus Christ and was convinced of his Divine Sonship.

His tremendous struggle for God-realization extended over twelve years. During this period and the remaining eighteen years of his life he had varied mystical experiences and realizations repeatedly, saw myriads of spiritual visions, and dwelt in sublime ecstatic moods. In his spiritual practices he was mostly guided by adepts who came to him at the hour of need, directed as it were by the Divine Will.

He attained to the pinnacle of spiritual realization—the transcendental experience of the Supreme Consciousness, the One without a Second, free from all distinctions. Once he stayed in that state continuously for six months; indeed, so accustomed did he become to its sublime height that the natural tendency of his mind was to soar beyond time and space, name and form, to the Limitless One. However, by means of spiritual practices he gradually trained his mind to occupy a unique position in the realm of the spirit: it remained usually on the borderland of the Absolute and the relative, where it could turn to either at any time. As a result, in the normal state of consciousness he always perceived the One in the many and the many in the One, and he was able to shift from the manifold experience to the Unitary Consciousness with ease.

Though the aspirant is very rare who can rightly practice even a single spiritual method and reach the goal after life-long struggle, it was thus the genius of Sri Ramakrishna to finish the whole course of the world's spiritual lessons, so to speak, within a few years; to demonstrate the truth that the Goal is the same, though the paths vary; that the Divine Spirit is both transcendental and immanent; and that It has many aspects and forms. In dealing with people he always looked upon them as Narayanas, the veritable manifestations of God.

It was revealed to Sri Ramakrishna by some of his spiritual experiences that he had a Divine Mission to fulfill, that his practices and realizations were intended not for his personal benefit but for the good of humanity: he was to establish a new religious order for the regeneration of India, for the spiritual awakening of mankind, and for the establishment of harmony among the different religions of the world. He foresaw that earnest seekers of various sects, communities and ranks of society would come to him for solace, inspiration, guidance, enlightenment—and during the last twelve years of his life just such a stream of people constantly flowed into his room.

Sri Ramakrishna had visions of his intimate disciples and devotees long before they came to him. Some of them, he knew, would be young—they were the potential monks especially chosen by the Divine Mother to carry out Her mission. They arrived one by one during the last six years of his life (1881–1886)—most of them were indeed very young—and he recognized each of them at first sight. It was not until the year 1886, during his last illness, that the entire band of his intimate disciples rallied round him.

Twelve of them, who constantly attended on him, organized themselves under the leadership of Narendranath (afterward Swami Vivekananda) and served the master with utmost care, love and veneration. Their whole-hearted love of God and devotion to the master and his ideals led to the formation of the brotherhood which soon after Sri Ramakrishna's death was to develop into the Ramakrishna Order. The master himself took decisive steps to lay its foundation.

He often exhorted the young disciples to follow the path of renunciation for the realization of God and for the service of God in man. On a certain occasion, charging Narendranath not to let his ideas die out after his death, he said to him, "I leave these boys in your charge; see that they develop spirituality and do not enter into the world." As preparatory to monastic life he once asked the young disciples to beg their food from door to door, regardless of caste. A few days later he presented to each of them a piece of ocher cloth, the emblem of the life of renunciation. Shortly before his passing, in August, 1886, he transmitted his powers to Narendranath, saying to him, "By virtue of this gift you will do immense good to the world, and not until then will you gain release."

III

At the time of Sri Ramakrishna's advent India was in a state of torpor. The decline of the Mughul sovereignty, dating from the beginning of the eighteenth century, had produced political and social chaos in the country. Then, in the latter part of the eighteenth century, the British power had begun to rise. With the establishment of British supremacy law and order had been restored, but English education was introduced, the evangelism of the Christian missionaries started, and Western customs and manners were transmitted on as vast a scale as was Western merchandise.

The political subjugation of the country by Britain had dealt a severe blow to the national self-esteem of the Indian people. With the spread of English education the materialistic views of Western science and philosophy infiltrated their minds. Dazed by the glare and self-assurance of Western civilization, they began to doubt the efficacy of their traditional ideals and ways of life. The Christian missionaries were overlooking no opportunity to vilify the social and religious beliefs and practices of the Hindus. It is not strange that under the circumstances English-educated Indians often lost faith in their own culture and religion and were ready to adopt Western ideals and methods for the salvation of their country. Not a few brilliant Indians actually deserted their time-honored faith and turned atheists or Christian converts. It seemed that the barge of Indian national life was going to be cut adrift from its ancient moorings.

But this was not to be: the inner spirit of India soon reacted to the cultural aggression of the West. Of the religious and social movements that sprang up to counteract the foreign influence, the most important were the Brahmo Samaj of Bengal and the Arya Samaj of the Punjab. But whether such movements were progressive or reactionary, liberal or conservative, none of them proved able to call forth the national genius of India; none pointed out to India's children the import of their voluminous scriptures, the universal character of their religion, the inner harmony of their multifarious beliefs, the fundamental unity of their national life despite divergencies of sect, creed, caste, color, custom, language and so forth; none could restore their faith in their ancient heritage and indicate how to accept the new on the basis of the old and apply the eternal religious principles to modern conditions. The life and teachings of Sri Ramakrishna furnished a clue to the fulfillment of all these needs and stimulated the slumbering self-consciousness of India. In him India found herself.

The spiritual realizations of Sri Ramakrishna verified the truths affirmed by Vedanta. Without studying the scriptures, he discovered them. His extraordinary purity, blissfulness, wisdom, compassion, and power to transform the lives of others by a mere touch, word, glance or wish testified to the validity of his inner experiences. His message, a restatement of the Vedantic truths, can be summed up as follows:

1. God alone is real.

2. To realize God is the goal of human life; man must live with that end in view.

3. God is one, but various are His names, forms and aspects. He is also without names and forms.

4. A person can choose whatever name, form or aspect of God appeals to him most, and he can reach Him thereby if he has real longing, steadfastness, purity and devotion.

5. Different religions are merely differing ways to God-realization, which is the one goal of all of them.

6. Religions in their essentials are utterly harmonious. The adherents of all religions should live in perfect harmony—there is no place for dogmatism or intolerance in religion.

7. God is manifest everywhere. See Him in all human beings and serve Him in them.

The four cardinal points of Sri Ramakrishna's message are thus seen to be that God is real, that He can be realized, that religions are essentially harmonious, and that man is to be served in the spirit of serving God. These truths have deep significance for the modern age; each of them has an important bearing on our life and thought.

Sri Ramakrishna's life was a beacon in an age of spiritual darkness: at the very time when religion was being classified as a relic of barbarism, as the last surviving superstition that humanity must outgrow in consequence of scientific knowledge, when "enlightened" people the world over were discarding all ideas of the supersensuous, God, soul, heaven and so forth and holding to the material universe as the sole reality, Sri Ramakrishna, turning his back upon the sense world, plunged into the unseen in search of the Real and came out with the discovery that God alone exists in the true sense.

His experience was a challenge to materialism and its concomitants such as scepticism, naturalism, agnosticism and atheism, which dominated human thought with the progress of the physical sciences during the nineteenth century. By declaring the Ultimate Reality to be Pure Consciousness he rendered inestimable service to the cause of human knowledge. His experience corroborates the logical truth that the fundamental concept cannot be inert matter, energy, life-force or blind will, that it can be nothing but Absolute Consciousness. Every existence presupposes Consciousness, which alone is Self-existent, Self-intelligent. Every branch of knowledge, in order to come to right conclusions, must conform to the basic Reality. No philosophic or scientific view, if contrary to It, can be correct.

Sri Ramakrishna placed before humanity one supreme ideal— God-realization. Not only it is indispensable to ultimate freedom and eternal bliss, but also to worldly peace, security, happiness and prosperity. Man cannot be great and glorious even here unless he directs his life to that goal, unless he cultivates his physical, mental and moral powers and establishes social, economic and political systems with that end in view. As long as earthly power and prosperity constitute the goal of life, man's intellectual, esthetic and ethical natures will be subservient to material interests and tend to degenerate, and there can be no possibility of peace and harmony in individual or collective life.

On the contrary, when man turns to the spiritual ideal and regulates his entire existence accordingly, he will raise himself physically, mentally and morally. Only better men and women can make a better world. Laws and institutions do not make men; it is men who make them. The peace and progress of the world depend in the last analysis on human nature. In rendering service to the world the Ramakrishna Movement gives first consideration to the human factors and directs its best attention to the development of man's inner life.

Religious bigotry, fanaticism and feuds have caused untold misery to human beings. As long as these exist men can never live in peace and amity. But for mutual understanding and co-operation among the different religions, a spirit of mere tolerance is not enough; no religious unity can be achieved by eclecticism or syncretism. Sri Ramakrishna's harmony of religions is based on the recognition of the fundamental principle underlying them; it views religions as varied expressions of one eternal religion—as so many methods of God-realization intended for men and women of diverse capacities and conditions of life. The seeming unity of a religious system formed by the eclectic method is artificial, like that of a bouquet of flowers. It has no root in the soil of life, it does not spring from the living experience of God-men. Syncretism stresses the similarities and disregards the differences. Sri Ramakrishna seeks harmony not in spite of, but with, the differences, because in his view differences have a deep significance.

Sri Ramakrishna's idea of serving God in man is really the keynote of the Ramakrishna Movement. One day in 1884, in course of a conversation with Narendranath and other devotees, the master said, "Kindness to living beings! Who are you to be *kind* to them? Serve them as manifestations of God. Does not God exist in all?" These words went straight into the heart of Narendranath; he found in them the answer to how he would channel the knowledge of Vedanta into practical life. Sri Ramakrishna himself was the living example of this teaching—he saw God in all and treated them as such. He would bow down even to fallen women, who were to him but the Divine Mother in disguise.

Even his own wife he worshiped as the very image of the Divine Mother when at the age of eighteen, fourteen years after their marriage, she came to live with him, and always he regarded her as such. She in her turn became his disciple and always looked upon him as the "Divine Master." She was, at one and the same time, virgin and wife. Younger than Sri Ramakrishna by seventeen years, she outlived him thirty-three years and played an important role in strengthening the spiritual foundation of the Ramakrishna Movement. She is called by the Order the "Holy Mother."

IV

Shortly after the passing of the Master in August, 1886, the young disciples banded themselves into the Ramakrishna Order, which was in line with the Vedantic Order of sannyasins (monks) to which Sri Ramakrishna and his monistic teacher, Totapuri, had belonged. The young monks were joined by an elderly disciple, who was older than the master. This made their number sixteen. Foremost among them was Swami Vivekananda, their leader, and second only to him, Swami Brahmananda, the spiritual son of Sri Ramakrishna. With the help of Sri Ramakrishna's lay disciples a monastery was started in a rented house near Dakshineswar. This was the nucleus of the Ramakrishna Math. But most of the young disciples did not at first stay in the monastery; though they had experienced communion with God at the touch or blessing of Sri Ramakrishna, they were eager to make Divine Communion their permanent possession. Many of them went out on pilgrimages to the Himalayas and other parts of India, living solitary lives and practicing meditation and austerities. But one of them, Swami Ramakrishnananda, was all along in the monastery as its pivot. With rare devotion and steadfastness he performed the daily worship and other duties for ten long years, until at the leader's call he went to Madras to establish a new monastery there.

Swami Vivekananda, as an itinerant monk, for about six years traveled all over India, from the Himalayas to Cape Comorin, and in course of his wanderings came in close touch with people of all classes and ranks, from the Maharajas to the peasants, from the learned brahmins to the pariahs. His heart bled at the sight of the abject poverty, misery and ignorance of the Indian masses. He concluded that he must, in particular, shoulder two arduous tasks for the regeneration of India: the upliftment of the people in general and the improvement of the condition of women.

He observed the weaknesses as well as the strength of India; he studied her various problems—economic, political, social, educa-

tional, religious and so forth—and he decided what was necessary
for their solution. Underlying all diversities of doctrines, rites, customs, etc. he discerned the spiritual unity of Indian life; he found
that spirituality was the very lifeblood of India, that her national
regeneration must be on a spiritual basis.

As Swami Vivekananda, filled with deepest compassion for the
suffering millions of India, awaited an opportunity to start his work,
there arose an occasion for his coming to America: he was to represent Hinduism at the Parliament of Religions held at the World's
Fair in Chicago in September, 1893. This he hailed as an opening
for his contemplated mission.

His message of the divinity of man and the harmony of religions,
delivered from the depth of his realizations, made a profound impression on the audiences at the Parliment of Religions and paved
the way for his preaching the universal gospel of Vedanta in the
Western world. For nearly three years he stayed in America lecturing before popular and learned audiences, holding classes and conversations in drawing rooms and clubs, giving interviews to people
of various ranks, and gaining admirers, friends, and followers by his
all-comprehensive teachings and forceful, luminous personality in
many places from the Atlantic to the Mississippi. Before leaving the
country in April, 1896, he placed his work on a permanent basis by
establishing the Vedanta Society of New York and summoning from
India his brother disciple, Swami Saradananda, to take charge.
Moreover, his books on *Raja Yoga, Karma Yoga,* and *Bhakti Yoga,*
containing many of his collected addresses as well as original writings
by him, were published or ready for publication.

During his stay in London in 1896 the Swami lectured mostly on
Jnana Yoga. His spiritual fervour, breadth of vision, dignified bearing and saintly purity deeply impressed many minds and attracted
to him some very talented and devoted disciples. Chief among them
were Miss Margaret E. Noble and Mr. and Mrs. Sevier. Miss Noble
dedicated her life to the education of Indian girls and became
known as Sister Nivedita (the consecrated one). The Ramakrishna
Mission Girls' School in Calcutta, named after her, owes its origin
to her tireless and self-sacrificing efforts. Mr. and Mrs. Sevier took
up the cause of Vedanta, followed Swami Vivekananda to India,
and established the retreat known as the *Advaita Ashrama* in the
Himalayas, which was dedicated to the culture of Nondualism and

became the principal publication center of the Ramakrishna Order.

It was at this time that Swami Vivekananda met the great Orientalist, Professor Max Müller of Oxford University, who had already written for the *Nineteenth Century* an article on Sri Ramakrishna, entitled "A Real Mahatman," and who wanted to know more about the saint. The facts supplied by Swami Vivekananda as well as Swami Saradananda, who at Swami Vivekananda's request was also in London, helped the professor substantially to bring out his book *The Life and Sayings of Sri Ramakrishna.*

After a tour of the continent, during which he met Professor Paul Duesson at Kiel, Swami Vivekananda returned to India in January, 1896, accompanied by Mr. and Mrs. Sevier and Mr. J. J. Goodwin, another English disciple, who joined him in America, to whose tireless labor and faithful transcripts we are indebted for many of the Swami's recorded lectures.

From the time of his arrival in America the Swami had been struck by the material achievements, the technical efficiency, the scientific knowledge, the capacity for organized work, and the orderliness of the Western people. Simultaneously there arose in his mind the dark picture of misery and suffering in India, which by contrast became all the more harrowing, making him feel India's distress the more keenly. Then again, he perceived the lack of spiritual understanding in the Western world; he saw the precarious condition of the West. Beneath its activities and enjoyments, its pomp and power, were sense attachment, disquietude, confusion and despair.

His experiences in the East and the West confirmed his view that spirituality was the chief characteristic of India's national existence and that she had maintained it under the most adverse conditions. He noticed that while the West, for strengthening its civilization and culture, needed the spiritual wisdom, inner strength, calmness, patience and contentment of Indian life, India, for her national reconstruction on the existing spiritual foundation, needed the technical efficiency, the scientific knowledge, the power of co-ordination and organization of the West. The Swami's historical knowledge and insight revealed to him the fact that India's special gift to the world throughout the ages had been the profound truths of spiritual life, and that on her regeneration depended the regeneration of the world.

Thus Swami Vivekananda's mission has a twofold significance, national and universal, and the two aspects are closely allied. On the one hand, it calls for the consolidation of the spiritual consciousness of India and setting her to the task of national reconstruction on the religious basis; on the other hand, it calls for the spiritual awakening of the world at large by sending out special messengers trained for the purpose from India, and for the fellowship, based on mutual appreciation and acceptance, of the various world religions.

Throughout his stay in the West Swami Vivekananda, by letters and writings, was urging his brother disciples, friends and students all over India to prepare themselves for the noble mission. As a result, the Vedantic tribune, *The Brahmavadin,*—and afterward another journal, *Prabuddha Bharata*—was started in Madras as early as 1893. One of his brother disciples undertook educational work for the masses in Rajputana early in 1894. Others, renouncing their pilgrimages and solitary wanderings, went back to the monastery near Calcutta, and novices began to join it.

V

An unprecedented welcome was accorded Swami Vivekananda on his return to the motherland: everywhere he received ovations. As the nation's hero he proceeded from Colombo to Calcutta, awakening India by his soul-stirring addresses. He set to work immediately. With the help of brother monks and young men who at his clarion call joined the Order, he started in Bengal and Madras monastic Centers as well as Centers for continuous service which would carry on operations to relieve suffering and want. Visitors poured in to discuss with him various problems of the country. On May 1, 1897, with the monastic and lay disciples of Sri Ramakrishna, he organized the Ramakrishna Mission. Then he undertook a lecture tour in Northern India, bearing enlightenment on his plan of work to everyone from the Maharajas to the common people. The response his message evoked from his countrymen was gratifying.

In July, 1897, he wrote to a friend in America: "Only one idea was burning in my brain—to start the machine for elevating the Indian masses; and that I have succeeded in doing to a certain extent. It would have made your heart glad to see how my boys are working in the midst of famine and disease and misery—nursing the cholera-stricken pariah and feeding the starving chandala, and the

Lord sends help to me and to them all. I must see my machine in strong working order, and then knowing for sure that I have put in a lever for the good of humanity, in India at least, which no power can drive back, I will sleep without caring what will be next, and may I be born again and again, and suffer thousands of miseries, so that I may worship the only God that exists, the only God I believe in, the sum total of all souls. And above all, my God the wicked, my God the miserable, my God the poor of all races, of all species, is the special object of my worship."

To organize the growing activities of the Math and the Mission, Swami Saradananda was called back from America in 1898. Swami Abhedananda went from London to New York to take charge of the Vedanta Society there. The present site of the Ramakrishna Math and the Ramakrishna Mission headquarters at Belur was occupied in January, 1899. The next year Swami Vivekananda formed the Board of Trustees of the Belur Math, and did not include himself on it. Swami Brahmananda was elected President of the Board and therefore of the Math and the Mission, Swami Saradananda, Secretary.

Swami Akhandananda founded an orphanage and Swami Trigunatita started the Bengali review *Udbodhan* early in 1899. At this time, an important part of Swami Vivekananda's work was the training of the Western disciples, who came to India for the education of Indian girls. With the blessings of the Holy Mother the Sister Nivedita Girls' School was started in November, 1898.

In the latter part of 1899, Swami Vivekananda, visiting America for the second time, was accompanied by Swami Turiyananda, a brother monk whose spiritual fervor and ascetic habits were remarkable. In taking Swami Turiyananda with him, Swami Vivekananda's object was to present to America an ideal spiritual personality, rather than a preacher. After a short stay in the East, where the work was being ably conducted by Swami Abhedananda, the Swamis went to California. From December to May Swami Vivekananda gave several courses of lectures in Los Angeles, San Francisco and adjoining places. This created a stir in intellectual circles, and several groups of students were formed in both northern and southern California. To stabilize the work, the Vedanta Society of San Francisco was organized. The Swami received a gift of 160 acres of land in the valley of San Antonio, twelve miles from Lick Observatory on Mt. Hamilton, where Swami Turiyananda established Shanti Ashrama (Peace Retreat) with a group of earnest students.

Meanwhile the work Swami Vivekananda had started and organized in India was continued with unabated zeal, in his absence, under the direction of Swami Brahmananda. Besides religious, educational and other regular activities the Mission conducted relief operations in different parts of India, for helping in times of famine, epidemics, floods, landslides and the like. Swami Brahmananda, following the rules laid down by Swami Vivekananda, took special care to mould the lives of the young monks and the novices, who gradually increased in number. He enjoined on them regular practice of meditation along with other essentials for the development of their spiritual natures, for only by developing spiritually could they be truly helpful to themselves and to others.

After attending the Congress of the History of Religions in Paris, before which he spoke twice, Swami Vivekananda returned to India in December, 1900. Shortly after his arrival he made a trip to Advaita Ashrama at Mayavati in the Himalayas. The journey was very strenuous—it was winter, the whole region was snow-bound, and the Swami was not feeling well. Next, upon leaving Mayavati he visited several places in East Bengal and Assam and gave public lectures. To serve the diseased and the destitute hospitals were founded by him in Benares and Kankhal. But the Swami's health was fast declining. Everyone was deeply concerned about him—he was asked to take a complete rest.

His attention at this time was directed especially to the training of the young monks and the novices by holding study classes and giving spiritual instructions. Even on the last day of his life, the fourth of July, 1902, he conducted a class in Sanskrit Grammar for about three hours in the afternoon. In the evening he sat for meditation, and calmly withdrawing from his body, entered into Mahasamadhi (the highest state of Divine Communion, from which there is no return).

VI

The sudden passing of the mighty leader at the early age of thirty-nine was a tremendous shock to the whole Movement. Though the loss was irreparable, the work continued to grow under the able guidance of Swami Brahmananda, Swami Saradananda and other great disciples of Sri Ramakrishna. Swami Brahmananda emphasized the spiritual side of the Movement, of which he was President till the end of his life—April 10, 1922. Most of the administrative work was taken care of by Swami Saradananda, who was Secretary of the Math and the Mission until his death on August 19, 1927, that is, for a period of about thirty years.

At the present time the Ramakrishna Math and Mission have nearly 150 permanent Centers, of which 13 are in the U.S.A.; one each in Argentina Republic, England, France, Mauritius, Fiji, and Straits Settlements; two in Burma, five in Ceylon, and the rest in different parts of India. Some of the Centers conduct mainly cultural and religious work; others, educational or medical work. Indeed, the activities are most varied—and in all Centers service is rendered free, irrespective of color, creed, caste or sex. More specifically, the different types of work are as follows:

1. Religious and Cultural Work: This is done by almost all the Centers in some form or other. Its main items are lectures and classes, publication of books and periodicals, maintenance of libraries and reading rooms, and the public celebration of festivals. In India the Headquarters (Belur), the Institute of Culture (Calcutta), Advaita Ashrama (Himalayas), and the Centers in Madras, Bombay and Karachi are prominent in this field. The Occidental Centers are intended especially for religious and cultural work. The Swamis are sent to the West by the Headquarters at the invitation of groups interested in Vedanta. They are guest teachers and not missionaries. They do not seek converts. The Order publishes five monthlies (two English, one Bengali, one Tamil, one Malayalam), two bi-monthlies (English), and one quarterly bulletin (English).

2. Educational Work: There are about 150 educational institutions with nearly 18,000 students of whom 13,000 are boys and 5,000 girls. These include 2 colleges, 23 secondary schools, 3 Sanskrit academies, 4 industrial schools, 18 night schools, and nearly 100 middle, primary, vocational and other schools. Besides, 45 Ashramas (Retreats) provide nearly 1,500 students with free board and lodging. The chief residential institutions are the Students' Homes in Calcutta and Madras, the Vidyapith at Deoghar (S.P.), the Vidyalaya in Coimbatore (S.I.), and the Boys' Home at Rahara (24 Perganas). The monks of the Order teach in most of the institutions.

The students live in an environment conducive to moral and spiritual growth.

3. Medical Treatment and Nursing: The Mission has ten well-equipped indoor hospitals, in which about 12,000 patients are treated annually. Besides, there are over sixty outdoor clinics that treat nearly two million patients a year. The principal indoor hospitals are those in Benares, Kankhal and Rangoon. The Mission has also established Child-welfare and Maternity Home in Calcutta, Invalid Women's Home in Benares, Tuberculosis Sanatorium-Hospital in Ranchi, and so forth. Usually the monastic workers attend on the patients. Home nursing is also undertaken.

The Mission serves the indigent and the distressed in various other ways.

4. Temporary Relief Work: From its very inception the Ramakrishna Mission has organized relief operations to minister to the victims of such calamities as famine, flood, cyclone, epidemics and so forth. It is the pioneer in this field. In 1942 and 1943 the Mission carried on Burma Evacuee Relief in co-operation with the Government and A.R.P. Relief in collaboration with the Calcutta Corporation. It also conducted Bengal Distress Relief, Burdwan Flood Relief, Bengal and Orissa Cyclone Relief and Malaria Relief in Assam. Some of these relief activities, along with the new ones, have continued during 1944 and 1945.

VII

Since the time of Ramakrishna-Vivekananda there has been the resurgence of a new life in India. The national consciousness has manifested itself not only in the religious but also in the social, cultural, economic, and political life of the country. The present political movement is only a phase of a deeper national awakening. While rousing the spiritual consciousness of India, the Ramakrishna Movement has created, among the people, a desire to serve others. As a result, the country is dotted over with charitable organizations, many of which, however, do not belong to the Ramakrishna Order. The selfless activities of all these organizations have tended to create an atmosphere of unity between the classes and the masses, between the literate and the illiterate.

Sri Ramakrishna is worshiped today by millions in India and

abroad as a God-man, one in line with Krishna, Buddha and Christ. Swami Vivekananda was the first Hindu to carry to the Western Hemisphere the spiritual message of India. He interpreted in modern terms the ancient wisdom of India illustrated in the life of Sri Ramakrishna, a wisdom which he himself also realized. The lives Sri Ramakrishna and Swami Vivekananda lived and the message they delivered have been the source of inspiration to millions of human beings in different parts of the world; and millions more have been directly or indirectly influenced by them. This has contributed to the setting in of a new spiritual current among men. In fact, the world is witnessing a spiritual rebirth. Materialistic ideas have been losing ground; men and women are veering to spiritual idealism; religions are crying for rapprochement. The conditions on the physical plane are no doubt deplorable, but these are perhaps the after effects of the dying materialism. In the spiritual realm the situation is very hopeful.

BIBLIOGRAPHY

Publications of Advaita Ashrama, 4 Wellington Lane, Calcutta, India:

Life of Sri Ramakrishna—compiled from various authentic sources (1936).
Life of Ramakrishna—by Romain Rolland (translated from French) (1931).
Teachings of Sri Ramakrishna—culled from different sources (1934).
The Disciples of Sri Ramakrishna—a collection of 22 lives (1943).
The Life of Swami Vivekananda—by his Eastern and Western disciples (1933), 2 vols.
The Life of Vivekananda and the Universal Gospel—by Romain Rolland (1931), (translated from the French).
The Complete Works of Swami Vivekananda—in 7 vols. (1935).
Selections from Swami Vivekananda—a representative volume (1944).
Spiritual Talks—Conversations of disciples of Sri Ramakrishna (1936).
With the Swamis in America—by a Western Disciple (1938).
Letters of Swami Vivekananda—303 epistles in one vol. (1940).

Publications of Sri Ramakrishna Math, Mylapore, Madras, India:
Inspired Talks—notes of class-talks by Swami Vivekananda (1938).
Sri Ramakrishna and His Mission—by Swami Ramakrishnananda (1946).

Sri Ramakrishna, His Unique Message—by Swami Ghanananda (1937).

Sayings of Sri Ramakrishna—an exhaustive collection (1938).

Sri Sarada Devi, The Holy Mother—Her Life and Conversations (1940).

Publications of the Ramakrishna-Vivekananda Center, 17 E. 94th Street, New York City:

The Gospel of Sri Ramakrishna—recorded by M.—a direct disciple, English translation with Introduction by Swami Nikhilananda (1942).

(1) *Jnana Yoga*, (2) *Raja Yoga*, (3) *Karma and Bhakti Yoga*— Swami Vivekananda's lectures in 3 vols. (1939).

Other Publications:

The Life and Sayings of Ramakrishna—by Prof. F. Max Müller (London, 1923).

The Master As I Saw Him—Intimate account of Swami Vivekananda, by Sister Nivedita (Calcutta, 1939).

The Eternal Companion—Swami Brahmananda's Life and Teachings —By Swami Prabhavananda (Hollywood, Calif., 1944).

Sri Ramakrishna and Spiritual Renaissance—by Swami Nirvedananda (The Ramakrishna Mission Institute of Culture, Calcutta, India, 1940).

NATURALISTIC HUMANISM

Religious Humanism is a twentieth-century religion having its roots in the development of a scientific culture. It is fitting that Dr. Roy Wood Sellars is the spokesman for this movement. He wrote the first draft of the now famous "Humanist Manifesto"— its most representative statement— which was issued in May, 1933. To this group belong many of the intellectual leaders of American thought in the fields of religion, art, literature, philosophy and the sciences.

Dr. Sellars was born in Seaforth, Ontario, Canada, in 1880. He took his bachelor's degree in 1903 and his Ph.D. in 1908 at the University of Michigan. He studied at the Hartford Theological Seminary, at the Universities of Wisconsin and Chicago and in France and Germany. He has been on the faculty at the University of Michigan since 1905, where he is now its distinguished professor of philosophy.

He is one of America's leading philosophers, well known for his works on metaphysics, logic and epistemology and especially for his defense of a neo-materialism and for critical realism. Throughout the years he has contributed many scholarly articles to professional magazines. In 1923 he served as president of the Western Division of the American Philosophical Association and he has been vice-president of its Eastern Division. His books (other than those mentioned in the bibliography) include: "Critical Realism" (1916); "The Next Step in Democracy" (1916); "The Essentials of Logic" (1917); "The Essentials of Philosophy" (1917); "Essays in Critical Realism" (1921); "Evolutionary Naturalism" (1921); "Principles and Problems of Philosophy" (1926); and "The Philosophy of Physical Realism" (1932).

Editor

NATURALISTIC HUMANISM

ROY WOOD SELLARS

NATURALISTIC HUMANISM, I would begin by saying, is largely a contemporary development, at once religious, scientific and philosophical, which postulates the necessity of an overt, conscious and decisive break with the framework and emphases of theism or supernaturalism, orthodox or esoteric. It counsels this frank shift of perspective in all charity and in continuing gratitude to the moral idealism which the great historic religions have at their best nourished. It is not its intention, or desire, to draw up a balance-sheet of good and evil, of progress and frustration, for the actual working of religion in the past. It sees all phases of the past as part of man's immemorial march toward mastery of himself and his environment, a march begun in ignorance but, in these days, illumined by ever-increasing knowledge and—what is still more encouraging—the means and methods for extending and deepening that knowledge.

But modern humanism is not a mere form of rationalism. It differs from those past movements called agnosticism, free-thought and atheism in that these were dominated by an intellectual battle with orthodox beliefs and were, accordingly, essentially negative and rejective in their interest and emphasis. Instead, naturalistic humanism is affirmative and constructive in interest and concern. It seeks to develop, for man, a positive perspective within the framework of a mature type of naturalism, capable of doing justice to the actualities of human life. It is thus, in essence, an attempt at a reorientation of religion, holding, as it does, that the heart of religion is man's need to possess a working complex of attitudes, sentiments and ideas about the meaning of life, the human situation, the kind of universe man is in, and the ideals he should embrace. Humanism holds that religion is not a static thing but something which evolves and reflects the stage of human culture. And it is convinced that the time is ripe for a step forward in religious matters, that explorations and reconsiderations are in order.

To many humanists it is as though the tables had turned, and not they but their opponents were on the defensive. It is an age of science; and science and scientific method have expanded to encompass both man and nature. It is, also, an age of social and political change, with need for new emphases and institutions. A democratic way of life must be worked out. And this can hardly be done soundly and adequately without weighing the whole context and setting of human life, itself. Is man the creature he seems to be in the light of the best knowledge of our time? Or is Christian, or Buddhist, anthropology a truer account? Such questions are imperative and unavoidably on the agenda of the time.

Naturalistic humanism is a religion in that it seeks to reckon with, and do justice to, the unchanging need of man to assess his life in the light of the far-flung nature of things. It recognizes that descriptive and factual knowledge—important as it is—is not enough. It must be wedded to values in harmony with it. From this marriage, it is to be expected, wisdom will be born, a wisdom relevant to, and at home in, the culture of the present; a culture which promises to be global and increasingly sustained and impelled forward by the thoughts and deeds of human beings of diverse races and climes.

It is in this respect, perhaps, that the peculiar genius of humanism discovers itself. It is not tied down to the past or to some geographical area with its somewhat fixed pieties and institutions. It can, therefore, act as a leaven and rallying point for people of like minds wherever they may be. Probably its influence will not come so much from churches—although they will play a rôle—as from literature, science, associations of various kinds, and from what the sociologists call culture-contacts. It will be in the air, in the steady advance of the sciences, in the creative forward-movement of the arts, in progressive education. And, if this be not the case, then the very fact means that naturalistic humanism is not an expression of the cultural forces at work in this day and of their elective insight into the world and the human situation there. Time will, of course, alone give the answer to such questions.

In another respect naturalistic humanism is exceptional, if not unique. The major religions of the past have had Founders in the sense of individuals who initiated the gospel of salvation or enlightenment from which the religion stemmed. Of course, the labors and insights of many apostles were added, through the centuries, to what was transmitted from the origins. In contrast, naturalistic humanism makes no pretense to be anything but a cooperative development of men of good will, who see the human scene in this naturalistic and humanistic fashion. It is, by its very genius, empirical and exploratory, seeking to bring together, in a fruitful way, the best methods of approach to human problems, personal and social. All are welcome to make their contribution.

Perhaps, the primary thing to remember about humanism is that it is a term for a cultural watershed which contains many streams and rivers. In the United States, the background is largely that of liberalism, though, in these days, it is a more realistic liberalism than was once the case, a new liberalism with its feet more on the ground and aware of racial, economic, political and educational problems. Pragmatism has had its influence here, as has the swing from romantic idealism to realism. In England, where pragmatism has had less influence, rationalism and scientific humanism seem to predominate. In France and Latin America, the main stream is that of rationalism, positivism and free-thought. But here, also, there have been increasing signs of the affirmative emphasis upon human values and ideals, within a mature and accepted naturalism, more assured of itself and less on the defensive.

But it would be foolish to ignore the fact that Marxism, in all its variations, belongs to the same cultural watershed. And it is interesting to note that, in the Soviet Union, the term humanism is frequently used as descriptive of the mellower ideals which are envisaged. The background of Soviet thought is, as is well known, naturalistic after the principles of dialectical—as opposed to mechanical—materialism. Those historically minded should not forget that the churches of Marx's and Engels's time were socially conservative as well as intellectually rigid and uncritical. The warfare between science and religion was hardly a misnomer. What is usually called modernism in religion was largely in the future.

It follows that the humanist is in the main concerned with the development in the Soviet Union of democratic ways of life and with the enlargement in other countries of the pattern of ideals to include securities in employment and education for the masses. All of which means that humanism cannot be—and does not desire to be—merely something literary, theoretically scientific, and philosophic. It is these things, for, otherwise, it could not be creative and interpretative. But it must have its roots in all the significant movements of the age.

While, then, naturalistic humanism proposes a conscious break with the hitherto dominant religious frameworks of the past, it fully recognizes the heritage of moral values which have been worked out through the interaction of a sympathetic, moral imagination on the part of ethical leaders and the pressure of events. In the eyes of the humanist, all this is human but, in no invidious sense, too human. But ethical insights and demands must be expressed in civic and cultural institutions and not treated as something purely personal in an otherworldly sense. Perhaps the historical weakness of Christianity was the separation of idealism from the full range of human activity. Certainly to-day every healthy activity must be recognized, that it may find its place and function. The guiding principle of this humanist ideal might well be that of a healthy mind, in a healthy body, in a healthy society.

I would regard humanism as tolerant in principle and insistent on understanding situations, and yet firmly desirous of giving leadership to mankind, a leadership of a cooperative rather than of a competitive type and resting on principles and methods to be continuously subject to the test of their furtherance of human welfare. So conceived, humanism would seem to be universal or ecumenical by its very nature, much as science is. Analogies which come to my mind in this connection are the spread of democratic ideas, of humanitarianism, of social movements. What is desired and desirable is not some type of uniformitarianism, or superficial cosmopolitanism, but attitudes and rational directions. As a teacher of more than one generation of foreign students in an American university, I have always been impressed by the essential likeness of men and women from all countries. Accordingly, I anticipate a process of give-and-take in the clarification of human values, nor do I consider that the American temper does not need counsel from other lands. Property values may rank too high in our scale, and haste may defeat serenity. For the humanist, intelligent living is a high art but one to which all human beings are apprenticed, the modest and unassuming as well as the conspicuous.

So much for the intention and expected mode of working of humanism. It will, I expect, spread after the nature of the spirit of an age, such as that of the Enlightenment of the eighteenth century or the earlier, more literary, humanism of the Renaissance. Simply the base and foundation should, in these days, be broader and more securely established. Yet, of course, as we all well know in this period of World Wars and international friction, there is no guarantee. We can only believe that sanity and enduring massiveness of human life will prevail over nationalistic and economic rivalry.

Let us turn now to the main tenets of naturalistic humanism. I shall here use the theses of the "Humanist Manifesto" as the point of departure. At the suggestion of the humanist center in Chicago I wrote the first draft of the document which was then reworked and much improved by Reese, Bragg, Wilson and others in that center. As is well known, this drafting occurred in 1933. Many, from all walks in life, found themselves able to affix their signatures to it as a public pronouncement of their faith. That is, that these theses expressed their view of the human situation and their general conception of the methods and aims which human beings would do well to keep before themselves in the business of living.

There are fifteen theses in all. Since I shall not have the space to comment on all, I shall select those which are most controversial and which involve the sharpest break with the framework of theism. I do so particularly because I wish to make it clear that the humanist does not believe that he has a monopoly of ideals. Fortunately, indeed, he is not the sole advocate of democratic ways of life and thought and of inter-racial understanding.

First, then, to the statement of the alternative to theism. Religious humanists regard the universe as self-existing and not created.

The point of this preliminary thesis of the *aseity* of nature as a going concern is the querying of traditional proofs for the existence of a creative God and the doubt that there is any genuine, empirical evidence for theism or special revelation. Do we not have, in theism and in sacred writings, a tradition handed down from the fathers of long ago and native to their culture? How it is transmitted through families and churches from generation to generation all are aware. But the same holds for all religions and customs.

The acceptance of the universe as an eternally going concern, an all-inclusive, autonomous process, merely runs counter to the theistic postulate of special creation. Even the early Christian Fathers had difficulty with this notion writ large in the Old Testament. Aristotle thought of the world as eternal and as primarily changing only in the regions in and near the earth.

But, leaving aside history, the term creation would seem best to cover a belief in omnipotent power for which there is no parallel or strict analogy in human experience and the distinction between what are called contingent and necessary being. But this distinction is, itself, scarcely empirical since we know of no necessary beings, that is, beings whose existence is intrinsic to their essence. The humanist would hold that the very terminology is question-begging. Are there essences? And is existence something which can be added to subordinate essences? This traditional terminology seems to me outworn.

Since Hume's and Kant's day, existence is seldom regarded by philosophers as a simple, undefinable property. Much of the difficulty has come through the imperfections of language. To say that a thing exists is really tautologous. It can't be a thing without existing. When we ask whether lions or sea-serpents exist we are really asking whether the concepts have application in the public world of reality which we all accept. Thus we live and think within existence, within a world of things which can be pointed out and given a location and date. This is the truth of a valid existentialism.

It is, so it would seem, just a characteristic of our universe that there is an unceasing process of integration and disintegration, and that, on our little planet, this process has taken an evolutionary, emergent direction leading to living things in all their astounding variety, and to man. I suppose the outstanding fact here is the rise of what we call the personal from what strikes us as a non-personal basis. But there are so many intermediate stages that close study shows transition with novelty. The humanist is not one who has no scientific and speculative interest in such emergence but merely one who sees no evidence of something supernatural about it. In what sense would that be explanatory or throw light upon it?

But, interesting as this first thesis is, and much as I should like to consider it from all sides, I am forced to pass on. To sum up: There is no logical need for a First Cause if we take the universe to be eternal, much as theists take God to be. In the second place, there is no empirical reason to hold that there is some intrinsically

Necessary Being. Nature would appear to be self-sufficient and self-conserving. In the third place, the universe shows no evidence of being *deiform,* that is, teleological and replete with purpose and plan. It *might* be better if that were the case. But how such providence would manifest itself and yet leave man to his own decisions has always been a puzzling thing to conceive! The naturalistic humanist takes the human scene as the evidence shows it. The other approach and its problems reflect a framework whose origins we have evidence for. In his famous Appendix to Book One, Spinoza said, perhaps, the ultimate word upon it. I refer, of course, to his *Ethics.*

The second thesis: Humanism believes that man is a part of nature and that he has emerged as the result of a continuous process.

This thesis needs little comment. It is that of biological evolution. The fact of evolution is well established; the methods are still being explored.

Third: Holding an organic view of life, humanists find that the traditional dualism of mind and body must be rejected.

This thesis is no simple matter either in its theory or its implications. The chief implication for religion is the exclusion of personal immortality. Far Eastern religions have laid far less stress upon personal immortality than has Christianity, for which it has been central. Christianity was, along with so much else, a salvation-immortality religion.

There are two main types of Christian dualism: the Christian Aristotelian and the Platonic-Cartesian. Roman Catholics favor the first and infer a bodily resurrection through God's power. The soul is so much the organized form of the body that it is incomplete without it. Protestant modernists are vague but tend to leave the body behind. Their idealism and Platonism make for indistinctness in these matters. Still more indistinct are esoteric cults; but, perhaps, nearer primitive ideas.

Science, definitely, and philosophy, increasingly, are redefining both terms. Mind has become largely adverbial, a term for activities and processes. The body is the living organism with its high-level structure and capacities. Shall we not speak of the living organism as minded and integrative and adaptive? And is not each one in his consciousness participating in the integrative process of awareness so essential to action?

I have written much on this subject and regard it as one of the most fascinating of problems. The human organism is a most remarkable kind of emergent. Let no one despise it. The day of reductiveness to the inorganic is passing. The living being is a plastic, and yet responsive and desirous, whole. A human being is lifted up above the beast by his capacity for symbolization and social inheritance. The very content of a human self reflects the culture in which he has grown to man's estate.

The humanist knows that many are reluctant to accept mortality. But the more he studies the human self biologically, socially and psychologically, the more he sees him as a gifted organism with a marvelous nervous system reared in the stimulating context of a social environment. Should we not aim, then, at a culture in which people can live alertly and creatively and grow old gracefully? A religion, so pointed, is a religion of this world and yet not a "worldly" religion.

I shall pass over the fifth, sixth, seventh, and eighth theses as largely self-explanatory and come to the more controversial ninth and tenth. The ninth is as follows: In place of the old attitudes involved in worship and prayer, the humanist finds his religious emotions expressed in a heightened sense of personal life and in a cooperative effort to promote social well-being. The tenth predicts that there will be no uniquely religious emotions and attitudes, of the kind hitherto associated with belief in the supernatural.

The import of these declarations is that the framework and *dramatis personae* of religion will alter; and with this basic shift from heaven to earth will come new attitudes, aims, and procedures. Worship will become, at most, cosmic emotion, an almost aesthetic sense of what Santayana calls piety to the roots of our being. But such piety can scarcely have the full flavor of worship which, I take it, involves a personality-attitude or something continuous with it. Already, prayer has many forms from petitionary to meditative. It may be that social ritual will evolve within the new setting with its different horizon. But the philosopher must leave such a question to the churches. Much will, I take it, depend upon the evolution of our culture. A richer and less competitive culture might well find the need to express itself dramatically and artistically. It must not be forgotten that we are in an age of change if not of transition.

In the remaining theses the social and institutional aspects of humanism are unfolded, ending in the affirmation of life and the extension of its full promise to all.

Perhaps, the chief significance of naturalistic humanism lies in its frank and fearless presentation of an alternative direction to religion than that dominant in the past. It had been customary to assume that all who deviated from the traditional framework were condemned to negation and frustration. Here, on the other hand, is something affirmative and constructive which offers a life-plan and a perspective. And it is my guess that far more religious people and people of good-will have been moving in this direction than is usually admitted by the Churches. The stream of our culture is flowing in this direction and carries people along, hardly aware of the different scenery on the banks as they go past, and yet affected by it in this way and that. Each generation will diverge in this fashion from the one before it. I am already an old enough man to have observed many changes in these matters. And I am persuaded that the current is becoming swifter. Let us hope that the wide sea lies beyond with its stars and calm. The era of merely physical science, of improved means for unimproved ends, may give place to cooperative living on a global scale. The texture and temper of human life will then be essentially one with its religion.

It may be well at this point to introduce a few remarks upon the applicability of the term religion to naturalistic humanism, especially so because "religion" has both a broad and a narrow usage. Etymologically it is, of course, a word adopted in the Western World from the Latin *religio,* probably connected with the notion of tabu and restraint. It is notorious that Roman religion had this marked primitive element in it. It was an affair of ritual adjustments to impersonal powers. Other regions had their religions without, necessarily, any word for them of this generic sort. And so, for lack of a better term, religion has become a covering word for all this vast variety of basic attitudes, beliefs, and procedures. And the process of generalization and inclusion has continued so that anything from conscientiousness to emotional fervor about nationalism or social reform is called a religion.

In a lexicographical sense, then, religion is what the dictionaries define it as being. And dictionaries are being constantly revised to include new developments in thought and knowledge. It is not too much to say that all serious scholars of the subject recognize the fact that those expressions of human living which are tied in with anxieties and hopes as these involve beliefs about what must be taken account of and what must be done are called religious; and the configuration of feeling, belief and procedure is, taken together, a religion.

Anthropology and the history of religions have made the student familiar with the kaleidoscopic variety which changes in any one of these ingredients makes possible. At any one general cultural level, alone, the possible variations are manifold. With the rise in Asia and Europe of nations with historically evolving political and ecclesiastical institutions a distinctive level emerged. If, at its aliterate stage, religion knew only of mana, ghosts, spirits, magic and prescribed ritual, with shamans and medicine-men the authorities, it now conceived of gods and theologies and cosmologies with priests and prophets as the experts and advisors. Time, place and history gave coloring and emphases. But it must not be forgotten that, at the heart of it all, were human beings as individuals and groups with their needs and values, their beliefs and customs, their prescriptions and ideals. Burtt and Haydon, I take it, express the position of most, if not all, scholars, when they assert that human values, the hopes, needs and interests of human beings, constitute the central and controlling element in all religions. One must keep one's eye on this in all its varying attachments to beliefs and ideals and procedures. Man confronted by his fate; man praying to his gods; man seeking the good life.

The *main* stream of religious history now divides into the Near East and the Far East. And the Near East found in the tormented and passionate culture of the Jewish people a development of theism which unfolded the dramatic possibilities of a personal god attested to by revelation and a sacred literature. And Christianity grew out of this into a gentile world with emphasis upon salvation and faith. This, then, became religion *par excellence* for those in this tradition. If science and philosophy, as they did, gradually began, after the seventeenth century of our era, to undermine the credibility of this framework, so credible in the eyes of Jewish prophet and Christian apostle, did it mean that religion was at an end? Surely not. Man must still appraise, interpret and direct his life, even if the old Heavens are rolled back like a curtain, or vanish like a summer mist, to be replaced by the immensities of nebular space. What is startling about Judaism and Christianity is its romantic intensity and its dramatic personnel. Faith, revelation, immortality, salvation, to many these are the defining essence of religion.

But the Far East took, on the whole, a calmer and more serene direction. The religion of the masses with its ritual, magic and faith persisted while religious leaders arose to speculate and teach. Buddha sought release from the Wheel of Rebirth through the path of reflection which undercuts the roots of desire and leads to Nirvana. Here, as many have pointed out, we have something akin to Stoicism with a different cosmology and less emphasis upon action. In China, along with a retention of the belief in the Order of Heaven, Confucius formulated a social ethics which stressed loyalty to station and its pieties and duties. There was a touch here of what is often called positivism and this-worldliness. The entrance into China of Buddhism added the note of speculation and mysticism. But I do not wish to oversimplify a complex culture.

These, then, are some of the frameworks within which men have sought to interpret and direct their lives. Yet life must go on. And it is for us, the living, in our own day to consummate and express our lives in the relatively new framework of naturalism. I suspect that a decreasing belief in personal immortality will be one of the indices of this shift. Certainly it would strike at the very basis of orthodox Christianity, as Paul recognized. And the Buddhist presupposition of the Wheel of Rebirth and karma would be challenged. I suspect that traditional religions fostered almost as much anxiety as hope. During any transitional period there might well be relief as well as regret. After all, in these matters much depends upon what an individual has been encouraged to believe.

So much for the perspective and quality of naturalistic humanism. There remains to give some information about its history and the vital statistics of groups, explicitly religious or otherwise, associated with it.

It is not surprising to find that the humanist controversy broke out, first of all, in the Unitarian Church in America. It seems to have less hold in the corresponding Churches in England and on the Continent, though there are signs of its growing impact there.

In the United States, humanist ideas were first openly advocated by Curtis Reese, now dean of the Abraham Lincoln Centre in Chicago, and by John Dietrich, a minister in Minneapolis. At much the same time, I published a book called *The Next Step in Religion* in which the concluding chapter was devoted to *The Humanist's Religion*. While a tolerant Church the frankness and completeness of the shift from theocentrism to anthropocentrism took Unitarianism by surprise. Dr. Richard Boynton of Buffalo and Albert C. Dieffenbach acted as moderators; and the spirit of liberalism gained the day. It must be remembered that Unitarianism reflected the spirit of the Enlightenment in its origins. It is a pleasure to record the utterance at this time by John Howland Lathrop, a liberal theist, of the following judgment: "Divergent views that would cause a revolt in an orthodox body, prove in the fellowship of the free to be the very stimulus to development and growth. . . . Liberty is the true means to unity." At present writing, an influential section of the Unitarian ministry is humanist, many of the individuals occupying important administrative positions. The organ for the expression of humanism had a humble enough beginning in a manifolded leaflet sent out from Chicago. It was later replaced by a magazine for a long time now edited by Edwin H. Wilson with headquarters at 569 South 13th Street, Salt Lake City, Utah. With him are associated, as associate editors, Van Meter Ames, Raymond Bragg, Edward Fiess, Harold Larrabee, Max C. Otto, Donald Piatt, Harold Scott. It is of interest to look over current numbers and find contributing many of the intellectual leaders of American thought in science, art, literature and philosophy.

It should not be forgotten that many liberal Jewish leaders are representative humanists and that both in England and in America Ethical Societies find themselves in sympathy with the general program of naturalistic humanism.

Another stream of humanism is that usually called scientific humanism. It stresses, as Sir Richard Gregory points out, verifiable knowledge acquired by observation and experiment. Julian Huxley is another brilliant representative of scientific *humanism,* which means to him the cooperation of science in all its reaches with the life of the community.

So far as I can judge, there has been no marked alteration in naturalistic humanism except the deeper note that came with the rise of Fascism and the outbreak of war. Professor Burtt was led to query any residue of eighteenth-century perfectionism and mystical belief in the "natural" goodness of man. The result was that **more** attention was directed to the historical, economic and social conditions of human personality. But there was no inclination to stress the "demonic" and finite pride.

The movement has been enriched by the men and women who have come to its support. One always thinks of A. E. Haydon, John Dewey, Max Otto, C. F. Potter, Oliver Reiser, Arthur Morgan, J. A. Auer, Corlis Lamont, and C. Judson Herrick, to mention only a few. I very much doubt that any other religious movement has as firm a foundation in method and knowledge.

BIBLIOGRAPHY

J. A. C. F. AUER, *Humanism States Its Case* (1933).

J. DEWEY, *A Common Faith* (1934).

A. E. HAYDON, *Man's Search for the Good Life* (1937).

M. C. OTTO, *Natural Laws and Human Hopes* (1926).

C. F. POTTER, *Humanism, A New Religion* (1930).

J. H. RANDALL AND J. H. RANDALL, JR., *Religion and the Modern World* (1929).

C. W. REESE, *Humanist Religion* (1931).

———, *The Meaning of Humanism* (1945).

G. SANTAYANA, *Reason in Religion* (1905).

J. WALKER, *Humanism as a Way of Life* (1932).

J. S. HUXLEY, *Religion Without Revelation* (1927).

R. W. SELLARS, *The Next Step in Religion* (1919).

———, *Religion Coming of Age* (1928).

RECONSTRUCTIONISM

Born in Swenziany, Lithuania, in 1881, Mordecai Kaplan was brought to the United States when but a mere boy. He graduated with a bachelor's degree from the College of the City of New York in 1900; took his master's at Columbia two years later. He became a rabbi after studying at the Jewish Theological Seminary of America, his seminary honoring him in 1929 with the D.H.L. degree. From 1903 to 09 he was rabbi of the Congregation Kehilath Jeshurum. For many years he has been professor at the Jewish Theological Seminary in New York, organizer and dean of its Teachers' Institute. He has taught also at the Graduate School of Jewish Social Work and Teachers College, Columbia University. In 1937 until 1939 he was a visiting professor at the Hebrew University of Jerusalem.

His first published volume "Judaism as a Civilization" revealed the trend of his developing thought. Early in 1935 a group joined him in editing a magazine, now widely circulated and of which he is the editor, called "The Reconstructionist." This magazine is sponsored by friends associated with the Society for the Advancement of Judaism which Dr. Kaplan had founded in 1922 and the Jewish Reconstructionist Foundation (New York) which was organized in 1940.

Reconstructionism, we are told, does not aim to set up another denomination. It is dedicated to serve as a unifying force within Judaism according to its own naturalistic orientation.

Other of Dr. Kaplan's publications are: "Judaism in Transition" (1936); "The Meaning of God in Modern Jewish Religion" (1937), "The Future of the American Jew" (1947) and works of editorship.

Editor

RECONSTRUCTIONISM

MORDECAI M. KAPLAN

RECONSTRUCTIONISM is a philosophy of Jewish life designed to effect a creative adjustment of that life to the conditions under which it must be lived in the modern world. Such a creative adjustment would be one that makes the maximum use of the Jewish social and cultural heritage for insuring the survival of Jewry, for enriching the personal life of the individual Jew with spiritual values, and for enabling the Jewish people to contribute its best to the enhancement of human life in general.

To carry out this program, Judaism should be conceived as a religious civilization, the civilization of the Jewish people. The term *Judaism* would then apply not merely to the religion of the Jewish people, but to its entire way of life, just as the term Hellenism applies to the whole way of life of the Hellenic people. Judaism involves, in addition to Jewish religion, also the social and economic interests Jews have in common, their relation to their Palestinian homeland, their traditions, their laws and mores, their language, literature and art, and every other aspect of their collective life. In Jewish civilization, however, religion has always played and, from the Reconstructionist viewpoint should continue to play, a dominant role.

To view Jewish religion as an inseparable function of a living, evolving Jewish civilization carries with it certain implications with regard to the nature of religion in general and of Jewish religion in particular. These we shall here endeavor to set forth.

I

Reconstructionism implies that *religion is a natural social process which arises from man's intrinsic need of salvation or self-fulfillment.* That conception of religion is obviously a definite departure from the conception of religion held universally among Jews until the period of their emancipation from ghetto conditions and their integration into the political and cultural life of the peoples among whom they lived. It is no less a departure from the conception of religion held by all the orthodox faiths of the Western World. All of these faiths, in common with traditional Judaism, have assumed that religious truth is something to which man cannot attain by the exercise of his natural powers, but only by the miraculous intervention of Deity in human affairs in the form of a supernatural revelation of His will.

The considerations that have led great multitudes of men of all religions to abandon faith in miracles and to seek to ground religion in a philosophy of life that accepts ungrudgingly the assumption of the uninterrupted processes of nature are too well-known to need repetition. But among those who accept naturalism and renounce belief in miraculous revelation there is still great confusion as to the true nature of religion, its function in the evolution of human life and the manner in which it must endeavor to realize its purpose.

This is a particularly crucial problem for Jews. Since they constitute a minority group they can preserve their own religious civilization only by much conscious effort. Moreover, Jews feel the widespread antipathy against their people which exists in the Gentile world, an antipathy that varies in its manifestations from efforts at exterminating them, such as were practiced by the Nazis, to forms of social snobbishness that merely hurt their pride. They know that this antipathy is not directed against them as individuals but against their people, that it is tantamount to a denial of the worth of the Jewish people and its right to a continuing collective existence. If they are to experience their life as worthwhile, they must possess what their fathers possessed before emancipation from the ghetto, a religious faith capable of investing Jewish efforts at collective survival and the cultivation of the Jewish cultural heritage with universal significance. Yet they cannot go back to a belief in the miraculous and supernatural, which was the presupposition of Jewish religion before the Emancipation.

Nor have more modern trends in Jewish religious thinking afforded them the kind of religious experience that they need. Reform Judaism, which was the first effort on the part of Jews to repudiate the miraculous and supernaturalist formulation of **Jewish** religion, arose from a misconception of the nature of religion. That misconception was current in the world in the days of the emancipation of Jewry from ghetto conditions and the incorporation of Jews in the bodies politic of the modern nations. It was born of the desire to validate and make possible the toleration of religious differences within the civic community. The notion then prevailed that the different religions were different theistic philosophies and that one's adherence to a particular religion expressed merely a personal opinion about God and man's relation to him, a predilection for certain theological doctrines. The various religious communions were conceived as societies organized to give effect to their respective theistic philosophies.

The unorthodox among the Jews were therefore inclined to accept the notion that the only thing that mattered in Jewish civilization was Jewish religion, and that the only things that mattered in Jewish religion were the idea of God and the ethical conduct it implied. All else was merely a means to the implementation of the God idea, and, if its relation to the God-idea could not be demonstrated, it might as well be discarded. It was assumed that the difference between Jewish religion and other religions was based on a difference in the way Jews conceived of God.

But religion is more than the fruit of metaphysical speculation. Metaphysical theory is never the true basis of religious unity. The conclusions of metaphysical schools have always cut across religious denominational lines. All **Kantians have** more in common in their conception of God than have all **Jews** or all Christians. Religion is not a philosophical doctrine originating in the mind of an individual and communicated by him to his fellows; it is a product of a people's life, the soul of its civilization. The essence of religion is the effort to discover what makes life worth while, and to bring life into conformity with those laws on which the achievement of a worthwhile life depends. Religion is thus a human institution, a product of man's life on earth, of his efforts to make the most of his life, to make the best and most satisfying use of the powers with which he is endowed.

II

To many who have been habituated to think in traditionalist terms such a conception may seem a derogation of the role of religion, if not a denial of the fundamentals of religion itself. If religion is a human institution, where does God come in? What justification have we for calling a human institution by the name of religion? But a further analysis of this premise will show that faith in God is one of its clear implications.

Religion is man's quest for self-fulfillment or salvation, and *the need of self-fulfillment presupposes that reality is so patterned as to contain the means of satisfying it.* Man is distinguished from the brute by possessing not merely a will to live but a will to life abundant and enduring. His quest for abundant life makes him continually aware of his dependence on other persons and objects. He is aware that his conduct will bring him full satisfaction only if the goals he seeks and the means by which he seeks them conform to a law not of his own creation, that his own purposes emanate from and point to a life that transcends his own. That spiritual purpose which transcends his and which gives significance to the events of life and direction to his own purposes is what religion means by the will of God. Faith in God means faith that there is an unfailing Power at work in the universe on which man can depend for salvation or self-fulfillment, if he conforms with the required conditions, which constitute the law of God.

Since all civilizations depend on the willingness of men to cooperate in the pursuit of ends considered to be life enhancing, at least for their own adherents, they cannot dispense with religion. Even when they avow atheism, their atheism rests on certain unproved assumptions that they consider contributory to self-fulfillment of the group. The loyalty that they command is essentially a religious loyalty, although they will not admit that it is, for it assumes the inherent and supreme value or holiness of their own civilization.

Religions result from the fact that every civilization identifies the more important elements of its life as sancta, i.e., as media through which its people can achieve salvation or self-fulfillment. Among the *sancta* of a civilization are all those institutions, places, historic events, heroes and all other objects of popular reverence to which superlative importance or sanctity is ascribed. These *sancta,* the attitude toward life that they imply and the conduct that they inspire are the religion of that people. In Jewish religion, such *sancta* are, among others, the Torah, the synagogue, Sabbaths and holy days, the Hebrew language, Moses and the Patriarchs, etc.

American civilization also has its *sancta*: the Constitution, the Declaration of Independence, Thanksgiving Day, the Fourth of July and other national holidays, the Stars and Stripes. They and what they imply represent American religion. The American Jew sees no contradiction in reverencing both groups of *sancta* any more than American Christians see any contradiction in reverencing these American *sancta* as well as the Cross, the New Testament, the Church and its sacraments and sacred days, which are among the *sancta* of Christian civilization. Religions are not necessarily mutually exclusive; they are so only when their *sancta* are interpreted as implying contradictory doctrines. Thus Judaism cannot include the New Testament among its *sancta* because its fundamental premise is the inadequacy of the Torah, which Judaism holds sacred, as a guide to salvation. Therefore, the Christian and Jewish religions exclude one another but the American religion excludes neither and neither should exclude the American religion.

III

If then every civilization has religious *sancta*, what do Reconstructionists mean when they speak of Judaism as specifically a religious civilization? Traditionally, the Jewish people assumed from its early beginnings, that it was the "Chosen People," that it stood in a unique relationship to God, since to it, and to it alone, God miraculously imparted the supreme revelation of His will, the Torah. But that doctrine is inconsistent with our premise that religion is a natural social process. The need for salvation being inherent in all peoples and the quest of salvation being a natural process evident among all human societies, we must assume that the way of salvation is available to all men and peoples everywhere and on the same terms. Reconstructionism, therefore, renounces all pretensions to Israel's being God's chosen people. While profoundly grateful for all the manifestations of the divine spirit in the history and civilization of Israel, Reconstructionists do not assume that Israel must necessarily at all times possess that spirit in higher degree than any other people. Loyalty to Judaism and Jewish religion does not require any assumption of the superiority of Jewish religion over all others, any more than an individual's fidelity to his personal ideals, his aspiration to make the most of his personal abilities and talents for the enhancement of human life, requires a belief in his own superiority over other individuals. The worth of one person is incommensurate with the worth of any other, and the same is true of the collective personalities of groups.

What Reconstructionists have in mind when they speak of Judaism as a religious civilization is the historic truth that the Jewish people, under the leadership of its law-givers, prophets and sages, considered the chief function of its collective life to be the fostering of its *sancta*. It sought consciously to make its collective experience yield meaning for the enrichment of the life of the individual Jew.

That is how the entire life of the Jew came in time to be invested with *mitzvot*, ritual acts designed to impress on him the moral and spiritual value which had emerged from the process of Jewish living. The performance of every one of these *mitzvot* is preceded by a *berakah* (blessing) which begins with the formula, "Blessed be Thou, O Lord our God, King of the universe, who hast sanctified us by Thy *mitzvot* . . . ," implying that the *mitzvot* are intended to sanctify, that is to confer worth on, Jewish life.

In contrast to certain secularist interpretations of Judaism, which have resulted from the reaction against Orthodox dogma on the one hand and against the Reform movement's repudiation of all the secular aspects of Jewish civilization, on the other, Reconstructionism stresses the religious emphasis on the *mitzvot* as a vital need for modern Jewish life. Without this religious emphasis it is inconceivable that Judaism could have survived in the diaspora until the present time, or that it will be able to survive in the future. When a people lives on its own soil, its civilization perpetuates itself with a minimum of conscious purpose. Not being challenged by any competing civilization, its *sancta* are taken for granted by its adherents who think of them only occasionally, while devoting most of their energies to the pursuit of secular, individualistic and materialistic interests. But when the Jewish people was exiled and its state destroyed, the only way in which Judaism could survive at all was by stressing its *sancta* and emphasizing their value for the individual and for the group.

This was true during the Middle Ages, when Jewish communities were autonomous and Jews were excluded from Gentile society.

It is even more obviously true in our day, when, in democratic countries, Jews live simultaneously in two civilizations. Under such conditions, Jews have no motive for retaining their connection with the Jewish people, unless they derive from that connection values which they cannot find elsewhere. Moreover, these values must be relevant not only to life in an exclusively Jewish environment, but to life in the two civilizations in which the Jew lives. Now, of all Jewish values, the most universal are those that make the Jew feel he has a place in human society and that help him to understand what he must do to fulfill his destiny as an individual, as a Jew, and as a member of the human race, in a word, the religious values of Judaism. Without these values, the Jew becomes a drifter, uprooted, socially impotent and unhappy. His American inheritance by itself will not suffice to satisfy his need for salvation, because American religion is pluralistic. It assumes that, in addition to being loyal to the *sancta* of Americanism, its adherents will seek salvation through loyalty to one or another of the great religious traditions that existed long before America came into being. The Jew who is out of touch with Jewish life and out of sympathy with its spiritual culture thus feels himself spiritually isolated and generally forlorn. He needs for his salvation *Jewish religion,* for he is conditioned by his early training, his associations and the consciousness of his Jewish identity against accepting as his own, the *sancta* of any of the other historic religions.

But religious values cannot be realized except in association with all the other elements in the civilization which would apply them. When abstracted from its life, they are mere verbalizations. As we have already pointed out, religions are not metaphysical schools of thought or the attempts of the adherents of such schools to implement a theoretic doctrine. Religions are not organizations; rather are they organic functions of the civilization of some particular societal group or people. Only in relation to the life of that group can their religion be understood, and only in relation to that life can it be effective.

It is therefore incorrect to think of Jewish religion as the elaboration of a specifically Jewish conception of God. There is no single Jewish conception of God. What distinguishes Jewish religion from all others is that it is a specifically Jewish application of the God idea, one which associates belief in God with the *sancta* of Judaism.

The Jews have changed their conception of God considerably in the course of Jewish history. In the visions of the prophets, God is represented as manifesting himself to the human senses; but ever since the termination of the controveries between the adherents and opponents of Maimonides, the denial of corporeal attributes to God has become a dogma of traditional Judaism. Moreover even in any particular age, conceptions of God have varied. While Maimonides was denying all corporeal attributes to God, Jewish mystics speculated on God's dimensions. Certainly in our day, one will find, even among Jewish worshipers in the same synagogue great variation in their conception of the God they worship.

The difference between Jewish religion and all others does not consist so much in the uniqueness of its conception of God as in the uniqueness of its *sancta*. The distinctive character of Jewish religion resides in the fact that it is an endeavor to apply the God idea to the sanctification of Jewish life, to enable the Jew to see God in the events of his own history, in the products of his own culture, in the experience of applying ethical standards to the regulation of Jewish conduct, in the emotional response evoked by Jewish symbols. Jewish religion, in a word, is the conscious endeavor of the Jewish people to make its collective experience contribute to the spiritual growth and self-realization of the individual Jew, the Jewish people, and all mankind.

IV

In the light of this analysis of the place of religion in Judaism, the indifference to religion on the part of many modern Jews becomes intelligible. In part, that indifference is due to the fact that Jewish religion is identified in the minds of most Jews with a particular traditional doctrine to which they find it intellectually impossible to subscribe, rather than with the whole process by which a living civilization evolves its *sancta*. In part it is due to the disorganization of Jewish life that resulted from the loss of the communal autonomy which Jews enjoyed in the ghetto, and the constant pressure of the majority culture, making it difficult to maintain such *sancta* as the Jewish Sabbath, the dietary regulations and other elements of Jewish religion. For, since religion is a function of Jewish community life, it thrives or languishes, equally with all other aspects of Jewish civilization, in proportion as that life is vigorous or feeble.

This gives us a clue to what needs to be done to revitalize Jewish religion. In the first place it must be emancipated from bondage to dogmatism. This bondage arises from the fear that any departure from the specific doctrines that were taught as religion in the past undermines religion itself. But this fear is seen to be groundless, if we regard Jewish religion as a function of Jewish civilization. A living civilization is, of necessity, a changing civilization. But change in civilization does not mean loss of identity, any more than the individual's growth from childhood to maturity means loss of identity. Religion must change in keeping with all the changes in all the other functions of a civilization.

To make this possible, the traditional *sancta* of religion must be reinterpreted in each generation so that their meanings are kept relevant to the needs of that generation. Tradition must not be a source of authority, imposing restrictions on the creativity of later generations, but a source of wisdom and inspiration awakening new creative powers. When *sancta* have become meaningless, they cease, in the nature of the case, to be *sancta*. But this need not trouble us so long as the people lives and creates, for then it will produce new *sancta*. To keep religion vital, religious thought must be free. It is a sad commentary on the intellectual level of religious thought that a *free thinker* is identified in the popular mind with an atheist.

Freedom of thought will, of course, emancipate religion from all association with magic and supernaturalism. In opposing supernaturalism, it is not intended to affirm that nothing is real except that which has been scientifically classified as natural law. *What is condemned as supernaturalism is the notion that God's power manifests itself in the suspension or abrogation of natural law.* To revitalize Jewish religion, it must discountenance the use of ritual for the purpose of influencing the course of events in other ways than by its influence on the mind and heart of the worshiper. Nor should any ritual that is morally or aesthetically offensive be retained merely because in an earlier state of Jewish culture it was legally enjoined.

Stated affirmatively, Jewish worship must be directed to influencing the worshipers to bring their life into harmony with God as the Power that determines the conditions by which man in general and the Jewish people in particular can achieve an abundant and harmonious life. All that is not intellectually and emotionally attuned to this purpose should be eliminated. But that is not enough. The liturgy should be enriched by the writing of new prayers, meditations, hymns that express the religious experiences of our generation. Traditional forms should be retained wherever these have something of positive value to contribute to the services; but they must be supplemented by additional material directly relevant to the interests, needs, problems and ideals of our day. Though Reconstructionism stresses the importance of reinterpreting or revising traditional *sancta* where these have lost their value for considerable numbers of Jews, it does not insist on the acceptance of its own scale of values as the measure of religious loyalty in Judaism. It recognizes the need for a certain religious pluralism within Jewish religion itself. The unity of Jewish religion must henceforth be based not on uniformity of theological belief or ritual practice but on a common purpose to sanctify Jewish life. For those Jews who find that they cannot accept as valid all the tenets of traditional Jewish religion or cannot practice all the traditional religious rites and observances, Reconstructionism seeks a new rationale for faith in God and in Jewish spiritual values, and new forms of Jewish religious expression. But Reconstructionism does not seek to win adherents away from any institutional loyalty to organizations that are not committed to Reconstructionism or may even be opposed to it. The Reconstructionist movement seeks rather to cooperate with all elements in Jewry in every enterprise that may contribute to preserving or enhancing Jewish life. It seeks to embody the principle of diversity within unity in the organization of democratic, federated forms of Jewish communal life that safeguard the right to be different and organize the will to cooperate.

V

Reconstructionism maintains that in all aspects of Jewish civilization, the emphasis must be on universal values. The distinctiveness of Jewish religion must not appear in any difference of aim between it and other religions but solely in the fact that Jewish religion assumes special responsibility for the Jewish sector of the front in the battle against evil and, accordingly, uses the resources which are available in Jewish tradition for the discharge of its responsibility.

All Jewish institutions, and particularly Jewish religious institutions, must endeavor to improve human relations in accordance with the profoundest insights of religion. From time immemorial this has been a major interest of Jewish civilization. The conception of the fatherhood of God, which plays so important a part in Jewish religion, was based on the insight that a community of interest binds together the whole human race and that this community of interest must transcend all differences. The realization of the ideal unity of the human race cannot be effected by imposing one uniform standard of conduct upon all men. Implied in the concept of brotherhood is the sort of unity that prevails among brothers in a happy family in which all members help one another to achieve each his own purpose. Judaism must strive for the establishment of a social order that satisfies at one and the same time two contrary requirements: the maximum of human cooperation and the maximum of personal liberty. To this end Judaism must seek an equitable distribution not merely of the material goods needed for human living but also of responsibility and power in the control of human affairs.

VI

To summarize the Reconstructionist viewpoint—Reconstructionism is designed to provide a rationale and a program that would make possible the survival, progress and beneficent functioning of Judaism, the civilization of the Jewish people, under the conditions of modern life. With this end in view, it is deeply concerned with such social, political and cultural problems as the establishment of the Jewish national home in Palestine, the organization of Jewry along democratic lines, the development of the Hebrew language and literature and of Jewish music and art. But it regards the achievement of all of these as dependent on religion, on a spiritual attitude toward Jewish life which would invest it with sanctity or supreme importance for the Jew.

Jewish religion cannot meet the needs of modern Jews unless it conforms to a clear and correct understanding of the role of religion in human life and its relation to human civilization. Its function is to point out those elements of Jewish civilization, past and present, which contribute most to making Jewish life worth while and to utilize them to this end. In pursuing this common religious purpose, there must be full freedom of thought and its inevitable concomitant, diversity of expression. Freedom of thought should be used to reinterpret the old *sancta* of Judaism in the light of the best spiritual insight of our times. Judaism must renounce all pretensions to superiority or chosenness and base Jewish loyalty on the need for experiencing the worthwhileness of Jewish life. And it should participate in every human striving for the social advancement of the human race.

The principles of Reconstructionism, though conceived with special reference to Jewish religion and Jewish civilization can be applied as well to other religions, and, if so applied, would serve the following ends which to us seem wholly desirable.

1. Their application would make it possible for people to retain their allegiance to their religious faiths without surrender of freedom of thought in the interest of any authoritarian dogma. For the Reconstructionist conception of religion renders the survival and development of a religion independent of any notion of the immutability of specific doctrines. The survival of the religion would be assured by its natural connection with an evolving civilization. There would be no need of insistence on dogmatic adherence to a specific creed or on conformity to a specific code of ritual practice.

2. The Reconstructionist conception of religion makes the adherent's loyalty to his faith independent of any pretensions to superiority and thus affords the only sound basis for interfaith goodwill. Reconstructionism recognizes that every religion possesses universal values which it applies to its own group life by relating them to the specific *sancta* of its own civilization. These values are communicable and can be adopted by other religions without imposing the condition that the adherents of those religions discard their own *sancta* or adopt those of any other. Unless this viewpoint is universally accepted, religionists must assume that their own religion is the only, or, at any rate, the best religion that there is, an assumption which nullifies mutual respect and frustrates mutual goodwill and interfaith cooperation.

3. The recognition of the functional character of religion and its relation to all other aspects of a people's civilization answers the charge so often brought against religion that it is concerned only with the hereafter, or with abstract platitudes and not with live

issues. Operating with the conception of religion as a functional aspect of a civilization, religions can demonstrate the relevance of the values they cherish to the vital issues which preoccupy the minds of the living generation of their adherents.

BIBLIOGRAPHY

SAMUEL DININ, *Judaism in a Changing Civilization* (1933).
EUGENE KOHN, *The Future of Judaism in America* (1934).
MORDECAI M. KAPLAN, *Judaism as a Civilization* (1934) (out of print).
———, *Judaism in Transition* (1936).
IRA EISENSTEIN, *Creative Judaism* (1936).
M. M. KAPLAN, editor, *Reconstructionist Papers* (1936).
———, *The Meaning of God in the Jewish Religion* (1937).
IRA EISENSTEIN, *What We Mean by Religion* (1938).
MILTON STEINBERG, *A Partisan Guide to the Jewish Problem* (1945).
MORDECAI M. KAPLAN, *The Future of the American Jew* (1947).

Pamphlets

M. M. KAPLAN, *The Meaning of Reconstructionism* (1940).
MILTON STEINBERG, *To Be or Not to Be a Jew* (1940).
M. M. KAPLAN, *The Reconstructionist Viewpoint* (1941).
ANON., *The Reconstructionist Platform* (1942).
M. M. KAPLAN, *The Freedom to Be Jews* (1945).
———, *Jewish Survival and Its Opponents* (1945).
EUGENE KOHN, *What Is Jewish Religion?* (1945).
HANNAH L. GOLDBERG, *Introduction to Reconstructionism* (1945).
IRA EISENSTEIN, *Interfaith Relations and How to Improve Them* (1946).
MILTON STEINBERG, *The Common Sense of Religious Faith* (1947).
ANON., *Zionism Explained* (1947).
The Reconstructionist Magazine, Volume I and continuing.

All books and pamphlets may be obtained through the Jewish Reconstructionist Foundation, 15 W. 86th Street, New York, 24, N. Y.

INDEX

447